Implementing
a Microsoft Windows 2000
Network Infrastructure

Implementing
a Microsoft Windows 2000
Network Infrastructure

iUniverse.com, Inc.

San Jose   New York   Lincoln   Shanghai

Implementing a Microsoft Windows 2000 Network Infrastructure

Published by iUniverse.com, Inc.

For information address:
iUniverse.com, Inc.
5220 S 16th, Ste. 200
Lincoln, NE 68512
www.iuniverse.com

Cover Creation by Shay Jones

Graphic Production by Matt Bromley, Associate Consultant
Domhnall CGN Adams, Corporation Sole—http://www.dcgna.com
5721-10405 Jasper Avenue
Edmonton, Alberta—Canada T5J 3S2
(780) 416-2967—dcgna@yahoo.com

ISBN: 0-595-14819-0

Printed in the United States of America

Acknowledgments

We are pleased to acknowledge the following people for their important contributions in the creation of this study guide.

Technical Writer—Barb Young

Editors—Grace Clark and Nina Gettler

Indexer—Loral Pritchett

Proofreaders—Nina Gettler and Kerry Holland

Cover Creation, Text Conversion and Proofing—Shay Jones, AA, MCSE, MCP

Technical Reviewer—Jay Graham, MCSE+I

Graphic Designer—Matt Bromley

V.P., Publishing and Courseware Development— Candace Sinclair

Course Prerequisites

The Implementing a Microsoft Windows 2000 Network Infrastructure study guide targets individuals who are new to Microsoft Windows 2000 and will be responsible for the installation, configuration, management, and support of a network infrastructure that uses Microsoft Windows 2000 Server products.

Prerequisites including the ability to perform the following tasks:

- Install or upgrade to Windows 2000

- Configure Windows 2000

- Connected Windows 2000 client computers to various networks

- Create and manage user accounts

- Use groups to manage resource access

- Configure the NTFS file system for managing data

- Provide network access to various file types

- Configure and manage disks and their partitions

- Monitor and optimize Windows 2000

- Implement Windows 2000 security

- Configure printing connectivity and print options

- Set up mobile computing capabilities

- Implement a disaster protection plan

- Install and configure Terminal Services

- Implement Windows 2000-based servers and client computers

- Thorough understanding of TCP/IP

In addition, we recommend that you have a working knowledge of the English language so that you can understand the technical words and concepts presented in this study guide.

To feel confident about using this study guide, you should have the following knowledge or ability:

- The desire and drive to become a certified MCSE through our instructions, terminology, activities, quizzes, and study guide content

- Basic computer skills, which include using a mouse, keyboard, and viewing a monitor

- Basic networking knowledge including the fundamentals of working with Internet browsers, e-mail functionality, and search engines

- IP, remote connectivity and security

Hardware and Software Requirements

To apply the knowledge presented in this study guide, you will need the following minimum hardware:

- For Windows 2000 Professional, we recommend 64 megabytes of RAM (32 megabytes as a minimum) and a 1-gigabyte (GB) hard disk space.

- For Windows 2000 Server, we recommend a Pentium II or better processor, 128 megabytes of RAM (64 megabytes minimum), and a 2-GB hard drive. If you want to install Remote Installation Server with Windows 2000 Server, you should have at least two additional gigabytes of hard disk space available.

- CD-ROM drive

- Mouse

- VGA monitor and graphics card

- Internet connectivity

To apply the knowledge presented in this study guide, you will need the following minimum software installed on your computer:

- Microsoft Windows 2000 Advanced Server

- Microsoft Windows 2000 Professional

Symbols Used in This Study Guide

To call your attention to various facts within our study guide content, we've included the following three symbols to help you prepare for the Implementing a Microsoft Windows 2000 Network Infrastructure exam.

 Tip: The Tip identifies important information that you might see referenced in the certification exam.

 Note: The Note enhances your understanding of the topic content.

 Warning: The Warning describes circumstances that could be harmful to you and your computer system or network.

How to Use This Study Guide

Although you will develop and implement your own personal style of studying and preparing for the MCSE exam, we've taken the strategy of presenting the exam information in an easy-to-follow, ten-lesson format. Each lesson conforms to Microsoft's model for exam content preparation.

At the beginning of each lesson, we summarize the information that will be covered. At the end of each lesson we round out your studying experience by providing the following four ways to test and challenge what you've learned.

Vocabulary—Helps you review all the important terms discussed in the lesson.

In Brief—Reinforces your knowledge by presenting you with a problem and a possible solution.

Activities—Further tests what you have learned in the lesson by presenting ten activities that often require you to do more reading or research to understand the activity. In addition, we have provided the answers to each activity.

Lesson Quiz—To round out the knowledge you will gain after completing each lesson in this study guide, we have included ten sample exam questions and answers. This allows you to test your knowledge, and it gives you the reasons why the "answers" were either correct or incorrect. This, in itself, enhances your power to pass the exam.

You can also refer to the Glossary at the back of the book to review terminology. Furthermore, you can view the Index to find more content for individual terms and concepts.

Introduction to MCSE Certification

The Microsoft Certified Systems Engineer (MCSE) credential is the highest-ranked certification for professionals who analyze business requirements for system architecture, design solutions, deployment, installation, and configuration of architecture components, as well as troubleshooting system problems.

When you receive your MCSE certification, it proves your competence by having earned a nationally recognized credential as an information technology professional who works in a typically complex computing environment of medium to large organizations. It is recommended that a Windows 2000 MCSE candidate should have at least one year of experience implementing and administering a network operating system environment.

The MCSE exams cover a vast range of vendor-independent hardware and software technologies, as well as basic Internet and Windows 2000 design knowledge, technical skills and best practice scenarios.

To help you bridge the gap between needing the knowledge and knowing the facts, this study guide presents Implementing a Microsoft Windows 2000 Network Infrastructure knowledge that will help you pass this exam.

 Note: This study guide presents technical content that should enable you to pass the Implementing a Microsoft Windows 2000 Network Infrastructure certification exam on the first try.

Study Guide Objectives

Successful completion of this study guide is realized when you can competently understand, explain and identify the tasks involved in Implementing a Microsoft Windows 2000 Network Infrastructure.

You must fully comprehend each of the following objectives and their related tasks to prepare for this certification exam:

- Understand the Windows 2000 Network Infrastructure components

- How to automate Internet Protocol (IP) address assignment as it relates to DHCP

- Implementing Name resolution by using DNS and WINS

- Configuring Network Security by using a Public Key infrastructure

- Configuring Network Securing by using IPSec

- Supporting Remote Network Access

- Using IAS

- Configuring a Windows 2000 Server as a router

- Configuring network Internet access

- Configuring a Web Server

- Using RIS for Windows 2000 Professional deployment

- Managing a Windows 2000 network

- Troubleshooting Windows 2000 network services

- Configuring network connectivity between operating systems

Figures

List of Tables

Table of Contents

Lesson 4
Remote Access Configuration and Management 161

Lesson 5
Network Protocol Installation and Administration 255

Lesson 8
Network Address Translation Installation and Administration............445

Lesson 9
Certificate Services Installation and Administration 485

Lesson 10
Network Traffic Security and Cross-Platform Authentication..............541

Windows 2000 Networking Infrastructure

Windows 2000 is designed specifically for large enterprise systems. With this new operating system, Microsoft intends to not only surpass Novell NetWare but also challenge IBM's mainframe dominance in major corporations.

Windows 2000 presents significant improvements on Microsoft Windows NT 4.0, namely, increased reliability, enhanced security and scalability, and more user-friendly administrative tools. Many of the difficulties from Microsoft Windows NT 4.0 are largely reduced, such as the need to reboot when changing parameters. Depending on the version of Windows 2000, up to 32 processors can be supported. Furthermore, digital certificates replace user IDs and passwords for identification and authentication, providing much desired security.

Many of the services and processes from Microsoft Windows NT 4.0 are included, particularly those related to Transport Control Protocol/Internet Protocol (TCP/IP), the most widely used networking protocol. Experienced Microsoft Windows NT 4.0 administrators will find the organization of the administrative interface different. The inclusion of Active Directory will take some adjustment as well, but it will ultimately lead to more streamlined administration.

This lesson introduces you to the components of a typical Windows 2000 network and describes how to provide connectivity with different operating systems.

After completing this lesson, you should have a better understanding of the following topics:

- Overview of Windows 2000 Networking Infrastructure

- Network Components Identification

- Connectivity between Windows 2000 and Other Operating Systems

Overview of Windows 2000 Networking Infrastructure

Any kind of network has two functions. The first is to provide services, such as centralized file storage, shared printers and other hardware resources, fax services, and enhanced communication through e-mail. The second function is to secure those services through a process of authentication and authorization of the users and computers.

These functions must perform seamlessly together across a variety of platforms, since it is uncommon you will have a pure Windows 2000 enterprise network. You will more likely need to integrate legacy equipment running older Windows operating systems, computers running Novell NetWare or Apple Macintosh, or IBM mainframes and AS/400s running UNIX and other operating systems into your network (Figure 1.1).

Figure 1.1 Mixed Windows 2000 Network

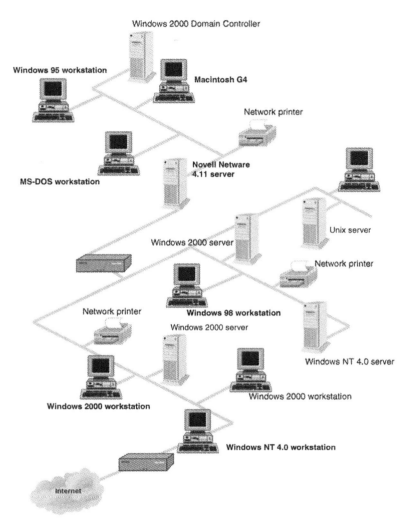

With Microsoft Windows NT 4.0, accessing resources in a mixed network was cumbersome. You needed to enter separate usernames and passwords to access NetWare resources to an Oracle database. However, Windows 2000 allows centralized logon through the Active Directory, since Active Directory is built on the Lightweight Directory Access Protocol (LDAP). This makes it possible for application developers to write to the LDAP standard and integrate security for their products with Windows 2000 built-in security.

Windows 2000 Active Directory is a significant change and is important for managing network resources and services. Active Directory permits one administrative reference point for all resources, including users, files, peripheral devices, host connection, databases, Web access, services, and network resources. Most of the key features of Windows 2000 require Active Directory in order to function. By deploying it, you integrate multiple namespaces from various operating systems into one directory.

However, Windows 2000 is not completely different from Microsoft Windows NT 4.0. Much of Microsoft Windows NT 4.0's basic foundation has been incorporated, including the internal kernel structure, how drivers are designed, and multitasking.

The tools for managing the underlying structure are very different. The Microsoft Management Console (MMC) holds administrative tools that are seen as consoles (Figure 1.2). The tools are built with modules called snap-ins to allow for customization. These custom tools can be shared through e-mail, the Web, or put into a network folder to allow specific users and groups to accomplish many administrative tasks.

Figure 1.2 Microsoft Management Console

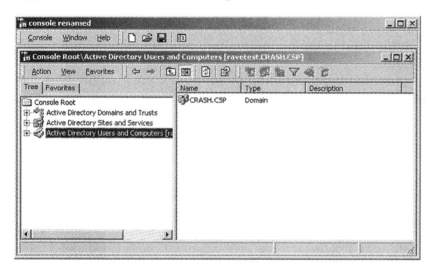

As a result of significantly improved administrative interfaces, the Total Cost of Ownership (TCO) for a Windows 2000 network may end up lower compared to other network operating systems. Although Microsoft Windows NT 4.0 hardware and software were relatively inexpensive compared to mainframe components, Windows NT 4.0 required a heavy investment in administrative support.

A highlight of Windows 2000 is its built-in Internet functionality. Server support exists for most Internet protocols, so that a Windows 2000 server can act as a Web server, File Transfer Protocol (FTP) server, Simple Mail Transport Protocol (SMTP) host, or Network News Transfer Protocol (NNTP) host. TCP/IP is highly integrated, making Dynamic Host Configuration Protocol (DHCP), Domain Name System (DNS) and other transport stack services vital to the proper functioning of Active Directory and Windows 2000 clients.

The exception is Windows Internet Naming Service (WINS), Microsoft's name resolution service. Due to the reliance on DNS to resolve names to Internet Protocol (IP) addresses, you only need WINS if you have a network containing more than Windows 2000 servers and Windows 2000 clients, however, keep in mind that applications may utilize WINS. Since the administrative tools work as well on remote computers as they do on local ones, these changes make it easier to administer Windows 2000 servers remotely. The command-line tool is also more powerful. Another great improvement over Microsoft Windows NT 4.0 is the Windows 2000 Plug-and-Play feature that supports many types of hardware and improves support to laptops.

Note: Many Microsoft Windows NT 4.0 drivers do not work in Windows 2000.

Security is tighter in Windows 2000 than in Microsoft Windows NT 4.0. Windows NT 4.0's LAN Manager (NTLM) authentication system is replaced by the Kerberos v5 security protocol, which is used in the UNIX world and works well in larger systems. This is supplemented by a second, even more scalable, security system—a public key system based on the X.509 standard, the most widely used standard for defining digital certificates.

Kerberos and the public key infrastructure permit transitive trust relationships not available in Microsoft Windows NT 4.0. A transitive trust is the two-way trust relationship between Windows 2000 domains in a domain tree or forest, between trees in a forest, or between forests. Transitive trusts are automatically established when a domain joins an existing forest or domain tree. This simplifies user and group administration in multi-domain networks. The Security Configuration and Analysis snap-in on the Microsoft Management Console (MMC) allows an administrator to check the state of a system's security against one or more security templates and make desired modifications (Figure 1.3). The security template can then be applied to computer groups. Intranets, extranets, dial-in access and ordinary users are all protected configurations.

Figure 1.3 System Security Analyzer

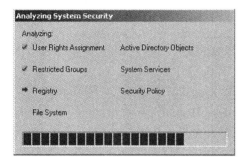

Network Components Identification

Managing an enterprise Windows 2000 network is impossible without a thorough understanding of the various components that allow for smooth communication. A number of services need to be deployed to support Active Directory and Windows 2000 client functioning. Many of these components are the same as those found in Microsoft Windows NT 4.0. Their configuration windows are different, but the underlying architecture and function of these services remain much the same.

Defining Network Infrastructure Components

Following are the typical parts of a Windows 2000 enterprise network:

Network Protocols—TCP/IP is a set of protocols providing communication among diverse networks. Since it accommodates different architectures and operating systems, TCP/IP is the most commonly used Internet protocol. It includes standards and conventions on how computers and networks are connected and traffic is routed. Another common protocol is NWLink, Microsoft's implementation of Novell's Internetwork Packet Exchange/Sequenced Packet Exchange (IPX/SPX) protocol. Windows 2000 Local Area Networks (LANs) can operate with the NWLink protocol alone. NWLink is used more often, however, to provide interconnectivity with NetWare networks. Once the protocols are installed and configured, you need to manage the network traffic through regular monitoring to assess bandwidth usage, optimizing network bindings, and implementing packet filters to increase security.

Domain Name System (DNS)—This is the hierarchical naming system used to locate domain names on the Internet and on private TCP/IP networks. The DNS service maps DNS domain names to IP addresses and vice versa, allowing users, computers, and applications to query the DNS for remote systems by Fully Qualified Domain Names (FQDN) rather than by IP addresses. Installing, configuring, and optimizing the service is a routine administrative task.

Dynamic Host Configuration Protocol (DHCP)—This is a networking protocol that simplifies TCP/IP network configuration and dynamically configures IP addresses for clients. DHCP ensures that address conflicts do not occur, and it streamlines the use of IP addresses through centralized address allocation. Installing, configuring, and troubleshooting this service properly is vital to smooth network functioning.

IP Routing Protocols—The most common IP routing protocols are Routing Information Protocol (RIP) and Open Shortest Path First (OSPF). RIP and OSPF are protocols that define how routers share routing information. RIP transfers whole tables while OSPF transfers only routing information that has changed since the last transfer. The proper installation, configuration, monitoring, and administration of IP routing protocols are vital to optimizing connectivity between networks. You also need to know how to configure TCP/IP filters, how to implement demand-dial routing, as well as how to integrate routers with network services such as DNS and DHCP. By using Windows 2000 computers as IP routers, you can also allocate bandwidth and give preferential access to different users through Quality of Service (QoS).

Remote Access Service (RAS)—This is a Windows service that allows remote networking for mobile workers and for system administrators who monitor and manage servers at multiple sites. You need to learn how to configure outbound as well as inbound connections, manage routing, create Virtual Private Networks (VPNs) and troubleshoot problems. Remote Authentication Dial-In User Service (RADIUS) is the most common authentication protocol used by Internet service providers. Running on an Internet Authentication Service (IAS) server with Windows 2000, RADIUS can be used to manage the access policies of remote access servers.

Windows Internet Name Service (WINS)—This is a software service that dynamically maps IP addresses to Network Basic Imput/Output System (NetBIOS) (computer names). This allows users to access resources by name instead of by IP address. Important concepts include installing and configuring the service, replicating and maintaining the WINS database, and supporting non-WINS clients.

Network Address Translation (NAT)—This is a service that hides your actual IP address from computers beyond the device doing the actual translation. Windows 2000 Server provides basic NAT capabilities, which you will learn to install and administer.

Microsoft Certificate Services—An optional component of Windows 2000 that lets you issue digital security certificates, certify them as valid, and revoke undesired certificates. After you have installed and configured Certificate Services, it can be used to provide enterprise security through the Public Key Infrastructure (PKI). Using the public key technology, Internet Protocol Security (IPSec) provides robust security for network packets. Create, test, implement IPSec policies, and optimize TCP/IP to ensure maximum server security. Managing and troubleshooting Certificate Services is part of any administrator's job, especially given the current climate of heightened Internet security fears.

Identifying Processes for Computers on a Network

With its flexibility and scalability, client-server computing is competing with the traditional mainframes for Information Technology (IT) infrastructure dollars. The process by which a client identifies itself to a server on the network is critical to understanding overall network functionality. In an enterprise system, determination of where computers and resources reside is done mainly by the computer browser service that runs in Microsoft Windows NT 4.0 and Windows 2000 environments. It helps to decide which of the computers on a particular subnet will be designated as a browser. This browser computer then keeps and updates the browse list, a summary of what computers and shared resources are available across the network.

Browser Roles

Browser roles can be ranked in order of power, from the highest level to the lowest level:

Domain master browser—It builds and manages the inventory of Novell NetWare, Microsoft Windows NT 4.0 and Windows 2000 servers within the entire domain. The domain master browser also trades new information with master browsers in order to update the inventory list. The domain master browser is always located on a domain controller.

Master browser—It performs the same function as the domain master browser only within its subnet rather than in the whole domain. Master browsers give copies of its inventory list to backup browsers in the same subnet.

Backup browser—It keeps an inventory list of resources on the local subnet.

Potential browser—It waits for notification of promotion to backup browser from the subnet's master browser.

Non-browser—It acts as a client browser.

Computers move between these different roles as a result of automatic browser elections, usually stemming from a hardware failure. The most technologically advanced and powerful computer (usually a domain controller) becomes the domain master browser by default, with the other computers falling into respective positions based on their stature in the domain and hardware composition. If one of the browsers cannot meet the browser role, understudies are available. Figure 1.4 shows the types of computers that can play the different roles.

Figure 1.4 Types of Browser Roles

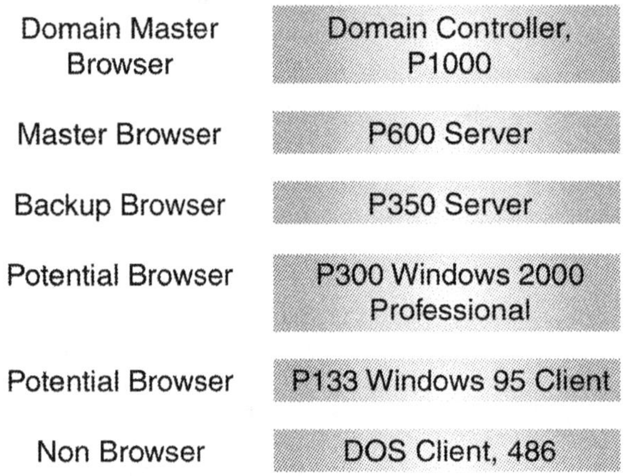

Role	Computer
Domain Master Browser	Domain Controller, P1000
Master Browser	P600 Server
Backup Browser	P350 Server
Potential Browser	P300 Windows 2000 Professional
Potential Browser	P133 Windows 95 Client
Non Browser	DOS Client, 486

As a computer logs on to a network, it broadcasts its existence. Devices identify themselves through an IP address or a 48-bit Media Access Control (MAC) address on the Network Interface Card (NIC). After a session in which name resolution takes place, the nearest master browser compares the computer name of the transmitting computer to its master browse listing and adds the transmitting computer, if it is not already there.

The master browsers list is updated every 15 minutes and copies are distributed to domain master browsers. Backup browsers update every 12 minutes. To maintain the integrity of the browser list, browser announcements are made every few minutes from all other browsers to the Master Browser.

Icons are available in the My Network Places window to browse the Local Area Network (LAN) or Wide Area Network (WAN) (Figure 1.5), while the Add Network Place icon helps to connect your Windows 2000 computer with shared folders, Web folders and FTP sites. When you browse resources through these icons, your computer makes a request to the master browser on the local subnet for the desired item. It then needs to resolve the computer name into the corresponding network IP address.

Figure 1.5 Entire Network View

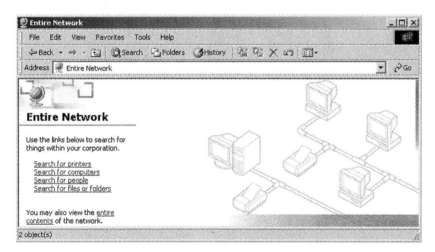

Name Resolution

The two services WINS and DNS are available to resolve names. In a pure Windows 2000 environment, DNS is used to resolve IP addresses to user-friendly names such as www.toyota.com. But WINS is required in older networks to integrate computers running legacy versions of Windows, as well as applications that rely on NetBIOS. WINS maps NetBIOS names to IP addresses. On smaller networks, name resolution can occur with NetBIOS over TCP/IP (NetBT) alone. NetBT is a feature that layers the NetBIOS programming interface over the TCP/IP transport protocol.

By default, Windows 2000 is configured to use DNS for name resolution. Windows 2000 has a new implementation of DNS that dynamically updates, stores and retrieves computer names and IP addresses. Using DNS as the sole name-resolution service requires that you implement Active Directory. In addition, NetBT needs to be disabled to prevent the usage of NetBIOS-based name queries.

The information found by the computer browser service is then published in the Active Directory using Global Catalogs (Figure 1.6). A Global Catalog is a Windows 2000 service and data store that holds a partial replica of each object found in the Active Directory, along with commonly accessed attributes. It knows, for instance, every user and from which domain the user originates. When a user begins browsing a Windows 2000 network, the associated computer will contact the Active Directory Global Catalogs to look up a specific computer name. A Global Catalog's attribute listing is smaller than the listing in the full Active Directory so that indexing is faster. After name resolution, the desired resource is available on the user's desktop if the user has appropriate permissions.

Figure 1.6 Global Catalog Server Creation

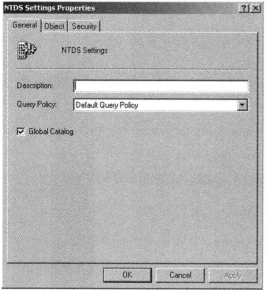

Network Communications Analysis

The ability of a business to effectively manage its data determines its health. As a result, the network infrastructure becomes pivotal in either helping or hindering business growth. Windows 2000 has enhancements that provide simple and reliable communication. These include built-in Internet support for e-mail, chat, and newsgroups on Windows 2000 Professional and client support for Virtual Private Networks (VPNs) through the Point-to-Point Tunneling Protocol (PPTP) or Layer Two Tunneling Protocol (L2TP). Both of these protocols enable branch offices to connect securely to other networks over the Internet. These links extend a private network and turn it into a VPN.

You must consider factors that impact the network plan before you address implementation and support concerns. Planning is essential for any project, but it is especially crucial for a network because a poorly designed infrastructure will impede business growth and be difficult to administer.

When migrating or upgrading your network to Windows 2000, consider the following:

- How do your business requirements and IT capabilities match currently?

- What are your business and IT goals?

Start your analysis with individual departments. What does each area do now or would like to do in the future? What are the departmental goals? You should consider both routine activities and special initiatives.

Once you have identified business needs, rank the enterprise functions that are required to meet those needs. Include the following:

- A breakdown of the TCO, identifying where network upgrades can reduce costs

- An analysis, giving Return on Investment (ROI) for improvements to the IT infrastructure

- Additional business that may occur due to improved communication abilities after an upgrade

- Potential risks of not upgrading the network

 Tip: Microsoft has a useful TCO and ROI calculator at http://www.microsoft.com/ntwork-station/basics/features/lowesttco/tcocalculator.asp

To better define your ideal network infrastructure, you must address the following points:

- What the organization will look like in one, three, or five years

- What the geographical boundaries are

- How many users you expect

- What their work patterns are—virtual project teams, telecommuters, on client sites, contract staff, or field staff

Next, to assess your current network, perform the following activities (Figure 1.7):

Hardware and software—Document both hardware and software on the network. Which items need to be supported? Are preparatory upgrades needed? Are there incompatible operating systems and applications that support specific departmental needs?

Physical linkages—Make a graphical representation of the physical linkages using Visio 5 or some other drawing tool. This includes workstation, servers, routers, switches, hubs, and wiring closets. You can then better determine where the network can be expanded, optimal traffic routing, and placement of equipment.

Network traffic patterns—To determine the quantity and best placement of hubs, switches and routers, use a sniffer product. Get information on bandwidth needs of workstations as well as future needs for network management software. The traffic patterns may dictate a specific type of WAN connectivity. For instance, because Windows 2000 Active Directory servers compress data before sending it over slow WAN links, Windows 2000 uses less bandwidth than Microsoft Windows NT 4.0. The whole domain structure can be different.

Interoperability—Decide if current interoperability with other operating systems such as UNIX or NetWare needs to be maintained.

External connectivity—Determine the kind of external connectivity you have and what will be needed in the future. External connections could be videoconferencing lines, fax services, the Internet, WAN linkages, dial-up networking, or remote network management.

Security—Analyze current security measures and projected security requirements.

Figure 1.7 Factors to Assess in Your Network

Tip: Microsoft's IT Advisor is a handy tool to analyze your current network infrastructure and how IT spending can affect business results. It is found at http://www.microsoft.com/enterprise.

Be realistic in your assessment, bearing in mind the availability of technical support staff, money, and time. Consider also the changing technological landscape. Some new technology on the horizon may better accommodate projected needs than current standards. Only then can you decide on the desired infrastructure. Aim for simplicity, consistency, and flexibility in your network. Reduce the number of technologies deployed in order to save time and money, prevent mistakes, and simplify administration.

Windows 2000 Connectivity with Other Operating Systems

Because of the heterogeneous nature of networking environments, connectivity between different architectures and operating systems is a major concern. Windows 2000 provides several advances on Microsoft Windows NT 4.0 that allow for greater interoperability between Windows 2000 and UNIX, NetWare and Macintosh computers. The interoperability features allow a gradual migration to Windows 2000 or continued operation as a mixed environment.

Providing Access to Macintosh Users

Since the Apple Macintosh has a devoted following among graphic designers, Web enthusiasts, and video producers, integration of Macintosh users into your Windows 2000 environment is likely. Windows 2000 retains the two Microsoft Windows NT 4.0 services that allow Macintosh users to share files and printers. The File Server for Macintosh (FSM) service manages the publishing of shared files, while the Print Server for Macintosh (PSM) service permits Windows and Macintosh computers to use each other's printers. Microsoft's implementation of the AppleTalk network protocol is also included.

To allow Macintosh users access to Windows files, simply share folders and files on your server, and then enable Macintosh file sharing on the share. The share becomes known as a Macintosh-Accessible Volume (MAV) and appears as a volume to Macintosh clients (Figure 1.8). The Macintosh clients use Apple's file-sharing software to connect to the MAV on the Windows 2000 server. Windows clients, on the other hand, see the share as an ordinary file or folder and access it normally.

Figure 1.8 A MAV to a Macintosh Client

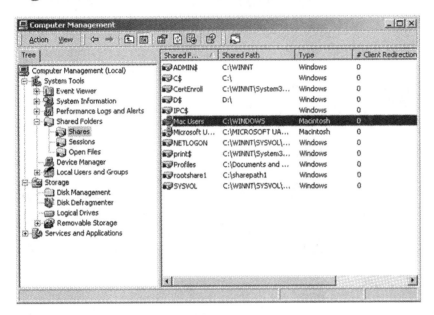

AppleTalk

Install the AppleTalk protocol before installing and configuring Macintosh file and print services. The AppleTalk protocol handles AppleTalk routing as well as regular network communication with Macintosh clients. If you install the AppleTalk protocol without FSM or PSM, the Windows 2000 server can route AppleTalk network traffic or manage remote Macintosh users who are calling in through RAS (Figure 1.9).

Note: AppleTalk is available in Phase 1 and Phase 2 versions. Only the Phase 2 version supports FSM and PSM.

Figure 1.9 Local Area Connection

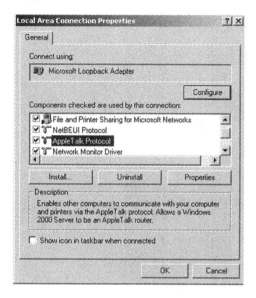

File Server for Macintosh (FSM)

To integrate Macintosh clients into a Windows 2000 network, install FSM on a Windows 2000 domain controller to which the Macintosh clients will log on. This must be done on a New Technologies File System (NTFS) partition. Designed for Microsoft Windows NT 4.0 and Windows 2000, NTFS is the file system that provides data security, file system reliability, and file system recoverability. FSM is layered on top of the standard Windows 2000 Server service. It converts standard NTFS shares to MAVs and manages the creator, type, and icon data needed by the Macintosh OS Finder. As with NTFS, Macintosh file-naming conventions are not case-sensitive.

Both FSM and PSM can be installed easily through the Windows Components Wizard. Configurable FSM options include presenting a user-friendly name, providing a logon message to Macintosh users, selecting the desired type of authentication, and limiting the number of concurrent users (Figure 1.10).

Figure 1.10 File Services for Macintosh

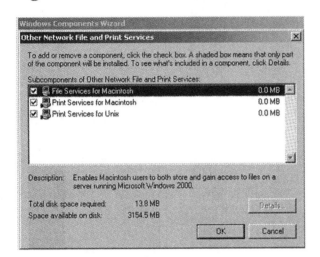

FSM translates between Windows 2000 extensions and Macintosh operating system creator codes through a map in the registry. Macintosh operating system clients will see icons that behave like regular Macintosh volumes when they work with MAVs. However, you may need to alter the mapping associations, since the current version of FSM does not support extensions such as .BMP, .GIF, .JPG, .HTM, .PNG, and .JS by default. Do this alteration through the File Association tab of the File Server for Macintosh Properties window (Figure 1.11).

Figure 1.11 Macintosh File Association Property Page

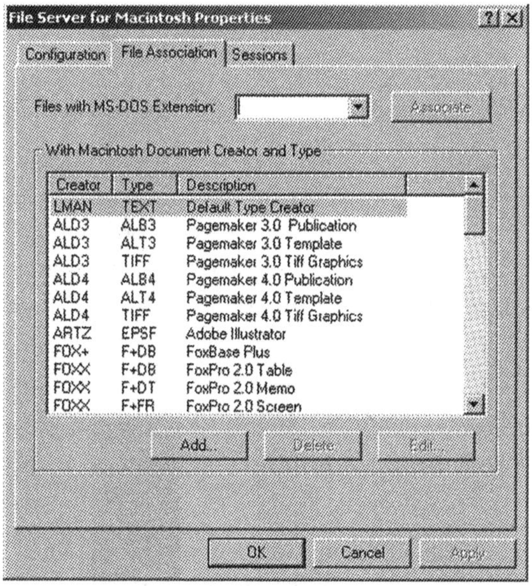

To share files using FSM, first create MAVs in one of two ways. You can create a new Windows share using the Create Shared Folder Wizard through the Shared Folders snap-in. Alternatively, create a MAV for a pre-existing Windows share by using the wizard to form a Macintosh share pointing to the same item.

Note: Do not create MAVs at the root level of your drives because you cannot create a MAV inside another MAV.

Once you have created your share, assign permissions to the folders. Since the Macintosh operating system does not support regular Windows file-level security, file-level permissions apply only if they are more restrictive than permissions on the corresponding folder.

Follow are several types of Macintosh default user permissions:

- Full Control: read, write, execute, delete, change permissions, and take ownership

- Change: read, write, execute, and delete files and folders

- Read: read and execute

- No access: none of the above actions

Macintosh and NTFS permissions differ particularly with respect to inheritance, group permissions, and guest access.

Since both FSM and PSM get account information from the Windows 2000 Active Directory service, Macintosh clients need an account in the directory or guest access to servers in order to log on to FSM and PSM servers. Guests can be allowed access to FSM volumes either through a Macintosh operating system client using the Windows 2000 Guest account or the Macintosh operating system Guest account. The Windows 2000 Guest account requires a password, while the Macintosh operating system Guest account does not.

To increase security, you can encrypt Macintosh authentication. You can do this by configuring your server to accept Apple-encrypted authentication or by installing a Microsoft user authentication module on the Macintosh client.

Not included in Windows 2000 Server is a utility that would allow Windows clients to access files on a Macintosh computer. To do this, purchase a third party NetBIOS network package especially for the Macintosh.

Print Server for Macintosh (PSM)

Using PSM, all printers available to Windows clients become accessible to Macintosh computers and vice versa. PSM converts PostScript output from Macintosh clients into device-independent bitmap files that are supported by Windows 2000 printer drivers. PSM also permits the creation of printer pools and the prioritization of print jobs through a process known as capturing the printer. AppleTalk clients send print requests to a Windows 2000 server queue that forwards them to the captured printer. Although AppleTalk clients can print directly to an uncaptured printer, you cannot then audit, control, or prioritize the print jobs from a Windows 2000 server.

To share a Windows printer with Macintosh users once PSM is installed, create a standard shared printer, either by creating a new printer using the Add Printer Wizard or by sharing an existing printer (Figure 1.12). To share a Macintosh printer with Windows users, capture the printer so that both Windows and Macintosh computers print to the corresponding queue on the Windows PSM server.

Figure 1.12 Printer Port Selection

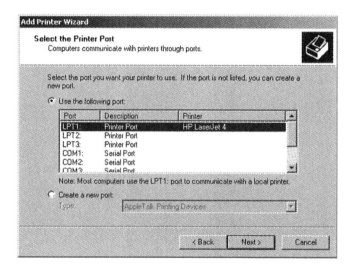

Interoperability between Windows 2000 and IBM Hosts

Connectivity between workstations and IBM hosts has been difficult because of vast differences in architecture between both IBM's mainframes and AS/400 computers and desktop computers. Particularly in larger organizations, much time and money have been invested in hardware and the specialized applications running on these platforms.

Windows 2000 provides services for file and print sharing with IBM mainframes through a Systems Network Architecture (SNA) Server, a Microsoft BackOffice suite application. IBM created SNA to facilitate communications between its large systems and the varied terminals, peripherals, and peer computers on today's network.

SNA Server acts like a gateway between mainframes and PCs. PCs can communicate directly with a host computer (mainframe or AS/400) or through a card in the PC similar to a Network Interface Card that transforms the PC into a dumb terminal with the help of terminal emulation software.

Microsoft's SNA Server provides host connectivity through a manageable interface. The PC-host connection is started and managed by a Windows 2000 server running the SNA Server service. The host connects to the Windows 2000 server, which maintains resources available from the host. The server manages the list of users with permissions to access its resources. The users are then presented with file or print resources through host sessions as if the host resources were any other Windows 2000 server resources. The SNA server can distribute a limited number of concurrent terminal sessions on a first-come basis (Figure 1.13). Install SNA Server on an NTFS partition for increased security.

Figure 1.13 Basic Structure of an SNA Server

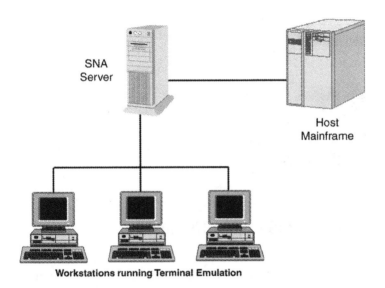

SNA
Server

Host
Mainframe

Workstations running Terminal Emulation

An SNA server provides the following benefits:

- Increased security, because Windows 2000 security is applied to the host session

- The PC workstation no longer needs a host cable or adapter card

- Only one physical connection to the host needs to be managed to retain client connectivity

- Client connections to the host are not limited by physical connections as would be the case with a direct connection

SNA server supports most communications adapters, cabling, wiring, modems, and controllers. It can connect to multiple hosts or peer computers through a number of connections including 802.2 Token Ring or Ethernet, Synchronous Data Link Control (SDLC), X.25 and Distributed Function Terminal (DFT). SDLC is a link service used most often in SNA networks. It allows for communication through full or half-duplex synchronous modems over switched or leased telecommunications lines. X.25 is a packet-switching protocol, and DFT is a link service that runs over coaxial cable.

Configuring Access to UNIX Resources

Interoperability with a variety of UNIX products is vital in an enterprise system, since UNIX is often involved in the routing and generation of network services for larger organizations. UNIX is a powerful, portable, 32-bit, multiprocessing operating system that has been around for decades. Small UNIX hosts used by Internet service providers have increased in popularity because of the Internet boom.

Windows 2000 is very Internet-oriented and comes with basic connectivity tools for UNIX. HyperText Transfer Protocol (HTTP), the protocol used to transfer information on the Word Wide Web, and File Transfer Protocol (FTP), a protocol and application that transfers files from one computer to another over the Internet, are both supported. Also built into Windows 2000 is the dumb terminal emulation protocol Telnet.

Because of the Internet focus, similarities exist between UNIX and Windows 2000, although their underlying architectures are different (Table 1.1).

Table 1.1 Windows 2000 and UNIX Comparison

Windows 2000	UNIX
Designed for client-server operation	Designed for host-based terminal computing
Expanded file metaphor, with all UNIX devices including device rights being seen as objects	All devices such as printers and tape drives appear as ordinary files
Security Reference Monitor, the Logon Process protected subsystem, and Security protected subsystem provide security	Security provided by add-ons such as Kerberos
More powerful group status. Can define new group types, have built-in groups and user accounts, and can belong to more than one group at a time	File and directory permission can only be given to the owner, group, or world
Individual permissions: Read, Write, Execute, Delete, Change Permissions, and Take Ownership	Only three basic permissions: Read, Write, and Execute
Multiple user and group associations with a file	Three user associations with a file: the file owner, a member of the same group as the owner, and everyone else
Filename extensions .COM, .EXE, .BAT or .CMD indicate executability	No relationship between file extension and execution status

Microsoft Windows NT Services for UNIX (SFU)

The Microsoft Windows NT Services for UNIX (SFU) package released in 1999 contains expanded functions to facilitate interoperability between Windows 2000 and UNIX. It includes Network File System (NFS), Telnet, the UNIX Korn shell and utilities, and a password synchronization daemon.

Network File System was developed by Sun Microsystems to share files and directories across a network. Windows computers, however, use Server Message Blocks (SMBs) to perform network file-sharing. Until SFU was released, products bridging this gap needed to be purchased from third-party vendors.

The default mechanism for SFU is the broadcast User Datagram Protocol (UDP) because older NFS implementations do not support TCP. Although SFU allows for transparent access to UNIX resources, it is not suitable for large file transfers since NFS file transfers between Windows 2000 and UNIX systems are slow.

Products also exist to translate SMBs to packets understood by UNIX. One of these is Samba, a widely distributed SMB server freeware that has ports for many versions of UNIX.

Note: Older Samba versions may not work with Windows 2000 because the encrypted LAN Manager password is no longer enabled in the default Windows 2000 configuration.

Commercial vendors also have their own workgroup SMB servers, and some UNIX vendors offer Microsoft Windows NT 4.0 domain SMB servers. SMB servers transfer files faster than NFS solutions, with the bonus that SMB domain servers have the same graphical interface as a Microsoft Windows NT 4.0 server. On the other hand, these SMB domain servers may not operate in the new Windows 2000 security model.

SFU has the following three basic parts:

- Connectivity services: Telnet server, Telnet client, and password synchronization daemon

- File services: NFS client and server support

- Usability services: UNIX utilities and a Korn shell

Connectivity Services

The Telnet server is administered through the TLNTDMN.EXE program. You can use the program to list current users, terminate a user, display and modify the server registry settings, and start or stop a service. Registry settings can be modified either through the TLNTDMN.EXE program, or through REGEDIT or REGEDT 32, the two Windows registry editors. The Telnet client provides a variety of terminal emulations.

With the password synchronization daemon, you can manage user passwords for both Windows 2000 and UNIX clients from the Windows 2000 Server. Changes to a Windows 2000 or UNIX client's password are automatically recorded on the server. The precompiled binary daemons run on the UNIX server. SFU incorporates password synchronization daemons for three versions of UNIX: HP-UX, Sun Microsystems OS, and Digital UNIX. For other UNIX versions, you can use clear text password synchronization with RLOGIN, which is supported by most versions of UNIX.

UNIX hosts are grouped into pods for administrative purposes, with password synchronization occurring per pod. Different UNIX pods can use different encryption keys, but all hosts within a pod must use the same key.

Warning: UNIX accounts are case sensitive, unlike Windows 2000 accounts. When you are adding Windows 2000 accounts into a UNIX environment, make password and account synchronization simpler by creating corresponding Windows 2000 accounts in lowercase.

File Services

Windows 2000 provides a network file system through its network redirector and server components. UNIX implementations have similar functionality. Most versions use NFS, which allows directories and files to be shared and accessed across a network as if they were local resources. NFS works transparently by attaching the share from the remote file system onto a stub of the local file system. The NFS client makes the request to the NFS server, with any computer having the potential to be a client or server. Install and configure the NFS client and server after you have installed SFU.

The NFS server provides resources from a Windows 2000 computer to any computer supporting NFS. It allows you to manage permissions and shares by groups of computer, so that you can share file system resources for client groups instead of just by specific computers. Permissions for these shares are similar to that of UNIX permissions. UNIX file systems are viewed as subdirectories of the root file system while Windows 2000 has each drive letter shared as a separate file system.

The addition of NFS client and server allows for seamless connectivity. You can map exported file systems from UNIX servers as if they were native Windows 2000 shares. Using Windows Explorer, you can connect to an NFS export (share) just as you would to any other shared file system network resource. Use the Windows syntax \\server\share, the UNIX syntax server:/share, or a command-line Net Use command. The UNIX syntax is typically faster.

Usability Services

SFU has only a limited number of the many UNIX command-line utilities on which it is based. It provides basic file and directory utilities, text utilities, programming utilities, and security-related utilities. If you want more UNIX functionality, you can buy a third party add-on.

Windows computers can print to a UNIX computer using Line Printer Remote (LPR), a network protocol in the TCP/IP suite. With the LPR protocol, a client application on one computer sends a print job to the spooler on another computer. The print service is called Line Printer Daemon (LPD). You can also use Samba to allow UNIX workstations to share their attached printers with Windows clients or to have UNIX computers print to Windows computers.

You can use several emulations of UNIX shells to Windows 2000. SFU provides an implementation of the UNIX Korn shell in Windows 2000, which makes concessions to the Windows environment such as case-insensitivity and the Windows drive letter syntax. UNIX scripts can be ported to this shell with minor modifications. Another emulation is the Interix Portable Operating System Interface Standard (POSIX) implementation from Softway Systems. Interix is a POSIX subsystem that integrates into the Windows 2000 kernel. Unlike the modified Korn shell, the Interix POSIX shell implements UNIX conventions into Windows 2000.

Configuring Access to Novell NetWare Networks

Novell NetWare still holds a large share of the enterprise market, so Windows 2000 keeps the features of Microsoft Windows NT 4.0 that allow for interoperability between the two operating systems. The following are the main features that Windows 2000 has kept:

NWLink—This is Microsoft's version of the NetWare communication protocol IPX/SPX. NWLink allows for connectivity between Windows 2000 and NetWare computers.

Gateway Service for NetWare (GSNW)—This permits a Windows 2000 server to connect to NetWare servers operating NetWare v4.x and v5.x, which run Novell Directory Services (NDS). NDS is a distributed database that maintains information about every resource on the network and provides access to these resources, much like the Windows 2000 Active Directory. Included is support for login scripts. The GSNW creates a gateway on a Windows 2000 server through which Windows clients can access NetWare resources.

File and Print Services for NetWare (FPNW)—Allows NetWare clients to directly access files and printers on a Windows 2000 server.

Novell also provides access to Windows resources through client software aimed at all Windows variations.

NWLink

To install and configure NWLink, follow these steps:

1. Right-click on **My Network Places** and select **Properties**.

2. Right-click on the local area connection where you want to install NWLink. Choose **Properties**, and select **Install**.

3. Choose **Protocol**, and select **Add**.

4. Select **NWLink IPX/SPX Compatible Transport Protocol** from the list, and click OK.

5. In the Local Area Connection Properties page (Figure 1.14), select **NWLink**, and choose **Properties**. Three components are needed to configure NWLink: the **network number** and **frame type** are automatically selected by Windows 2000 during installation of NWLink and a default **internal network number** is also provided. However, you need to change this to match the internal number for your network if GSNW or IPX Routing is enabled.

Figure 1.14 Local Area Connection Properties

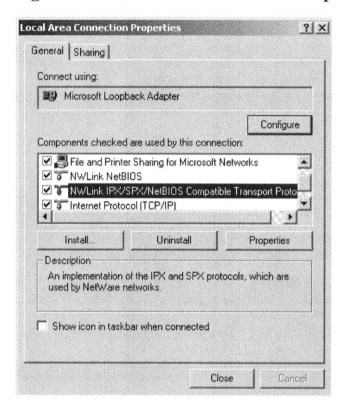

 Note: The Microsoft and Novell version of TCP/IP were not compatible until NetWare v5, so you need NWLink to communicate with NetWare v4.x and earlier servers.

The frame type defines the way the network adapter card formats data. Windows can usually autodetect the network frame type, but you can also enter the frame type manually. A unique network number for each network segment is needed for each frame type. In order for all hosts on a segment to communicate, they must have the same network number. To get configuration details on NWLink after you have configured it, use the **IPXROUTE CONFIG** command at the command prompt.

Tip: A common communication problem in mixed NetWare environments is an incorrect frame type. Client/server communication can only take place using a common frame type. This item has appeared on previous certification exams.

GSNW

Client Services for NetWare (CSNW) and Gateway Services for NetWare (GSNW) found in Microsoft Windows NT 4.0 have been combined in Windows 2000 Server to form Gateway (and Client) Services for NetWare (GSNW). Because the client services feature is included in Windows 2000 Professional as CSNW, Windows 2000 Workstations can make direct connection to resources on NetWare computers operating NetWare v2.x and later without using GSNW. They just need to have an associated user account with the correct permissions on the NetWare server and have NWLink installed.

For enterprise computing, save time on installing and configuring each workstation with CSNW by using GSNW on a Windows 2000 server (Figure 1.15). It is more difficult, however, to customize security on an individual basis when using GSNW. Each user profile takes a separate share on the gateway, limiting the number of shares to the number of unused drive letters.

With the installation of GSNW on a Windows 2000 server, you can run many common NetWare utilities and NetWare-specific applications from the command prompt.

Note: GSNW does not support utilities for NetWare v4.x or earlier.

Figure 1.15 Gateway (and Client) Services for NetWare

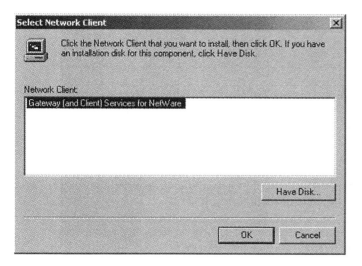

FPNW

Microsoft offers an add-on package called Microsoft Services for NetWare, which includes File and Print Services for NetWare (FPNW) and Directory Service Manager for NetWare (DSMN). FPNW allows a Windows 2000 server to provide file and print services to NetWare v4.x and earlier clients operating in bindery emulation mode. No additional configuration on the part of the NetWare client is needed.

Active Directory and DSMN work together to streamline management of the resulting mixed Windows 2000 and NetWare environment. DSMN copies NetWare user accounts to Active Directory and brings back any changes to the NetWare server.

Vocabulary

Review the following terms in preparation for the certification exam.

Term	Description
Active Directory	The directory service included with Windows 2000 Server. Active Directory stores information about objects on a network in a hierarchical view and provides a single point of administration for all network objects.
AppleTalk	The communication protocol used by Macintosh clients. AppleTalk must be installed on a computer running Windows 2000 Server for Macintosh clients to connect to it.
Computer browser service	A service used by Windows computers that maintain an updated list of shared resources on a network or subnet. Computers take on browser roles through elections.
CSNW	Client Service for NetWare is a service included with Windows 2000 Professional that allows clients to connect directly to resources on servers running NetWare 2.x and later.
Daemon	A process that runs in the background and performs a specified operation at predefined times or in response to certain events.
DHCP	Dynamic Host Configuration Protocol is a networking protocol that simplifies TCP/IP network configuration and dynamically configures IP addresses for clients. DHCP ensures that address conflicts do not occur by centralizing address allocation.

Term	Description
DNS	Domain Name System is the hierarchical naming system used to locate domain names on the Internet and on private TCP/IP networks. The DNS service maps DNS domain names to IP addresses and vice-versa.
FPNW	File and Print Services for NetWare is part of an add-on package called Microsoft Services for NetWare. It runs on a Windows 2000 server and emulates a NetWare server, providing resources for NetWare clients.
FSM	File Server for Macintosh is a Windows 2000 service that manages the publishing of shared files and allows Macintosh users file access.
FTP	File Transfer Protocol is a protocol that defines how to transfer files from one computer to another over the Internet. It is also a client/server application that moves files using this protocol.
Global Catalog	A Windows 2000 service and data store that holds a partial replica of each object found in the Active Directory, along with commonly accessed attributes. When a user begins browsing the network, the associated computer will contact a Global Catalog to look up a specific computer name.
GSNW	Gateway Service for NetWare is a service that creates a gateway in which Microsoft clients can access NetWare resources through a Windows 2000 server.
HTTP	HyperText Transfer Protocol is the protocol used to transfer information on the World Wide Web. It defines how messages are formatted and transmitted.

Term	Description
IPSec	Internet Protocol Security is a set of industry-standard, cryptography-based protection services and protocols. IPSec protects all protocols in the TCP/IP suite.
IPX/SPX	Internetwork Packet Exchange/Sequenced Packet Exchange is Novell NetWare's networking protocol. Microsoft has its own version of IPX/SPX called NWLink.
Kerberos	The default user and host authentication protocol for Windows 2000. Internet Protocol security may use the Kerberos protocol for authentication.
Kernel	The essential part of an operating system that provides basic services. It manages memory, processes, tasks, and disks.
LDAP	Lightweight Directory Access Protocol is a directory service protocol that runs over TCP/IP and is the primary access protocol for Active Directory.
LPD	Line Printer Daemon, which originally was a UNIX component, acts like print server. It receives print jobs from LPR clients and sends them to a printer.
LPR	Line Printer Remote is a command-line utility provided by Windows 2000. LPR directs and monitors print jobs aimed for UNIX host printers.
L2TP	Layer 2 Tunneling Protocol is a tunneling protocol that encapsulates Point-to-Point frames to be sent over IP, X.25, Frame Relay, or ATM networks.
MAC address	Media Access Control address is the address used for communication between network adapters on the same subnet. Each network adapter has an associated MAC address.

Term	Description
MAV	Macintosh Accessible Volume is a Windows shared folder or file that appears as a volume to Macintosh clients who use Apple's file-sharing software to connect to the MAV.
Microsoft Certificate Services	An optional component of Windows 2000 that lets you issue digital security certificates, certify them as valid, and revoke undesired certificates.
MMC	Microsoft Management Console is a framework for hosting administrative consoles. A console is defined by the items on its console tree. It has windows that provide views of the tree as well as the administrative properties, services, and events that are acted on by items in the console tree.
NAT	Network Address Translation is a protocol that allows a network with private addresses to access information on the Internet through an IP translation process.
NDS	Novell Directory Services is a distributed database that operates on Novell NetWare 4.x and 5.x networks. NDS maintains information about every resource on the network and provides access to these resources.
NetBIOS name	A name recognized by WINS, the service that maps a computer name to its IP address.
NetBT	NetBIOS over TCP/IP is a feature that provides the NetBIOS programming interface over the TCP/IP protocol. It is used for monitoring routed servers that use NetBIOS name resolution.
NNTP	Network News Transfer Protocol is part of the TCP/IP suite and is used to distribute network news messages on the Internet from a central database on a server.

Term	Description
NT	New Technologies is Microsoft's version of Windows previous to Windows 2000.
NTFS	New Technologies File System is a file system designed for Windows NT and Windows 2000. It provides data security, file system reliability, and file system recoverability.
NTLM	New Technologies LAN Manager is a Microsoft client login authentication system that gives a transparent connection to the host while ensuring that clear text passwords do not pass over the network.
NWLink	Microsoft's implementation of IPX/SPX, Novell's transport protocol that supports routing and client-server applications.
OSPF	Open Shortest Path First is a protocol that defines how routers share routing information. OSPF transfers only new routing information, to conserve bandwidth.
PKI	Public Key Infrastructure includes the laws, standards, policies, and software that regulate certificates and public and private keys. This system of digital certificates and certification authorities authenticate the validity of each party in an electronic transaction.
Pods	Groupings of UNIX hosts that simplify administration.
PPTP	Point-to-Point Tunneling Protocol is a tunneling protocol that encapsulates Point-to-Point frames for transmission over the Internet or a private intranet.
PSM	Print Server for Macintosh is a Windows 2000 service that permits Windows and Macintosh computers to share each other's printers.

Term	Description
QoS	Quality of Service is a set of quality assurance standards and mechanisms for data transmission in Windows 2000.
RADIUS	Remote Authentication Dial-In User Service, the most common authentication protocol used by Internet service providers. Running on an Internet Authentication Service server with Windows 2000, RADIUS can be used to manage the access policies of remote access servers.
RAS	Remote Access Service is a Windows service that permits remote networking for mobile workers and for system administrators who monitor and manage servers at multiple sites.
RIP	Routing Information Protocol. A protocol that specifies how routers exchange routing information. Because RIP exchanges entire routing tables, it is being replaced by the more efficient OSPF protocol.
Samba	A popular SMB server freeware that has ports for many versions of UNIX.
SDLC	Synchronous Data Link Control is a protocol used for communication in IBM's SNA networks.
SFU	Windows NT Services for UNIX is a Microsoft package that facilitates interoperability between Windows 2000 and UNIX hosts.
SMB	Server Message Block is a file-sharing protocol that allows networked computers to transparently access files residing on remote systems over a variety of networks.

Term	Description
SMTP	Simple Mail Transport Protocol is a protocol used to transfer mail on the Internet. SMTP is independent of the transmission subsytem.
SNA	Systems Network Architecture is a communications interface used to establish a link with IBM mainframes and AS/400 hosts.
TCO	Total Cost of Ownership. The total cost of purchasing an item, including implementation and administrative costs, and lost employee productivity.
TCP/IP	Transport Control Protocol/Internet Protocol is a set of protocols that provides communication among diverse networks. Because it accommodates different architectures and operating systems, TCP/IP is the most commonly used Internet protocol.
Telnet	A terminal emulation program that is used on the Internet to log on to network computers.
Transitive trust	The trust relationships between Windows 2000 domains in a domain tree or forest, between trees in a forest, or between forests. Transitive trusts are automatically established when a domain joins an existing forest or domain tree.
UDP	User Datagram Protocol is a TCP/IP component that transmits data through a connectionless service but does not guarantee the delivery or sequencing delivery of sent packets.
VPN	Virtual Private Network is the extension of a private network that encompasses links across shared or public networks such as the Internet.

Term	Description
WINS	Windows Internet Name Service is a Microsoft software service that dynamically maps IP addresses to computer names. This allows users to access resources by name instead of by IP address.
X.25	A popular protocol used in packet-switching networks.
X.509	The most widely used standard for defining digital certificates. An X.509 certificate includes the public key and information about the person or entity to whom the certificate is issued, as well as information about the certificate.

In Brief

If you want to...	Then do this...
Migrate or upgrade your network to Windows 2000	Consider current business requirements and IT capabilities. Then determine your business and IT goals. Be realistic in your assessments, keeping in mind available technical support, money, and time.
Provide Macintosh users access to your Windows 2000 network	Install and configure the AppleTalk protocol. Implement the File Server for Macintosh (FSM) and Print Server for Macintosh (PSM) services. Purchase a third-party utility to allow Windows clients to access files on a Macintosh computer.
Configure interoperability between Windows 2000 and IBM hosts	Use SNA Server to provide services for file and print sharing. Establish a PC-host connection and manage host resources through the Windows 2000 server.
Configure access to UNIX resources	Implement Microsoft's Windows NT Services for UNIX (SFU) package. Functions include Network File System, Telnet, the UNIX Korn shell and utilities, and a password synchronization daemon.
Configure access to Novell NetWare networks	Install and configure the NWLink protocol. Then implement Gateway Service for NetWare (GSNW) to create a gateway on a Windows 2000 server through which the Windows client can access NetWare resources. Novell can also access Windows resources through client software targeting all Windows variations.

Lesson 1 Activities

Complete the following activities to better prepare you for the certification exam.

1. Describe the protocol on which the Active Directory is built and explain its significance.

2. Discuss the factors to consider and activities to perform when assessing a network for an upgrade or a migration.

3. Explain how to provide a Macintosh client access to a file on your Windows 2000 server.

4. Describe the advantages of SNA server over direct PC-IBM host connections.

5. List the three basic parts of Windows NT Services for UNIX (SFU).

6. Discuss the advantages and disadvantages of installing Client Services for NetWare (CSNW) versus Gateway Services for NetWare (GSNW).

7. Explain why Windows 2000 built-in Internet functionality is important in a network environment.

8. Discuss the relationship between WINS and DNS in Windows 2000.

9. List four differences between Windows 2000 and UNIX.

10. Explain briefly Microsoft Certificate Services.

Answers to Lesson 1 Activities

1. The Active Directory is built on the Lightweight Directory Access Protocol (LDAP). Application developers can write to this standard and integrate security for their products with Windows 2000 built-in security.

2. Document both hardware and software on the network to determine which items need to be supported and if preparatory upgrades are needed. Then decide if there are incompatible operating systems and applications that support specific departmental needs.

    Next, make a graphical representation of the physical linkages to better assess where the network can be expanded, optimal traffic routing, and placement of equipment. Monitor network traffic patterns using a sniffer product to determine the number and best placement of hubs, switches and routers. Get information on bandwidth needs of workstations as well as future needs for network management software. The traffic patterns may dictate a specific type of WAN connectivity.

    Decide if current interoperability with other operating systems such as UNIX or NetWare needs to be maintained. Determine the kind of external connectivity you have and what will be needed in the future. Then analyze current security measures and projected security requirements.

3. To integrate a Macintosh client into a Windows 2000 network, first install the AppleTalk protocol on your network. Then install File Server for Macintosh (FSM) on an NTFS partition on the Windows 2000 domain controller to which the Macintosh client will log on. FSM will convert standard Windows NTFS shares to Macintosh Accessible Volumes (MAVs). Either create a new share by using the Create Shared Folder Wizard or create a MAV for a pre-existing Windows share by using the wizard to form a Macintosh share pointing to the same item.

4. Advantages of SNA server include:

    *   Increased security because Windows 2000 security is applied to the host session

    *   The PC workstation no longer needs a host cable or adapter card

    *   Only one physical connection to the host needs to be managed to retain client connectivity

    *   Client connections to the host are not limited by physical connections as they would be with a direct connection

5. SFU has three basic parts:

    *   Connectivity services: a Telnet server, a Telnet client, and password synchronization daemon

- File services: NFS client and server support

- Usability services: UNIX utilities and a Korn shell

6. Because CSNW is included in Windows 2000 Professional, Windows 2000 workstations can connect directly to resources on NetWare computers operating NetWare 2.x and later. For enterprise computing, you can save time spent installing and configuring each computer with CSNW by using GSNW. However, customizing client security becomes a problem, because all GSNW clients are treated the same. Also, each user profile uses a separate share on the gateway, limiting the number of concurrent shares to the number of unused drive letters.

7. One highlight of Windows 2000 is its built-in Internet functionality. Since server support exists for most Internet protocols, a Windows 2000 server can act as a Web server, File Transfer Protocol (FTP) server, Simple Mail Transport Protocol (SMTP) host, or Network News Transfer Protocol (NNTP) host.

8. Windows Internet Naming Service (WINS) is a proprietary Microsoft service that resolves IP addresses to NetBIOS (computer) names. Domain Name System (DNS) is a standard service that maps Internet DNS domain names to IP addresses. In Windows 2000, DNS is the default name resolution service. Because of this reliance on DNS, you only need WINS if you have a network containing more than Windows 2000 servers and Windows 2000 clients.

9. Windows 2000 characteristics:

- Designed for client-server operation

- Has expanded file metaphor, with all UNIX devices including device rights being seen as objects

- The Security Reference Monitor, the Logon Process protected subsystem, and Security protected subsystem provide security

- Individual permissions are Read, Write, Execute, Delete, Change Permissions, and Take Ownership

- Multiple user and group associations with a file

- Filename extensions .COM, .EXE, .BAT or .CMD indicate executability

UNIX characteristics:

- Designed for host-based terminal computing

- All devices such printers and tape drives appear as ordinary files

- Security provided from add-ons such as Kerberos

- File and directory permission can only be given to the owner, group, or world

- Three basic permissions are Read, Write, and Execute

- Three user associations with a file: the file owner, a member of the same group as the owner, and everyone else

- No relationship between file extension and execution status

10. Microsoft Certificate Services is an optional component of Windows 2000 that lets you issue digital security certificates, certify them as valid, and revoke undesired certificates. It is used with the Public Key Infrastructure (PKI) to provide enterprise security.

Lesson 1 Quiz

These questions test your knowledge of features, vocabulary, procedures, and syntax.

1. Why does your computer contact the Active Directory Global Catalogs when you begin to browse a Windows 2000 network?
    A. Global Catalogs contain more comprehensive information than Active Directory.
    B. A Global Catalog's attribute listing is smaller than the listing in the full Active Directory, so indexing is faster.
    C. There is no particular browse order. Depending on the resource desired, your computer contacts either a Global Catalog or the Active Directory.
    D. The Active Directory is always contacted directly first.

2. What are some factors to consider when assessing an upgrade or migration for you network?
    A. Availability of technical support staff
    B. Money
    C. Time
    D. New technologies

3. Why would you alter the mapping associations between the Windows 2000 extensions and Macintosh operating system creator codes on a Windows 2000 FSM server?
    A. You do not need to alter the mapping associations for newer extensions, just for older extensions that support legacy Windows operating systems.
    B. You should not alter the mapping associations. They are configured and optimized automatically.
    C. The map needs to be customized for your particular network.
    D. The current version of FSM does not support .BMP, .GIF, .JPG and .HTM extensions by default.

4. Which of the following are Internet related security protocols?
    A. HTTP
    B. IPX/SPX
    C. IPSec
    D. Kerberos

5. What is the file-sharing protocol that Windows uses to access files over a network?
    A. Samba
    B. SMTP
    C. SMB
    D. SDLC

6. What is the main difference between Open Shortest Path First (OSPF) and Routing Internet Protocol (RIP)?
    A. OSPF is faster than RIP.
    B. RIP is more efficient in exchanging routing table entries.
    C. OSPF transfers only new routing information.
    D. RIP is faster than OSPF.

7. Which protocol(s) allows for the creation of a Virtual Private Network?
    A. L2TP
    B. PPTP
    C. NNTP
    D. LPD

8. Which of the following describes the SFU password synchronization daemon?
    A. A compiled binary daemon that runs on a Windows 2000 server
    B. A daemon that allows you to manage user passwords for both Windows 2000 and UNIX clients from a Windows 2000 server
    C. A daemon that allows you to manage user passwords for both Windows 2000 and Sun Microsystem's version of UNIX only
    D. A daemon that automatically records a Windows 2000 or UNIX client's password onto the UNIX server

9. You want to access resources on a NetWare server from a Windows 2000 Professional computer. What do you need to obtain access?
    A. Administrator privileges
    B. NWLink
    C. A user account on the NetWare server
    D. GSNW

10. What is a common communication problem in mixed NetWare environments?
    A. Incompatible protocols
    B. Cabling problems
    C. Network adapter card problems
    D. Incompatible frame types

Answers to Lesson # Quiz

1. Answer B is correct. A Global Catalog is derived from entries in the Active Directory. It has fewer attribute listings for the same objects than Active Directory, so indexing is faster.

    Answer A is incorrect. The Active Directory contains more comprehensive information than a Global Catalog.

    Answers C and D are incorrect. By default a Global Catalog is contacted first.

2. Answers A, B, C, and D are all correct. When planning an upgrade or migration for your IT infrastructure, keep in mind the availability of technical support staff, money, time, and new technology.

3. Answer D is correct. Mapping associations in the Windows 2000 registry are created by FSM automatically. However, the current version of FSM does not support newer applications with extensions such as .BMP, .GIF, .JPG and .HTM by default. You need to map the associations through the File Association tab of the FSM Properties Window.

    Answer A is incorrect. The reverse is true.

    Answer B is incorrect. As with any other automatically configured registry setting, make changes to the map if needed to optimize performance.

    Answer C is incorrect. You are not required to customize the mapping associations for your network.

4. Answers C and D are correct. Internet Protocol Security (IPSec) is a set of industry-standard protection services and protocols. IPSec protects all protocols in the TCP/IP suite through cryptography.
    Kerberos is the default user and host authentication protocol used by Windows 2000. IPSec uses Kerberos for authentication.

    Answer A is incorrect. HyperText Transfer Protocol (HTTP) defines how messages are formatted and transmitted across the World Wide Web.

    Answer B is incorrect. Internetwork Packet Exchange/Sequenced Packet Exchange (IPX/SPX) is Novell NetWare's networking protocol.

5. Answer C is correct. Server Message Block (SMB) is a file-sharing protocol used by Windows computers to transparently access files residing on remote systems over a variety of networks.

    Answer A is incorrect. Samba is a widely available SMB server freeware that can communicate with many versions of UNIX.

Answer B is incorrect. Simple Mail Transport Protocol (SMTP) transfers mail on the Internet independently of the transmission subsystem.

Answer D is incorrect. Synchronous Data Link Control (SDLC) is the communication protocol used by IBM's SNA networks.

6. Answer C is correct. OSPF is a recent protocol that defines how routers share routing information. Unlike RIP which transfers whole routing tables, OSPF transfers only routing information that has changed since the last transfer, which conserves bandwidth.

    Answer A is incorrect. The main difference is the conservation of bandwidth, not so much the speed.

    Answer B is incorrect. OSPF is more efficient in exchanging routing table entries than RIP.

    Answer D is incorrect. RIP is not faster than OSPF.

7. Answers A and B are correct. Layer 2 Tunneling Protocol (L2TP) encapsulates Point-to-Point frames, which can then be sent over IP, X.25, Frame Relay, or ATM networks. Point-to-Point Tunneling Protocol (PPTP) is another tunneling protocol that encapsulates Point-to-Point frames for transmission over the Internet or a private intranet.

    Answer C is incorrect. Network News Transfer Protocol (NNTP) is used to distribute network news messages on the Internet from a central database on a server.

    Answer D is incorrect. Line Printer Remote (LPR) is used by Windows 2000 to direct and monitor print jobs aimed for printers attached to UNIX hosts.

8. Answer B is correct. The SFU password synchronization daemon automatically records changes to a Windows 2000 or UNIX client's password on the Windows 2000 server.

    Answer A is incorrect. The SFU password synchronization daemon is a precompiled binary daemon that runs on the UNIX server.

    Answer C is incorrect. The daemon allows you to manage user password for Windows 2000 clients as well as HP-UX, Sun Microsystems OS, and Digital UNIX hosts.

    Answer D is incorrect. The passwords are recorded and managed from the Windows 2000 server not the UNIX hosts.

9. Answers B and C are correct. A user accessing a NetWare server directly requires a user account on the NetWare server. In order to have a common communication protocol, NWLink needs to be installed and configured.

Answer A is incorrect. You do not need administrator privileges.

Answer D is incorrect. Gateway Service for NetWare (GSNW) is not needed because Client Service for NetWare (CSNW) is part of Windows 2000 Professional.

10. Answer D is correct. Client-server communication can only take place using a common NetWare frame type.

Answer A is incorrect. The protocol is common. The frame types that are set to be autodetected are different, however. Simply manually configure the frame types.

Answer B is incorrect. Cabling problems are frequently the cause of communication problems in any network, but they are not unique to a mixed NetWare system.

Answer C is incorrect. Problems with network adapter cards often result in communication problems in any network, but they are not unique to a mixed NetWare system.

Lesson 2

DNS Installation and Configuration

Domain Name Service (DNS) provides name resolution for hosts using Transport Control Protocol/Internet Protocol (TCP/IP), the Internet's communication protocol. After you configure the DNS with a list of host names and corresponding Internet Protocol (IP) addresses, users can connect to other computers through friendly names instead of by IP addresses. Windows 2000 is the first Microsoft operating system that uses DNS by default for name resolution. Other improvements over previous versions of Windows DNS include an easier administrative interface and dynamic updating capabilities.

DNS uses Fully Qualified Domain Names (FQDN), such as netadmin.lightpointlearning.wa, to determine the IP address of a system. The hierarchical DNS structure consists of a root domain, which is indicated by a single dot. The root domain encompasses all other domains. Next are top-level domains organized according to their function or country of origin, such as .gov for government or .wa for Washington. Unique second-level domains that represent a business or organization, such as lightpointlearning.wa, provide further name refinement. Finally, the host name specifies a single computer or private network, such as netadmin.lightpointlearning.wa.

After completing this lesson, you should have a better understanding of the following topics:

- DNS Overview

- DNS Server Service Installation

- DNS Server Service Configuration

- Cache-Only Server Configuration

- DNS Script Configuration

- DNS Server Service Monitoring

DNS Overview

A DNS server retains the DNS data for its network as well as a list of other DNS servers to which it can refer requests for hierarchical name resolution (Figure 2.1). Historically, one drawback to DNS was the static DNS tables used to resolve host names to IP addresses. You needed to enter this information manually before replicating it over your network or over the Internet to other DNS servers. This manual administration of DNS tables required in Microsoft Windows NT 4.0 has been replaced in Windows 2000 with a dynamic update of DNS records.

Figure 2.1 Hierarchical FQDN Resolutions

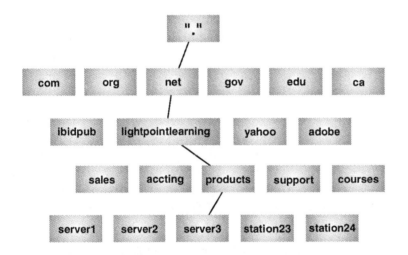

You can use DNS exclusively only if all clients on your network are running Windows 2000. Otherwise, you need Windows Internet Naming Service (WINS) for name resolution in a network with computers running legacy versions of Windows. WINS dynamically maps IP addresses to Network Basic Input/Output System (NetBIOS) (computer names).

The Microsoft Windows version of DNS can be integrated easily with WINS and other Windows TCP/IP services, such as Dynamic Host Configuration Protocol (DHCP). DHCP dynamically configures and allocates IP addresses for clients. However, the full functionality of DNS is only realized when it works with Active Directory. Active Directory is a Windows 2000 feature which stores information about network objects in a hierarchical view and provides a single point of administration for all network objects.

Windows 2000 features several wizards to help you install and configure the DNS Server service. In particular with mixed environments involving UNIX clients, make sure of the correct configuration so that UNIX computers can also use DNS. In UNIX systems, DNS is referred to as Berkeley Internet Name Domain (BIND).

DNS Server Service Installation

The DNS Server service is key to name resolution functionality in Windows 2000 and is essential to Active Directory. Ideally, you would install DNS on every domain controller so that a DNS server can use the Active Directory to store zone information. Zones are a particular domain or area within a domain housing a subset of DNS records that are grouped together for administrative purposes. A DNS server holding the relevant zone database file handles queries for name resolution. You can have multiple DNS servers within a zone, and DNS servers can store information for more than one zone.

With Active Directory, DNS administration is simplified with full replication of records between authoritative DNS servers in different zones. An authoritative server is the primary DNS server within a zone. This server keeps an updated master copy of DNS records and the zone's configuration files, which simplifies fault tolerance.

You can create the following four types of Windows 2000 DNS servers:

Active Directory-integrated primary—A DNS server, fully integrated with Active Directory and with all DNS data stored in the Directory, is one type of DNS server. You can automatically install DNS with a default configuration when you install the first domain controller on an Active Directory network or promote a computer to be a domain controller.

The benefits of a fully integrated DNS server include support for any domain controller to access DNS data. In addition, clients that obtain dynamically updated DNS records through DHCP can get information from any DNS server within a zone. Other benefits of full integration are simplified replication of DNS information throughout the network, the ability to use directory security to screen access to DNS information, and easier DNS administration.

Primary server—As the authoritative DNS server for a domain that is only partially integrated with Active Directory, the primary server stores a master copy of DNS records and the domain's configuration files as text at %SystemRoot%\System32\ Dns. Updates are handled by the primary

DNS server for the zone. The main drawback of partial integration is increased administrative complexity as DNS information is stored and replicated separately from Active Directory. This can increase network traffic and delay replication of DNS changes.

Secondary server—Acting as a backup to the primary DNS server, the secondary server keeps an updated copy of DNS records it receives from a primary DNS server through zone transfers. This provides fault tolerance and load balancing with the primary server. On startup, secondary servers get a full copy of the DNS information from a primary server.

Cache-only server—This type of server always passes DNS requests to other servers but caches DNS information after lookups. Cache-only servers do not get full copies of a zone's database files. On startup, its database is empty.

Installing the DNS Server

To enable DNS on your network, install the DNS Server service and configure DNS clients to have the IP addresses of DNS servers on the network. Complete the following steps to install a DNS server on a member server for the first time:

1. From the **Start** menu, choose **Settings**, **Control Panel**, and select **Add/Remove Programs**.

2. From the left pane of **Add/Remove Programs**, choose **Add/Remove Windows Components**.

3. From **Windows Components**, choose **Networking Services** and **Details**.

4. From **Networking Services**, choose the **Domain Name System (DNS)** checkbox, click **OK**, and select **Next**.

5. Specify the location for the installation files, and, from **Completing the Windows Components**, choose **Finish** (Figure 2.2).

Figure 2.2 Networking Services Window

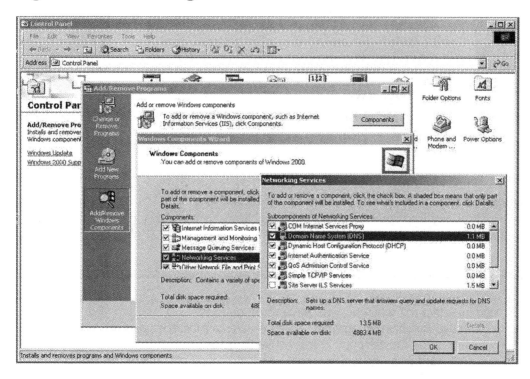

Warning: Assign your Windows 2000 server a static IP address before you install the DNS service to avoid network problems associated with a dynamically assigned IP address.

The management tool for DNS is added to the Administrative Tools folder once you have installed your first DNS server.

Configuring a DNS Zone

After you finish the installation, you need to set up DNS and configure server zones. A New Zone Wizard is available to simplify the creation and initial configuration of zones:

1. From the **Start** menu, choose **Programs**, **Administrative Tools**, and then **DNS**.

2. Choose **Next** and within **Root Servers** (if your server cannot find a root server on the network, you must decide between two options), you can either make your server the root server, by selecting **This is the first DNS server on this network**, or you can type the IP address of the root server, and then select **Next**.

3. Within Add Forward Lookup Zone, choose Forward lookup zone and then Next.

4. Within **Select a Zone Type**, choose **Standard secondary** (Figure 2.3) if you have fully integrated Active Directory into your network, otherwise, **Standard primary** is selected by default, and then choose **Next**.

 Note: Within Select a Zone Type, you have three options:
- Active Directory integrated, which creates a master copy of a new zone and stores the master copy in the Active Directory
- Standard primary, which creates a master copy of a new zone and stores the master copy in a text file
- Standard secondary, which creates a replica of an existing zone

Figure 2.3 Zone Type Selection

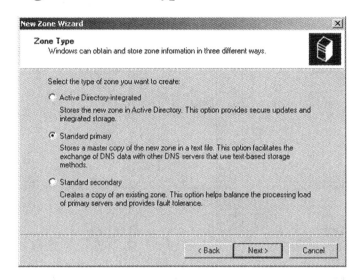

5. Within **Zone Name**, type the name of the zone, and choose **Next**.

6. From **Add Reverse Lookup Zone**, choose **Yes** if desired, and choose **Next**.

Note: Reverse lookup occurs when IP addresses are resolved to names instead of the usual names to IP addresses. A reverse lookup zone, while not mandatory, is useful because it allows you to record names instead of IP address in your Internet Information Server log files. Internet Information Server (IIS) is Microsoft's web server. Also, reverse lookup must be enabled to run troubleshooting tools such as NSLOOKUP.

Note: The reverse DNS entry will return a value different from the actual one if a message has been sent through a firewall.

7. If you selected **Yes,** choose a zone type in the window that appears, and select **Next.**

8. Specify the reverse lookup zone by typing either the network ID and subnet mask, or the name of the reverse lookup zone.

 Tip: Determine the name of the reverse lookup zone by reversing all octets but the last one in the IP address and appending them to "in-addr.arpa". For example, the IP address 200.120.50.24 would get the reverse zone name of 50.120.200.in-addr.arpa.

9. Choose **Next,** select to create a new file, and then **Next** again.

10. Review the summary of your server's configuration, and choose **Next.**

11. Type the network class and subnet mask of your network, choose **Next** and then **Finish.**

The DNS Server service is vital to a smoothly functioning Active Directory and to an overall TCP/IP network. As a result, Microsoft recommends that you configure multiple DNS servers in each zone for fault tolerance, with one DNS server per zone fully integrated into Active Directory.

Once you have finished creating a DNS zone for a server, many of the remaining configuration parameters can be accessed through the Properties sheet for that zone.

Configuring a DNS Zone Transfer Process

Each zone you create has six associated property pages. To access them, right-click on the zone you wish to configure and choose Properties. The six pages are:

General—This tab lets you manage and configure dynamic updates for the zone. Information is available on the operational status and type of zone. From this tab, you can change the zone type and select the kind of dynamic updates you require. The options available are to permit no dynamic updates, allow all dynamic updates or, when the zone is integrated with Active Directory, restrict updates to certain IP to name mappings (Figure 2.4). You can also set up aging and scavenging parameters to scavenge records that have not been refreshed in a long time. Doing so prevents the unrestricted growth of a DNS database.

Figure 2.4 Zone General Property Page

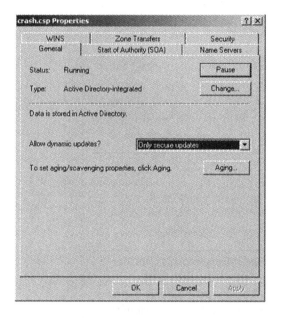

Start of Authority (SOA)—The SOA defines the authoritative name server for a zone and controls how DNS information is propagated throughout the network. Fields in the SOA tab of the zone Properties sheet are listed in Table 2.1.

Table 2.1 SOA Fields

Field	Description
Serial number	The version of the DNS database files. When you change zone files, this number is automatically updated. Secondary servers compare the serial number of their database files with that of the primary server and can request updated DNS zone records whenever the primary server's version shows new records.
Primary server	Enter the Fully Qualified Domain Name for the name server, followed by a period.
Responsible person	Gives the e-mail address of the person in charge of the domain.
Refresh interval	The time interval in which a secondary server checks for zone updates.
Retry interval	The time the secondary server waits after a failed zone database transfer request before asking again.
Expires after	The period of time the zone information is considered valid on the secondary server, after which the secondary DNS server will stop responding to queries if it cannot get updated database files from the primary DNS server.
Minimum (default) TTL	Gives the minimum Time-to-Live for cached records on a secondary server.
TTL of this record	This entry defines the Time-to-Live value for the SOA record and is usually the same as the minimum TTL (Figure 2.5).

Tip: To reduce network traffic, set the minimum TTL to a high number, such as 24 hours. Balance efficiency with the need to propagate updates through the Internet.

Figure 2.5 Zone SOA Property Page

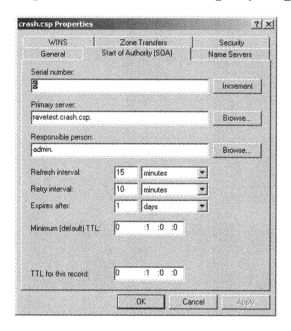

WINS—You need to integrate WINS with DNS if you have a mixed environment where earlier versions of Windows exist. The WINS page of the zone properties sheet permits you to configure forward lookups using NetBIOS (computer names), reverse lookups, and caching and time-out values for WINS resolution. Simply add a WINS and WINS Reverse (WINS-R) record to the zone where you want WINS lookup to be supported.

During a WINS lookup in DNS, the DNS server looks for an address record for the specified FQDN. If it does not find a record, the server extracts the host name and uses WINS to try to resolve the name as a NetBIOS name (Figure 2.6).

Figure 2.6 WINS Property Page

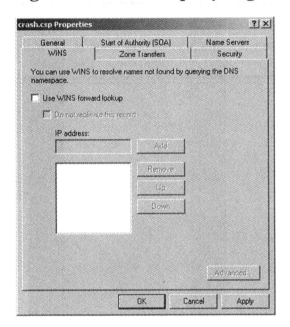

Configuring reverse WINS lookup is very much like configuring WINS lookup in DNS. The difference is that you are configuring the resolution of an IP address to a NetBIOS name. The DNS server looks for a record for the specified IP address. If it does not find one, the server sends a request to WINS, which returns a NetBIOS name for the IP address. This host domain is then appended to the computer name (Figure 2.7).

Figure 2.7 WINS-R Property Page

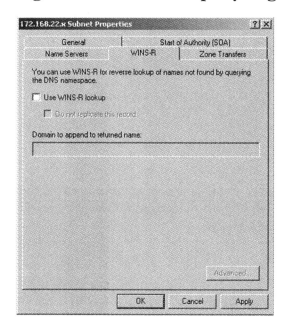

If you integrate WINS with DNS, set WINS caching and time-out values through the Advanced dialog box in the WINS or WINS-R pages. The caching field determines the length of time records returned from WINS remain valid, while the time-out value determines the length of time DNS will wait for a response from WINS before timing out (Figure 2.8).

Figure 2.8 Time-Out Values

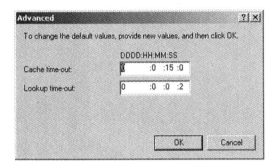

Name Servers—This page allows you to specify the names and IP addresses of other name servers. When you choose Add, a New Resource Record dialog box appears for each entry. The name servers are accessed in order of entry on the Name Servers page (Figure 2.9).

Figure 2.9 New Resource Record

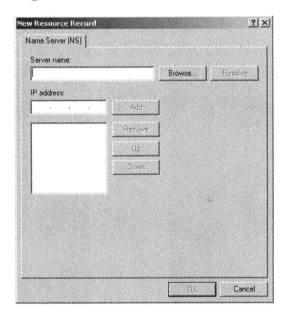

Security—You manage control of and access to a zone by users and groups through this property page (Figure 2.10).

Figure 2.10 Zone Security Property Page

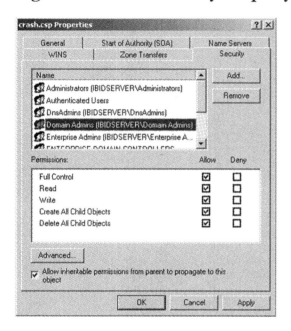

Zone Transfers—Use this page to configure zone transfers which replicate and synchronize all copies of the zone file used by each server hosting a particular zone. The primary server in a zone is configured by default to perform zone transfers with any DNS server requesting the service, while secondary DNS servers in a zone are pre-configured to perform zone transfers with the primary server in the zone. Modify these default settings to prevent unauthorized DNS servers from obtaining your zone data.

Options on the Zone Transfers page include to not perform zone transfers, perform zone transfers to any server, allow zone transfers only to servers named in the Name Servers property page, or allow transfers only to servers with specified IP addresses. You can also notify secondary servers in your zone when the zone file is updated (Figure 2.11).

Figure 2.11 Zone Transfers Property Page

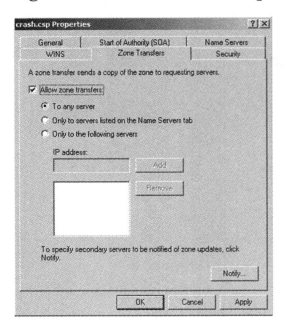

Zone transfers between DNS servers managing a zone can happen in several ways. Active Directory handles the zone replication for fully integrated DNS servers that use Active Directory to store their zone data. In this case, zones transfer updated records instead of full zone records, following the multimaster model. In multimaster replication, any domain controller accepts and replicates database changes to any other domain controller.

Incremental zone transfer is a database transfer method in which a secondary DNS server pulls only the zone changes it needs to synchronize its copy of the zone data with that of the primary server. A higher serial number is given to a DNS database whenever its records change. By checking the serial number of the primary DNS server's zone file against that of the secondary DNS server file's serial number, the secondary DNS server knows when updates become available.

Incremental zone transfer only works if both servers support it, and only for standard zone files. Only Windows 2000 computers support this feature; a full zone transfer occurs with other DNS servers such as Microsoft Windows NT 4.0 DNS servers. In this case, the secondary server pulls the entire zone file from the primary DNS server.

Note: Windows 2000 DNS servers are configured by default to perform fast zone transfers with data compression and multiple resource records sent in each message to all Windows DNS servers and BIND v4.9.4 or later DNS servers. Disable fast zone transfer for BIND servers running earlier versions.

Configuring a Zone for the Root Domain

As you previously saw, the Windows 2000 Configure DNS Wizard provides a convenient method of creating a root DNS server. The root DNS server is the first DNS server on a network. The wizard creates a root server whose initial zone configuration parameters can be fine-tuned in the zone's Properties sheet. Details about options in the zone properties page are found in Configuring a DNS Zone. The basic DNS zone parameters created by the wizard include defining the forward lookup zone type as being integrated into Active Directory, primary or secondary. A reverse lookup zone can also be defined with the same zone type options.

Delegating Authority for a Zone

The root DNS server provides the highest level of name resolution services within a hierarchically organized DNS infrastructure. Extra DNS servers can be created from this focal point. Each of these is responsible for answering DNS queries from a subset of computers on the network or their own zones. By creating additional zones and configuring more DNS servers, administrative responsibilities are more clearly divided.

For example, Figures 2.12 and 2.13 show two DNS options for LightPoint Learning Solutions. In the first option, one DNS server is authoritative for all of the organization's computers. In the second, part of the name resolution responsibilities handled by the top-level lightpointlearning.net DNS server has been offset to the acctg.lightpointlearning.net and sales.lightpointlearning.net DNS servers. Queries involving accounting or sales department computers are handled by their respective DNS servers. The lightpointlearning.net DNS server has delegated authority for a subset of lightpointlearning names.

Figure 2.12 DNS Options

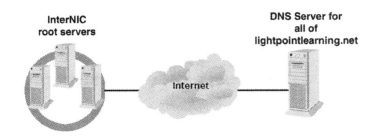

Figure 2.13 Three DNS Zones

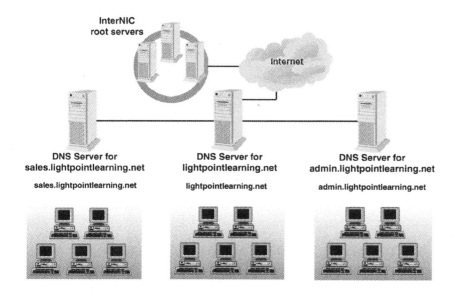

Each of the two options is valid. It depends on your Information Technologies (IT) infrastructure and the division of administrative duties within your organization.

Delegating authority is a three-part process:

- Notify the upper level domain that there will be a lower-level domain or zone under another computer's control

- Notify the DNS server of the upper-level domain where to find a DNS server for the new zone

- Configure the DNS server of the new lower-level zone

To notify the upper level domain that there will be a lower-level domain or zone under another computer's control, follow these steps:

1. From the **Start** menu, choose **Programs, Administrative Tools,** and then **DNS.**

2. Within the DNS console, right-click the upper-level domain and choose **New Domain.**

3. Type the name of the new domain, and click **OK.**

To notify the DNS server of the upper-level domain where to find a DNS server for the new zone, you need to create a host record for the new DNS server for the subdomain by following these steps:

1. From the **Start** menu, choose **Programs**, **Administrative Tools**, and then **DNS**.

2. Within the DNS console, right-click the new lower-level domain or zone, and choose **New Host**.

3. Type in the name of the DNS server that will be responsible for the new zone and its static IP address, choose **Add Host**, and click **OK**.

4. Within the DNS console, right-click the upper-level domain's folder, choose **New Delegation** and then **Next**.

5. Within **Name Servers**, choose **Add**, type the FQDN and IP address of the new DNS server responsible for the lower-level domain, click **OK**, select **Next** and then **Finish**.

To configure the DNS server of the new lower-level zone:

1. From the **Start** menu of the new DNS server, choose **Programs**, **Administrative Tools**, and then **DNS**.

2. Within the DNS console, right-click **Forward Lookup Zones**, choose **New Zone**, and the New Zone Wizard appears.

3. Proceed through the wizard steps to configure a DNS zone.

Delegating authority for a subset of your company's computers makes name resolution for an outside server slightly slower. Instead of answering most name queries, the root DNS server will usually refer questions to lower level DNS servers. This slight delay is compensated for in the clear delineation of responsibilities between DNS servers within a network. If an extra computer is added to a network, only the DNS server responsible for that computer's namespace needs to add a new DNS name record.

The distinction between DNS domains, or zones, and Windows 2000 domains must be made clear. Within your network, you can create as many DNS domains as needed to meet your organization's administrative needs. Creating additional DNS zones does not affect the computer or user division that is part of Windows 2000 domains.

DNS Server Service Configuration

The initial installation and configuration wizards help you establish a DNS server. The remaining configuration tasks can be done using standard UNIX Request for Comment (RFC) text files or property sheets on the graphical DNS Management console (Figure 2.14)

Figure 2.14 DNS Management Console

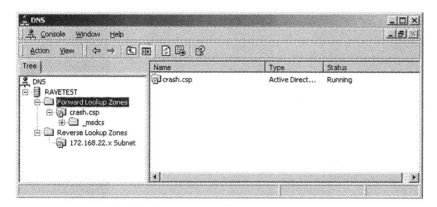

Access the seven property pages associated with a server by right-clicking the desired DNS server in the DNS Management console tree and selecting Properties. Configuration options available on each tab include:

Interfaces—This page permits you to restrict a DNS server to listen to requests only from specified IP addresses. By default, the DNS Service accepts DNS requests from all IP addresses configured for the server. If your server has multiple IP addresses, you can restrict which IP address the server listens to by selecting **Listen on only the following IP addresses** and entering the respective addresses (Figure 2.15)

Figure 2.15 Interfaces Property Page

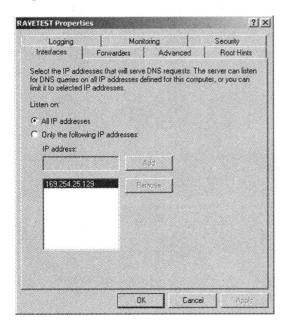

Forwarders—This is a DNS Server configured to give recursive support for other DNS servers by passing an unresolved query to another server. To configure forwarding, follow these steps:

*   From the **Start** menu, choose **Programs**, **Administrative Tools**, and then **DNS**.

*   Within the console tree, right-click the desired DNS server, and choose **Properties**.

*   Choose **Forwarders** and then **Enable forwarders**.

*   Type the IP addresses of the DNS servers to which you want to forward resolution queries, and choose **Add** (Figure 2.16).

Figure 2.16 DNS Forwarders Property Page

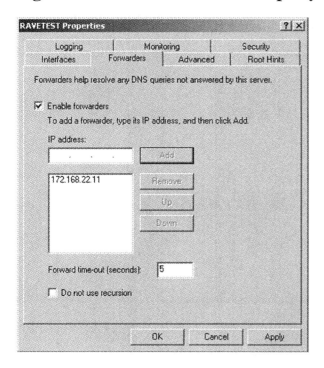

Advanced—A number of advanced server options are offered in this page, including the desired method of loading the DNS Server with database files and resolution methods. DNS supports three methods for resolving DNS names:

Strict RFC, where any names not compliant with RFC rules are treated as errors

Non RFC, where any names not compliant with RFC rules can still be used with the DNS server

Multibyte, the most lenient resolution method, which uses the Unicode 8 bit translation encoding scheme; this is the name resolution method used by default as it provides the greatest degree of inter-operability with other DNS servers (Figure 2.17)

Figure 2.17 DNS Advanced Property Page

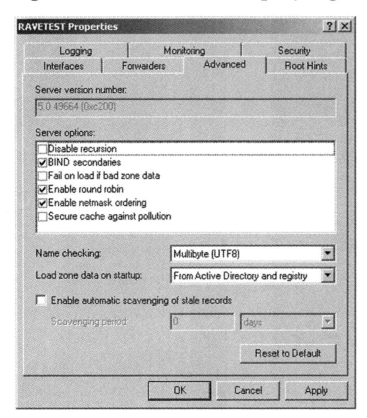

Root Hints—This page lists the Name Server resource records. Root Hints help a DNS server discover and use other servers managing zones located at a higher level in the DNS hierarchical namespace. The Root Hints page contains a default list of hints regarding upper level servers on the Internet generated from the cache.dns file. If you are using DNS in your private network, enter pointers to the appropriate DNS servers on your network by choosing Edit. (Figure 2.18)

Figure 2.18 Root Hints Property Page

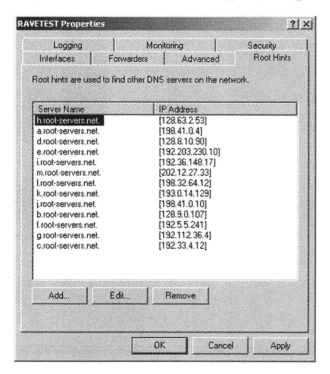

Logging—This page is used mainly for troubleshooting. You can set many different DNS debugging logging options.

Monitoring—The Monitoring property page allows you to configure and perform tests on your DNS server. Details are available in the DNS Server Service Monitoring portion of this lesson.

Security—The Security property page sets object permissions by user and group (Figure 2.19).

Figure 2.19 DNS Security Property Page

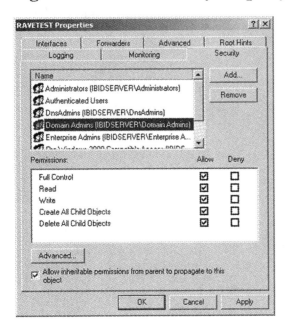

Tip: For added network security, establish external host names different from your internal NetBIOS names. This helps to prevent outside hackers from accessing your server.

Cache-only Server Configuration

Cache-only DNS servers are DNS servers that cache the results of queries that they perform on behalf of their clients. The cache-only servers do not host zones and are not authoritative for any domains. Using this type of server reduces network traffic from zone transfers across slow Wide Area Network (WAN) links to other DNS servers. It also allows for better response times and less DNS traffic for frequently accessed sites.

To install and configure a cache-only DNS server, you would follow these steps:

1. Install the DNS service on a server.

2. Configure the server with a static IP address.

3. From the **Start** menu, choose **Programs, Administrative Tools,** and then select **DNS.**

4. From the **Action** menu, choose **Connect to Computer** (Figure 2.20).

5. From **Select Target Computer**, choose **The following computer,** type the name of the DNS server from which you want to cache, and click **OK.**

 Note: After this procedure, the DNS server is added to the DNS console on the caching server, which in turn answers recursive queries from its clients and accumulates records.

---

6. To clear the cache on a cache DNS server, within the DNS console, right-click the server's name, and choose **Clear Cache.**

Figure 2.20 Select Target Computer

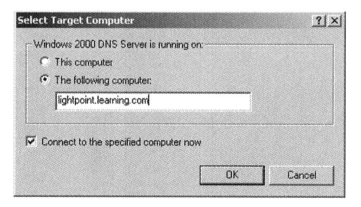

Reducing Network Traffic

By judiciously placing secondary and cache DNS servers on your network, you can reduce communication traffic and optimize the response time to client requests. A secondary server keeps an updated copy of DNS records that it gets from a primary DNS server through zone transfers. This provides redundancy if the primary DNS server is not functioning. Secondary servers also reduce network traffic in a heavily queried zone through load balancing. To provide protection from a network failure, you place secondary servers on a different subnet with routed LANs or across a WAN link.

Cache-only DNS servers can also help reduce network traffic from zone transfers to other DNS servers across slow WAN links. They allow for better response times and less DNS traffic for frequently accessed sites.

DNS Script Configuration

The DNS creates the Start of Authority and Name Server records automatically when a zone is created. However, you can add to and configure resource records in the zone files at any time, depending on your organization's needs, by following these steps:

1. Right-click on the desired zone, choose **New**, and select the type of record you want from a list, or select **Other Record** to obtain an alternative record from a list.

2. Choose the record you want and then **Create Record**.

3. Within **New Resource Record** (Figure 2.21), you will be prompted for information relevant to that record.

Figure 2.21 New Resource Record

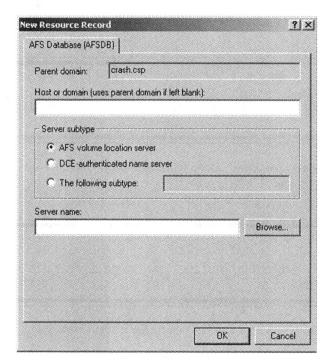

DNS records must exist for any computers that need to be accessed from Active Directory and for DNS domains. You should become familiar with the different types of DNS records so that you know how to configure them, as well as spot problems when troubleshooting. Common DNS records and their abbreviated names as seen in the database include the following ones:

Address (A)—An Address maps a host name to an IP address. If a computer has multiple adapter cards or IP addresses (multihomed), it should have corresponding multiple address records.

Canonical Name (CNAME)—This record establishes an alias for a host name, allowing one host to appear to be multiple computers.

Host Information (HINFO)—This item identifies the Central Processing Unit (CPU) and operating system in use by the host.

Mail Exchange (MX)—A Mail exchange record identifies a mail exchange server for the domain that processes mail within the domain. Multiple MX records within a domain allow for fault tolerance and load balancing on multiple computers. You are prompted during configuration to enter a preference number for the host from 0 to 65,535. The preference number indicates the server's priority in the domain, with the lowest preference number given the highest priority.

 Tip: When assigning preference numbers for mail servers, leave gaps in the numbering to allow for network growth.

Name Server (NS)—By specifying the primary and secondary name server for the domain, a Name Server record allows DNS lookup within zones.

 Note: Remember to input a Name Server record for your secondary name services if they come from an Internet service provider.

Pointer (PTR)—This sets a pointer that maps an IP address to a host name for reverse lookups.

Service (SRV)—The Service record lists which servers are hosting a particular service.

Start of Authority (SOA)—An SOA record defines the host that has the best DNS information for the zone. It is created automatically when you add a zone (Figure 2.22).

Figure 2.22 Zone Database File with Resource Records

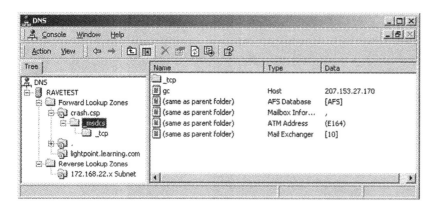

DNS Server Service Monitoring

Windows 2000 has built-in features allowing you to check that the DNS is configured properly. Monitoring can be configured manually or automatically using the following steps:

1. From the **Start** menu, choose **Programs**, **Administrative Tools**, and then select **DNS**.

2. Within the DNS console, right-click the desired server and select **Properties**.

3. From the **Monitoring** tab, you can elect to do one of two tests: a simple query against the selected DNS server or a recursive query to other DNS servers in which the query initiates itself.

4. You can choose to perform a manual test by selecting **Test Now**, or schedule the server for automatic monitoring by selecting **Polling interval**.

Test results are shown in the bottom window and include information about when the test was conducted as well as the result, such as Pass or Fail. Multiple failures indicate a DNS resolution problem, whereas a single failure is usually caused by a transient network problem (Figure 2.23).

Figure 2.23 DNS Monitoring Property Page

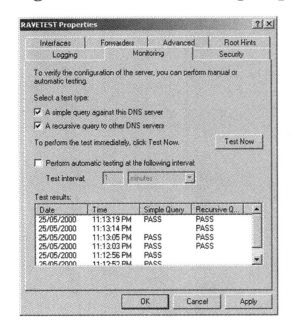

Tip: Set the DNS Server Service Monitoring to automatic monitoring every 15 seconds if you are troubleshooting a DNS problem. Standard monitoring can occur with an interval of two or three hours.

The DNS Server Event Log is a useful tool to track DNS. Accessed through the Event View node in Computer Management, the log can record all DNS events. You configure the log options through the Logging page of a DNS server's property page. By default, none of the options are selected. You must be careful when selecting debugging options as they take up considerable disk space and can impact server performance.

The following are several debugging options:

• Query, which logs all queries received by the DNS service from clients

• Notify, which logs all notification messages received by the DNS service from other servers

• Update, which logs all dynamic updates received by the DNS service (Figure 2.24)

Figure 2.24 DNS Server Event Log

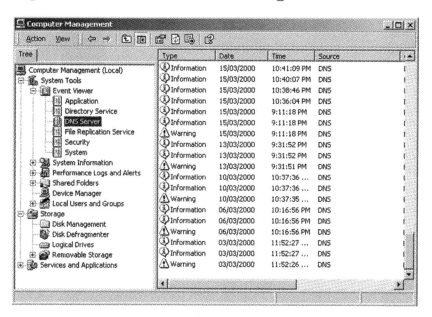

Tip: Unlike Microsoft Windows NT 4.0 MCSE certification exams, Windows 2000 exams have fewer theoretical questions and more drag-and-drop or dialog box selection questions requiring hands-on experience. Beta exam takers warn that over half of the questions in exam 70-216 Implementing and Administering a Microsoft Windows 2000 Network Infrastructure are based on DNS, DHCP and WINS topics.

Vocabulary

Review the following terms in preparation for the certification exam.

Term	Description
A	An Address record in the DNS database maps a host name to an IP address.
Active Directory	The directory service included with Windows 2000 Server. Active Directory stores information about objects on a network in a hierarchical view and provides a single point of administration for all network objects.
authoritative server	The primary DNS server within a zone that is responsible for keeping an updated master copy of DNS records and the zone's configuration files.
BIND	Berkeley Internet Name Domain is a UNIX service that is equivalent to DNS in Microsoft products.
cache-only server	A server that always passes DNS requests to other servers, but caches DNS information after lookups.
CNAME	Canonical Name is a DNS record that establishes an alias for a host name, allowing one host to appear to be multiple computers.
CPU	The Central Processing Unit is the device that processes and transmits data, and where most calculations take place.
DHCP	Dynamic Host Configuration Protocol is a networking protocol that simplifies TCP/IP network configuration and dynamically configures IP addresses for clients. DHCP ensures that address conflicts do not occur by centralizing address allocation.

Term	Description
DNS	Domain Name System is the hierarchical naming system used to locate domain names on the Internet and on private TCP/IP networks. The DNS service maps DNS domain names to IP addresses and vice-versa.
forward lookup	A query in which the DNS name for the computer is used to determine the IP address.
FQDN	Fully Qualified Domain Name is a domain name that indicates the precise location of a computer in the hierarchical domain namespace tree.
HINFO	The Host Information DNS record identifies the CPU and operating system used by the host.
IP	Internet Protocol specifies the format of packets and the addressing scheme.
LAN	A Local Area Network spans a relatively small area, connecting workstations and resources.
multihomed	A computer that has multiple network adapters installed.
multimaster replication	A replication model in which any domain controller accepts and replicates directory changes to any other domain controller.
MX	A Mail Exchange DNS record identifies a mail exchange server for the domain that processes mail within the domain.
namespace	A set of distinct names for the resources in a network. The names in a namespace can be resolved to the objects they represent. For DNS, namespace is the hierarchical structure of the domain name tree.

Term	Description
NetBIOS name	A name recognized by WINS, the service that maps a computer name to its IP address.
NS	A Name Server record in the DNS database allows DNS lookup within zones by specifying the primary and secondary name server for the domain.
NT	New Technology is Microsoft's version of Windows previous to Windows 2000.
NTFS	New Technologies File System is a file system designed for Microsoft Windows NT 4.0 and Windows 2000. It provides data security, file system reliability, and file system recoverability.
primary server	The authoritative DNS server for a domain. Primary servers come in two versions. An Active Directory-integrated primary server is fully integrated with Active Directory and stores all DNS data in the Directory. An ordinary primary server is only partially integrated with Active Directory and stores all DNS data as text files.
PTR	A Pointer record in the DNS database maps an IP address to a host name for reverse lookups.
reverse lookup	A query in which the IP address is used to determine the DNS name for the computer.
RFC	Request For Comments is a document that defines a TCP/IP standard. RFCs are published by the Internet Engineering Task Force and other working groups.
secondary server	A backup DNS server to the primary server. A secondary server keeps an updated copy of DNS records it receives from a primary DNS server through zone transfers.

Term	Description
SOA	The Start Of Authority is a DNS record that is created automatically when you add a zone. It defines the host that has the best DNS information for the zone.
SRV	A Service record in the DNS database lists which servers are hosting a particular service.
TCP/IP	Transport Control Protocol/Internet Protocol. A set of protocols that provides communication among diverse networks. Because it accommodates different architectures and operating systems, TCP/IP is the most commonly used Internet protocol.
TTL	Time To Live specifies the duration a process can occur or record can be kept before the process is ended or the record discarded.
WAN	A Wide Area Network spans a large geographical area and typically consists of two or more LANs.
WINS	Windows Internet Name Service is a Microsoft software service that dynamically maps IP addresses to computer names. This allows users to access resources by name instead of by IP address.
WINS-R	A Windows Internet Name Service Reverse record dynamically maps the reverse of WINS, computer names to IP addresses.

Term	Description
zone	In a DNS database, a zone is a domain or an area within a domain that is administered as a distinct entity by a DNS server. The zone contains resource records for all the names within the zone.
zone transfer	The process by which DNS servers interact to maintain and synchronize authoritative data. A secondary server periodically queries the primary DNS server. If the zone version kept by the primary DNS server is different from the version kept by the secondary server, the secondary server will pull zone information from its primary server.

In Brief

If you want to...	Then do this...
Install a DNS server on a member server for the first time	1. From the **Start** menu, choose **Settings, Control Panel**, and select **Add/Remove Programs**.
	2. From the left pane **of Add/Remove Programs**, choose **Add/Remove Windows Components**.
	3. From **Windows Components**, choose **Networking Services and Details**.
	1. From **Networking Services**, choose the **Domain Name System (DNS)** checkbox, click **OK**, and select **Next**.
	2. Specify the location for the installation files, and, from **Completing the Windows Components**, choose **Finish**.

If you want to...	Then do this...
Create and configure a DNS zone	1. From the **Start** menu, choose **Programs, Administrative Tools,** and then select **DNS.**
	2. Choose **Next** and within **Root Servers** (if your server cannot find a root server on the network, you must decide between two options), you can either make your server the root server, by selecting **This is the first DNS server on this network,** or you can type the IP address of the root server, and then select **Next.**
	3. Within **Add Forward Lookup Zone,** choose **Forward lookup zone** and then **Next.**
	4. Within **Choose a Zone Type,** choose **Standard secondary** (Figure 2.3) if you have fully integrated Active Directory into your network, otherwise, **Standard primary** is selected by default, and then select **Next.**
	5. Within **Zone Name,** type the name of the zone, and choose **Next.**
	6. From **Add Reverse Lookup Zone,** choose **Yes** if desired, and choose **Next.**
	7. If you selected **Yes,** choose a zone type in the window that appears, and select **Next.**
	8. Specify the reverse lookup zone by typing either the network ID and subnet mask, or the name of the reverse lookup zone.
	9. Choose **Next,** select to create a new file, and then **Next** again.
	10. Review the summary of your server's configuration, and choose **Next.**
	11. Type the network class and subnet mask of your network, choose **Next** and then **Finish.**
	Once you have finished creating a DNS zone for a server, many of the remaining configuration parameters can be accessed through the Properties sheet for that zone.

If you want to...	Then do this...
Install and configure a cache-only server	1. Install the DNS service on a server. 2. Configure the server with a static IP address. 3. From the **Start** menu, choose **Programs, Administrative Tools,** and then **DNS**. 4. From the **Action** menu, choose **Connect to Computer**. 5. From **Select Target Computer,** choose **The following computer,** type the name of the DNS server from which you want to cache, and click **OK**.
Add to or configure a DNS script	1. Right-click on the desired zone, choose **New**, and select the type of record you want from a list, or select **Other Record** to obtain an alternative record from a list. 2. Choose the record you want and then **Create Record**. 3. From **New Resource Record,** you are prompted for information relevant to that record. Common DNS records and their abbreviated name as seen in the database include: **Address (A)**—An Address maps a host name to an IP address. If a computer has multiple adapter cards or IP addresses (multihomed), it should have corresponding multiple address records.

If you want to...	Then do this...
	Canonical Name (CNAME)—This record establishes an alias for a host name, allowing one host to appear to be multiple computers.
	Host Information (HINFO)—This item identifies the CPU and operating system in use by the host.
	Mail Exchange (MX)—A Mail Exchange record identifies a mail exchange server for the domain that processes mail within the domain. Multiple MX records within a domain allow for fault tolerance and load balancing on multiple computers. You are prompted during configuration to enter a preference number for the host from 0 to 65,535. The preference number indicates the server's priority in the domain, with the lowest preference number given the highest priority.
	Name Server (NS)—The Name Server record specifies the primary and secondary name server for the domain, allowing DNS lookup within zones.
	Pointer (PTR)—This item sets a pointer that maps an IP address to a host name for reverse lookups.
	Service (SRV)—This lists which servers are hosting a particular service.
	Start of Authority (SOA)—A SOA record is created automatically when you add a zone, defining the host that has the best DNS information for the zone.

If you want to...	Then do this...
Monitor the DNS server services	1. From the **Start** menu, choose **Programs, Administrative Tools,** and then **DNS**.
	2. Within the DNS console, right-click the desired server and choose **Properties**.
	3. From the **Monitoring** tab, you can elect to do one of two tests: a simple query against the selected DNS server or a recursive query to other DNS servers in which the query initiates itself.
	4. You can choose to perform a manual test by selecting **Test Now**, or schedule the server for automatic monitoring by selecting **Polling interval**.

Lesson 2 Activities

Complete the following activities to better prepare you for the certification exam.

1. Describe how to check whether you have DNS configured properly.

2. Define the four types of Windows 2000 DNS servers and explain how they differ.

3. Describe some of the configurable options found in the Start of Authority (SOA) record.

4. List three steps you can take to reduce DNS traffic in your network.

5. Describe the function of four of the seven property pages associated with a DNS server property sheet.

6. Describe briefly the process by which you delegate authority for a zone.

7. Discuss how the DNS Server Event Log can help you track DNS.

8. Define some common DNS records found in zone files.

9. Describe the three methods DNS can use to resolve DNS names.

10. Discuss an advantage and a disadvantage of delegating authority.

Answers to Lesson 2 Activities

1. Windows 2000 has built-in monitoring options accessible from the Monitoring page of the server Properties sheet. You can elect to do a simple query against the selected DNS server or a recursive query to other DNS servers. You can also perform a manual test immediately or schedule the server for automatic monitoring. Test results are shown in the bottom window. Multiple failures indicate a DNS resolution problem, while a single failure is usually caused by a transient network problem.

2. The four types of Windows 2000 DNS servers are:

    Active Directory-integrated primary—This is a DNS server fully integrated with Active Directory, with all DNS data stored directly in the Directory.

    Primary server—Updates are handled by the primary DNS server for the zone, the authoritative DNS server for a domain that is only partially integrated with Active Directory.

    Secondary server—The secondary server keeps an updated copy of DNS records that it gets from a primary DNS server through zone transfers, acting as a backup DNS server to the primary one.

    Cache-only server—This is a server that always passes DNS requests to other servers but caches DNS information after lookups.

3. Some of the configurable options in the Start of Authority (SOA) record are:

    Serial number—This indicates the version of the DNS database files. When you change zone files, this number is automatically updated. Secondary servers compare the serial number of their database files with that of the primary server and can request updated DNS zone records whenever the primary server's version shows new records.

    Primary server—Enter the Fully Qualified Domain Name for the name server, followed by a period.

    Responsible person—This gives the e-mail address of the person in charge of the domain.

    Refresh interval—This is the time interval in which a secondary server checks for zone updates.

    Retry interval—This is the time the secondary server waits after a failed zone database transfer request before asking again.

Expires after—This is the time period in which the zone information is considered valid on the secondary server, after which the DNS will stop responding to queries if it cannot get updated database files from the primary server.

Minimum (default) TTL—This gives the minimum Time-to-Live for cached records on a secondary server.

TTL of this record—This entry defines the Time-to-Live value for the SOA record and is usually the same as the minimum TTL

4. To reduce DNS traffic in your network:

   • Place secondary servers on a different subnet with routed LANs or across a WAN link, which protects you from a network failure and reduces network traffic in a heavily queried zone through load balancing

   • Cache-only DNS servers can also help reduce network traffic from zone transfers to other DNS servers across slow WAN links, and they also allow for better response times and less DNS traffic for frequently accessed sites

   • Set the minimum Time-to-Live (TTL) value for the SOA record to a high number, such as 24 hours (the TTL gives the minimum Time-to-Live for cached records on a secondary server) because the longer a database is considered operational, the fewer the updates that are needed

5. The seven property pages of a DNS server's property sheet are:

   • Interfaces, which permits you to restrict a DNS server to listen to requests from only specified IP addresses

   • Forwarders, which allows you to configure a DNS server to give recursive support to other DNS servers by passing an unresolved query to another server

   • Advanced, where you select a number of advanced options including the desired method of loading the DNS server with database files and resolution methods

   • Root Hints, where the Name Server resource records help a DNS server discover and use other servers managing zones located at a higher level in the DNS hierarchical namespace.

   • Logging, which permits you to set DNS debugging logging options during troubleshooting

   • Monitoring, which allows you to configure and perform tests on your DNS server

   • Security, which sets object permissions by user and group

6. Delegating authority is a three-part process:

    •   Notify the upper level domain that there will be a lower-level domain or zone under another computer's control

    •   Notify the DNS server of the upper-level domain where to find a DNS server for the new zone

    •   Configure the DNS server of the new lower-level zone

7. The DNS Server Event Log is a useful tool to track DNS. Accessed through the Event View node in Computer Management, the log can record all DNS events. You configure the log options through the Logging page of a DNS server's Properties sheet. By default, none of the options are selected. You must be careful when selecting debugging options as they take up considerable disk space and can impact server performance. Some of the more frequently used options are:

    •   Query, which logs all queries received by the DNS service from clients

    •   Notify, which logs all notification messages received by the DNS service from other servers

    •   Update, which logs all dynamic updates received by the DNS service

8. Some common DNS records found in zone files are:

    Address (A)—An Address maps a host name to an IP address. If a computer has multiple adapter cards or IP addresses (multihomed), it should have corresponding multiple address records.

    Canonical Name (CNAME)—This record establishes an alias for a host name, allowing one host to appear to be multiple computers.

    Host Information (HINFO)—This item identifies the CPU and operating system in use by the host.

    Mail Exchange (MX)—A Mail Exchange record identifies a mail exchange server for the domain that processes mail within the domain. Multiple MX records within a domain allow for fault tolerance and load balancing on multiple computers. You are prompted during configuration to enter a preference number for the host from 0 to 65,535. The preference number indicates the server's priority in the domain, with the lowest preference number given the highest priority.

    Name Server (NS)—The Name Server record specifies the primary and secondary name server for the domain, allowing DNS lookup within zones.

Pointer (PTR)—This item sets a pointer that maps an IP address to a host name for reverse lookups.

Service (SRV)—This lists which servers are hosting a particular service.

Start of Authority (SOA)—A SOA record is created automatically when you add a zone, defining the host that has the best DNS information for the zone.

9. DNS supports the following four methods for resolving DNS names. Configuration of the resolution method is done through the Advanced page of the server Properties sheet:

    •   Strict RFC, where any names not compliant with RFC rules are treated as errors

    •   Non RFC, where any names not compliant with RFC rules can still be used with the DNS server

    •   Multibyte, the most lenient resolution method, which uses the Unicode 8 bit translation encoding scheme; this is the name resolution method used by default as it provides the greatest degree of interoperability with other DNS servers

    Any character, allows any character, including UTF-8 characters

10. One advantage of delegating authority is clear division of administrative responsibilities between DNS servers within a network. If an extra computer is added to a network, only the DNS server responsible for that computer's namespace needs to add a new DNS name record.

    A disadvantage of delegating authority is that name resolution for an outside server will be slightly slower because the root DNS server refers most questions to lower level DNS servers.

Lesson 2 Quiz

These questions test your knowledge of features, vocabulary, procedures, and syntax.

1. Why would you assign a static IP address to your Windows 2000 server before installing the DNS service?
    A. It is easier than having DHCP provide an address.
    B. A static IP address is a requirement for installation of the DNS service on a Windows 2000 server.
    C. A static IP address will prevent network problems associated with a dynamically assigned IP address.
    D. It makes no difference whether the IP address is static or dynamic.

2. Why is it not possible to configure an incremental zone transfer between a Windows 2000 DNS server and a Microsoft Windows NT 4.0 DNS server?

    A. Incremental zone transfer is designed to occur between Windows 2000 and UNIX computers.
    B. This occurs by default, so you do not need to configure it.
    C. Windows 2000 does not support this feature.
    D. Microsoft Windows NT 4.0 does not support this feature.

3. Why is a reverse lookup zone useful?
    A. It reduces network traffic.
    B. It permits you to use an IP address to obtain a corresponding host name.
    C. It allows you to record names instead of IP addresses in your Internet Information Server.
    D. Reverse lookup must be enabled to run troubleshooting tools such as NSLOOKUP.

4. What is the reverse lookup zone for the IP address 200.120.50.24?
    A. 50.120.200.in-addr.arpa
    B. 24.50.120.200.in-addr.arpa
    C. In-addr.arpa.50.120.200
    D. In-addr.arpa.24.50.120.200

5. By default, the primary server in a zone is configured to perform zone transfers with any DNS server requesting the service. Why would you want to modify this setting?
    A. Do not modify the setting as it has been optimized.
    B. It is better to configure the primary server to automatically transfer database updates to secondary servers.
    C. To prevent unauthorized DNS servers from obtaining your zone data.
    D. To reduce network traffic.

6. What happens during multimaster replication?
   A. Active Directory handles zone replication.
   B. A secondary DNS server pulls only the needed zone changes to synchronize its copy of the zone data with that of the primary server.
   C. A Windows 2000 DNS server performs slow zone transfers without data compression.
   D. Any domain controller accepts and replicates DNS database changes to any other domain controller.

7. Under what conditions would you integrate WINS with DNS?
   A. You do not ever need to integrate WINS with DNS.
   B. You have a mixed environment involving UNIX computers.
   C. You have a mixed environment involving legacy versions of Windows.
   D. You have a mixed environment involving DOS and NetWare computers.

8. How is a zone different from a domain?
   A. A domain is a subset of a zone.
   B. Creating a zone does not affect domain computer or user division.
   C. A zone is a subset of a domain.
   D. A zone can be a domain.

9. What is a field from the Start of Authority Page of a zone's Properties sheet?
   A. Primary server
   B. Responsible person
   C. Serial number
   D. Minimum (default) TTL

10. What is an authoritative server?
    A. A server that always passes DNS requests to other servers.
    B. A server responsible for keeping an updated master copy of DNS records for a zone.
    C. A server that receives an updated copy of DNS records.
    D. Permits logon of users like domain controllers.

Answers to Lesson 2 Quiz

1. Answer C is correct. A DNS server should have a static IP address so that it can be contacted consistently by other DNS servers and clients.

    Answer A is incorrect. It is easier to have DHCP configure the DNS server's IP address, but a dynamically assigned IP address would lead to network problems.

    Answer B is incorrect. A static IP address is not a requirement for installation of the DNS service on a Windows 2000 server.

    Answer D is incorrect. It does make a difference whether the IP address is static or dynamic. A dynamically assigned IP address would lead to network problems.

2. Answer D is correct. Incremental zone transfer only works if both servers support it and then only for standard zone files. Only Windows 2000 computers support this feature. Other DNS servers will participate in full zone transfers.

    Answer A is incorrect. UNIX computers do not support incremental zone transfers, so they will participate in full zone transfers.

    Answer B is incorrect. Zone transfers do not occur by default. They must be configured.

    Answer C is incorrect. Windows 2000 does support incremental zone transfers.

3. Answers B, C and D are correct. A reverse lookup zone permits you to use an IP address to obtain a corresponding host name, to record names instead of IP addresses in your Internet Information Server, and to run troubleshooting tools such as the command line NSLOOKUP.

    Answer A is incorrect. A reverse lookup zone does not necessarily reduce traffic.

4. Answer A is correct. Determine the reverse zone name by reversing all octets but the last one in the IP address and appending them to "in-addr.arpa".

    Answer B is incorrect. You do not include the octet representing the host in the reverse zone name. Only the network octets are included.

    Answer C is incorrect. "In-addr.arpa" should be appended to the back of the reversed octets, not the front.

Answer D is incorrect. You do not include the octet representing the host in the reverse zone name. Only the network octets are included. Besides, "in-addr.arpa" should be appended to the back of the reversed octets, not the front.

5. Answer C is correct. By leaving the default configuration in which the primary server in a zone is set to perform zone transfers with any DNS server requesting the service, you leave your network open to attack from unauthorized DNS servers who can take your zone data. Instead, use one of the options on the Zone Transfers page of the Zone Properties sheet. You can allow zone transfers only to servers named in the Name Servers property page or to servers with specified IP addresses.

Answer A is incorrect. The default setting has not been optimized for your network.

Answer B is incorrect. Configuring the primary server to "push" or automatically transfer database updates to secondary servers is not necessarily better.

Answer D is incorrect. Allowing zone transfer to take place with any DNS server requesting the service would lead to increased network traffic.

6. Answer D is correct. During multimaster replication, any domain controller within a network can accept and replicate DNS database changes to any other domain controller within the network.

Answer A is incorrect. Although DNS is integrated into the Active Directory, the Active Directory itself does not handle zone replication.

Answer B is incorrect. An incremental zone transfer occurs when a secondary DNS server pulls only the needed zone changes to synchronize its copy of the zone data with that of the primary server.

Answer C is incorrect. A Windows 2000 DNS server is configured by default to perform fast zone transfers with data compression and multiple resource records sent in each message to all Windows DNS servers and BIND v4.9.4 or later DNS servers.

7. Answer C is correct. WINS is Microsoft's proprietary name resolution service. Versions of Windows previous to Windows 2000 use WINS not DNS as the default service to resolve computer names to IP addresses.

Answer A is incorrect. You need to integrate WINS with DNS in a mixed network involving legacy versions of Windows.

Answer B is incorrect. UNIX uses DNS for name resolution.

Answer D is incorrect. Novell NetWare computers cannot use WINS, since WINS is a proprietary service developed by Microsoft.

8. Answers B, C and D are correct. You can create as many DNS domains as needed without affecting the computer or user division that is part of Windows 2000 domains. A zone is a domain or a subset of a domain that is administered as a distinct entity by a DNS server.

Answer A is incorrect. A domain is not a subset of a zone. The reverse is true.

9. Answers A, B, C and D are all correct. The SOA defines the authoritative name server for a zone and controls how DNS information is propagated through the network. In the Primary server field, enter the Fully Qualified Domain Name for the name server; in the Responsible person field, enter the e-mail address of the person in charge of the domain; and in the Minimum (default) TTL field, enter the minimum Time-to-Live for cached records on a secondary server. The Serial number field tells you the version of the DNS database files.

10. Answer B is correct. An authoritative server is the primary DNS server within a zone that is responsible for keeping an updated master copy of DNS records and the zone's configuration files.

Answer A is incorrect. A cache-only server always passes DNS requests to other servers but caches DNS information after lookups.

Answer C is incorrect. A secondary server is a backup to the authoritative or primary DNS server. It keeps an updated copy of the DNS records it receives from a primary DNS server through zone transfers. This provides fault tolerance and load balancing with the primary server.

Answer D is incorrect. An authoritative server cannot log on users like domain controllers. It only handles the DNS service.

DHCP Installation and Administration

Transport Control Protocol/Internet Protocol (TCP/IP) plays an important role in the smooth functioning of a network. It is vital that the parameters enabling a computer to use this protocol are configured properly. The required configuration information includes an Internet Protocol (IP) address, servers for name resolution such as Domain Name System (DNS) and Windows Internet Name Service (WINS), a gateway address, and the subnet class of the network.

Dynamic Host Configuration Protocol (DHCP) reduces administrative effort by automating the TCP/IP client configuration process. It is especially useful in a dynamic network environment, as all client parameters are dynamically reconfigured.

Windows 2000 DHCP has new features that decrease the DHCP administrative overhead found in Microsoft Windows NT 4.0. These features include a more intuitive administrative interface, support for Microsoft Windows NT name space, integration into Active Directory, auditing capabilities, and a default behavior when a DHCP server cannot be found.

After completing this lesson, you should have a better understanding of the following topics:

* DHCP Overview

* DHCP Server Service Installation

* DHCP Server Service Configuration

* DHCP Integration

* DHCP Support

107

DHCP Overview

The DHCP service has been a core network service starting with Microsoft Windows NT 3.5. It automates the process of keeping track of a list of computers and their corresponding IP addresses. DHCP is based on Bootstrap Protocol (BOOTP), a TCP/IP protocol that allows diskless workstations to boot up and access a TCP/IP network. A BOOTP server hands out IP addresses according to its table, which maps Media Access Control (MAC) addresses to each computer's network adapter card. DHCP works in much the same way, by providing IP addresses to computers requesting access to the Local Area Network (LAN).

DHCP has many benefits, as shown in Table 3.1.

Table 3.1 DHCP TCP/IP Configurations

Manual TCP/IP Configuration	DHCP TCP/IP Configuration
Administrators assign IP addresses and configure TCP/IP information, creating overhead and possibility of errors from assigning duplicate addresses or incorrect configuration information	IP addressing and TCP/IP configuration information is automatically supplied to clients, without administrator overhead
Ideal for small networks	Useful for medium to large networks
Larger pool of IP addresses is needed	Smaller pool of IP addresses is needed since not all IP addresses are used all the time
Administrative overhead caused by moving clients to different subnets and manual reconfiguration of IP addresses, subnet masks, default gateway, and WINS and DNS information	Reduced administrative overhead if you need to move clients to different subnets

Tip: Do not implement DHCP without some thought. If you have a dynamic network, a DHCP server is useful as it centralizes TCP/IP configuration changes.

However, in a small network, implementing DHCP could be more work than it is worth. Additionally, you might need static IP addresses for your workstations to work with legacy software.

A DCHP client obtains an IP address from a DHCP server in the following ways:

DHCPDISCOVER—The client broadcasts a request to all DHCP servers asking for the location of a DHCP server and IP address information. The source address of the message is 0.0.0.0 since the client does yet have an IP address, and the destination address is the broadcast 255.255.255.255. The message contains the client's MAC address and computer name so that a responding DHCP server can identify the client. The communication protocol used is User Datagram Protocol (UDP), not TCP, as an IP address does not yet exist. UDP is part of the TCP/IP suite (Figure 3.1).

DHCPOFFER—Each available DHCP server responds to the client's MAC address with a broadcast message offering an IP address, a subnet mask, the lease duration, and the IP address of the offering server (Figure 3.2).

DHCPREQUEST—The client selects the best offer, or the first received if all offers appear equal, and broadcasts back a UDP packet to all DHCP servers confirming its acceptance of an offer. The message includes the IP address of the server whose offer it accepted, and a request for additional configuration information such as a default gateway. The other servers then retract their offers, returning their offered IP addresses to their respective pools (Figure 3.3).

DHCPACK (DHCP Acknowledgement)—The server handing out the IP address acknowledges the request by broadcasting a message containing a lease for an IP address and other TCP/IP configuration information, such as the default gateway, WINS server, and DNS server. When the DHCP client receives the message, it completes its TCP/IP binding. Now the client can use TCP/IP to communicate over the network (Figure 3.4).

Figure 3.1 DHCPDISCOVER

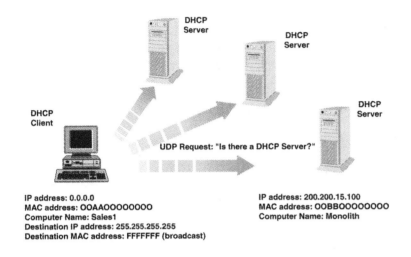

IP address: 0.0.0.0
MAC address: OOAAOOOOOOOO
Computer Name: Sales1
Destination IP address: 255.255.255.255
Destination MAC address: FFFFFFF (broadcast)

IP address: 200.200.15.100
MAC address: OOBBOOOOOOOO
Computer Name: Monolith

Figure 3.2 DHCPOFFER

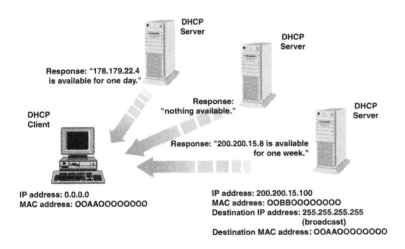

IP address: 0.0.0.0
MAC address: OOAAOOOOOOOO

IP address: 200.200.15.100
MAC address: OOBBOOOOOOOO
Destination IP address: 255.255.255.255
(broadcast)
Destination MAC address: OOAAOOOOOOOO

Figure 3.3 DHCPREQUEST

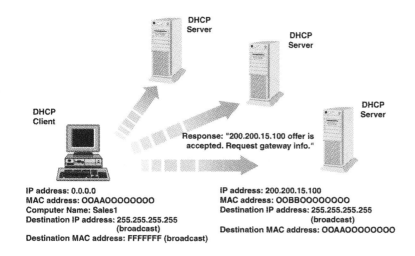

IP address: 0.0.0.0
MAC address: OOAAOOOOOOOO
Computer Name: Sales1
Destination IP address: 255.255.255.255
(broadcast)
Destination MAC address: FFFFFFF (broadcast)

IP address: 200.200.15.100
MAC address: OOBBOOOOOOOO
Destination IP address: 255.255.255.255
(broadcast)
Destination MAC address: OOAAOOOOOOOO

Figure 3.4 DHCPACK

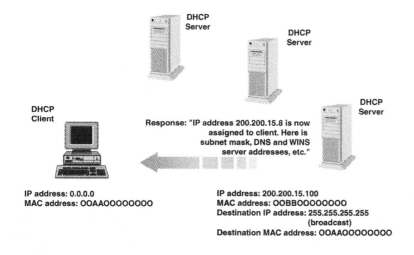

IP address: 0.0.0.0
MAC address: OOAAOOOOOOOO

IP address: 200.200.15.100
MAC address: OOBBOOOOOOOO
Destination IP address: 255.255.255.255
(broadcast)
Destination MAC address: OOAAOOOOOOOO

If the DHCPREQUEST fails, the DHCP server broadcasts a DHCPNACK (DHCP Negative Acknowledgement). This can happen when the IP address or configuration information is invalid because the client computer has been moved to a different subnet, the client is trying to lease an unavailable IP address, or because of a mechanical failure on the server.

The DHCP client remembers its IP address and the lease time. In Windows 2000 workstations, this information is kept in the registry. If the client is rebooted during the half-life of its DHCP lease, it will request the same IP address of the server from which it originally received the address. The DHCP server would acknowledge the request, since it remembers the MAC address associated with an IP address.

The DHCP client attempts to renew its lease when 50% of the lease time has passed. It sends a DHCPREQUEST message every two minutes to the DHCP server from which it obtained the lease until it receives a response. If the DHCP server is available, it renews the lease and sends the client a DHCPACK message with the new lease time and updated TCP/IP configuration parameters. If the lease request is unsuccessful and lease time is still available, the DHCP client continues to use the same IP address until the next attempt to renew the lease, at 87.5% of the lease period.

The client then broadcasts a DHCPDISCOVER. Any DHCP server can respond with a DHCPACK message that renews the lease or a DHCPNACK message, which forces the client to obtain a lease with a new IP address. If the lease expires without a new one, the client loses functions associated with TCP/IP.

DHCP Server Service Installation

If you are implementing a DHCP server on a smaller LAN, map out which computers can immediately become DHCP clients, which computers need static IP addresses, and the desired TCP/IP configurations for the DHCP server to hand out. For a larger LAN, more factors need to be considered prior to installing DHCP.

Installing the DHCP Server Service

Before you install the DHCP service on a Windows 2000 server, configure your server with a static IP address, subnet mask, and default gateway because a DHCP server cannot give itself a dynamic IP address.

Then follow these steps to install the DHCP service on a server:

1. From the **Start** menu, choose **Settings, Control Panel,** and then **Add/Remove Programs**.

2. Choose **Add/Remove Windows Components**, and select **Networking Services**.

3. Choose **Details**, and from **Subcomponents of Networking Services**, select **Dynamic Host**

4. **Configuration Protocol (DHCP)**, and click **OK**.

5. From **Windows Components**, choose **Next** and type in the location of the installation files.

6. From **Completing the Windows Components**, choose **Finish** (Figure 3.5).

Figure 3.5 Windows Components Wizard

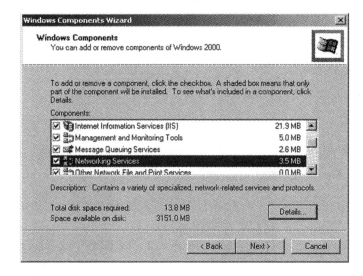

Once you install the DHCP service, the DHCP snap-in to the Microsoft Management Console (MMC) is installed. If you want to manage remote servers running DHCP without installing the DHCP service itself, you can install the DHCP snap-in by running the command line utility ADMIN-PAK.MSI.

Note: Although there is no theoretical limit to how many clients a DHCP server can support, Microsoft recommends at least one on-line DHCP server and one backup for every 10,000 clients to reduce network traffic and increase speed.

DHCP Client

DHCP works only if the TCP/IP software on a workstation has a built-in DHCP client. To be a DHCP client, a computer needs to have one of the following operating systems:

- Microsoft Windows NT 3.51 or later

- Windows 2000

- Windows 95 or later

- Windows for Workgroups 3.11 running TCP/IP-32

- MS DOS with the Microsoft Network Client 3.0 with the real mode TCP/IP driver

- LAN Manager 2.2c, except for the OS/2 version

To configure DHCP on a Windows 2000 client, follow these steps:

1. From the **Start** menu, choose **Settings**, **Control Panel**, and double-click **Network and Dial-up Connections**.

2. Double-click **Local Area Connection**, and choose **Properties**.

3. From **Local Area Connection** Properties, choose **Internet Protocol (TCP/IP)** and then **Properties**.

4. From the **General** property page, choose **Obtain an IP address automatically**, and click **OK** (Figure 3.6).

Figure 3.6 Internet Protocol (TCP/IP) Properties

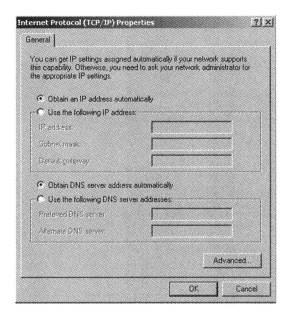

Authorizing the DHCP Server

Windows 2000 solves the problem of rogue DHCP servers handing out non-functioning IP addresses. In earlier versions of DHCP, clients broadcast IP address requests to the nearest DHCP server, which would then provide addresses along with TCP/IP configuration information. This led to situations where a test DHCP server could give out incorrect TCP/IP information, supplanting a legitimate production DHCP server. DHCP clients receiving the faulty information would then be unable to access network resources because of their faulty TCP/IP configuration.

In Windows 2000, you must authorize your DHCP server with Active Directory services before you can assign IP addresses. Authorization is a security precaution in which only authorized DHCP servers are permitted to operate on a network. When the Windows 2000 DHCP service is started, the server contacts the Active Directory to see if it is on the list of authorized DHCP servers. If it is not, Active Directory stops the service, preventing network problems.

Note: Legacy DHCP servers will continue to operate.

To authorize a Windows 2000 DHCP server, follow these steps:

1. From the **Start** menu, choose **Programs**, **Administrative Tools**, and then select **DHCP**.

2. From the console tree, choose the desired DHCP server.

3. From the menu bar choose **Action**, **Authorize**, and then select the **F5** key to refresh the display.

 Note: A green arrow pointing up appears next to the server indicating it has been authorized, replacing the earlier red arrow pointing down, which signifies an unauthorized DHCP server (Figures 3.7 and 3.8).

Figure 3.7 Unauthorized DHCP Server

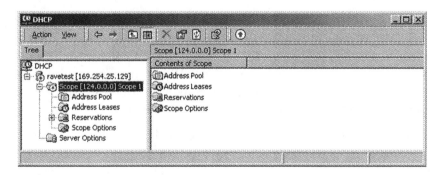

Figure 3.8 Authorized DHCP Server

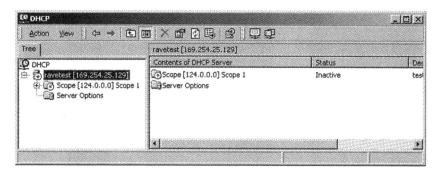

4. You can authorize a number of DHCP servers at the same time; instead of choosing a specific DHCP server from the console, select the **DHCP icon** and from the **Action** menu, select **Manage authorized servers**.

5. From **Manage Authorized Servers**, choose **Authorize**, type in the name or IP address of the DHCP server you want to authorize (Figure 3.9), click **OK**, choose **Yes** and then select **Close**.

Figure 3.9 DHCP Authorized Servers

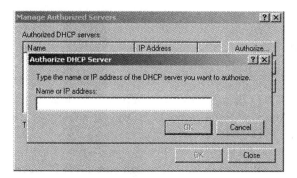

DHCP Server Service Configuration

After installing the DHCP service and making sure it is running, you need to create a scope or range of valid IP addresses that can be released to clients. The scope then needs to be configured.

The basic guidelines for configuring the DHCP service are as follows:

- Create multiple DHCP servers if you are administering a multi-domain network, because a DHCP server can only issue IP addresses to clients in the domain in which the server is participating

- Create at least one scope for every DHCP server

- Create one scope per subnet (in most cases)

- May create multiple scopes on one DHCP server to centralize administration, but only one scope can apply to a specific subnet

- When you create scopes on multiple DHCP servers, make sure the scopes do not overlap because DHCP servers do not share scope information; otherwise, you will assign duplicate IP addresses and create network anomalies

- Implementation of separate scopes possible to meet the needs of specific user groups

- For administrative ease, you can group multiple scopes into one large superscope, in which case you define two or more scopes on a DHCP server, right-click the server, choose New Superscope, and add as many scopes to the superscope as you like

- Exclude static IP addresses from the range of available IP addresses

- For fault tolerance, many administrators run DHCP on at least two servers. Configure each DHCP server with multiple scopes that refer to the same subnet. However, the range of addresses in the scope do not overlap. For example, DHCP Server 1 gives out addresses for one subnet from 203.15.39.10 through 203.15.39.25, while DHCP Server 2 gives out addresses for the same subnet from 203.15.39.26 through 203.15.39.40. In this way, although one DHCP server may fail, computers on any given subnet can still access network resources by obtaining IP information from the other DHCP server (Figure 3.10).

Figure 3.10 DHCP Fault Tolerance

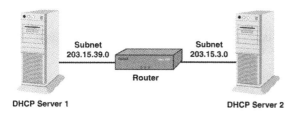

DHCP Server 1   DHCP Server 2

Scope 1 IP addresses:
203.15.39.10 — 203.15.39.25

Scope 3 IP addresses:
203.15.39.26 — 203.15.39.40

Scope 2 IP addresses:
203.15.3.5 — 203.15.3.20

Scope 4 IP addresses:
203.15.3.21 — 203.15.3.35

One major configuration parameter is the lease time or the duration a client may use a particular IP address. You consider the needs of the clients and the number of available addresses when deciding on appropriate lease times. If you have many clients and many addresses, set long lease times because longer lease times result in fewer renewal broadcasts and less network traffic. If you have many clients and comparatively few IP addresses, set shorter lease times so that the IP addresses can be reused for another client. In the long term, though, you should get more IP addresses.

Tip: Have your DHCP clients renew their IP address leases frequently if it does not significantly increase network traffic. In that way, when configuring a new network you can lease a dummy set of IP addresses for LAN connectivity while waiting for final configuration approval from the client or while waiting for your Internet Service Provider (ISP) to provide real Internet IP addresses. Once you have implemented a new IP addressing configuration, the DHCP clients automatically seek the new information.

You also need to consider the exclusion range, a small range of IP addresses that are excluded from being leased to DHCP clients. You might need to configure addresses in this range as static for the following clients:

- HP JetDirect printers that are connected directly to the network, which operate dynamically through BOOTP, not DHCP

- Other DHCP servers

- DNS servers

- Non-DHCP clients such as Macintosh computers or workstations supporting videoconferencing that need a fixed, real Internet-registered IP address

- Diskless workstations

- Remote Access Service (RAS) clients (RAS is a Windows service that provides remote networking for mobile workers)

- Point-to-Point Protocol (PPP) clients (PPP is a protocol suite supporting point-to-point links in transporting multi-protocol datagrams)

- Routers

 Tip: Always create an exclusion range. You will likely need the addresses later on to support new hardware or processes.

Configuring the DHCP Service

The configuration of Windows 2000 DHCP is simpler than that of Microsoft Windows NT 4.0 DHCP because wizards help you establish a scope and configure scope options. To create a scope and modify the initial configuration, follow these steps:

1. From the **Start** menu, choose **Programs, Administrative Tools,** and then select **DHCP.**

2. In the DHCP console snap-in, double-click the server you want to configure.

3. From the menu bar, choose **Action, New Scope** and then select **Next.**

4. Within **Scope Name,** type the name of the scope, include a brief description, and then choose **Next.**

5. Within IP Address Range, type the Start IP and End IP addresses for the scope, the subnet mask, and the number of bits from the IP address used to specify the host, and choose Next (Figure 3.11).

Figure 3.11 IP New Scope Wizard

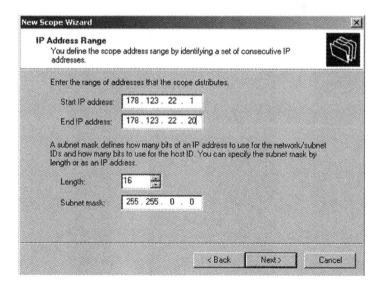

6. Within **Add Exclusions**, type the Start IP and End IP addresses for the exclusion range, choose **Add** and then **Next** (Figure 3.12).

Figure 3.12 New Scope Exclusions

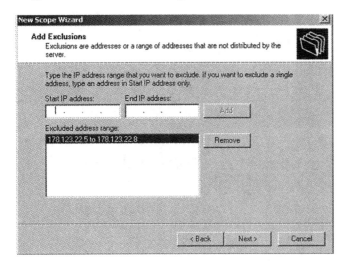

7. Within Lease Duration, change the default lease period of 8 days to the days, hours, and minutes you prefer, and choose Next (Figure 3.13).

Figure 3.13 New Scope Lease Duration

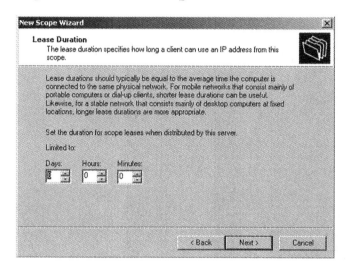

8. Within **Configure DHCP Options**, you must decide when you wish to configure common DHCP options.

9. If you choose **No, I will configure these options later**, choose **Next**, and from **Completing The New Scope**, choose **Finish** (an icon representing the new scope appears in the DHCP console and you can finish the configuration at any time).

10. If you choose **Yes, I want to configure these options now**, choose **Next**, and within **Router (Default Gateway)**, type the IP addresses of routers to be used by clients, in the order that you want the routers to be accessed, and after entering each IP address, choose **Add** and then **Next** (Figure 3.14).

Figure 3.14 Router (Default Gateway) New Scope Wizard

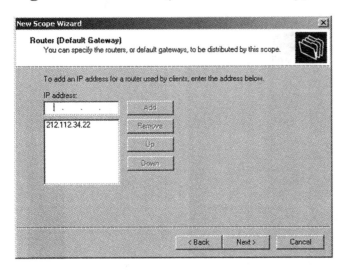

11. Within **Domain Name and DNS Servers**, type the name of the parent domain that you want client computers on your network to use for DNS name resolution, specify the names and IP addresses of DNS servers on your network, in the order that you want the servers to be accessed, and after entering each server choose **Add** and then **Next** (Figure 3.15).

Figure 3.15 Domain Name and DNS Servers

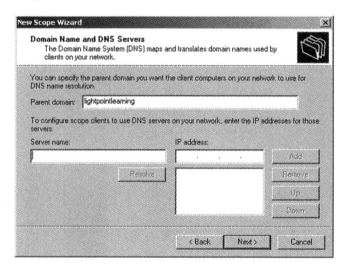

12. Within **WINS Servers**, type the names and IP addresses of WINS servers on your network, in the order that you want the servers to be accessed and aAfter entering each server, choose **Add** and then **Next** (Figure 3.16).

Figure 3.16 WINS Servers Wizard

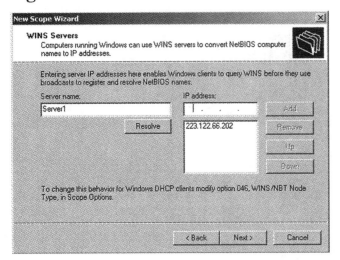

13. Within **Activate Scope**, choose **Yes** and then **Next**.

 Note: You must activate a scope before it becomes available to give out IP addresses.

14. Within **Completing the Scope**, choose **Finish**, and exit the wizard (the DHCP console now looks different (Figure 3.17)).

Figure 3.17 DHCP Console with Activated Scope

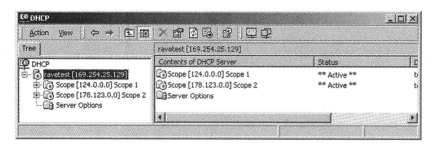

Configuring Server Options

The DHCP snap-in allows you to control any DHCP server from a central location. Once you have created a DHCP scope, you can configure options for DHCP clients on three levels: server, scope, and client. Server options are used for those parameters that need to remain the same for all DHCP clients on all subnets.

To configure server options, follow these steps:

1. From the **Start** menu, choose **Programs**, **Administrative Tools**, and **DHCP**.

2. In the left pane of the DHCP console, choose the desired **server**, and, in the right pane, the corresponding **Server Options** folder.

3. From the **Action** menu, choose **Configure Options**.

4. Within **Server Options** (appears with a **General** and an **Advanced** page (Figure 3.18)), choose **Advanced** to make further refinements regarding vendor and user class and, when you have finished configuring, click **OK** .

Figure 3.18 Server Options

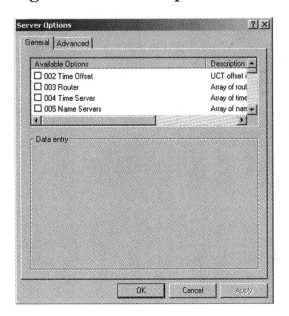

Of the more than 75 available TCP/IP options, some of the more common from the General page of the Server Options page are seen in Table 3.2.

Table 3.2 Server Configuration Options

Option	Description
003 Router	The IP address of a router, usually the default gateway
005 Name Servers	Specifies an ordered list of IP addresses for Internet Engineering Notes (IEN) name servers available to the client
006 DNS Servers	The IP address of a DNS server

Option	Description
014 Merit Dump File	Specifies the path name for the crash dump file
015 DNS Domain Name	The DNS domain name for client resolutions
044 WINS/NBNS Servers	The IP address of a WINS/NetBIOS Name Server (NBNS) server. WINS is Microsoft's proprietary NetBIOS or computer name resolver, while NBNS refers to generic name resolvers.
046 WINS/NBT Node Type	The type of NetBIOS over TCP/IP name resolution to be used by the client, whereby the options are: B-node (broadcast), P-node (peer), M-node (mixed), and H-node (hybrid).

Configuring Server Properties

DHCP server parameters are found in the server's Properties page. To configure the server's Properties page, follow these steps:

1. From the **Start** menu, choose **Programs**, **Administrative Tools**, and **DHCP**.

2. In the left pane of the DHCP console, right-click the desired server, and choose **Properties**.

3. From the General page, specify whether you want to automatically update statics and the desired interval to do so in hours and minutes.

 Note: You can also enable DHCP audit logging, and show the BOOTP table folder, which contains the configuration entries to support BOOTP clients.

Figure 3.19 DHCP Server General Property Page

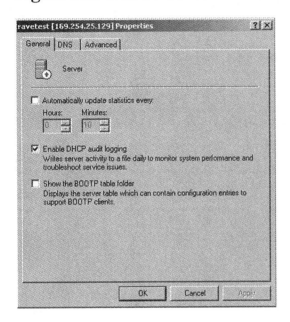

 Note: On the DNS page of the DHCP server Properties page, you can allow an automatic update of DHCP client information in DNS, either on an ongoing basis or only when requested by a DHCP client. You can also discard forward (name-to-address) lookups when the DHCP lease expires. Another configuration option on this page is to enable updates for DNS clients that do not support dynamic updates. Only Windows 2000 supports dynamic updates of DNS information. This option confers the same knowledge to older computers running legacy versions of Windows DNS (Figure 3.20).

Figure 3.20 DNS Property Page

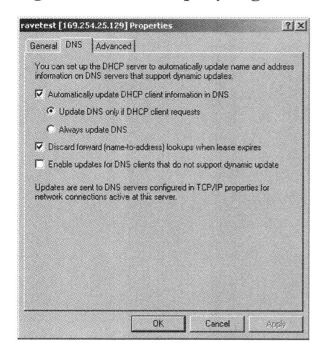

Note: On the Advanced page of the DHCP server Properties page, you can enter the number of times the server should attempt conflict detection for an IP address before the server leases the address to a client. You can also specify the audit log file path as well as the path to store the DHCP database. Another configuration option on this page is to change the server connections bindings (Figure 3.21).

Figure 3.21 DHCP Advanced Property Page

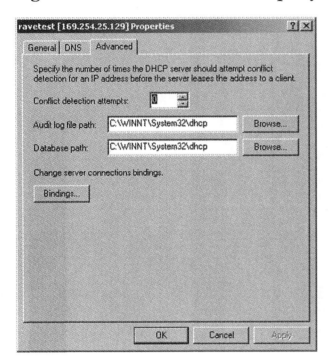

Configuring Scope Options

Each server can support a number of subnets, with one scope for each subnet. Within the scope, you can control the following four subfolders that hold configuration information.

Address Pool—This subfolder specifies the range of IP addresses to be distributed. You can change the address pool at any time by right-clicking the Address Pool folder and selecting New Exclusion Range. Then enter the Start and End IP addresses for a new exclusion range.

Address Leases—You manage client leases through this folder, which details client IP addresses and corresponding names in the right pane, along with lease expiration information and MAC addresses.

Reservations—This subfolder holds a list of reserved IP addresses and corresponding clients. Reservations are IP addresses that are reserved for specific clients, such as for computers that often need to be moved to different subnets. You can change the reservations list at any time by following these steps:

1. From the **Start** menu, choose **Programs, Administrative Tools,** and **DHCP.**

2. In the DHCP console, right-click on **Reservations** and choose **New Reservation.**

3. Within **New Reservation** (Figure 3.22), type the client name and the corresponding reserved IP address, type in the **MAC address** without hyphens, and enter a brief description in the **Description** text box.

4. Under **Supported types,** choose **DHCP only, BOOTP only,** or **Both,** and choose **Add** and then **Close.**

 Note: A BOOTP client could be a legacy terminal or router that does not use DHCP.

Figure 3.22 New Reservation Dialog Box

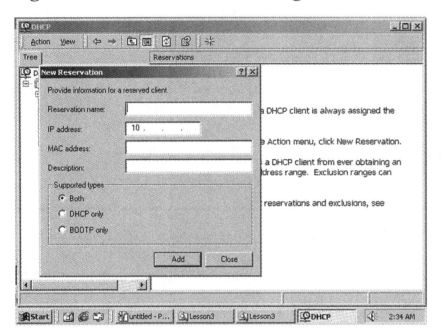

Scope Options—Scope options detail specific TCP/IP settings that the DHCP server should give to clients who obtain an IP address from a specific scope. Scope options are usually used to specify special parameters for a particular subnet, such as a default gateway, and they override server options.

Configuring Client Options

Client options override both server and scope options. Client options designate parameters available only to specific clients with reserved DHCP addresses. To configure client options, select the specific client reservation and then from the Action menu, select Configure Options.

Tip: If you get an error message that the DHCP client could not obtain an IP address or the DCHP client could not renew the IP address lease, make sure the DHCP server service is running on the target DHCP server and the client's network connection is working. Also, check that the DHCP server has free IP addresses to give.

DHCP Integration

The DHCP service needs to be integrated into your Information Technology (IT) infrastructure. Historically, routers were designed not to forward broadcasts in order to reduce network traffic. However, Request for Comments (RFC) 1542 was devised. RFCs are documents that define TCP/IP standards and are published by the Internet Engineering Task Force.

Routers that support RFC 1542 recognize and forward BOOTP broadcasts, known as BOOTP forwarding. Newer routers generally comply with RFC 1542, while older ones do not. This becomes important in an enterprise network because DHCP clients must first broadcast their IP requests to a DHCP server.

Integrating DHCP in a Routed Environment

You can work around the problem of supporting DHCP client broadcasts in several ways. One solution is to make sure that all routers in your network connecting subnets are RFC 1542-compliant so that they can forward DHCP requests across subnets. Many vendors have DHCP Relay Agents and BOOTP forwarding built into their networking products. The DHCP Relay Agent listens for a DHCP client broadcast on a local subnet, takes the broadcast and converts it to a point-to-point message destined for a DHCP server on another subnet. Routers are designed by default to forward point-to-point messages. For example, Cisco has a setting on their routers called a Helper Address, which acts much like a Microsoft DHCP Relay Agent. Older routers may need a software upgrade.

Another option is to configure a DHCP server on each subnet to service the subnet locally. Unfortunately, this defeats the purpose of centralized TCP/IP management and can get expensive.

One common solution is to turn a Windows 2000 server into a DHCP Relay Agent. Only Windows 2000 Server has the software to support the DHCP Relay Agent—Windows 2000 Professional does not. This is unlike Microsoft Windows NT 4.0, which had the DHCP Relay Agent built in to both the workstation and server editions. You should have only one DHCP Relay Agent on each subnet, with the proviso that the DHCP server should never be a DHCP Relay Agent.

Tip: Questions regarding DHCP relay agents and BOOTP forwarding invariably appear on MCSE certification exams.

To create a Windows 2000 DHCP Relay Agent, follow these steps:

1. From the **Start** menu, choose **Programs, Administrative Tools,** and **Routing and Remote Access**.

2. From the **Routing and Remote Access** console, right-click the desired server's name, choose **Configure and Enable Routing and Remote Access** and then **Next**.

3. Choose **Manually configured server** from the five possible common configurations, then **Next**, and finish the wizard.

4. From **Routing and Remote Access**, open the **IP Routing** object by selecting the plus sign, right-click on **DHCP Relay Agent**, and choose **Properties**.

5. Within **DHCP Relay Agent Properties**, type the IP address of the DHCP server, choose **Add**, and then click **OK**.

6. Right-click **DHCP Relay Agent**, choose **New Interface** and then **Local Area Connection**.

Another method of supporting DHCP client broadcasts is to configure a Windows 2000 or Microsoft Windows NT computer as a router. Both Windows 2000 and Windows NT routing software are compliant with RFC 1542. First, create a dual-homed computer having two or more Network Interface Cards (NICs) with IP addresses belonging to each subnet interface. You can also create a dual-homed system by binding multiple IP addresses to a single network adapter card, with each address belonging to the subnets that you want to connect. Next, install and configure the DHCP server service. Enable IP routing in the Routing and Remote Access Service (RRAS) snap-in, and the server will be able to support multiple subnets.

DHCP Support

The DHCP service is easier to support now because of improvements to Windows 2000 from Microsoft Windows NT 4.0. A snap-in within the Microsoft Management Console (MMC) provides an icon-based user interface that shows error states for the DHCP service and free addresses within a scope. From the interface, you can also create and modify scopes, view address leases, create and modify client reservations, and configure server, scope, and client reservation options.

Unlike previous versions of Windows in which WINS was heavily integrated with DHCP, DNS is now the primary method of resolving names. As a result, whenever a computer needs to be given a new IP address such as during a move to a different subnet, the DNS configuration information is automatically updated, leading to fewer DHCP and DNS administration tasks. Windows 2000 offers improved detection of unauthorized DHCP servers.

Another improvement is the default behavior when a DHCP client cannot locate a DHCP server. With Microsoft Windows NT 4.0, the client displayed an error message and was blocked from all network resources. Now, the Microsoft Automatic Private IP Address built in to each Windows 2000 computer assigns an IP address that does not conflict with the rest of the network from a pool of addresses that the Internet reserves for private networks. The client then tries to contact a DHCP server every five minutes until one is located. Meanwhile, the client can access local network resources but not remote network resources.

A further improvement from Microsoft Windows NT 4.0 is that administrators at the organizational unit level can manage scopes for DHCP servers within their respective organizational units. Previously, only domain administrators could manage DHCP scopes.

Support for superscopes and multicast scopes is now available. A superscope allows one DHCP server to issue IP addresses for multiple logical subnets. Multicast DHCP, in which clients having a multicast IP address can message a whole group within an intranet, is needed by multimedia clients participating in collaborative application sessions. It acts independently from regular unicast scopes, which are used for point-to-point data transfer. Multicast DHCP is configured through scopes using the Multicast Scope wizard.

Windows 2000 provides improved reporting as well, offering DHCP monitoring and statistical reports, some of which are graphical.

Maintaining and Troubleshooting DHCP

Built-in utilities are available to help you administer and troubleshoot your DHCP service.

IPCONFIG

Ipconfig is a command line utility used to display IP configuration and other options. You can obtain DHCP configuration parameters on a local computer by typing **ipconfig /all** from the command line (Figure 3.23). To erase DHCP information, type **ipconfig /release** from the command line, and to obtain new configuration parameters from DHCP, type **ipconfig /renew**. Other switches can be used with ipconfig, permitting you to register DNS or display DNS information.

Figure 3.23 Host Information Provided by Ipconfig /all

```
C:\Documents and Settings\Administrator>ipconfig /all

Windows 2000 IP Configuration

        Host Name . . . . . . . . . . . . : ravetest
        Primary DNS Suffix  . . . . . . . : CRASH.CSP
        Node Type . . . . . . . . . . . . : Hybrid
        IP Routing Enabled. . . . . . . . : Yes
        WINS Proxy Enabled. . . . . . . . : No

Ethernet adapter Local Area Connection:

        Connection-specific DNS Suffix  . :
        Description . . . . . . . . . . . : Microsoft Loopback Adapter
        Physical Address. . . . . . . . . : 02-00-4C-4F-4F-50
        DHCP Enabled. . . . . . . . . . . : Yes
        Autoconfiguration Enabled . . . . : Yes
        Autoconfiguration IP Address. . . : 169.254.25.129
        Subnet Mask . . . . . . . . . . . : 255.255.0.0
        Default Gateway . . . . . . . . . :
        DNS Servers . . . . . . . . . . . :

C:\Documents and Settings\Administrator>
```

Tip: Run the **ipconfig /release** and **ipconfig /renew** program on computers if you have changed parameters significantly on your DHCP server to prevent network anomalies.

Ipconfig works on DOS, Windows for Workgroups and Microsoft Windows NT computers. Windows 95 and Windows 98 computers have a graphical version called Winipcfg.

DHCP Logs

Windows 2000 has auditing to allow for monitoring of the DHCP server. A separate log is kept for each day of the week in \winnt\system32\dhcp to facilitate record recovery. The logs are in American Standard Code for Information Interchange (ASCII), the standard code for representing English characters as numbers and can be read with Notepad.

However, since Windows 2000 also has disk quotas, you need to make sure the DHCP activity logs do not fill up all the available disk space. To change the log settings, edit the registry key: HKEY_LOCAL_MACHINE\SYSTEM\CurrentControlSet\Services\DHCPServer\Parameters.

The main log parameters are defined as follows:

- DhcpLogFilePath-Allows you to specify the full path to the log file

- DhcpLogMinSpaceOnDisk-Allows you to specify the minimum amount of disk space remaining before audit logging stops

- DhcpLogDiskSpaceCheckInterval-The number of times the audit log is written to before disk free space is checked

- DhcpBackupInterval-Default is 60 minutes, but you can specify in minutes the interval between backups

- DhcpLogFileMaxSize-The maximum size of the log file in megabytes (Figure 3.24)

Figure 3.24 DHCP Server Parameters Registry Key

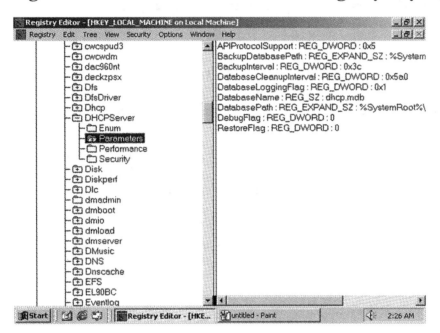

Backup copies of the DHCP database are found in:
%systemroot%\System32\Dhcp\Backup\Jet\newfolder

By default, the DHCP service restores a corrupt DHCP database automatically when you restart the DHCP service. You can also restore a database manually by editing the RestoreFLag registry key:

HKEY_LOCAL_MACHINE\System\CurrentControlSet\Services\DHCPServer\

To change parameters, Set the RestoreFlag key to 1. After the database is restored, the server changes the key to 0 again.

You can also restore the DHCP database file by copying the contents of the %systemroot%\System32\Dhcp\Backup\Jet folder to the %systemroot%\System32\Dhcpfolder and then restarting the DHCP service.

Vocabulary

Review the following terms in preparation for the certification exam.

Term	Description
Active Directory	The directory service included with Windows 2000 Server. Active Directory stores information about objects on a network in a hierarchical view and provides a single point of administration for all network objects.
ASCII	American Standard Code for Information Interchange is a code for representing English characters as numbers.
BOOTP	Bootstrap Protocol is a set of standards enabling computers to connect to one another. It is used mainly on TCP/IP networks to configure diskless workstations. DHCP is based on this protocol.
BOOTP forwarding	The act of forwarding BOOTP broadcasts across subnets.
DHCP	Dynamic Host Configuration Protocol is a networking protocol that simplifies TCP/IP network configuration and dynamically configures IP addresses for clients. DHCP ensures that address conflicts do not occur by centralizing address allocation.
DHCP Relay Agent	A DHCP Relay Agent forwards client DHCP requests directly to a DHCP server on another subnet.
DNS	Domain Name System is the hierarchical naming system used to locate domain names on the Internet and on private TCP/IP networks. The DNS service maps DNS domain names to IP addresses and vice versa.
exclusion range	A small range of IP addresses that are excluded from being leased to DHCP clients.

Term	Description
ISP	An Internet Service Provider is a private company that offers connectivity to the Internet for individuals or organizations.
LAN	A Local Area Network consists of a limited number of computers connected together in a common area within a limited physical space. It combines hardware and software technologies that allow users to share resources such as data, programs, storage devices, printers and other peripherals.
lease	The duration a DHCP client is permitted to retain an IP address.
MAC address	Media Access Control address is the address used for communication between network adapters on the same subnet. Each network adapter has an associated MAC address.
MMC	Microsoft Management Console is a framework for hosting administrative consoles. A console is defined by the items on its console tree. It has windows that provide views of the tree as well as the administrative properties, services and events that are acted on by items in the console tree.
Multicast DHCP	DHCP clients having a multicast IP address can message a whole group within an intranet.
multihomed	A computer that has multiple network adapters installed.
NBNS	A NetBIOS Name Server resolves a computer name to and IP address.
NetBIOS name	A name recognized by WINS, the service that maps a computer name to its IP address.

Term	Description
NetBT	NetBIOS over TCP/IP is a feature that provides the NetBIOS programming interface over the TCP/IP protocol. It is used for monitoring routed servers that use NetBIOS name resolution.
NIC	A Network Interface Card is a device that allows the network cable to connect the computer to the network.
PPP	Point-to-Point Protocol is an industry standard suite of protocols for the use of point-to-point links to transport multiprotocol datagrams.
RAS	Remote Access Service provides remote networking for telecommuters, mobile workers, and system administrators who manage servers at multiple sites.
reservation	An IP address that is reserved for a specific client, such as a computer that often needs to be moved to different subnets.
RFC	Request For Comments is a document that defines a TCP/IP standard. RFCs are published by the Internet Engineering Task Force and other working groups.
scope	The range of IP addresses a DHCP server can assign.
superscope	Multiple scopes grouped together for administrative ease.
TCP/IP	Transport Control Protocol/Internet Protocol is a set of protocols that provides communication among diverse networks. Because it accommodates different architectures and operating systems, TCP/IP is the most commonly used Internet protocol.

Term	Description
UDP	User Datagram Protocol is a TCP component offering connectionless packet delivery. While it is direct, it does not guarantee delivery or correct sequencing of packets.
WINS	Windows Internet Name Service is a Microsoft software service that dynamically maps IP addresses to computer names. This allows users to access resources by name instead of by IP address.

In Brief

If you want to...	Then do this...
Install the DHCP server service	1. From the **Start** menu, choose **Settings**, **Control Panel**, and then **Add/Remove Programs**. 2. Choose **Add/Remove Windows Components**, and select Networking Services. 3. Choose **Details**, and from **Subcomponents of Networking Services**, select **Dynamic Host Configuration Protocol (DHCP)**, and click **OK**. 4. From **Windows Components**, choose **Next** and type in the location of the installation files. 5. From **Completing the Windows Components**, choose **Finish**.

If you want to...	Then do this...
Authorize the DHCP server	1. From the **Start** menu, choose **Programs**, **Administrative Tools**, and **DHCP**.
	2. From the **console tree**, choose the desired **DHCP server**, from the **Action** menu, select **Authorize**, and select the **F5** key to refresh the display.
	3. You can authorize a number of DHCP servers at the same time; instead of choosing a specific DHCP server from the console, select the **DHCP icon** and from the **Action** menu, select **Manage authorized servers**.
	4. From **Manage Authorized Servers**, choose **Authorize**, type in the name or IP address of the DHCP server you want to authorize, click **OK**, select **Yes** and then **Close**.
Configure the DHCP server service	1. From the **Start** menu, choose **Programs**, **Administrative Tools**, and **DHCP**.
	2. In the DHCP console snap-in, double-click on the desired server, and **Configure the DHCP Server** appears.
	3. From the **Action** menu, choose **New Scope** and then **Next**.
	4. Within **Scope Name**, type the name of the scope, include a brief description, and then choose **Next**.
	5. Within **IP Address Range**, type the Start IP and End IP addresses for the scope, the subnet mask, and the number of bits from the IP address used to specify the host, and choose **Next**.

If you want to...	Then do this...
Configure the DHCP server service	6. Within **Add Exclusions**, type the Start IP and End IP addresses for the exclusion range, choose **Add** and then **Next**.
	7. Within **Lease Duration**, change the default lease period of 8 days to the days, hours, and minutes you prefer, and choose **Next**.
	8. Within **Configure DHCP Options**, you must decide when you wish to configure common DHCP options.
	9. If you choose **No, I will configure these options later**, choose **Next**, and from **Completing The New Scope**, select **Finish** (you can finish the configuration at any time).
	10. If you choose **Yes, I want to configure these options now**, choose **Next**, and within **Router (Default Gateway)**, type the IP addresses of routers to be used by clients, in the order that you want the routers to be accessed, and after entering each IP address, select **Add** and then **Next**.
	11. Within **Domain Name and DNS Servers**, type the name of the parent domain that you want client computers on your network to use for DNS name resolution, specify the names and IP addresses of DNS servers on your network, in the order that you want the servers to be accessed, and after entering each server choose **Add** and then **Next**.

If you want to...	Then do this...
Configure the DHCP server service	12. Within **WINS Servers**, type the names and IP addresses of WINS servers on your network, in the order that you want the servers to be accessed and after entering each server, choose **Add** and then **Next**. 13. Within **Activate Scope**, choose **Yes** and then **Next**. 14. Within **Completing the Scope**, choose **Finish**, and exit the wizard.
Integrate DHCP in a routed environment	Work around the problem of supporting DHCP client broadcasts in several ways: • Make sure that all routers in your network connecting subnets are RFC 1542-compliant, so that they can forward DHCP requests across subnets (newer routers support RFC 1542 while older routers may need a software upgrade) • Configure a DHCP server on each subnet to service the subnet locally • Turn a Windows 2000 Server into a DHCP Relay Agent • Configure a Windows 2000 or NT computer as a router (create a dual-homed computer, install and configure the DHCP server service, and enable IP routing in the TCP/IP configuration)

If you want to...	Then do this...
Maintain and troubleshoot DHCP	Use built-in utilities to manage your DHCP service: **Ipconfig**—This command line utility displays IP configuration and other options. You can obtain DHCP configuration parameters on a local computer by typing **ipconfig /all**. To erase DHCP information, type **ipconfig /release**, and to obtain new configuration parameters from DHCP, type **ipconfig /renew**. Ipconfig works on DOS, Windows for Workgroups and NT computers. Windows 95 and Windows 98 computers have a graphical version called Winipcfg. **DHCP logs**—Windows 2000 has auditing to allow for monitoring of the DHCP server. A separate log is kept for each day of the week in \winnt\system32\dhcp to facilitate record recovery. Make sure that the DHCP activity logs do not fill up all the available disk space. To change the log settings, edit the registry key: HKEY_LOCAL_MACHINE\SYSTEM\ CurrentControlSet\Services\DHCPServer\ Parameters Backup copies of the DHCP database are found in: %systemroot%\System32\Dhcp\Backup\ Jet\newfolder By default, the DHCP service restores a corrupt DHCP database automatically when you restart the DHCP service. You can also restore a database manually by editing the RestoreFLag registry key. Set the RestoreFlag key to 1.

If you want to...	Then do this...
Maintain and troubleshoot DHCP	You can also restore the DHCP database file by copying the contents of the %systemroot%\System32\Dhcp\Backup\ Jet folder to the %systemroot%\System32\Dhcpfolder and then restarting the DHCP service.

Lesson 3 Activities

Complete the following activities to better prepare you for the certification exam.

1. Describe the four steps in the DHCP lease process.

2. Describe and compare the manual configuration of TCP/IP with DHCP.

3. List three common configurable options at the server, scope, or client level.

4. You want to limit the size of the DHCP activity logs so that they do not fill up all the available hard disk space. Describe what you would do.

5. Explain the considerations for establishing a lease time.

6. Describe the function of the Ipconfig command line utility.

7. Describe the default behavior of a Windows 2000 DHCP client when it cannot locate a DHCP server.

8. List the basic guidelines for configuring the DHCP service.

9. Describe how you would configure a DHCP Relay Agent.

10. List some of the activities you can perform from the DHCP snap-in to the MMC.

Answers to Lesson 3 Activities

1. A DCHP client gets an IP address from a DHCP server in four steps:

    DHCPDISCOVER—The client broadcasts a request to all DHCP servers asking for the location of a DHCP server and IP address information. The source address of the message is 0.0.0.0 since the client does not yet have an IP address, and the destination address is the broadcast 255.255.255.255. The message contains the client's MAC address and computer name so that a responding DHCP server can identify the client. The communication protocol used is User Datagram Protocol (UDP), not TCP, since an IP address does not yet exist. UDP is part of the TCP/IP suite.

    DHCPOFFER—Each available DHCP server responds to the client's MAC address with a broadcast message offering an IP address, a subnet mask, the lease duration, and the IP address of the offering server.

    DHCPREQUEST—The client chooses the best offer, or the first received if all offers appear equal, and broadcasts back a UDP packet to all DHCP servers confirming its acceptance of an offer. The message includes the IP address of the server whose offer it accepted and a request for additional configuration information such as a default gateway. The other servers then retract their offers, returning their offered IP addresses to their respective pools.

    DHCPACK (DHCP Acknowledgement)—The server handing out the IP address acknowledges the request by broadcasting a message containing a lease for an IP address and other TCP/IP configuration information, such as the default gateway, WINS server, and DNS server. When the DHCP client receives the message, it completes its TCP/IP binding. Now the client can use TCP/IP to communicate over the network.

2. Manual TCP/IP configuration:

    *   Administrators assign IP addresses and configure TCP/IP information, creating overhead and possibility of errors from assigning duplicate addresses or incorrect configuration information

    *   Ideal for small networks

    *   Larger pool of IP addresses is needed

    *   Administrative overhead caused by moving clients to different subnets and manual reconfiguration of IP addresses, subnet masks, default gateway, and WINS and DNS information

DHCP TCP/IP configuration:

- IP addressing and TCP/IP configuration information is automatically supplied to clients, without administrator overhead

- Useful for medium to large networks

- Smaller pool of IP addresses is needed because not all IP addresses are used all the time

- Reduced administrative overhead if you need to move clients to different subnets

3. Of the more than 75 available TCP/IP options, some of the more common options are the following:

- 003 Router (IP address of a router, usually the default gateway)

- 005 Name Servers (Specifies an ordered list of IP addresses for name servers available to the client)

- 006 DNS Servers (IP address of a DNS server)

- 014 Merit Dump File (Specifies the path name for the crash dump file)

- 015 DNS Domain Name (DNS domain name for client resolutions)

- 044 WINS/NBNS Servers (IP address of a WINS/NetBIOS Name Server (NBNS) server)

- 046 WINT/NBT Node Type (Type of NetBIOS over TCP/IP name resolution to be used by the client, whereby the options are: B-node (broadcast), P-node (peer), M-node (mixed), and H-node (hybrid)

4. You will need to change the log settings by editing the registry key: HKEY_LOCAL_MACHINE\SYSTEM\CurrentControlSet\Services\DHCPServer\ Parameters.

The log parameters you would be interested in are:

- DhcpLogFilePath-Allows you to specify the full path to the log file

- DhcpLogMinSpaceOnDisk-Allows you to specify the minimum amount of disk space remaining before audit logging stops

- DhcpLogDiskSpaceCheckInterval-The number of times the audit log is written to before disk free space is checked

- DhcpLogFileMaxSize-The maximum size of the log file in megabytes

5. Decrease the lease time if most of the clients have portable computers, are dialing in, move their computers often, or if many clients on the network have a comparatively limited supply of IP addresses. A shorter lease time results in faster reuse of IP addresses and quicker changes in configuration parameters.

    Increase the lease time if you have many clients and many addresses, because longer lease times result in fewer renewal broadcasts and less network traffic.

6. Ipconfig is used to display IP configuration and other options. You can obtain DHCP configuration parameters on a local computer by typing **ipconfig /all** from the command line. To erase DHCP information, type **ipconfig /release**, and to obtain new configuration parameters from DHCP, type **ipconfig /renew**. Other switches can be used with ipconfig, permitting you to register DNS or display DNS information.

7. One improvement of Windows 2000 over Microsoft Windows NT 4.0 is the default behavior when a DHCP client cannot locate a DHCP server. With Microsoft Windows NT 4.0, the client displayed an error message and was blocked from all network resources. Now, the Microsoft Automatic Private IP address built in to each Windows 2000 computer assigns an IP address that does not conflict with the rest of the network from a pool of addresses that the Internet reserves for private networks. The client then tries to contact a DHCP server every five minutes until one is located. Meanwhile, the client can access local network resources but not remote network resources.

8. The basic guidelines for configuring the DHCP service are as follows:

    *   Create multiple DHCP servers if you are administering a multi-domain network because a DHCP server can only issue IP addresses to clients in the domain in which the server is participating

    *   Create at least one scope for every DHCP server

    *   Create one scope per subnet (in most cases)

    *   May create multiple scopes on one DHCP server to centralize administration, but only one scope can apply to a specific subnet

    *   When you create scopes on multiple DHCP servers, make sure the scopes do not overlap because DHCP servers do not share scope information; otherwise, you will assign duplicate IP addresses and create network anomalies

    *   Implementation of separate scopes possible to meet the needs of specific user groups

- For administrative ease, you can group multiple scopes into one large superscope, in which case you define two or more scopes on a DHCP server, right-click the server, choose New Superscope, and add as many scopes to the superscope as you like

- Exclude static IP addresses from the range of available IP addresses

9. One method of solving the need to convey a DHCP client's broadcast messages to a DHCP server across subnets is to turn a Windows 2000 Server into a DHCP Relay Agent.

   To create a Windows 2000 DHCP Relay Agent, follow these steps:

   1. From the **Start** menu, choose **Programs, Administrative Tools**, and **Routing and Remote Access**.

   2. From the **Routing and Remote Access** console, right-click the desired server's name, choose **Configure and Enable Routing and Remote Access** and then **Next**.

   3. Choose **Manually configured server** from the five possible common configurations, then **Next**, and finish the wizard.

   4. From **Routing and Remote Access**, open the **IP Routing** object by selecting the plus sign, right-click on **DHCP Relay Agent**, and choose **Properties**.

   5. Within **DHCP Relay Agent Properties**, type the IP address of the DHCP server, choose **Add**, and then click **OK**.

   6. Right-click **DHCP Relay Agent**, choose **New Interface** and then **Local Area Connection**.

10. A snap-in within the Microsoft Management Console (MMC) provides an icon-based user interface that shows error states for the DHCP service and free addresses within a scope. From the interface, you can create and modify scopes, view address leases, create and modify client reservations, and configure server, scope, and client reservation options.

Lesson 3 Quiz

These questions test your knowledge of features, vocabulary, procedures, and syntax.

1. What are the benefits of using DHCP?
   A. Dynamic IP configuration
   B. Centralized IP name resolution
   C. Dynamic NetBIOS name registration
   D. Reduced administrative overhead

2. What is a superscope?
   A. A scope with DHCP clients that have multicast IP addresses
   B. Multiple scopes grouped together for administrative ease
   C. A large unicast scope
   D. A scope that encompasses more than one domain

3. When do you need more than one DHCP server on an internetwork?
   A. For support of multihomed computers
   B. For fault tolerance purposes
   C. For a multi-domain network
   D. For routers that are not BOOTP-enabled when no DHCP Relay Agent exists

4. Which of the following hosts need to have static addresses?
   A. DHCP server
   B. Router
   C. Remote Access Service client
   D. Non-DHCP client

5. When does a DHCP client attempt to renew its lease?
   A. 1/3 life
   B. 1/2 life
   C. 3/4 life
   D. 7/8 life

6. Which of the following items are used to administer a DHCP database?
   A. DHCP Relay Agent
   B. DHCP snap-in within the MMC
   C. The registry key: HKEY_LOCAL_MACHINE\SYSTEM\CurrentControlSet\Services\
      DHCPServer\Parameters
   D. Ipconfig

7. Clients on the same subnet as the DHCP server can get access to the Internet, while a DHCP client on a remote subnet cannot. The client can communicate with the rest of the clients on that remote subnet. What is the problem?
   A. DHCP client on remote subnet is malfunctioning
   B. Router is malfunctioning
   C. DHCP Relay Agent on local subnet is malfunctioning
   D. DHCP server is malfunctioning

8. What is an exclusion range?
   A. A range of IP addresses that are reserved for current specific clients
   B. A range of IP addresses set aside for future DHCP clients
   C. A small range of IP addresses that are excluded from being leased to DHCP clients
   D. A range of private IP addresses built in to each Windows 2000 computer

9. Which of the following statements are true?
   A. Client options override scope options
   B. Server options override scope options
   C. Scope options override client options
   D. Scope options override server options

10. Which of the following clients can use Windows 2000 DHCP?
    A. Windows for Workgroups 3.11 running TCP/IP-32
    B. Windows 95 or later versions
    C. LAN Manager 2.2c, except for the OS/2 version
    D. MS-DOS with the Microsoft Network Client 3.0 with the real mode TCP/IP driver

Answers to Lesson 3 Quiz

1. Answers A and D are correct. DHCP allows you to provide dynamic IP configuration for clients, thus reducing administration overhead. This is particularly true for larger networks or for those that change frequently.

    Answer B is incorrect. DHCP does not resolve names with IP addresses.

    Answer C is incorrect. Dynamic NetBIOS name registration is a service provided by WINS.

2. Answer B is correct. A superscope is simply a grouping of multiple scopes for the purpose of administering common configuration parameters.

    Answer A is incorrect. DHCP clients having a multicast IP address can message a whole group within an intranet.

    Answer C is incorrect. A unicast scope is a regular scope.

    Answer D is incorrect. A scope cannot encompass more than one domain, since a DHCP server can only provide IP addresses for clients in the domain in which the DHCP server belongs.

3. Answer B and D are correct. By configuring DHCP servers on different subnets with multiple non-overlapping scopes that refer to the same subnet, you provide fault tolerance. Broadcast requests by a DHCP client for an IP address cannot be heard across subnets by a DHCP server unless the routers support BOOTP forwarding, a DHCP Relay Agent exists on the client's subnet, or a multi-homed IP routing-enabled computer acts as a router.

    Answer A is incorrect. The presence of a multihomed computer may negate the need for multiple DHCP servers on an internetwork if IP routing is enabled in the multihomed computer's TCP/IP configuration.

    Answer C is incorrect. A DHCP server can issue IP addresses to clients in domains other than the domain in which the server is participating, so a multi-domain network doesn't need multiple DHCP servers.

4. Answers A, B, C and D are all correct. A DHCP server cannot assign itself a dynamic IP address. A router needs a static address so that all network components can find it. A RAS client needs a static address to obtain network access through a firewall that you have implemented for security reasons. Non-DHCP clients cannot use DHCP because they do not have the DHCP client built in to their operating systems.

5. Answers B and D are correct. A DHCP client first attempts to renew its lease when 50% of the lease time has passed. If the lease request is unsuccessful and lease time is still available, the DHCP client continues to use the same IP address until the next attempt to renew its lease at 87.5% (7/8) of the lease period.

   Answer A is incorrect. The first lease renewal attempt occurs at 1/2 life.

   Answer C is incorrect. The second lease renewal attempt occurs at 7/8 life.

6. Answers B, C and D are correct. The DHCP snap-in within the MMC provides an icon-based user interface that shows error states for the DHCP service, and free addresses within a scope. From the interface, you can create and modify scopes, view address leases, create and modify client reservations, and configure server, scope and client reservation options. The registry key HKEY_LOCAL_MACHINE\SYSTEM\CurrentControlSet\Services\DHCPServer\ Parameters holds settings for the DHCP activity logs. You can configure many of the log parameters. Ipconfig is a command line utility used to display IP configuration and other options. All, release, and renew are the switches most commonly used with Ipconfig.

   Answer A is incorrect. The DHCP Relay Agent plays no part in administering a DHCP database.

7. Answer C is correct. The DHCP Relay Agent on the remote subnet is probably malfunctioning, preventing broadcasts by DHCP clients on the remote subnet from being heard by the DHCP server.

   Answer A is incorrect. If the remote client can communicate with other hosts on its subnet, it is unlikely that the remote client is malfunctioning.

   Answer B is incorrect. If clients on the same subnet as the DHCP server are able to access the Internet through the router, it is unlikely that the router is malfunctioning.

   Answer D is incorrect. If the DHCP server were malfunctioning, clients on all subnets would be experiencing problems.

8. Answer C is correct. An exclusion range is a small range of IP addresses that are excluded from being leased to DHCP clients, since those IP addresses have been taken by hosts with static IP addresses.

   Answer A is incorrect. Reservations are used for DHCP clients requiring specific IP addresses.

   Answer B is incorrect. There is no such thing as a special range of IP addresses set aside for future DHCP clients.

Answer D is incorrect. The Microsoft Automatic Private IP Address feature built in to each Windows 2000 computer assigns an IP address, which does not conflict with the rest of the network, from a pool of addresses that the Internet reserves for private networks. This is done when a DHCP client cannot locate a DHCP server.

9. Answers A and D are correct. The more specific an option, the greater its precedence. Scope options override server options, and client options override scope options.

    Answer B is incorrect. The reverse is true. Scope options override server options.

    Answer C is incorrect. The reverse is true. Client options override scope options.

10. Answers A, B, C and D are all correct. All of these operating systems have a built in DHCP client.

Lesson 4

Remote Access Configuration and Management

Microsoft Windows NT Server 3.51 introduced the Remote Access Service (RAS) to provide a secure and reliable way to extend a network across communication links to remote computers. The improved version of this service, Routing and Remote Access Service (RRAS), was released in 1996 and integrated both remote access and multi-protocol routing services, turning a Microsoft Windows NT Server 4.0 into a mid-range dynamic software router.

The fully integrated version of RRAS found in Windows 2000 Server offers additional features that allow the server to function as a multi-protocol router, a demand-dial router, and a remote access server. RRAS works with many different hardware platforms and network adapters. As a result, it is less expensive than most dedicated routers or remote access server products.

When functioning as a remote access server, Windows 2000 creates connections to users in the outside world, to other servers, and to outside networks. In essence, this external connection behaves like a Network Interface Card (NIC) on a Local Area Network (LAN), allowing for access to resources on remote computers.

After completing this lesson, you should have a better understanding of the following topics:

*   Inbound Connections
*   Outbound Connections
*   Remote Access Server Configuration
*   Remote Access and Routing Management
*   RADIUS Overview

Inbound Connections

RRAS has the following three main functions that, when combined on the same computer, allow a Windows 2000 computer to become a Windows 2000 remote access router:

Multi-protocol router—A RRAS server can route Internet Protocol (IP), Internetwork Packet Exchange (IPX), and AppleTalk simultaneously. The IP protocol is responsible for the addressing, routing, and fragmentation and reassembly of IP packets, while IPX is a NetWare protocol that controls addressing and packet routing within and between LANs. AppleTalk is Apple computer's networking protocol.

Demand-Dial Router—A RRAS server can route IP and IPX over on-demand or persistent Wide Area Network (WAN) links, such as analog telephone lines or Integrated Services Digital Network (ISDN). ISDN is a communications standard for sending voice, video, and data over digital telephone lines, supporting 64 Kbps transfer per line.

Within demand-dial router function, a RRAS server can also use Point-to-Point Tunneling Protocol (PPTP) or Layer Two Tunneling Protocol (L2TP) with Internet Protocol Security (IPSec) to create Virtual Private Network (VPN) connections. PPTP is a tunneling protocol that encapsulates Point-to-Point Protocol (PPP) frames with IP datagrams for transmission over an IP-based Internetwork. PPP is simply a standard suite of protocols used to create point-to-point links for transporting multiprotocol datagrams. L2TP is a tunneling protocol that encapsulates PPP frames to be sent over IP, X.25, Frame Relay, or Asynchronous Transfer Mode (ATM) networks.

IPSec is a set of cryptography-based protection services and protocols that protects all protocols in the Transport Control Protocol/Internet Protocol (TCP/IP) suite and Internet communications using L2TP. A VPN is an extension of a private network, encompassing links across shared or public networks such as the Internet. ATM is a network technology based on transferring data in packets of a fixed size.

Remote Access Server—A RRAS server provides remote access connectivity to dial-up or VPN clients using IP, IPX, AppleTalk, or Network Basic Input/Output System (NetBIOS) Enhanced User Interface (NetBEUI), Microsoft's networking protocol for small networks.

Windows 2000 Server supports the following features:

*   Dial-up remote access as the client or server

*   VPN remote access as either client or server

- On-demand or persistent dial-up demand-dial routing as either the calling or answering router

- On-demand or persistent VPN demand-dial routing as either the calling or answering router

Adding RRAS Computers to a Tree

Since it has proven to be needed by a large number of users, when you install Windows 2000, RRAS is installed in a disabled state. One local server will be displayed as a RRAS server in the Routing and Remote Access snap-in. You can add more RRAS computers to the tree by following these steps:

1. From the **Start** menu, choose **Programs, Administrative Tools,** and **Routing and Remote Access.**

2. In the **Routing and Remote Access** console, right-click **Routing and Remote Access or Server Status,** and select **Add Server.**

3. From **Add Server,** as shown in Figure 4.1, select the desired server; alternatively, you can select **All Routing and Remote Access computers** within a domain or **Browse Active Directory** for a particular server.

4. Click **OK,** and the server is added to the console tree.

Figure 4.1 Add Server Specification

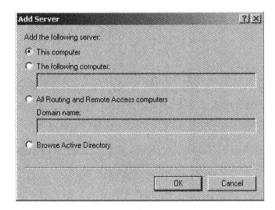

Understanding Remote Access Service

The Remote Access Service (RAS) component of RRAS permits remote access clients to connect, either to the remote access server's resources (point-to-point remote access connectivity) or to the remote access server's resources plus resources from its attached network (point-to-LAN remote access connectivity).

 Note: RAS is a robust, reliable, and manageable remote access service.

RAS connections are typically used to support users dialing in to a company network from a various locations, however, RAS can also connect corporate networks or link a LAN to a public network such as the Internet.

The following two methods of remote access connection are available:

Dial-up remote access—A remote access client uses the telecommunications infrastructure to create a virtual, temporary circuit to a port on a remote access server. The remaining connection parameters are negotiated once the temporary circuit is created.

VPN remote access—A VPN client uses an IP Internetwork to create a virtual point-to-point connection with a RAS server acting as the VPN server. As with dial-up remote access, the remaining connection parameters are negotiated once the virtual point-to-point connection is created.

Dial-up Remote Access Connections

A dial-up remote access connection consists of a remote access client, a remote access server, and the WAN infrastructure (Figure 4.2).

Figure 4.2 Remote Access Dial-Up Connections

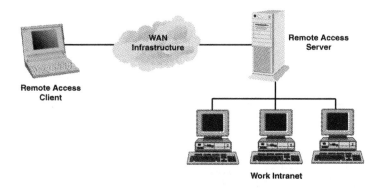

A Windows 2000 remote access server will accept dial-up connections and forward communication packets between remote access clients and the network to which the remote access server is attached. Remote access clients who could attach to a Windows 2000 remote access server could be computers running Microsoft Windows NT 3.5 or later, Windows 95 or 98, Windows for Workgroups, MS-DOS, or Microsoft LAN Manager. Most third party PPP remote access clients, such as UNIX and Apple Macintosh clients, are also candidates.

Various dial-up connections are possible, depending on the available telecommunications infrastructure and the equipment installed at both the remote access client and server. Care must be taken to choose compatible components when selecting the optimum connection type and hardware.

Tip: Make sure your remote access hardware is supported by Windows 2000 by checking the Hardware Compatibility List (HCL) at www.microsoft.com/hcl/default.asp.

Public switched telephone network (PSTN)—Transmission rates over an analog telephone system are slow, since it was not designed for digital data. The maximum rate supported by a PSTN connection is 33.6 Kbps. This is compensated by low cost, wide availability, and ease of use. To use this system, both the remote access client and server need analog modems (Figure 4.3).

Figure 4.3 PSTN Dial-up Connections

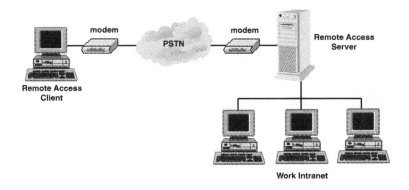

V.90—This new technology allows a RAS server to be connected to a central office through a digital switch rather than an analog PSTN switch, decreasing accumulated noise from digital to analog conversion. Remote access clients can send data at 33.6 Kbps and receive at 56Kbps (Figure 4.4).

Figure 4.4 V.90-based Dial-up PSTN Connection

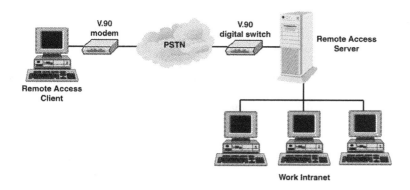

ISDN—ISDN provides standards to replace the PSTN with a digital equivalent. ISDN allows a single digital network to handle voice, data, fax, and other services over the existing wiring. ISDN works much like PSTN, however, it offers multiple data channels of 64Kbps each. This leads to higher rates of data transfer, and no analog -to-digital conversions are necessary. Remote access clients usually use two channels for data transfer, while large organizations use 23 channels. Costs run higher than with PSTN. Both the remote access client and server need ISDN adapters (Figure 4.5).

Figure 4.5 ISDN Dial-up Connections

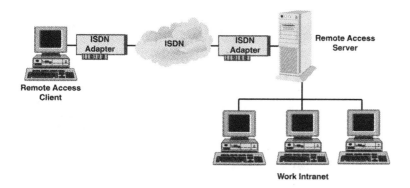

Tip: Microsoft offers a web site location at the following Internet address: www.microsoft.com/windows/getisdn, which explains ISDN and will put you in contact with a local provider.

X.25—This is a communications protocol standard for sending data across public packet-switching networks. The remote access client needs either an X.25 smart card that connects the client directly to the X.25 network or a modem to dial in to a Packet Assembler/Disassembler (PAD) of an X.25 carrier, which breaks data into chunks for reassembly at the destination point. The remote access server needs a direct connection to the X.25 network through an X.25 smart card (Figure 4.6).

Figure 4.6 X.25 Dial-up Connection

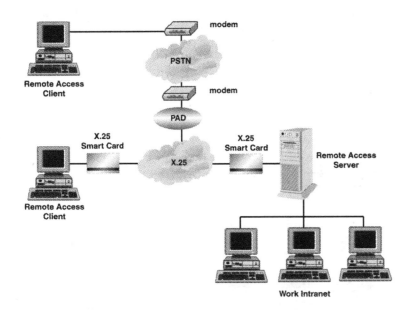

Asynchronous Transfer Mode (ATM) over Asymmetric Digital Subscriber Line (ADSL)— ADSL is a new technology for small business and residential customers. An ADSL connection offers

64 Kbps from the customer and 1.544 Mbps to the customer. An ASDL connection can be made to look like an Ethernet interface or a dial-up interface. When ASDL looks like an Ethernet interface, ASDL adapters at both the remote access client and server create connections similar to Ethernet connections to the Internet. When it appears as a dial-up interface, ASDL is used to make the physical connection, while ATM is used to send packets. You need to have ATM adapters with an ADSL port at both ends of the connection (Figure 4.7).

Figure 4.7 ATM over ADSL Connections

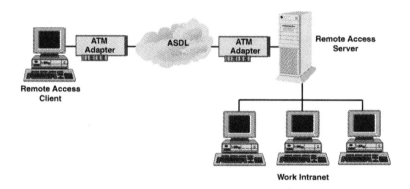

Work Intranet

Remote Access Protocols

The remote access protocol you can use is determined by the operating systems and LAN protocols in place at both ends of the connection. A Windows 2000 RAS server supports TCP/IP, the set of networking protocols used on the Internet that provide communications across diverse interconnected networks. The LAN protocols for IPX, AppleTalk and NetBEUI are also supported.

You can use the following two remote access protocols:

*   PPP, a standard set of protocols offering the best security, multi-protocol support, and interoperability

*   Microsoft remote access protocol, used by clients running Microsoft legacy operating systems such as Microsoft Windows NT 3.1, Windows for Workgroups, MS-DOS, and LAN Manager

Remote Access Security

Windows 2000 remote access security features include secure user authentication, mutual authentication, data encryption, callback, caller ID, and remote access account lockout.

Secure user authentication—You can configure a RAS server to require secure authentication and deny connections to any clients who cannot perform the required authentication. User credentials are encrypted and exchanged by using PPP with one of the following authentication protocols:

- Extensible Authentication Protocol (EAP), a method of attaching new security authentication schemes as they are developed

- Microsoft Challenge Handshake Authentication Protocol (MS-CHAP) versions 1 or 2, which allows you to encrypt an entire dial-up session, not just the original authentication

- Challenge Handshake Authentication Protocol (CHAP), a widely used method of encrypting client-server authentication sessions

- Shiva Password Authentication Protocol (SPAP), an encrypted password authentication method used by Shiva LAN Rover clients and servers and also supported by Windows 2000 Server

Mutual Authentication—To authenticate both ends of the connection, encrypted user credentials are exchanged from both server and client sides. This is done by using PPP with EAP-Transport Level Security (EAP-TLS) or MS-CHAP version 2. If either the remote access server or the client cannot execute the required authentication, the connection is terminated.

Data encryption—Remote access data encryption will support data encryption only on the communications link between the remote access client and server. It is based on a secret encryption key shared only by the RAS server and client and is generated during user authentication. You can permit data encryption over dial-up remote access links using PPP XE "multilink" with EAP-TLS or MS-CHAP. If you choose to configure the RAS server to require data encryption, and the remote client cannot perform the required encryption, the connection is rejected.

Callback—During callback, the remote access server calls the client back after verifying the user credentials. You configure the server to call back the client at a predetermined telephone number for greater security or, for convenience with traveling clients, to a number designated by the client at the time of the initial call.

Caller ID—Caller ID verifies that an incoming call is coming from a specified number. The feature is configured through the dial-in properties of the user account. All the dial-up equipment must support caller ID, including the caller's telephone line, the telephone system, the RAS server's telephone line and the Windows 2000 driver. If caller ID is configured for a user account and the caller ID is not passed from the client to the RAS server, then the connection is terminated. Caller ID is useful for supporting telecommuters.

Remote Access account lockout—This feature locks out remote access clients after a specified number of remote access authentication attempts have failed. It is useful for VPN connections over the Internet to prevent hackers from using dictionary attacks to break-in to an intranet. You need to determine the number of failed attempts allowable before attempts are denied, based on the types of users in your organization and the security required for your company's data. A successful authentication will reset the failed attempts counter to zero. You can also configure how often the failed attempts counter is reset.

Configuring Inbound Connections

Installing RAS is different from installing many other Windows services. You will need to be prepared with specific data and understand the results of the many configuration options. To install and configure a RAS server, in addition to your Windows 2000 computer, the following needs exist:

*   2 MB of hard drive space

*   A compatible communications device

*   The RAS communications device you will be using and the settings for both sides of the connection

*   Protocols available for RAS, since RAS support is configured automatically for most LAN protocols that have been previously installed on a server during the installation of RAS

To enable a RAS server to accept inbound Internet connections, follow these steps:

1. From the **Start** menu, select **Programs**, **Administrative Tools**, and **Routing and Remote Access**.

2. In the **Routing and Remote Access console**, right-click the desired server, and select **Configure** and then **Enable Routing and Remote Access**.

3. From **Routing and Remote Access Server Setup**, select **Next**.

4. From **Common Configurations** (Figure 4.8), choose **Remote Access Server** and then select **Next**.

Figure 4.8 Routing and Remote Access Server Setup Wizard

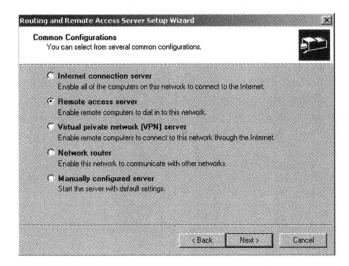

5. From **Remote Client Protocols**, verify that all of the protocols needed to support remote clients are listed, select **Yes, all of the required protocols are on this list** and then select **Next**.

6. If you select **No, I need to add protocols**, the wizard will prompt you to exit and add the required protocols from **Network and Dial-up Connections** in the control panel before running the wizard again.

7. From **Macintosh Guest Authentication** (assuming you have installed AppleTalk), you have the option of choosing **Allow unauthenticated access for all remote clients**, and then select **Next**.

8. From **IP Address Assignment**, select the method of assigning IP addresses to remote clients; choose either **Automatically**, for the DHCP server or the RRAS server to generate addresses automatically, or **From a specified range of addresses**, and select **Next**.

9. If you selected **From a specified range of addresses** in the previous step, type in the range for the server to use to assign addresses to clients in **Address Range Assignment**, and select **Next**.

10. From **Managing Multiple Remote Access Servers**, choose to either use a Remote Authentication Dial-In User Service (RADIUS) server, or select **No, I don't want to set up this server to use RADIUS now**, and then select **Next** (Figure 4.9).

Figure 4.9 Multiple Remote Access Servers

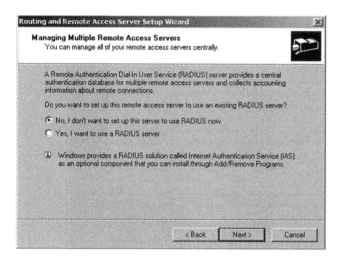

11. From **Completing the Routing and Remote Access Server,** choose **Finish.**

You can select one of five options from the Common Configurations Window, as described in Table 4.1. You can configure an RRAS server to be a combination of these options. You can use the Routing and Remote Access snap-in or the Net Shell (NETSH) command-line utilities to further configure parameters.

Table 4.1 Common Configuration Options

Configuration Option	Result
Internet connection server	Enables all the computers on the network to connect to the Internet
Remote access server	Enables remote computers to dial in to the network
Virtual Private Network (VPN) server	Enables remote computers to connect securely to the network through the Internet using PPTP and L2TP
Network router	Enables the network to transmit packets to other networks
Manually configured server	Starts the server with default settings that you can later alter using the Routing and Remote Access snap-in

When assigning IP addresses to your remote clients, you can use three blocks of IP addresses reserved by the Internet Assigned Numbers Authority for private network use (Table 4.2).

Table 4.2 Reserved IP Address Blocks

IP Address Class	Address Range
Class A	10.0.0.0 to 10.255.255.255
Class B	172.16.0.0 to 172.31.255.255
Class C	192.168.0.0 to 192.168.255.255

With a RADIUS server you can manage numbers of remote access servers locally. It provides a central authentication location and collects accounting information about remote connections. To use

RADIUS, you must have Internet Authentication Service (IAS) running. Windows 2000 uses IAS as the central component to authenticate, authorize, and audit users connecting to a network through VPN or dial-up access.

Your RAS server is now enabled, as is indicated by the green up arrow next to the server icon in the console tree. The default icons underneath your expanded RAS server are Ports, Remote Access Clients, IP Routing, Remote Access Policies, and Remote Access Logging. If you have installed AppleTalk and an Internetwork Packet Exchange/Sequenced Packet Exchange (IPX/SPX) compatible transport protocol, you will see AppleTalk Routing and IPX Routing icons as well (Figure 4.10).

Figure 4.10 Enabled RAS Server

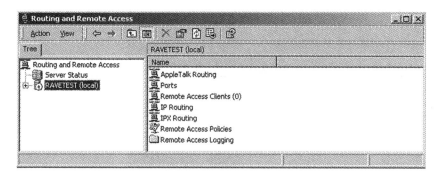

It is not easy to remove RRAS; however, you can disable it by using the Routing and Remote Access snap-in. In the console tree, right-click the appropriate server and choose Disable Routing and Remote Access. All configurations for the service are removed and all connected clients will be disconnected.

Outbound Connections

RAS in Windows 2000 Server, Windows 2000 Advanced Server and Windows 2000 Professional are backwards compatible with previous releases of Windows RAS. The only difference between the products is that in Windows 2000 Professional, only the user can connect from a remote site. Windows 2000 Server and Advanced Server support connections for the entire network.

Configuring Outbound Connections

You can configure outbound connections for a multitude of RAS clients. Windows 2000, Microsoft Windows NT 3.5 or later, Windows 95 or 98, Windows for Workgroups, MS-DOS, and Microsoft LAN Manager remote access clients can all connect to a Windows 2000 remote access server. In fact, almost any third party remote access clients using PPP, such as UNIX and Macintosh clients, can connect to a Windows 2000 RAS server.

Configuring an outbound RAS connection in Windows 2000 Server is almost identical to the process for Windows 2000 Professional. As a client, Windows 2000 Server can dial into a Serial Line Interface Protocol (SLIP) server. SLIP is a legacy dial-in protocol that does not offer the security, performance, or reliability of PPP. However, as a RAS server, Windows 2000 does not support incoming SLIP connections.

Private Network Connection

Before you start making any connections to another private network XE "multilink" , you will need the following information:

- Access telephone number to dial

- User name and password

- Protocol used on the remote network

- Authentication required by the remote network

To make a connection to another network, follow these steps:

1. From the **Start** menu, choose **Settings** and then **Network and Dial-up Connections**.

2. Double-click **Make New Connection**, and, from **Network Connection**, select **Next**.

3. From **Network Connection Type** (Figure 4.11), select **Dial-up to private network** and then **Next**.

Figure 4.11 Network Connection Wizard

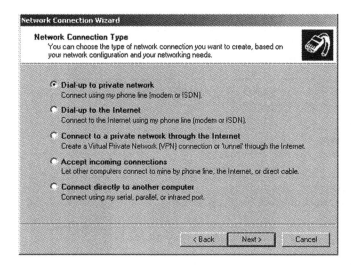

4. Within **Phone Number to Dial**, type the telephone number of the computer or network to which you want to connect, and select **Next**.

5. From **Connection Availability**, choose to make the connection available for all users or just yourself, and select **Next**.

6. Within **Completing the Network Connection Wizard**, type the name you want to use for the connection, and select **Finish**.

You can select one of five options from the Network Connection Type window, as described in Table 4.3. To edit these parameters and configure other parameters not seen in the wizard, use the Network and Dial-up Connections snap-in.

Table 4.3 Network Connection Options

Configuration Options	Result
Dial-up to private network XE "multilink"	Enables a connection using a modem or ISDN on a telephone line
Dial-up to the Internet	Allows a connection to the Internet using a modem or ISDN on a telephone line
Connect to a private network XE "multilink" through the Internet	Creates a Virtual Private Network (VPN) connection or tunnel through the Internet
Accept incoming connections	Lets other computers connect to yours by telephone line, the Internet, or direct cable
Connect directly to another computer	Allows you to connect using your serial, parallel, or infrared port

After using the wizard, double-check the default properties configured for the connection. Do this by checking the Connection Properties, which has the following five property pages:

- General

- Options

- Security

- Networking

- Sharing

General—As you can see in Figure 4.12, this page allows you to configure the connection device that you are using.

Figure 4.12 Internet Connections Properties

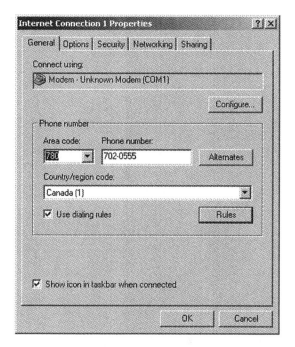

You can also run scripts during initialization, change the telephone number to which you wish to connect, as well as add alternate telephone numbers. Three pages are available on the Edit location property page:

- General, which allows you to specify the location from which you are dialing and rules to be used

- Area Code Rules, which determines how telephone numbers are dialed from your area code to other area codes and within your area code

- Calling Card, which allows you to select a calling card to use and enter its parameters

Options—This page allows you to configure dialing and redialing options. You can specify prompts for the telephone number, name, password, and certificate as well as whether to display progress while connecting. Redialing options include the number of redial attempts, time between redial attempts, and idle time before hanging up. You can also specify X.25 logon settings (Figure 4.13).

Figure 4.13 Connection Options

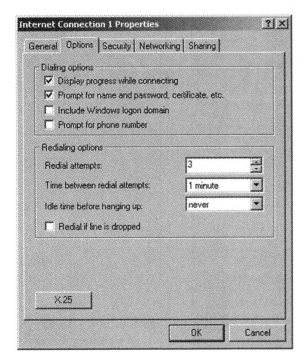

Security—From this page (Figure 4.14), you can specify the security options used to validate your identity. You can use the default typical settings for logon name, password, and data encryption.

Figure 4.14 Security Property Page

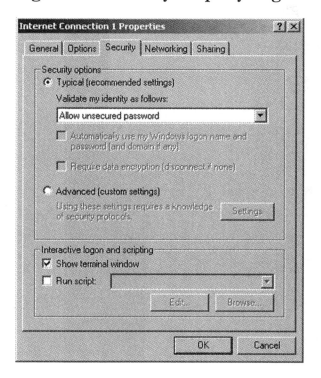

Alternatively, you can specify custom security settings through the Advanced Security Settings page (Figure 4.15). Options there include the data encryption type, logon security, and the protocols allowed. Interactive logon and scripting options are also available.

Figure 4.15 Advanced Security Settings

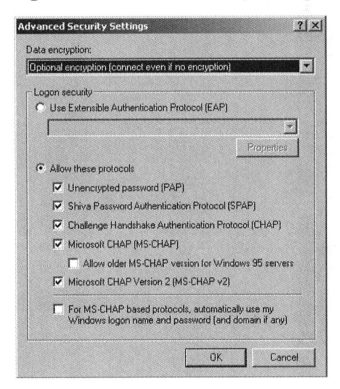

Networking—This page allows you to specify the type of server you are calling and the PPP settings to be used. You can also specify the networking components used by the connection, including transport protocols and file sharing services, such as Gateway (and Client) Services for NetWare (Figure 4.16).

Figure 4.16 Networking Property Page

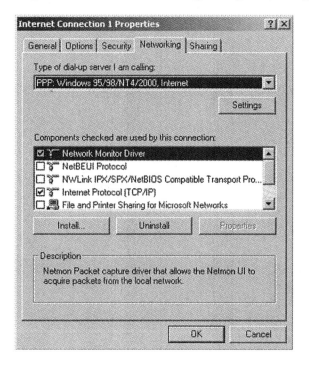

Sharing—This page allows you to implement Internet connection sharing so other computers on your local network can access external resources through your connection (Figure 4.17).

Figure 4.17 Connection Sharing Property Page

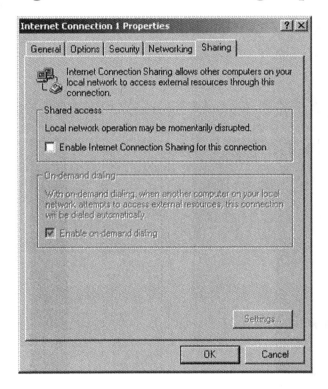

You further configure sharing through the Internet Connection Shared Settings pages (Figure 4.18).

Figure 4.18 Internet Connection Shared Settings

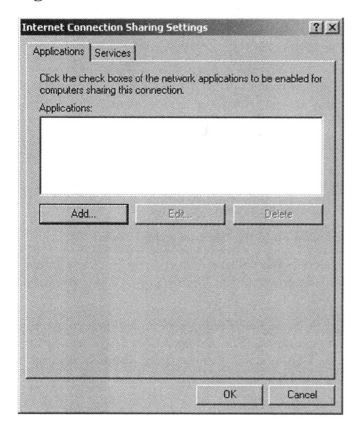

You can edit the properties for a dial-up connection by following these steps:

1. From the **Start** menu, choose **Settings** and then **Network and Dial-up Connections**.

2. Right-click the desired connection, and select **Properties**.

Internet Connection

Windows 2000 was designed so that accessibility to the Internet is a primary function. Another common use for dial-up networking is to allow your computer to dial into an Internet Service Provider (ISP). Before you start making a connection to the Internet, you will need the following information:

- A local access telephone number for the ISP

- User name and password

- Optionally, an IP address to assign the dial-up connection and Domain Name System (DNS) addresses to use, DNS being the hierarchical naming system used to locate domain names on the Internet

To create a connection to the Internet, follow these steps:

1. From the **Start** menu, choose **Settings** and then **Network and Dial-up Connections**.

2. Double-click **Make New Connection**, and, from **Network Connection**, select **Next**.

3. From **Network Connection Type**, select **Dial-up to the Internet** and then **Next**.

4. Within **Welcome to the Internet Connection Wizard**, choose to sign up for a new Internet account, transfer an existing Internet account, or set up your Internet connection manually, and then select **Next**.

5. If you have decided to set up your account manually, from **Setting up your Internet connection** specify if you connect to the Internet through a modem or through a LAN (if you already have in-house Internet connectivity, choose the LAN option; otherwise, select **Connect through a Phone Line and a Modem**), and then select **Next**.

6. In **Step 1 of Internet account connection information**, type your ISP's telephone number and country code, and select **Next**.

7. Alternatively, you can select **Advanced** to configure connection properties such as IP and DNS addresses through **Advanced Connection Properties** (Figure 4.19).

8. Click **OK**, and select **Next**.

Figure 4.19 Advanced Connection Properties

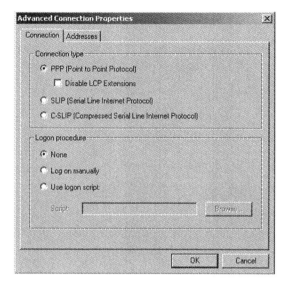

9. Within **Step 2 of Internet account connection information**, type the user name and password, and select **Next**.

10. Within **Step 3 of Internet account connection information**, type a friendly name and a descriptive connection name, and select **Next**.

11. At this point you can configure settings for your Internet mail client, and select **Next**.

12. From **Completing the Internet Connection Wizard**, select **Finish**.

You can edit the properties for an Internet connection by following these steps:

1. From the **Start** menu, choose **Settings** and then **Network and Dial-up Connections**.

2. Right-click the **ISP dial-up entry**, and select **Properties**.

The properties page for a dial-up Internet connection has five pages that are almost identical to those for a private network connection: General, Options, Security, Networking, and Sharing.

Remote Access Server Configuration

You can check your RAS configuration and change it at any time by expanding the objects in the left pane of the Routing and Remote Access console. Configurable objects include the RAS server, along with the associated icons for Remote Access Clients, Ports, IP Routing, Remote Access Policies, and Remote Access Logging. You can also see objects for IPX Routing and AppleTalk Routing, if you have installed those protocols.

Remote Access Server Properties Pages

To edit remote access server properties pages, in the console, right-click on your RAS server and select Properties. A Properties page for your server will appear, providing detailed information that you can modify.

General—This page allows you to enable the computer as either a router for the LAN, for both the LAN and demand-dial routing, or a remote access server.

Security—This page (Figure 4.20) allows you to select the authentication provider to validate credentials for remote access clients and demand-dial routers. You can choose to have either Windows Authentication or RADIUS Authentication. You can also select the authentication method from the following possibilities:

- Extensible Authentication Protocol (EAP)

- Microsoft Encrypted Authentication version 2 (MS-CHAP v2)

- Encrypted Authentication (CHAP)

- Shiva Password Authentication Protocol (SPAP)

- Unencrypted Password (PAP)

- Unauthenticated Access

From the Security page you can also choose to have either Windows Accounting or RADIUS Accounting. The accounting provider maintains a log of connection requests and sessions.

Figure 4.20 RAS Server Security

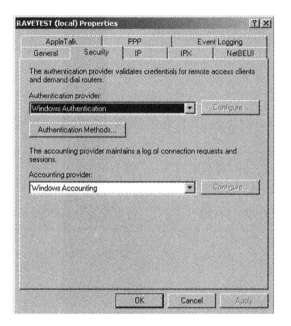

PPP—This page allows you to set PPP options. You can enable multilink connections with bandwidth control or software compression. Multilink allows clients to combine multiple physical connections into one logical connection. The settings for an individual connection are determined by remote access policies (Figure 4.21).

Figure 4.21 PPP Properties

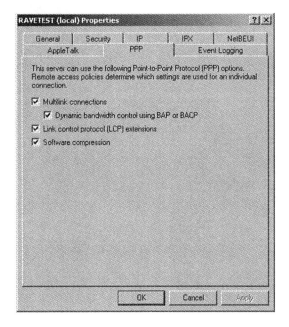

Event logging—Various event logging settings are available.

IP—You use this page (Figure 4.22) to enable IP routing and to allow IP-based remote access and demand-dial connections. This page is also used to define how the server can assign IP addresses, either by using Dynamic Host Configuration Protocol (DHCP) or a static address pool. DHCP simplifies TCP/IP network configuration by dynamically configuring IP addresses for clients.

Figure 4.22 RAS Server IP Property Page

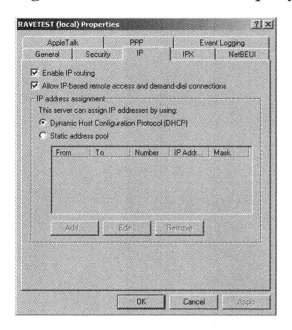

IPX—This page appears only if a IPX/SPX/NetBIOS Compatible Transport Protocol has been installed as a network protocol. The options are similar to those on the IP page. You can enable IPX-based remote access and demand-dial connections. You also assign IPX network numbers, either automatically or from a selected range. You can use the same network number for all IPX clients or allow remote clients to request an IPX node number (Figure 4.23).

Figure 4.23 RAS Server IPX Property Page

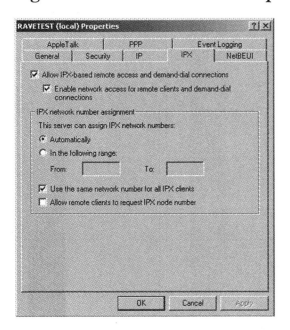

AppleTalk— This page appears only if AppleTalk has been installed as a network protocol. You can enable AppleTalk remote access from here.

Ports

Each communication port, along with the corresponding device and status, is shown in the right pane of the Routing and Remote Access console if you highlight the ports icon on the left pane.

To control the availability and use of the communication ports in a RAS server, follow these steps:

1. From the **Start** menu, choose **Programs**, **Administrative Tools**, and **Routing and Remote Access**.

2. From the left pane of the **Routing and Remote Access** console, expand the desired server, right-click **Ports**, and select **Properties** (Figure 4.24).

3. From **Devices**, choose the port you want, and select **Configure**.

4. From **Configure Device**, choose whether you want to use the port for inbound remote access connections or inbound and outbound demand-dial routing connections.

5. Type a telephone number for the device, set a maximum port limit if the device is meant to support multiple ports, click **OK**, then select **Apply**, and then click **OK** again.

Figure 4.24 Port Devices Property Page

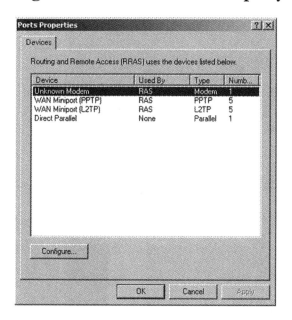

Remote Access Policies

Control and configuration of the users of the remote access server is done through Remote Access Policies. You can specify a set of conditions to be matched for the Remote Access Policy to apply. You then specify actions to be taken if the conditions are met. You can set policies for a specific user or a group of users.

To create a new policy, follow these steps:

1. From the **Start** menu, choose **Programs**, **Administrative Tools**, and **Routing and Remote Access**.

2. From the left pane of the **Routing and Remote Access** console, expand the desired server, right-click **Remote Access Policies**, and select **New Remote Access Policy**.

3. Within **Add Remote Access Policy**, type a friendly policy name, and select **Next**.

4. Within **Select Attribute** (Figure 4.25), specify the conditions to match, choosing **Add** between each selection, and select **Next**.

Figure 4.25 Attribute Selection

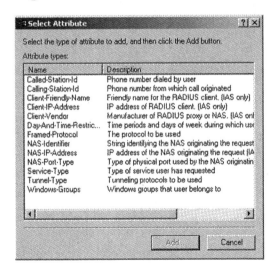

5. If a user matches the specified condition, select either **Grant remote access permission** or **Deny remote access permission**, and then select **Next**.

6. Select **Edit Profile**, type the desired configuration parameters in the six pages of the **Edit Dial-in Profile** page, and select **Finish**.

7. You can edit the profile of a group after it has been created by right-clicking the group in the right pane of the Routing and Remote Access console, selecting Properties and Edit Profiles. The Edit Dial-in Profile page contains the following six pages:

Dial-in constraints—This page allows you to cut the connection after a specified idle period, restrict the maximum session time, restrict access to specified days and times, restrict dial-in to a predetermined number, and specify the dial-in media permitted (Figure 4.26).

Figure 4.26 Dial-in Constraints Property Page

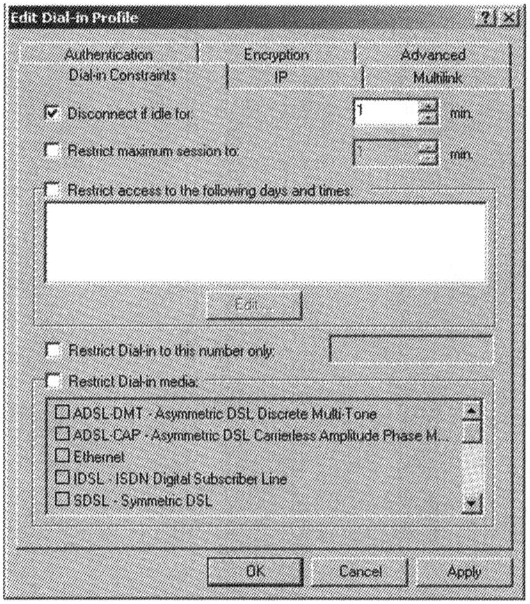

IP—This page (Figure 4.27) defines the IP address assignment policy for Routing and Remote Access. You can elect for the server to supply an IP address, the client to request an IP address, or server settings to define the policy. You can also define IP packet filters to apply during the connection—both from and to the client. Input filters control which packets can be received for processing on the server. You can specify the filter according to the destination IP address and protocol, selecting Add between each filter. Output filters control which packets can be processed and sent to the client. Alternatively, you can specify the filter according to the source IP address and protocol, selecting Add between each filter.

Figure 4.27 IP Page of Edit Dial-In Profile Page

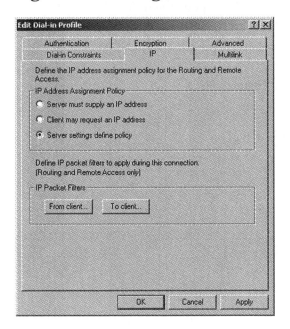

Multilink—You can configure the multilink settings from this page (Figure 4.28). You can choose to default to server settings, disable multilink, or allow multilink with a specified maximum number of ports. You can also configure Bandwidth Allocation Protocol (BAP) settings by choosing to reduce a multilink connection by one line if the lines fall below a predetermined percentage of capacity for a specified period of time, and to require BAP for dynamic multilink requests. BAP allows you to dynamically add or drop multiple connection links as needed in response to changing bandwidth needs.

Figure 4.28 Multilink Property Page

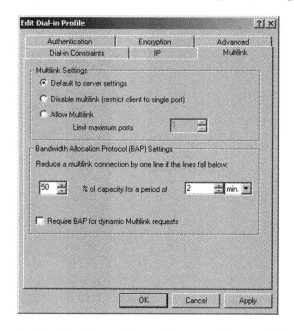

Authentication—From this page (Figure 4.29) you can specify the authentication methods allowed for the connection. You can make your choice from the following methods:

- Extensible Authentication Protocol (EAP)-MD5-Challenge, Smart Card, or other certificate

- Microsoft Encrypted Authentication version 2 (MS-CHAP v2)

- Microsoft Encrypted Authentication (MS-CHAP)

- Encrypted Authentication (CHAP)

- Unencrypted Authentication (PAP, SPAP)

- Unauthenticated Access

Figure 4.29 Authentication Property Page

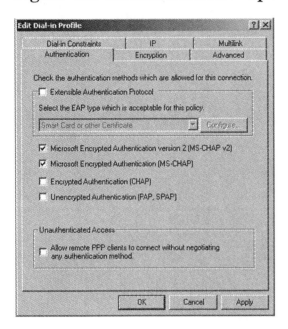

Encryption—You can select the required level of encryption from this page. Options include no encryption, basic encryption, and strong encryption.

Advanced—This page allows you to specify additional connection attributes to be returned to the remote access server. Dozens of RADIUS attributes and parameters supported by manufacturers of remote access hardware are listed.

Remote Access and Routing Management

Remote access management involves four main factors: managing users, addresses, access, and authentication.

User Management

Administration of user accounts can become complicated if there are multiple RAS servers. In this situation, you can streamline your work by setting up a master account table in the Active directory store or on a RADIUS server, which permits the RAS server to send authentication credentials to a central authentication device.

Address Management

For PPP connections involving IP, IPX, and AppleTalk, addressing information must be given to remote access clients when setting up the connection. The Windows 2000 RAS server needs to be configured to allocate IP addresses, IPX network and node addresses, or AppleTalk network and node addresses.

Access Management

Remote access connections are accepted based on the dial-in properties of a user account and the remote access policies. A remote access policy is a set of parameters that predefine the characteristics of the incoming connection. You can apply different sets of conditions to different RRAS clients or different requirements to the same client based on the parameters of the connection attempt.

The user account contains dial-in properties used when permitting or denying a connection attempt. For a standalone server, the dial-in properties are set through the dial-in page of the user account properties in the Local Users and Groups snap-in.

For a Windows 2000 server with Active Directory, you access dial-in properties by following these steps:

1. From the **Start** menu, choose **Programs**, **Administrative Tools**, and **Active Directory Users and Computers**.

2. From the left pane of the **Active Directory Users and Computers** console, right-click the desired user, and select **Properties**.

3.   Select the **Dial-in** page (Figure 4.30) and the remote access permissions and callback options, and click **OK**.

Figure 4.30 Dial-in Property Page

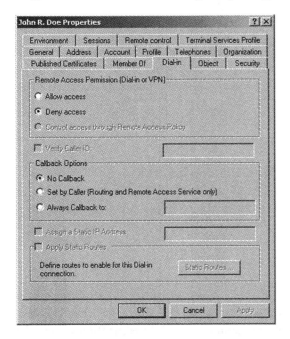

Dial-in or VPN remote access permissions include the following:

*   Allow access

*   Deny access

*   Control access through remote access policy

Callback options include the following:

*   No callback

*   Set by caller (Routing and Remote Access Service only)

- Always callback to a specified number

You can opt to verify caller ID and apply static routes, in which case you need to define those routes.

Authentication Management

A remote access server can be configured to use either Windows or RADIUS as an authentication provider. This is done through the Security page of the RAS server properties page.

Creating Inbound and Outbound Virtual Private Network (VPN) Connections

A VPN mimics the properties of a dedicated private network by creating encapsulated, encrypted, and authenticated links across shared or public networks. Point-to-point connections can be simulated through the use of tunneling, and LAN connectivity can also be simulated, allowing for secure data transfer between computers.

A branch office of a corporation can use either dedicated lines or dial-up lines to connect to networks over the Internet. If a dedicated line is used, both the branch office and corporate hub routers connect to the Internet through a dedicated circuit and local ISP, creating a VPN between the two routers. If a dial-up line is used, the branch office router calls its local ISP, creating a VPN between the branch office router and the corporate router. The corporate router must have a dedicated line to the local ISP and act as a VPN server, constantly monitoring for incoming VPN traffic.

Tunneling

Tunneling is the method of transferring data in a VPN. Frames produced by the originating node are encapsulated with an extra header that provides routing information for an intermediate Internetwork. Once the encapsulated frames are routed between the tunnel endpoints over the transit Internetwork, the frames are de-encapsulated and forwarded to their final destination. The logical path over the transit Internetwork, through which the encapsulated packets travel, is the tunnel (Figure 4.31).

Figure 4.31 Encapsulated Packets Transferred Through VPN

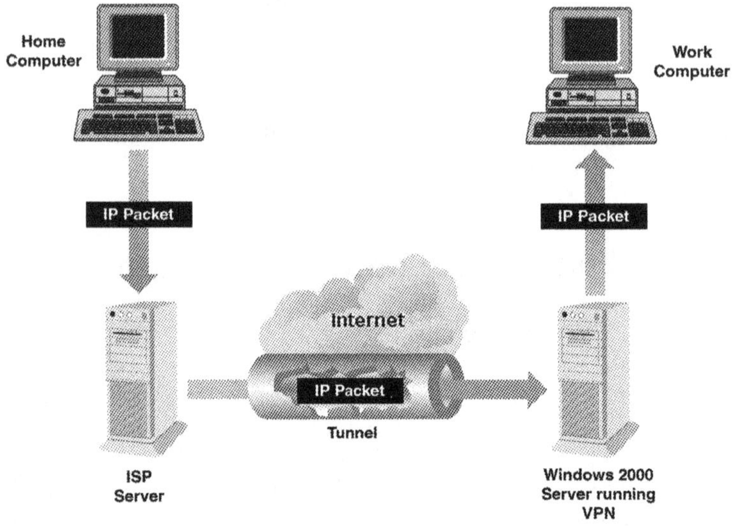

Both the tunnel client and tunnel server must use the same tunneling protocol. Windows 2000 Server supports the following three tunneling protocols for creating a VPN:

PPTP—Point-to-Point Tunneling Protocol encapsulates PPP frames with IP packets for transmission over an IP Internetwork, such as the Internet or a private network XE "multilink." The encapsulation authorizes the transport of packets that do not meet Internet addressing standards, such as IP, IPX, or NetBEUI packets. Since VPN provides transparent access to PPP clients, it works with UNIX, Macintosh, MS-DOS, and most Windows 16-bit clients. PPTP tunnels must be authenticated by using the same authentication protocols as PPP connections, such as PAP, MS-CHAP, CHAP, and EAP.

L2TP—Layer Two Tunneling Protocol is a combination of the features offered by PPTP and a Cisco protocol, Layer 2 Forwarding (L2F). L2TP encapsulates PPP XE "multilink" frames that are to be sent over IP, X.25, Frame Relay, or ATM networks. When IP packets are used to encapsulate the PPP frames, L2TP can be used as a tunneling protocol over the Internet or between two private LANs. Unlike PPTP, which is restricted to having an IP Internetwork as the transit intermediary, L2TP requires only that the tunnel media provide packet-oriented point-to-point connectivity. You need IPSec to provide encryption for L2TP.

IPSec—Internet Protocol Security is a layer 3 tunneling protocol, supporting the secured transfer of information across an IP Internetwork. IPSec is managed through the Internet Authentication snap-in to the Microsoft Management Console (MMC). IPSec Encapsulation Security Payload (ESP) Tunnel mode supports the encapsulation and encryption of entire IP datagrams for secure transfer across a private or public IP Internetwork.

Managing VPNs is similar to managing remote access. You first set up a master account database at a domain controller or on a RADIUS server to allow the VPN server to send authentication credentials to a central authenticating device. You can use the same account for both dial-in remote access and VPN-based remote access. For Windows 2000, authorization of VPN connections is determined by the dial-in properties on the user account and remote access policies.

Configuring a VPN server is much like configuring a remote access server. To install and configure a VPN server, follow these steps:

1. From the **Start** menu, choose **Programs**, **Administrative Tools**, and **Routing and Remote Access**.

2. In the **Routing and Remote Access** console, right-click desired server, and select **Configure** and then **Enable Routing and Remote Access**.

3. From **Routing and Remote Access Server Setup**, select **Next**.

4. From **Common Configurations**, select **Virtual private network (VPN) server** and then **Next**.

5. From **Remote Client Protocols**, verify that all of the protocols needed to support VPN clients are listed, select **Yes, all of the available protocols are on this list**, and then select **Next**.

6. If you select **No, I need to add protocols**, the wizard will prompt you to exit and add the required protocols from **the Network and Dial-up Connections** folder in the control panel before running the wizard again.

7. From **Macintosh Guest Authentication** (assuming you have installed AppleTalk), decide if you want to **Allow unauthenticated access for all remote clients**, and select **Next**.

8. Within **Internet Connection**, specify the single connection remote VPN clients and routers will use to access the server through the Internet, and select **Next**.

9. Within **IP Address Assignment**, select the method of assigning IP addresses to remote clients; choose either **Automatically**, and a DHCP server or the VPN server generates addresses automatically, or **From a specified range of addresses**, and select **Next**.

10. If you have selected **From a specified range of addresses**, type in the address range the server will use to assign addresses to clients in **Address Range Assignment**, and select **Next**.

11. From **Managing Multiple Remote Access Servers**, decide to use a **RADIUS server** or choose **No, I don't want to set up this server to use RADIUS now**, and then select **Next**.

12. From **Completing the Routing and Remote Access Server Setup**, select **Finish**.

 Note: MS-CHAP is important when it comes to setting up virtual private network XE "multilink" ing sessions. MS-CHAP v2 support is included in Windows 2000 for all types of connections and in Microsoft Windows NT 4.0 and Windows 95 / 98 for VPN connections.

You will need to check configuration parameters and confirm that you have the needed number of PPTP ports.

You can configure the client side of the connection by following these steps:

1. From the **Start** menu, choose **Settings** and then **Network and Dial-up Connections**.

2. Double-click **Make New Connection**, and, within **Network Connection**, select **Next**.

3. From **Network Connection Type**, select **Connect to a private network through the Internet**, and then **Next**.

4. From **Public Network**, decide to establish a public network (Internet) connection before a VPN connection is created; if you are connecting to a Windows 2000 device with a valid public IP address, select **Do not dial the initial connection** and click **OK**, otherwise select **Automatically dial this initial connection**.

5. Within **Destination Address**, type the host name or IP address of the target server, and select **Next**.

6. Within **Connection Availability**, choose to make the connection available for all users or just yourself, and select **Next**.

7. Within **Completing the Network Connection**, type the name you want to use for the connection, and select **Finish**.

For security, you need to filter packets based on their incoming or outgoing addresses. To set PPTP filters, follow these steps:

1. From the **Start** menu, choose **Programs**, **Administrative Tools**, and **Routing and Remote Access**.

2. In the console, expand the desired server, expand **IP Routing**, and select **General**.

3. From the details pane, right-click the interface to be filtered, and select **Properties**.

4. From the **General** page (Figure 4.32), choose **Input Filters** or **Output Filters** depending on how you would like to filter window packets, and type the source, destination, and protocol to be filtered, selecting **Add** between each filter.

5. Click **OK**, then select **Apply**, and then click **OK** again.

Figure 4.32 Local Area Connection General Property Page

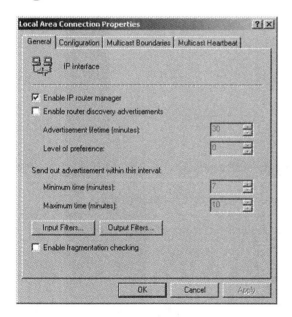

Your last step is to set up remote access policies.

Router-to-Router VPN Connections

A Windows 2000 router-to-router VPN connection has the following three parts:

VPN client—This is the calling router that initiates the VPN connection. Windows 2000 Server or Microsoft Windows NT Server 4.0 with RRAS can both be VPN clients.

VPN server—A VPN server is the answering router that accepts the connection from the calling router. Potential VPN servers are Windows 2000 Server or Microsoft Windows NT Server 4.0 with RRAS.

LAN and remote access protocols—LAN protocols such as TCP/IP are used to transport packets. Windows 2000 Server routes these packets by using PPP in a router-to-router VPN connection. Tunneling protocols encapsulate one network protocol inside another. VPN clients and VPN servers use tunneling protocols to manage tunnels and send tunneled data. Windows 2000 can use either PPTP or L2TP.

The VPN client or calling router needs to have a demand-dial interface configured with the following elements:

*   A host name or IP address of the interface of the VPN server on the Internet

*   A PPTP or L2TP port

*   A user name

*   A domain

*   A password for an account that can be validated by the VPN server

The dial-in permissions are obtained through the user account or remote access policies.

The VPN server or answering router must have a demand-dial interface configured with the following elements:

*   A host name or IP address of the interface of the VPN client on the Internet

*   A PPTP or L2TP port

*   The VPN's user name, domain, and password

To add a demand-dial interface, follow these steps:

1. From the **Start** menu, choose **Programs**, **Administrative Tools**, and **Routing and Remote Access**.

2. Expand the desired router in the console, select **Routing Interfaces**, and right-click **New Demand-dial Interface**.

3. Within **Demand Dial Interface**, type the **Interface name**, and select **Next**.

4. Type the **telephone number** to be dialed when establishing the demand-dial interface, adding alternate numbers as needed, and select **Next**.

5. From **Protocols and Security** (Figure 4.33), select the desired transports and security options for the connection, and then select **Next**.

Figure 4.33 Protocols and Security Window of Demand Dial Interface Wizard

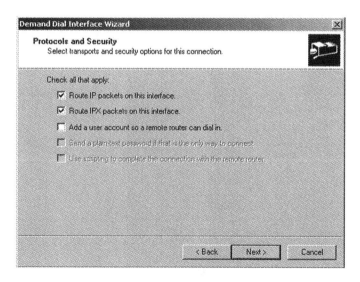

6. The remaining windows will vary depending on the options chosen from the previous window; type the appropriate information as required, click **OK**, and then select **Finish**.

For packets to be forwarded from router-to-router VPN connections, you must ensure each router has the appropriate routes in its routing tables. This can be done by adding static routes to the routing tables on both the sending and receiving computers or by enabling a routing protocol across a persistent router-to-router VPN connection.

To add a static route to the routing table, follow these steps:

1. From the **Start** menu, choose **Programs, Administrative Tools**, and **Routing and Remote Access**.

2. Expand the desired router in the console, select **IP Routing**, right-click **Static Routes**, and then select **New Static Route**.

3. In **Static Route**, select the interface, type the IP address for the destination router, and click **OK**.

Troubleshooting Remote Access Connection Problems

Windows 2000 has the following built-in tools to help you to administer and troubleshoot RRAS:

Routing and Remote Access snap-in—You can perform a variety of tasks from this interface, including enabling RRAS, managing routing interfaces, configuring IPX routing, creating a static IP address pool, and configuring remote access policies.

Net shell (NETSH) command-line utility—NETSH.EXE is a command-line utility that supports Windows 2000 networking components for both local and remote computers. You can use NETSH to save a configuration script in a text file for configuring other servers. The functionality of NETSH can also be extended by adding NETSH helper Dynamic Link Libraries (DLLs). A DLL is a library of executable functions or data that can be used by a Windows application. Each NETSH helper DLL provides a group of commands for a specific networking component. NETSH can run in two modes: online, in which each NETSH command issued at the command prompt is carried out, and offline, in which a batch file of accumulated NETSH commands can be run.

Authentication and accounting logging—If you enable Windows authentication or accounting, you can log information on PPP-based connection attempts. Authentication and accounting logging is useful in troubleshooting remote access problems. The log file ( ) is stored separately from the events recorded in the general system event log. It is stored in the %systemroot%\System32\Logfiles folder in a database format. Any database program can read it. From the properties page of the Remote Access Logging folder in either the Routing Access snap-in or the Internet Authentication Service snap-in, you can configure the type of activity to log as well as the log file settings.

Figure 4.34 PPP-Based Connections Log File

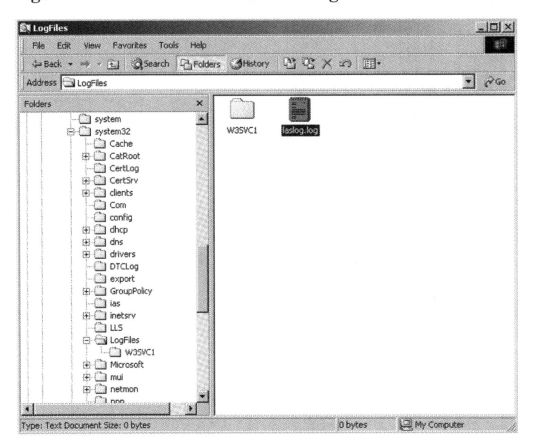

Event logging—You can use information from the system event log to troubleshoot routing or remote access processes. You can log errors only, log both errors and warnings, log the maximum amount of information, or disable event logging altogether. You can also enable PPP logging. Set the event logging parameters from the Routing and Remote Access snap-in or from the General page of the Properties page for IP Routing.

Warning: Use logging judiciously, as it consumes system resources. After you have identified the problem, reset logging to log errors only.

Tracing—Windows 2000 offers tracing capabilities that can help you troubleshoot network problems. You enable tracing for each routing protocol by setting values in the corresponding registry key. Tracing records internal component variables, function calls, and interactions. You can also separate routing and remote access component-tracing information to different files. Known as file tracing, it is enabled through HKEY_LOCAL_MACHINE\SOFTWARE\Microsoft\Tracing\Component.

Warning: Tracing is like logging in that it also consumes system resources. After you have identified the problem, disable tracing.

You can also obtain real time statistics on a remote access connection. To monitor a remote access connection, follow these steps:

1. From the **Start** menu, choose **Programs, Administrative Tools,** and **Routing and Remote Access**.

2. From the left pane of the console tree, choose **Remote Access Clients,** and, within the details pane, double-click the name of the desired connection.

3. From **Status** (Figure 4.35), observe the connection statistics, and select **Close**.

Figure 4.35 Remote Access Client Status

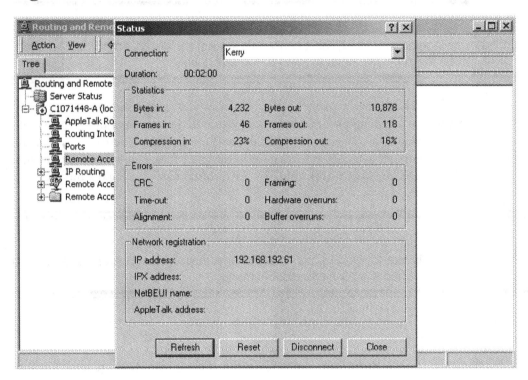

Available information from the Status window of a remote access client connection includes the following:

- Connection duration

- Data compression percentages

- Number of bytes being transferred in both directions

- Number of frames being transferred in both directions

- Cyclic Redundancy Check (CRC) errors, which is used to gauge data integrity

- Connection time-outs

- Buffer overruns

- Hardware overruns

- Framing errors

- Protocols registered

RADIUS Overview

To simplify the administration of remote access policies for multiple RAS servers, you can configure one Windows 2000 server with IAS as a RADIUS server, with the remote access servers as RADIUS clients. The IAS server provides centralized remote access authentication, authorization, accounting, and auditing. Auditing is the process of configuring and examining the logging of specified events. It can tell you about potentially dangerous conditions and leaves a trail of accountability.

RADIUS authenticates users through a series of communications between the remote access client and RADIUS server. Only after the user is authenticated, can the RAS client access network services.

If a remote access server has RADIUS installed and configured, the credentials and parameters of the connection attempt from the client are given as a series of RADIUS request messages to the RADIUS server for authentication and authorization.

The RADIUS server authenticates the client user and connection request against its authentication database. The RADIUS server can store a number of user and connection properties, such as maximum session time and static IP address assignment, and relay the information to the RAS server. RADIUS can also be configured to respond to authentication requests based upon the database from another database server, such as a generic Open DataBase Connectivity (ODBC) server, or a Windows 2000 domain controller.

Once the connection attempt is authenticated and authorized, the RADIUS server sends an accept message to the remote access server, and the connection attempt is accepted. However, if the connection attempt is either not authenticated or authorized, the RADIUS server relays a reject message to the RAS server and the remote client is denied a connection.

Configuring Authentication and Accounting

A Windows 2000 RADIUS server running IAS performs authentication through Windows 2000 security. Authorization, or the process of giving a user access to system objects based on the user's identity, is provided through the dial-up properties of the user account and the remote access policies stored on the IAS server.

You configure RRAS authentication in the Security page of the remote access server Properties page from the Routing and Remote Access console or by using the NETSH command-line utility.

Accounting is the process of maintaining a log of connection requests and sessions. It is also configured in the Security page of the remote access server Properties page from the Routing and Remote Access console or by using the NETSH command-line utility.

Configuring Authentication and Logging Capabilities

You can enable RADIUS authentication and accounting on a Windows 2000 RAS server to support the logging of accounting information for RAS connections at a RADIUS server. This logging is separate from the logging occurring in the system event log.

Defining the Network RADIUS Role

Managing a number of remote access servers can be simplified by using RADIUS, which allows localized administration of remote RAS servers. RADIUS is a client-server protocol that allows remote access servers acting as RADIUS clients to submit authentication and accounting requests to a RADIUS server.

The RADIUS server checks remote access authentication credentials against its user account information. If the user's credentials are verified, the RADIUS server authorizes the user's access based on predetermined conditions and logs the remote access connections as accounting events. RADIUS stores accounting data in a central location rather than on each RRAS server. Users connect to a RADIUS-compliant server, such as a Windows 2000 RRAS server, which then forwards requests to the centralized IAS server.

IAS is Microsoft's implementation of a RADIUS server. IAS performs centralized authentication, authorization, auditing, and accounting of connections for dial-up and VPN remote access and demand-dial connections. It can be used with Windows RRAS servers or a mixture of remote access or VPN servers from different manufacturers.

Identifying the Usage Scenarios for RADIUS

The following are reasons why you may want to use RADIUS in your network:

- You want to administer remote RRAS servers locally

- You want to administer multiple RRAS servers efficiently

- By configuring a primary and secondary RADIUS server, you support remote access fault tolerance and redundancy

- You want to administer heterogeneous remote access servers

To use RADIUS for dial-up or VPN connections, you need to install IAS, configure clients and servers, and set a remote access policy.

To install IAS on a Windows 2000 server, follow these steps:

1. From the **Start** menu, choose **Settings** and **Control Panel**.

2. From the **Control Panel**, double-click **Add/Remove Programs**, and select **Add/Remove Windows Components**.

3. Within **Windows Components**, highlight **Networking Services** and choose **Details**.

4. Select **Internet Authentication Service**, and within **Completing the Windows Components**, click **OK**, and select **Next** and then **Finish**.

Tip: For fault-tolerance purposes, configure both a primary and a secondary IAS server and copy the remote access policies from the primary server to the secondary one. Then configure each remote access server with two RADIUS servers corresponding to the IAS servers.

You should check settings after using any wizard, although, in many cases, the default IAS configuration is correct. To configure IAS, follow these steps:

1. From the **Start** menu, choose **Programs, Administrative Tools**, and **Internet Authentication Service**.

2. In the console tree, right-click **Internet Authentication Service** and choose **Properties**.

3. Within the **Service** page (Figure 4.36), you can change the description or event logging options.

Figure 4.36 Internet Authentication Service

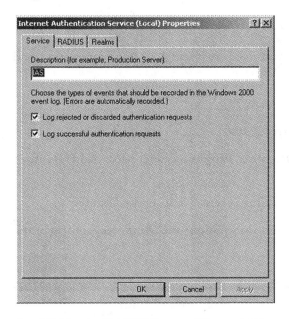

4. Within the **RADIUS** page (Figure 4.37), you can change the authentication and accounting User Datagram Protocol (UDP) ports.

Figure 4.37 RADIUS Property Page

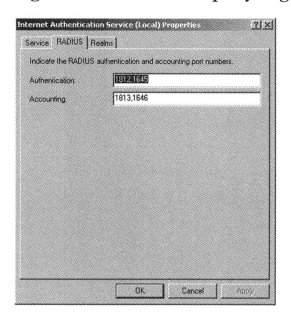

 Note: A realm is a rule or a particular parameter that IAS uses in a specified order to process user names in all accounting and authentication requests.

5. Within the **Realms** page (Figure 4.38), you can change the realm information, and click **OK**.

Figure 4.38 Internet Authentication Realms Property Page

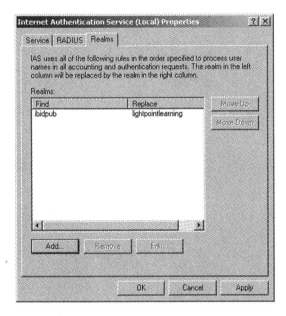

6. Next, you need to add the RRAS servers as clients on the IAS server. To configure clients for IAS, follow these steps:

7. From the **Start** menu, choose **Programs**, **Administrative Tools**, and **Internet Authentication Service**.

8. In the console tree, right-click **Clients**, and select **New Client**.

9. Type a name for the client, and select **Next**.

10. Type the client address and a shared secret, and select **Finish**.

 Note: A shared secret is a password used between an IAS server and other servers connected to it. It follows general password rules, and because you do not have to enter it in all the time as you do with regular passwords, you can make a shared secret longer, permitting greater security.

You can administer remote access policies for Windows IAS servers through the Internet Authentication snap-in and remote access policies for Windows RRAS servers through the Routing and Remote Access snap-in.

Configuring RADIUS Authentication

To change the properties of a Windows 2000 remote access server so that it uses RADIUS as the authentication provider, follow these steps:

1. From the **Start** menu, choose **Programs, Administrative Tools**, and **Routing and Remote Access**.

2. From the left pane of the **Routing and Remote Access** console, right-click the **server** name, and select **Properties**.

3. Choose the **Security** page, and, from **Authentication provider**, select **RADIUS Authentication** and then **Configure**.

4. From **RADIUS Authentication**, select **Add**, and within **Add RADIUS Server** (Figure 4.39), type the host name or IP address of the IAS server.

Figure 4.39 Add RADIUS Server Screen

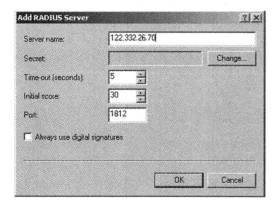

5. Type other configuration parameters, such as the **Time-out duration, Initial score, Port number,** and whether to **Always use digital signatures.**

6. Click **OK** three times to exit from screens and restart the Routing and Remote Access service.

Configuring RADIUS Accounting

To change the properties of a Windows 2000 remote access server so that it uses RADIUS as the accounting provider, follow these steps:

1. From the **Start** menu, choose **Programs, Administrative Tools**, and **Routing and Remote Access**.

2. From the left pane of the **Routing and Remote Access** console, right-click the **server** name and select **Properties**.

3. Choose the **Security** page, and, under **Accounting Provider**, select **RADIUS Accounting** and then **Configure**.

4. From **RADIUS Accounting**, select **Add**, and within **Add RADIUS Server**, type the host name or IP address of the IAS server.

5. Type other configuration parameters, such as the **Time-out duration, Initial score, Port number,** and whether to **Always use digital signatures**.

6. Click **OK** three times to exit from screens, and restart the Routing and Remote Access service.

After configuring a RAS server to use RADIUS accounting, register the remote access server as a client on the IAS server. Then only the remote access policies stored on the IAS server will be used, so that you need to copy the desired remote access policy from a RAS server to the IAS server. You can do this if both the source and destination computers are running the same version of Windows 2000 by following these steps:

1. From the **Start** menu, choose **Programs, Accessories,** and **Command Prompt**.

2. Type **netsh aaaa show config [path\file.txt**], which creates a text file that includes all of the configuration settings; the path can be relative, absolute or UNC.

3. Copy the text file to the destination IAS server.

4. From the command prompt at the destination server, type **netsh exec [path\file.txt]**.

Vocabulary

Review the following terms in preparation for the certification exam.

Term	Description
accounting	This process maintains a log of connection requests and sessions
Active Directory	The directory service included with Windows 2000 Server stores information about objects on a network in a hierarchical view. It provides a single point of administration for all network objects.
ADSL	Asymmetric Digital Subscriber Line is a new technology that supports faster rates of data transfer over existing copper telephone lines.
AppleTalk	The communication protocol used by Macintosh clients is AppleTalk. For Macintosh clients to connect to it, it must be installed on a computer running Windows 2000 Server.
ATM	Asynchronous Transfer Mode is a networking technology based on transferring packets of a fixed size across a fixed channel.
auditing	This process of configuring the logging and examination of predetermined events can tell you about potentially dangerous conditions, and besides, it leaves a trail of accountability.
authentication	In network access, authentication is the process by which the system validates the user's logon information. With IPSec, authentication is the process that verifies the origin and integrity of a message by assuring the identity of each computer.
authorization	This process gives a user access to system objects based on the user's identity.

Term	Description
BAP	The Bandwidth Allocation Protocol allows you to dynamically add or drop multiple connection links as needed in response to changing bandwidth needs.
callback	This security feature allows a RAS server to call the remote access client to establish a connection after the user credentials have been verified.
caller ID	A security feature is used to verify that an incoming call is coming from a specified telephone number.
CHAP	The Challenge Handshake Authentication Protocol is a challenge-response authentication protocol for PPP connections that uses Message Digest 5 to hash the response to a challenge issued by a remote access server.
CRC	Cyclic Redundancy Check is used to gauge data integrity.
demand-dial router	A router that supports the routing of packets over point-to-point on-demand WAN links.
DHCP	The Dynamic Host Configuration Protocol simplifies TCP/IP network configuration and dynamically configures IP addresses for clients. DHCP ensures that address conflicts do not occur by centralizing address allocation.
DLL	Dynamic Link Library allows executable routines serving specific functions to be stored separately as files with .DLL extensions. These are loaded only when requested by a program.
DNS	The Domain Name System is a hierarchical naming system used to locate domain names on the Internet and on private TCP/IP networks. The DNS service maps DNS domain names to IP addresses and vice-versa.

Term	Description
EAP	The Extensible Authentication Protocol is a method of attaching new security authentication schemes as they are developed.
EAP-TLS	Extensible Authentication Protocol-Transport Level Security is a new protocol devised by Microsoft. It combines the function of EAP, which supports additional authentication methods within PPP, with that of TLS, which supports mutual authentication, negotiation, and key exchange between computers. EAP-TLS also supports the fragmentation and reassembly of packets.
ESP	The Encapsulation Security Payload is a tunneling mode that supports the encapsulation and encryption of entire IP datagrams for secure transfer across a private or public IP Internetwork.
frame relay	This packet-switching protocol for connecting devices on a WAN supports data transfer across T1 and T3 lines. Although popular because of low costs, it is being replaced by the faster ATM.
GSNW	The Gateway Service for NetWare creates a gateway where Microsoft clients can access NetWare resources through a Windows 2000 server.
HCL	Hardware Compatibility List is maintained by Microsoft and lists approved operating systems.

Term	Description
IAS	The Internet Authentication Service is the central component in Windows 2000 for authenticating, authorizing, and auditing users who connect to a network through a VPN or dial-up access.
IP	The Internet Protocol is the routable protocol in the TCP/IP suite that is responsible for the IP addressing, routing, and fragmentation and reassembly of IP packets.
IPSec	Internet Protocol Security is a set of standard, cryptography-based protection services and protocols. It protects all protocols in the TCP/IP suite and Internet communications using L2TP.
IPX	The Internetwork Packet Exchange is the NetWare protocol that controls addressing and routing of packets within and between LANs.
IPX/SPX	The Internetwork Packet Exchange/Sequenced Packet Exchange is Novell NetWare's networking protocol. Microsoft has its own version of IPX/SPX called NWLink.
ISDN	Integrated Services Digital Network is a communications standard for sending voice, video, and data over digital phone lines.
ISP	The Internet Service Provider is a company that provides you with access to the Internet.
Kbps	A measure of data transfer speed, Kilobits per second is 1,000 bits per second.

Term	Description
Kerberos	The default user and host authentication protocol for Windows 2000. Internet Protocol security uses the Kerberos protocol for authentication.
L2F	Layer 2 Forwarding is a Cisco networking protocol upon which L2TP is based.
L2TP	The Layer Two Tunneling Protocol encapsulates Point-to-Point frames to be sent over IP, X.25, Frame Relay, or ATM networks.
LAN	A Local Area Network is a communications network connecting computers, printers, and other devices within a limited area.
MAC address	The Media Access Control address is used for communication between network adapters on the same subnet. Each network adapter has an associated MAC address.
MMC	Microsoft Management Console is a framework for hosting administrative consoles. A console is defined by the items on its console tree. It has windows that provide views of the tree as well as the administrative properties, services, and events that are acted on by items in the console tree.
MS-CHAP	Microsoft Challenge Handshake Authentication Protocol allows you to encrypt an entire dial-up session, not just the original authentication.
Multilink	With Multilink, clients can combine multiple physical connections into one logical connection.

Term	Description
multi-protocol router	A RRAS server that can act like a router, routing IP, IPX, and AppleTalk packets simultaneously.
NetBEUI	NetBIOS Enhanced User Interface is Microsoft's networking protocol for small LANs.
NetBIOS	Network Basic Input/Output System is an Application Programming Interface used by MS-DOS applications on a LAN to enable information transmission and sessions between nodes.
NetBIOS name	A name recognized by WINS, the service that maps a computer name to its IP address.
NetBT	NetBIOS over TCP/IP is a feature that provides the NetBIOS programming interface over the TCP/IP protocol. It is used for monitoring routed servers that use NetBIOS name resolution.
NETSH	Net Shell is a command-line utility that supports Windows 2000 networking components for both local and remote computers. You can use NETSH to save a configuration script in a text file for configuring other servers.
NIC	A Network Interface Card is the expansion board you insert into a computer so it can be connected to a network. NICs are usually designed for a particular network, protocol, and media.
NWLink	Microsoft's implementation of IPX/SPX, Novell's transport protocol that supports routing and client-server applications.

Term	Description
ODBC	Open DataBase Connectivity allows you to access any data in any application, no matter which database program handles the data.
packet-switching	This refers to protocols in which messages are divided into packets that are transmitted individually along different routes to their destination, where they are reassembled into the original message.
PAD	The Packet Assembler/Disassembler is a device that breaks data into packets for transmission over an X.25 network before reassembling them at the destination point.
PAP	The Password Authentication Protocol is the most basic form of authentication in which a user's name and password are transmitted over a network and compared with a table of name / password pairs.
PPP	The Point-to-Point Protocol is a method of connecting a computer to the Internet. It is more stable than the older SLIP protocol and supports error checking.
PPTP	The Point-to-Point Tunneling Protocol is a tunneling protocol that encapsulates Point-to-Point frames for transmission over the Internet or a private intranet.
PSTN	The Public Switched Telephone Network refers to the telephone system based on copper wires carrying analog voice data.

Term	Description
RADIUS	Remote Authentication Dial-In User Service is the most common authentication protocol used by Internet service providers. RADIUS running on an Internet Authentication Service server with Windows 2000 can be used to manage the access policies of remote access servers.
RAS	A Remote Access Service is a Windows service that permits remote networking for mobile workers and for system administrators who monitor and manage servers at multiple sites.
RRAS	The Routing and Remote Access Service is the Microsoft feature that integrates remote access and multi-protocol routing services. It can turn a Windows 2000 server into a dynamic software router.
SLIP	The Serial Line Internet Protocol is an older and simpler protocol used for connection on the Internet, which is being supplanted by PPP XE "multilink".
SPAP	The Shiva Password Authentication Protocol is an encrypted password authentication method used by Shiva LAN Rover clients and servers. It is also supported by Windows 2000 Server.
TCP/IP	The Transport Control Protocol/Internet Protocol is a set of protocols that provides communication among diverse networks. Since it accommodates different architectures and operating systems, TCP/IP is the most commonly used Internet protocol.

Term	Description
tunneling	Tunneling technology allows one network to send its data through another network's connections by encapsulating a network protocol within packets carried by the second network.
UDP	A User Datagram Protocol is a TCP/IP component that transmits data through a connectionless service but does not guarantee the delivery or sequencing delivery of sent packets.
VPN	A Virtual Private Network is the extension of a private network that encompasses links across shared or public networks, such as the Internet.
WAN	A Wide Area Network is a computer network that spans a large geographical area. It usually consists of two or more LANs.
WINS	The Windows Internet Name Service is a Microsoft software service that dynamically maps IP addresses to computer names. This allows users to access resources by name instead of by IP address.
X.25	This popular protocol is used in packet-switching networks.
X.25 smart card	This network connectivity hardware attaches directly to an X.25 network and uses the X.25 protocol to establish connections and send and receive data.

In Brief

If you want to...	Then do this...
Enable a RAS server to accept inbound Internet connections	1. From the Start menu, select Programs, Administrative Tools, and Routing and Remote Access.
	2. Within the Routing and Remote Access console, right-click the desired server, and select Configure and then Enable Routing and Remote Access.
	3. From Routing and Remote Access Server Setup, select Next.
	4. From Common Configurations, select Remote access server and then Next.
	5. From Remote Client Protocols, verify that all the protocols needed to support remote clients are listed, select Yes, all of the required protocols are on this list, and then Next.
	6. If you select No, I need to add protocols, the wizard will prompt you to exit and add the required protocols from Network and Dial-up Connections in the control panel before running the wizard again.
	7. From Macintosh Guest Authentication (assuming you have installed AppleTalk), decide if you want to Allow unauthenticated access for all remote clients, and select Next.

If you want to...	Then do this...
Enable a RAS server to accept inbound Internet connections	1. From IP Address Assignment, select the method of assigning IP addresses to remote clients; choose either Automatically, in which case a DHCP server or the RRAS server itself generates addresses automatically, or From a specified range of addresses, and then select Next.
	2. If you have selected From a specified range of addresses in the previous step, type the address range the server will use to assign addresses to clients in Address Range Assignment, and select Next.
	3. Within Managing Multiple Remote Access Servers, decide whether to use a server or not; select No, I don't want to set up this server to use RADIUS now, and select Next.
	4. From Completing the Routing and Remote Access Server, select Finish.
Configure an outbound connection to another network	1. From the **Start** menu, choose **Settings** and then Network and Dial-up Connections.
	2. Double-click Make New Connection, and, from Network Connection, select Next.
	3. From Network Connection Type, select Dial-up to private network and then Next.
	4. Within Phone Number to Dial, type the phone number of the computer or network to which you want to connect, and select Next.
	5. From Connection **Availability**, choose to make the connection available for all users or just yourself, and select **Next**..

If you want to...	Then do this...
Configure an outbound connection to the Internet	6. Within **Step 1 of Internet account connection information**, type your ISP's phone number and country code, and select **Next**.
	7. Alternatively, you can select **Advanced** to configure connection properties such as IP and DNS addresses through **Advanced Connection Properties**.
	8. Click **OK**, and select **Next**.
	9. Within **Step 2 of Internet account connection information**, type the user name and password, and select **Next**.
	10. Within **Step 3 of Internet account connection information**, type a friendly name and a descriptive connection name, and select **Next**.
	11. At this point you can **configure settings** for your Internet mail client, and select **Next**.
	12. From Completing the Internet Connection, select Finish.

If you want to...	Then do this...
Edit the default properties for an outbound connection	1. From the **Start** menu, choose **Settings** and then **Network and Dial-up Connections**.
	2. Right-click the icon for the desired connection, and choose **Properties**.
	3. You can view the following property pages:
	4. General allows you to configure the connection device
	5. Options allows you to configure dialing and redialing options
	6. Security allows you to specify the security options used to validate your identity
	7. Networking allows you to specify the type of server you are calling as well as PPP and the networking components to be used
	8. Sharing allows you to implement connection sharing with other computers on your LAN

If you want to...	Then do this...
Edit the default properties for a remote access server	1. From the **Start** menu, choose **Settings** and then **Network and Dial-up Connections**. 2. Right-click the icon for the desired server, and select **Properties.** You can see the following property pages: • General, which allows you to enable the computer as either a router for the LAN, for both the LAN and demand-dial routing, or a remote access server • Security, which allows you to select the authentication provider and method • PPP XE "multilink", which allows you to set PPP options • Event logging, which allows you to specify logging options • IP, which allows you to specify IP routing and remote access and demand-dial connections • IPX, which allows you to specify IPX transport protocol settings, appears only if an IPX/SPX compatible transport protocol has been installed • AppleTalk, which allows you enable the protocol if it has been installed

If you want to...	Then do this...
Control the availability and use of the communication ports in a RAS server	1. From the **Start** menu, choose **Programs**, **Administrative Tools**, and **Routing and Remote Access**.
	2. From the left pane of the Routing and Remote Access console, expand the desired server, right-click **Ports**, and select **Properties**.
	3. From Devices, select the port you want, and then select **Configure**.
	4. Within Configure Device, choose whether you want to use the port for inbound remote access connections or inbound and outbound demand-dial routing connections.
	5. Type a phone number for the device, set a maximum port limit if the device is meant to support multiple ports, click **OK**, select **Apply**, and then click **OK** again.
Create a new access policy	1. From the **Start** menu, choose **Programs**, **Administrative Tools**, and **Routing and Remote Access**.
	2. Within the left pane of the **Routing and Remote Access** console, expand the desired server, right-click **Remote Access Policies**, and select **New Remote Access Policy**.
	3. Within **Add Remote Access Policy**, type a friendly policy name, and select **Next**.
	4. Within **Select Attribute**, specify the conditions to match, selecting **Add** between each selection, and then select **Next**.

If you want to...	Then do this...
Configure a VPN server	1. From the **Start** menu, choose **Programs**, **Administrative Tools**, and **Routing and Remote Access**.
	2. In the **Routing and Remote Access** console, right-click the desired server, and select **Configure** and then **Enable Routing and Remote Access**.
	3. From **Routing and Remote Access Server Setup**, select **Next**.
	4. from **Common Configurations**, select **Virtual private network (VPN) server** and then **Next**.
	5. Within **Remote Client Protocols**, verify that all of the protocols needed to support VPN clients are listed, select **Yes, all of the available protocols are on this list**, and select **Next**.
	6. If you select **No, I need to add protocols**, the wizard will prompt you to exit and add the required protocols from **Network and Dial-up Connections** in the control panel before running the wizard again.
	7. From **Macintosh Guest Authentication** (assuming you have installed AppleTalk), decide if you want to **Allow unauthenticated access for all remote clients**, and select **Next**.
	8. Within **Internet Connection**, specify the single connection remote VPN clients and routers will use to access the server through the Internet, and select **Next**.

If you want to...	Then do this...
Configure a VPN server	1. From **IP Address Assignment**, select the method of assigning IP addresses to remote clients; choose either **Automatically**, in which case a DHCP server or the VPN server itself generates addresses automatically, or **From a specified range of addresses**, and select **Next**. 2. If you have selected **From a specified range of addresses** in the previous step, type the address range the server will use to assign addresses to clients in **Address Range Assignment**, and select **Next**. 3. Within **Managing Multiple Remote Access Servers**, decide whether to use a RADIUS server or not; select **No, I don't want to set up this server to use RADIUS now**, and select **Next**. 4. From **Completing the Routing and Remote Access Server Setup**, select **Finish**.
Configure a client VPN connection	1. From the **Start** menu, choose **Settings** and then **Network and Dial-up Connections**. 2. Double-click **Make New Connection**, and, within **Network Connection**, select **Next**. 3. From Network Connection Type, select Connect to a private network through the Internet, and select Next.

If you want to...	Then do this...
Configure a client VPN connection	4. From **Public Network**, decide whether you want to establish a public network (Internet) connection before a VPN connection is created; if you are connecting to a Windows 2000 device with a valid public IP address, select **Do not dial the initial connection** and click **OK**, otherwise select **Automatically dial this initial connection**.
	5. Within **Destination Address**, type the host name or IP address of the target server, and select **Next**.
	6. From **Connection Availability**, choose to make the connection available for all users or just yourself, and select **Next**.
	7. Within **Completing the Network Connection**, type the name you want to use for the connection, and select **Finish**.
Set PPTP filters	1. From the **Start** menu, choose **Programs**, **Administrative Tools**, and **Routing and Remote Access**.
	2. In the console, expand the desired the server, expand **IP Routing**, and select **General**.
	3. Within the details pane, right-click the interface to be filtered, and select **Properties**.

If you want to...	Then do this...
Set PPTP filters	4. From the **General** page, choose **Input Filters** or **Output Filters** depending on how you would like to screen packets, and type the source, destination and protocol to be filtered, selecting **Add** between each filter.
	5. Click **OK**, select **Apply**, and then select **OK** again.
Add a demand-dial interface	1. From the **Start** menu, choose **Programs**, **Administrative Tools**, and **Routing and Remote Access**.
	2. In the console, expand the desired router, select **Routing Interfaces**, and right-click **New Demand-dial Interface**.
	3. Within **Demand Dial Interface**, type the Interface name, and select Next.
	4. Type the phone number to dial when establishing the demand-dial interface, adding alternate numbers as needed, and select **Next**.
	5. From **Protocols and Security**, select the desired transports and security options for the connection, and select **Next**.
	6. The remaining screens will vary depending on the options chosen from the previous screen; type the information as required, click **OK**, and select **Finish**.

If you want to...	Then do this...
Add a static route to the routing table	1. From the **Start** menu, choose **Programs**, **Administrative Tools**, and **Routing and Remote Access**. 2. In the console, expand the desired router, select **IP Routing**, right-click **Static Routes**, and select **New static Route**. 3. Within **Static Route**, select the interface, type the IP address for the destination router, and click **OK**.
Monitor a remote access connection	1. From the **Start** menu, choose **Programs**, **Administrative Tools**, and **Routing and Remote Access**. 2. From the left pane of the console tree, choose **Remote Access Clients**, and, from the details pane, double-click the name of the desired connection. 3. Within **Status**, observe the connection statistics, and choose **Close**.
Administer and troubleshoot remote access connections	Use the following Windows 2000 built-in tools: • Routing and Remote Access snap-in, which allows you to enable RRAS, manage routing interfaces, configure IPX routing, and configure remote access policies • Net shell (NETSH) command-line utility, which supports Windows 2000 networking components for both local and remote computers • Authentication and accounting logging, which logs information on PPP-based connection attempts • Event logging, which logs system events • Tracing, which allows you to trace each protocol by setting values in the corresponding registry keys

If you want to...	Then do this...
Install IAS on a windows 2000 server	1. From the **Start** menu, choose **Settings** and **Control Panel**. 2. From the **Control Panel**, double-click **Add/Remove Programs**, and select **Add/Remove Windows Components**. 3. Within **Windows Components**, highlight **Networking Services**, and select **Details**. 4. Select **Internet Authentication Service**, from **Completing the Windows Components**, click **OK**, select **Next** and then **Finish**.
Edit the properties for an IAS server	1. From the **Start** menu, choose **Programs**, **Administrative Tools**, and **Internet Authentication Service**. 2. In the console tree, right-click **Internet Authentication Service**, and select **Properties**. 3. Within the **Service** page, you can change the description or event logging options. 4. Within the **RADIUS** page, you can change the authentication and accounting UDP ports. 5. Within the **Realms** page, you can change the realm information, and then click **OK**.

If you want to...	Then do this...
Add remote access servers as IAS clients	1. From the **Start** menu, choose **Programs**, **Administrative Tools**, and **Internet Authentication Service**.
	2. In the console tree, right-click **Clients**, and select **New Client**.
	3. Type a name for the client, and select **Next**.
	4. Type the client address and a shared secret, and select **Finish**.

Use RADIUS as the authentication provider	1. From the **Start** menu, choose **Programs**, **Administrative Tools**, and **Routing and Remote Access**. 2. From the left pane of the **Routing and Remote Access** console, right-click on the server name, and select **Properties**. 3. Select the **Security** page, and, from **Authentication provider**, select **RADIUS Authentication**, and then **Configure**. 4. From **Radius Authentication**, select **Add**, and within **Add RADIUS Server**, type the host name or IP address of the IAS server. 5. Type other configuration parameters, such as the **Time-out duration, Initial score, Port number**, and select or deselect **Always use digital signatures**. 6. Click **OK** three times to exit, and restart the **Routing and Remote Access** service.
Use RADIUS as the accounting provider	1. From the **Start** menu, choose **Programs**, **Administrative Tools**, and **Routing and Remote Access**. 2. From the left pane of the **Routing and Remote Access** console, right-click on the server name, and select **Properties**. 3. Choose the **Security** page, and, under Accounting provider, select **RADIUS Accounting** and **Configure**. 4. From **Radius Accounting**, select **Add**, and, within **Add RADIUS Server**, type the host name or IP address of the IAS server.

| Use RADIUS as the accounting provider | 1. Type other configuration parameters, such as the **Time-out duration, Initial score, Port number**, and select or deselect **Always use digital signatures**. |
| | 2. Click **OK** three times to exit, and restart the **Routing and Remote Access** service. |

Lesson 4 Activities

Complete the following activities to prepare for the certification exam.

1. Describe briefly some of the tools you can use to help you administer and troubleshoot RRAS.

2. Explain why you would want to use a RADIUS server.

3. Explain the difference between PPTP and L2TP.

4. Describe the four main factors you need to consider when managing remote access.

5. List and compare three types of dial-up connections.

6. Describe the procedure for copying a remote access policy from a RAS server to the IAS server if both the source and destination computers are running the same version of Windows 2000.

7. Explain the purpose of VPN and how it works.

8. Describe a good practice to follow after using a wizard and the reasons behind it.

9. Describe Windows 2000 remote access security features.

10. Define multilink.

Answers to Lesson 4 Activities

1. Windows 2000 has the following built-in tools to help you administer and troubleshoot RRAS:

    *   Routing and Remote Access snap-in, which allows you to enable RRAS, manage routing interfaces, configure IPX routing, configure remote access policies, and monitor remote access connections in real-time

    *   Net shell (NETSH) command-line utility, which supports Windows 2000 networking components for both local and remote computers

    *   Authentication and accounting logging, which logs information on PPP-based connection attempts

    *   Event logging, which logs system events

    *   Tracing, which allows you to trace each protocol by setting values in the corresponding registry keys

2. A RADIUS server simplifies the administration of multiple RRAS servers. RADIUS is a client-server protocol that provides centralized remote access authentication, authorization, accounting, and auditing for remote access servers acting as RADIUS clients. The Internet Authentication Service (IAS) is Microsoft's implementation of a RADIUS server. You may want to use RADIUS in your network for the following reasons:

    *   You want to administer remote RRAS servers locally

    *   You want to administer multiple RRAS servers efficiently

    *   By configuring a primary and secondary RADIUS server, you can support remote access fault tolerance and redundancy

    *   You want to administer heterogeneous remote access servers

3. **PPTP**—Point-to-Point Tunneling Protocol encapsulates PPP frames with IP packets for transmission over an IP Internetwork, such as the Internet or a private network. The encapsulation authorizes the transport of packets that do not meet Internet addressing standards, such as IP, IPX, or NetBEUI packets.

    L2TP—This protocol is a combination of the features offered by PPTP and a Cisco protocol, Layer 2 Forwarding (L2F). L2TP encapsulates PPP frames that are to be sent over IP, X.25, Frame Relay, or ATM networks. When IP packets are used to encapsulate the PPP frames, L2TP can be used as a tunneling protocol over the Internet or between two private LANs. Unlike PPTP, which is restricted to having an IP Internetwork as the transit intermediary, L2TP requires only that the tunnel media provide packet-oriented point-to-point connectivity. You need IPSec to provide encryption for L2TP.

4. Remote access management involves four main factors: managing users, addresses, access, and authentication.

    User Management— If there are multiple RAS servers, the administration of user accounts can be simplified by setting up a master account database in the Active directory store or on a RADIUS server, which permits the RAS server to send authentication credentials to a central authentication device.

    Address Management—For PPP XE "multilink" connections involving IP, IPX, and AppleTalk, addressing information must be given to remote access clients when setting up the connection.

    Access Management—Remote access connections are accepted, based on the dial-in properties of a user account and the remote access policies. A remote access policy is a set of parameters that predefines the characteristics of the incoming connection. You can apply different sets of conditions to different RRAS clients or different requirements to the same client based on the parameters of the connection attempt.

    The user account contains dial-in properties used when permitting or denying a connection attempt.

    Authentication Management—A remote access server can be configured to use either Windows 2000 or RADIUS as an authentication provider.

5. Various dial-up connections are possible, depending on the available telecommunications infrastructure and the equipment installed at both the remote access client and server.

    Public switched telephone network (PSTN)—Transmission rates over an analog telephone system are slow, as it was not designed for digital data. The maximum rate supported by a PSTN connection is 33.6 Kbps. This is compensated by low cost, wide availability, and ease of use.

    V.90—This new technology allows a RAS server to be connected to a central office through a digital switch rather than an analog PSTN switch, decreasing accumulated noise from digital to analog conversion. Remote access clients can send data at 33.6 Kbps and receive at 56Kbps.

ISDN—ISDN provides standards to replace the PSTN with a digital equivalent. ISDN allows a single digital network to handle voice, data, fax, and other services over the existing wiring. ISDN works much like PSTN; however, it offers multiple data channels of 64 Kbps each. This leads to higher rates of data transfer, and no analog -to-digital conversions are necessary. Costs run higher than with PSTN.

X.25—This is an older communications protocol standard for sending data across public packet-switching networks.

Asynchronous Transfer Mode (ATM) over Asymmetric Digital Subscriber Line (ADSL)— ADSL is a new technology for small business and residential customers. An ADSL connection offers 64 Kbps from the customer and 1.544 Mbps to the customer. An ASDL connection can be made to look like an Ethernet interface or a dial-up interface.

6. To copy a remote access policy from a RAS server to the IAS server, do the following:

   1. From the **Start** menu, choose **Programs**, select **Accessories**, and choose **Command Prompt**.

   2. Type **netsh aaaa show config [path\file.txt]**, which creates a text file that includes all of the configuration settings; the path can be relative, absolute, or UNC.

   3. Copy the text file to the destination IAS server.

   4. From the command prompt at the destination server, type **netsh   exec [path\file.txt]**.

7. A VPN mimics the properties of a dedicated private network XE "multilink" by creating encapsulated, encrypted, and authenticated links across shared or public networks. Point-to-point connections can be simulated through the use of tunneling, and LAN connectivity can be simulated, allowing for secure data transfer between computers.

   Tunneling is the method of transferring data in a VPN. Frames produced by the originating node are encapsulated with an extra header that provides routing information for an intermediate Internetwork. Once the encapsulated frames are routed between the tunnel endpoints over the transit Internetwork, the frames are de-encapsulated and forwarded to their final destination. The logical path over the transit Internetwork through which the encapsulated packets travel is the tunnel.

8. The wizards in Windows 2000 allow you to configure many objects and services easily and quickly. However, a wizard makes assumptions when creating default settings. So after you use a

wizard, check the configuration parameters through the properties pages for an object or service. These pages can usually be accessed by right-clicking on the desired object in the related MMC snap-in and selecting Properties.

9. Windows 2000 remote access security features include the following:

   Secure user authentication—You can configure a RAS server to require secure authentication and deny connections to any clients who cannot perform the required authentication. User credentials are encrypted and exchanged by using PPP with EAP, MS-CHAP, CHAP, or SPAP.

   Mutual Authentication—To authenticate both ends of the connection, encrypted user credentials are exchanged from both server and client sides. This is done by using PPP with EAP-Transport Level Security (EAP-TLS) or MS-CHAP v2. If either the remote access server or the client cannot execute the required authentication, the connection is terminated.

   Data encryption—Remote access data encryption is based on a secret encryption key shared only by the RAS server and client and is generated during user authentication. You can permit data encryption over dial-up remote access links using PPP with EAP-TLS or MS-CHAP. If you choose to configure the RAS server to require data encryption, and the remote client cannot perform the required encryption, the connection is rejected.

   Callback—During callback, the remote access server calls the client back after verifying the user credentials.

   Caller ID—Caller ID verifies that an incoming call is coming from a specified number. The feature is configured through the dial-in properties of the user account. If caller ID is configured for a user account and the caller ID is not passed from the client to the RAS server, then the connection is terminated.

   Remote Access account lockout—This feature locks out remote access clients after a specified number of remote access authentication attempts have failed. It is useful for VPN connections over the Internet, to prevent hackers from using dictionary attacks to break into an intranet.

10. Multilink is a technology that permits clients to combine multiple physical connections into one logical connection. You can configure multilink settings from the Multilink page of the Edit Dial-in Profile page. The Bandwidth Allocation Protocol (BAP) is often used with multilink. BAP allows you to dynamically add or drop multiple connection links as needed in response to changing bandwidth needs.

Lesson 4 Quiz

These questions test your knowledge of features, vocabulary, procedures, and syntax.

1. What is the central component in Windows 2000 for authenticating, authorizing, and auditing users who connect to a network through a VPN or dial-up access?
   A. IPSec
   B. IAS
   C. ISDN
   D. IPX

2. What information do you need prior to configuring connections to another private network?
   A. User name and password
   B. Access telephone number to dial
   C. Protocol used on the remote network
   D. Authentication required by the remote network

3. Which of the following is the process of verifying the origin and integrity of a message?
   A. Accounting
   B. Authorization
   C. Authentication
   D. Auditing

4. What is MS-CHAP?
   A. A tunneling protocol
   B. A WAN protocol
   C. A LAN protocol
   D. An authentication protocol

5. Which computers running the following operating systems can be RAS clients?
   A. Windows for Workgroups
   B. UNIX
   C. MS-DOS
   D. Macintosh

6. Why would you want to use RADIUS in your network?
   A. To administer a local RRAS server
   B. To administer heterogeneous remote access servers
   C. To administer a remote RRAS server locally
   D. To support remote access fault tolerance and redundancy

7. You have just finished using the Routing and Remote Access Setup Wizard to configure your remote access server, but you do not see the IPX page of the RAS Server Properties page. Why is that?
A. You need to configure client connections before you can see the IPX page.
B. The wizard cannot create an IPX page in the Properties page for a RAS server.
C. An IPX/SPX compatible protocol was never installed on the remote access server.
D. The LAN Protocol page handles configuration parameters for IPX, IP, and AppleTalk.

8. Which of the following are protocols that support tunneling?
A. PPTP
B. L2TP
C. IPSec
D. SLIP

9. How do you allow other computers on your LAN to use your Internet connection?
A. Configure the Sharing page of the Connection Properties page
B. Configure the Internet Connection Sharing Settings page of the Connection Properties page
C. Configure the Sharing page of the Remote Access Server Properties page
D. Configure the Sharing page of the IPX Routing Properties page

10. Where do you enable the authentication provider for a RAS server?
A. Authentication page of RAS Server Properties page
B. Security page of RAS Server Properties page
C. Authentication page of IAS Server Properties page
D. Security page of IAS Server Properties page

Answers to Lesson 4 Quiz

1. Answer B is correct. The Internet Authentication Service (IAS) in Windows 2000 is Microsoft's implementation of a RADIUS server. It performs centralized authentication, authorization, auditing, and accounting of dial-up connections, and remote access and demand-dial connections.

    Answer A is incorrect. A set of standard, cryptography-based protection services and protocols, Internet Protocol Security (IPSec) protects all protocols in the TCP/IP suite and Internet communications using L2TP.

    Answer C is incorrect. Integrated Services Digital Network (ISDN) is a communications standard for sending voice, video, and data over digital phone lines.

    Answer D is incorrect. Internetwork Packet Exchange (IPX) is the NetWare protocol that controls addressing and routing of packets within and between LANs.

2. Answers A, B, C, and D are all correct. During configuration of a connection to another private network using a wizard, you will be prompted for the user name and password, access telephone number to dial, protocol used on the remote network, and authentication required by the remote network.

3. Answer C is correct. Authentication is an IPSec process that verifies the origin and integrity of a message by assuring the identity of each computer. IPSec has many methods of authentication to support computers running legacy versions of Windows and non-Windows computers.

    Answer A is incorrect. Accounting is the process of maintaining a log of connection requests and sessions.

    Answer B is incorrect. Authorization is the process of giving a user access to system objects based on the user's identity.

    Answer D is incorrect. Auditing is the process of configuring the logging of predetermined events. Auditing can tell you about potentially dangerous conditions and leaves a trail of accountability.

4. Answer D is correct. Microsoft Challenge Handshake Authentication Protocol (MS-CHAP) versions 1 or 2 allows you to encrypt an entire dial-up session, not just the original authentication.

    Answers A, B, and C are all incorrect. MS-CHAP is not a tunneling, WAN or LAN protocol.

5. Answers A, B, C, and D are all correct. Other potential RAS clients include computers running Windows 2000, Microsoft NT 3.51 or later, Windows 95 or 98, or Microsoft LAN Manager. In fact, almost any third party remote access clients using PPP can connect to a Windows 2000 RAS server.

6. Answers B, C, and D are all correct. RADIUS allows you to administer a mixture of remote access servers from different manufacturers. It also supports the local administration of remote RRAS servers. Another reason to implement RADIUS is to provide fault tolerance and redundancy.

   Answer A is incorrect. You would establish RADIUS to administer multiple RRAS servers, not just one.

7. Answer C is correct. Wizards can only work with the given information. The IPX page cannot be seen because an IPX/SPX compatible protocol was never installed prior to using the wizard.

   Answer A is incorrect. You do not need to configure client connections before you can see the IPX page.

   Answer B is incorrect. You should install all desired protocols before using the Routing and Remote Access Setup Wizard because it can create an IPX page in the Properties page.

   Answer D is incorrect. A LAN Protocol page does not exist.

8. Answers A, B, and C are all correct. Point-to-Point Tunneling Protocol (PPTP) encapsulates PPP frames with IP packets for transmission over an IP Internetwork only. Layer 2 Transport Protocol encapsulates PPP frames that are to be sent over IP, X.25, Frame Relay, or ATM networks. Rather than having an IP Internetwork as the transit intermediary, L2TP requires only that the tunnel media provide packet-oriented point-to-point connectivity. Internet Protocol Security (IPSec) provides encryption when used with L2TP.

   Answer D is incorrect. Used for connection on the Internet, Serial Line Internet Protocol is an older and simpler protocol, which does not support tunneling.

9. Answers A and B are correct. The Sharing page of the Connection Properties page allows you to enable shared access and on-demand dialing. The Internet Connection Shared Settings pages are part of the Sharing page from the Connection properties page and permit detailed configuration of network applications to be enabled for computers sharing the connection and services to be provided the remote network.

   Answers C and D are incorrect. There are no Sharing pages in the Remote Access Server Properties or IP Routing Properties pages.

10. Answer B is correct. The Security page of the RAS Server Properties page allows you to select the authentication provider to validate credentials for remote access clients and demand-dial routers. You can choose to have either Windows Authentication or RADIUS Authentication. You can also select the authentication method from EAP, MS-CHAP v2, CHAP, SPAP, PAP, and Unauthenticated access.

Answer A is incorrect. An Authentication page does not exist within the RAS Server Properties page.

Answers C and D are incorrect. Although you can configure an IAS server, the decision to use a particular authentication provider is made on the RAS server through the Security page of its Properties page.

Network Protocol Installation and Administration

Protocols are industry-standard specifications for packets of data that make it possible for networks to share information. These packets are moved up and down the Open System Interconnection (OSI) Reference Model protocol stack before being relayed across the transmission media. A protocol suite or stack, is a combination of protocols that work together to achieve network communication.

The OSI Reference Model presents a layered approach to networking. Each layer of the model is responsible for a different part of the communication process. The model simplifies how network hardware and software work together and helps in troubleshooting by defining how components should function.

After completing this lesson, you should have a better understanding of the following topics:

*   Network Protocol Installation
*   Network Traffic Management
*   Network Binding Configuration
*   TCP/IP Packet Filter Configuration
*   Network Protocol Administration

Network Protocol Installation

Windows 2000 supports a number of network protocols including:

- Transmission Control Protocol/Internet Protocol (TCP/IP), a set of protocols that provides communication among diverse networks

- Asynchronous Transfer Mode (ATM), a networking technology based on transferring packets of a fixed size across a fixed channel

- Internetwork Packet Exchange/ Sequenced Packet Exchange (IPX/SPX), Novell NetWare's networking protocol

- Network Basic Input/Output System (NetBIOS) Enhanced User Interface (NetBEUI), Microsoft's networking protocol for small LANs

- AppleTalk, the protocol used by Macintosh clients

Installing TCP/IP

TCP/IP is the industry-standard suite of protocols supporting enterprise connectivity on Windows 2000 computers. A routable networking protocol supported by most operating systems, TCP/IP encompasses many utilities to facilitate data transfer. It also helps you access Internet resources.

Because Windows 2000 relies on TCP/IP for common functions such as logon, file and print services, and replication of information between domain controllers, TCP/IP is installed in the operating system by default. Microsoft's implementation of TCP/IP maps to the four-layer TCP/IP Reference Model, instead of the seven-layer OSI Reference Model.

Network Interface Layer—This layer puts frames on the wire and pulls frames off the wire. It includes the following Local Area Network (LAN) technologies:

*   Ethernet, one of the most widely implemented standards using a bus or star topology

*   Token Ring, a popular technology in which all computers are arranged in a logical circle and the computer that has possession of the token is able to send messages

*   Fiber Distributed Data Interface (FDDI), a set of protocols for sending digital data over a fiber optic cable

It also includes the following Wide Area Network (WAN) technologies:

*   Serial Lines, a sequential data transfer protocol

*   Frame Relay, a packet switching protocol

*   Asynchronous Transfer Mode (ATM), which transfers data in cells or packets of a fixed size

Internet Layer—The four protocols in this layer encapsulate packets in Internet datagrams and perform routing algorithms. They are described in Table 5.1.

Table 5.1 Internet Layer Protocols and Their Function

Protocol	Function
Internet Protocol (IP)	This protocol specifies the packet format and addressing scheme, but does not guarantee packet arrival or the correct packet sequence.
Address Resolution Protocol (ARP)	This protocol converts an IP address into a physical address. A host wanting to know a physical address broadcasts an ARP request that the host with the requested IP address answers with its physical address.
Internet Control Message Protocol (ICMP)	This protocol supports packets containing error, control and informational messages.
Internet Group Management Protocol (IGMP)	This protocol supports multicasting, a limited form of broadcasting in which clients having a multicast IP address can message a whole group within an intranet.

Transport Layer—The two protocols in this layer support communication sessions between computers. They are described in Table 5.2.

Table 5.2 Transport Layer Protocols and Their Function

Protocol	Function
Transmission Control Protocol (TCP)	This protocol provides connection packet delivery so that both the delivery of data and the order in which the packets are delivered are guaranteed.
User Datagram Protocol (UDP)	Used primarily for sending broadcast messages over the network, UDP is a connectionless protocol that does not guarantee packet delivery.

Application Layer— The two interfaces in this layer allow applications to gain access to the network. They are described in Table 5.3.

Table 5.3 Application Layer Interfaces and Their Function

Protocol	Function
Winsock	Windows Socket is an Application Programming Interface for developing Windows programs that can communicate with other computers through TCP/IP.
NetBT	NetBIOS over TCP/IP provides a standard interface for NetBIOS services as well as interactions between NetBIOS-based applications and TCP/IP protocols.

The various protocols in the TCP/IP stack and how they map to the four-layer TCP/IP Reference Model are seen in Figure 5.1.

Figure 5.1 Map of Microsoft's TCP/IP and the TCP/IP Reference Model

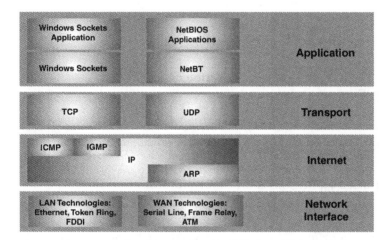

Before installing TCP/IP, you need to understand the services that work with TCP/IP.

DNS—The Domain Name System (DNS) is a distributed database of host and domain name to IP address mappings. DNS provides name resolution services for TCP/IP client applications. Each DNS server is responsible for maintaining a database of mappings for its Local Area Network (LAN), and is usually configured to contact other DNS servers when it cannot find a mapping requested by a client.

DHCP—Dynamic Host Configuration Protocol (DHCP) is the Microsoft service that provides automatic configuration of an IP address, a subnet mask, a default gateway, and DNS or Windows Internet Naming Service (WINS) server addresses for Windows clients. It supports centralized IP address management.

WINS—WINS dynamically resolves NetBIOS names to IP addresses. You need WINS in a mixed network environment where computers are running legacy versions of Windows and NetBIOS computer names need to be resolved for communication.

WINS clients register their name and corresponding IP address with a WINS server. These clients can then query the WINS servers to locate and communicate with other Windows resources on the network. Each time a WINS client boots up, it registers its current NetBIOS name and IP address mapping with the WINS server designated in the client's database. Whenever the client's IP addressing information changes, the client will also send updated information to the WINS database.

When the WINS client wants to communicate with another network resource, it issues a NetBIOS name query request to the WINS server. The WINS server looks for the relevant NetBIOS name/IP address mapping for the destination resource in its database, and returns the IP address to the client.

TCP/IP is installed on Windows 2000 by default if a network adapter was detected during installation of Windows 2000. It can be installed by following these steps:

1.   From the **Start** menu, choose **Settings** and then select **Network and Dial-up Connections**.

2.   From **Network and Dial up Connections**, right-click the connection for which you want to install TCP/IP, and choose **Properties**.

3.   Choose **Install**, highlight **Protocols**, and then select **Add**.

4.   From **Select Network Protocol**, highlight **Internet Protocol (TCP/IP)** (Figure 5.2) and click **OK**.

5.   Verify that **Internet Protocol (TCP/IP)** is selected and click **OK**.

Figure 5.2 Select Network Protocol

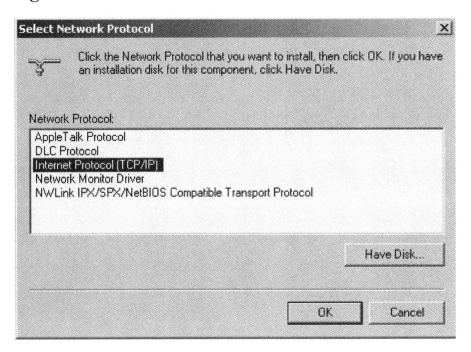

Configuring TCP/IP Properties

Once you have installed TCP/IP, you can configure the following seven property pages: General, IP Settings, DNS, WINS, Options, TCP/IP Filtering and IP Security.

General—The options are described in Table 5.4.

Table 5.4 Internet Protocol (TCP/IP) General Property Page

Option	Description
Obtain an IP address automatically	Allows you to obtain IP settings assigned automatically through DHCP.
Use the following IP address	Allows you to manually configure IP address settings. You can specify the IP address, subnet mask and default gateway.
Obtain DNS server address automatically	Allows you to obtain a DNS server address through DHCP.
Use the following DNS server addresses	Allows you to manually specify the DNS server address. You can type the IP address of the preferred DNS server and an alternate DNS server.

From the Advanced button on the General property, you reach four other property pages where you can configure advanced TCP/IP options. These are IP Settings, DNS, WINS and Options.

IP Settings—You can add, edit or remove IP addresses and their corresponding subnet masks from this page. You can also add, edit and remove gateway addresses and their associated metric (Figure 5.3).

Figure 5.3 Internet Protocol (TCP/IP) IP Settings Property Page

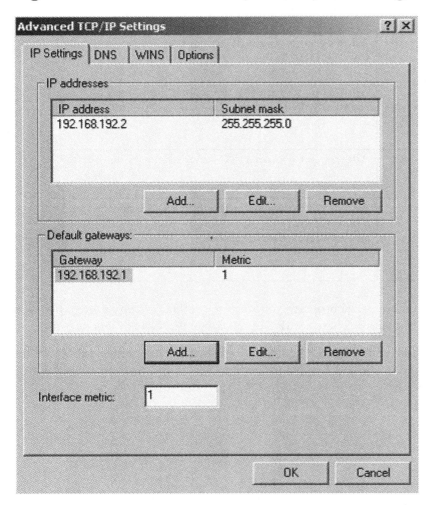

DNS— You can add, edit, remove or change the order of DNS server addresses from this page. Other options are described in Table 5.5.

Table 5.5 Internet Protocol (TCP/IP) DNS Property Page

Option	Description
Append primary and connection specific DNS suffixes	This option limits the resolution for unqualified names to domain suffixes and connection-specific suffixes.
Append parent suffixes of the primary DNS suffix	This option allows you to include parent suffixes up to the second-level domain in the resolution of unqualified names.
Append these DNS suffixes (in order)	This option specifies those specific domain suffixes that can be appended to unqualified domain names during name resolution. The primary and connection-specific suffixes will not be used if you specify domain suffixes here.
DNS suffix for this connection	This option overrides the parent DNS domain name specified for your computer on the Network property page of the System Properties Control Panel.
Register this connection's address in DNS	This option registers the full DNS name of your server's IP address with the DNS server.
Use this connection's DNS suffix in DNS registration	This option registers the IP addresses of your network connection in DNS based on the domain name of the connections and the Fully Qualified Domain Name (FQDN) for your computer. The FQDN indicates the precise location of a computer in the hierarchical domain namespace tree.

WINS— You can add, edit, remove or change the order of WINS server addresses from this page. The options are described in Table 5.6.

Table 5.6 Internet Protocol (TCP/IP) WINS Property Page

Option	Description
Enable LMHOSTS lookup	This option enables the import and use of an LMHOSTS file mapping NetBIOS (computer) names to IP addresses.
Enable NetBIOS over TCP/IP	This option enables NETBIOS over TCP/IP.
Disable NetBIOS over TCP/IP	This option disables NETBIOS over TCP/IP.
Use NetBIOS settings from the DHCP server	This option allows the DHCP server to automatically provide NetBIOS settings.

 Tip: LMHOSTS files are static. It can be an administrative burden to keep an LMHOSTS file current, which is not compensated by the small reduction in network traffic offered by an LMHOSTS file.

Options—You can choose to use a specific IP security policy from the IP Security property page (Figure 5.4), accessed through Properties on the Options page.

Figure 5.4 IP Security Property Page

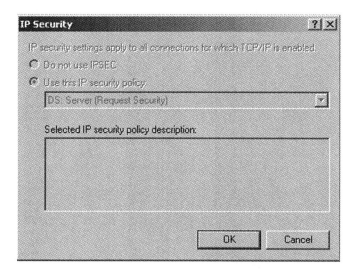

TCP/IP Filtering—You can access this property page (Figure 5.5) by highlighting TCP/IP filtering and selecting Properties from the Options property page. You can enable TCP/IP filtering for all adapters. You can also permit filters to apply to all or only to specified TCP ports, UDP ports and IP protocols.

Figure 5.5 TCP/IP Filtering Property Page

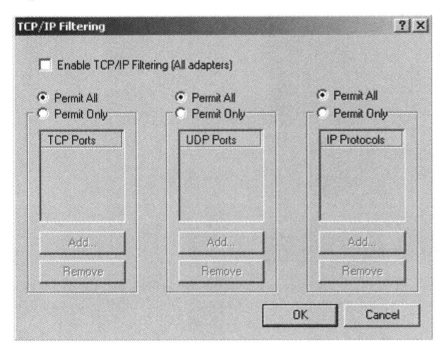

IP Security—You can access this property page by highlighting IP Security and selecting Properties from the Options property page. You can choose to use a specific IP security policy on all connections for which TCP/IP is enabled.

To configure the TCP/IP property pages, follow these steps:

1. From the **Start** menu, choose **Settings**, **Network and Dial-up Connections**, and then select **Local Area Connection**.

2. From **Local Area Connection Status**, choose **Properties**.

3. Highlight **Internet Protocol (TCP/IP)** and choose **Properties**.

4. From the **General** property page, choose the method of obtaining an IP address and a DNS server address.

5. Choose **Advanced** to specify a default gateway, a DNS name resolution method, WINS servers addresses, and security and filtering options, and click **OK**.

Installing the NWLink Protocol

NWLink is Microsoft's implementation of the IPX/SPX protocol. You will need to install it in order to communicate using IPX with computers running NetWare versions 3.X and early 4.x.

A frame type defines the way a network adapter formats data to be sent over a network. Before you install NWLink on a Windows 2000 server, you need to obtain the frame type used by the NetWare computers with which you wish to communicate, and a network address to use.

To install NWLink on your Windows 2000 computer, follow these steps:

1. From the Start menu, choose Settings, Control Panel, and then double-click Network and Dial-up Connections.

2. Right-click the desired local area network connection, and choose **Properties**.

3. From the **General** property page, choose **Install.**

4. Highlight **Protocol**, and choose **Add**.

5. Choose **NWLink IPX/SPX NetBIOS Compatible Transport Protocol** from the protocol list, and click **OK**.

After installation, you can check the defaults applied to the NWLink protocol by following these steps:

1. From the Start menu, choose Settings, Control Panel, and then double-click Network and Dial-up Connections.

2. Right-click the desired local area network connection, and choose Properties.

3. Highlight NWLink IPX/SPX/NetBIOS Compatible Transport Protocol and choose Properties.

4. From within the General property page (Figure 5.6), you can type an internal IPX network number.

5. IIf you want to manually configure the framing type that Windows 2000 uses for IPX packets, choose **Manual frame type detection**, select **Add**, and then type the appropriate framing information and IPX nework numbers.

6. Click **OK**.

Figure 5.6 NWLink IPX/SPX/NetBIOS Compatible Transport Protocol General Property Page

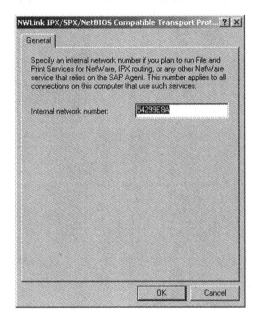

Table 5.7 describes several common network topologies and their associated NWLink frame types.

Table 5.7 Network Topologies and Frame Types Supported by NWLink

Topology	Supported Frame Type
Ethernet	Ethernet II, 802.3, 802.2 and Sub Network Access protocol (SNAP), which defaults to 802.2
Token Ring	802.5 and SNAP
Fiber Distributed Data Interface (FDDI)	802.2 and 802.3

On Ethernet networks, the standard frame type for NetWare 2.2 and NetWare 3.11 is 802.3. Newer versions of NetWare have a standard frame type of 802.2. NWLink automatically detects the frame type when loaded. If multiple frame types are detected in addition to the 802.2 frame type, NWLink defaults to the 802.2 frame type. If you manually configure the frame type, you can support multiple frame types simultaneously.

Configuring Network Protocol Security

After configuring the desired network protocols, you need to configure security to protect the integrity of your network and the data.

IPSec

Internet Protocol Security (IPSec) policies provide comprehensive security for network traffic using public key technology. It provides confidentiality, integrity and authentication to protect each IP packet. The two communicating computers agree on the highest level common security policy before individually handling security at each end. The computer initiating communication uses IPSec to encrypt data before sending it to the receiving computer, which then decrypts the data before passing it on to the destination. Any intermediary network equipment between the two computers forwards the encrypted IP packets, but is prevented from network eavesdropping.

To add the IP Security Policy Management snap-in to the Microsoft Management Console (MMC), follow these steps:

1. From the **Start** menu, choose **Programs**, **Accessories** and then select **Command Prompt**.

2. Type **MMC** at the command prompt and press the **Enter** key.

3. From the console menu, select **Add/Remove Snap-in**, and choose **Add**.

4. Choose **IP Security Policy Managment** from the list of snap-ins, and then select **Add**.

5. From **Select Computer**, choose the range of computers the snap-in will manage, whether the local computer only, the local computer's domain, another domain, or another computer, and then select **Finish**.

An IPSec policy comprehensively defines the correct procedures for all aspects of IP, from when to how to secure data. Table 5.8 explains the components of an IPSec policy.

Table 5.8 Components of an IPSec Policy

Component	Description
IP filter	The IP filter is a subset of potential network traffic based on the IP address, port and transport protocol. The IP filter secures both outbound and inbound traffic.
IP filter list	The IP filter list is a combination of one or more IP filters defining a range of network traffic.
Filter action	The filter action component describes how the IPSec driver should secure network traffic.
Security methods	Security methods describe the security algorithms and types used for authentication and key exchange.
Tunnel setting	If you are using IPSec tunneling to protect the packet destination, this setting gives the IP address or DNS name of the tunnel endpoint.
Connection type	The connection type describes the type of connection affected by IPSec policy, whether remote access, LAN or all network connections.
Rule	A rule is a combination of the various IPSec components that protect a specific subset of network traffic. You can have multiple rules for different traffic subsets.

Three predefined policies are available to be used as they are, or they can be changed to suit your particular needs.

Client (Respond Only)—This policy ensures that if the server requests security, the client will respond by securing the requested protocol and port traffic with that server. It is used on computers that normally do not send secured data.

Server (Request Security)—This policy protects all outbound transmissions; unsecured inbound transmissions are accepted but not resolved until IPSec requests security from the sender. It is used on both clients and servers to initiate secure communications.

Secure Server (Require Security)—This policy protects all outbound and inbound transmissions.

To create an IPSec policy, follow these steps:

1. From the **Start** menu, choose **Programs**, **Accessories** and then select **Command Prompt**.

2. Type **MMC** at the command prompt and press the **Enter** key.

3. From the console tree, choose the **IP Security Policy Management** snap-in.

4. Right-click **IP Security Policies on Local Machine**, and choose **Create IP Security Policy**.

5. From **Welcome to the IP Security Policy Wizard**, choose **Next**.

6. Type a policy name and description, and choose **Next**.

7. From **Requests for Secure Communication**, choose **Activate the default response rule** to have the policy allow negotiation with computers requesting IPSec.

8. Choose **Next**.

9. If you have enabled **Activate the default response rule**, from **Default Response Rule Authentication Method** choose the authentication method (Table 5.9) and then select **Next**.

10. From **Completing the IP Security Policy Wizard**, choose **Finish**.

Table 5.9 IPSec Default Response Rule Authentication Options

Option	Description
Windows 2000 default (Kerberos V5 Protocol)	Kerberos is the default authentication protocol and is supported only on computers that are members of a domain.
Use a certificate from this Certificate Authority (CA)	After choosing a CA corresponding to the certificate to be used, this option supports public-key authentication.
Use this string to protect the key exchange (pre-shared key)	Allows you to type in a pre-shared key known to the requesting computer for key exchange.

Functionality is added to an IPSec policy by creating rules that govern when and how security is applied. You can edit an IPSec policy after using the IP Security Policy wizard. You can use other wizards or you can right-click a policy and choose Properties. A total of seven property pages can be configured. These pages are Rules, IP Filter List, Filter Action, Authentication Methods, Tunnel Setting, Connection Type and General.

Rules—On this page (Figure 5.7), you can add, edit or remove IP security rules. If you choose Add, with the Use Add Wizard option turned off, you will access five more property pages, one for each element of a rule: IP Filter List, Filter Action, Authentication Methods, Tunnel Setting, and Connection Type.

Figure 5.7 IPSec Rules Property Page

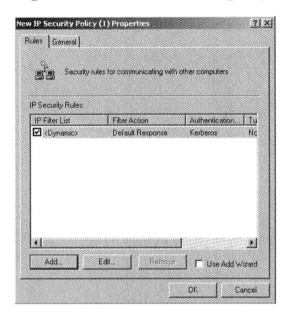

IP Filter List—On this page you define the filters specifying the network traffic to act on (Figure 5.8). By choosing the Add button, you can specify and configure filters to include in a customized filter list, which is composed of multiple subnets, IP addresses and protocols that can be combined into one IP filter.

Figure 5.8 IPSec IP Filter List Property Page

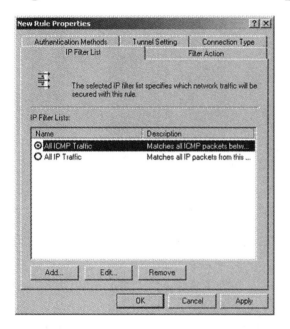

Filter Action—On this page (Figure 5.9) you can specify whether a rule negotiates for secure network traffic, and how it will secure the traffic. If you choose Add, with the Use Add Wizard option turned off, you will be able to progressively define the security methods.

Figure 5.9 IPSec Filter Action Property Page

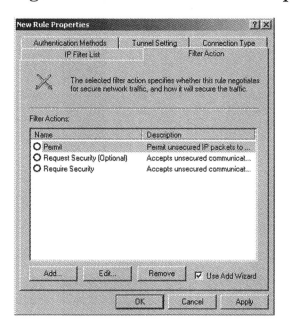

Authentication Methods—On this page (Figure 5.10) you specify how trust is established between two computers. When negotiating security with another computer, selecting Add can choose the authentication methods offered and accepted. The options are the same as in Table 5.9.

Figure 5.10 IPSec Authentication Methods Property Page

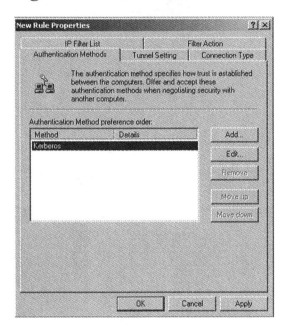

Tunnel Setting—If you opt to specify a rule for an IPSec tunnel, you can type the tunnel endpoint on this page (Figure 5.11). The tunnel endpoint is the tunneling computer closest to the IP traffic destination, as seen in the associated IP Filter List.

Figure 5.11 IPSec Tunnel Setting Property Page

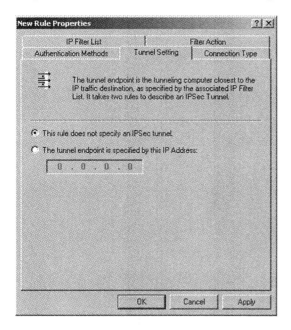

Connection Type—You can specify whether the rule applies to all network connections, LAN traffic, or remote access traffic.

General—On this page (Figure 5.12) you type the name of the IP security policy and a brief description. You can also specify the frequency with which to check for policy changes and advanced Key Exchange settings.

Figure 5.12 IPSec General Property Page

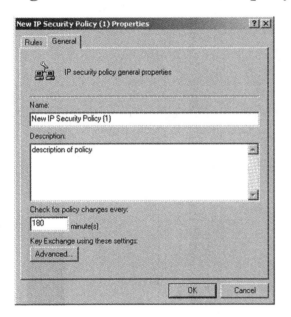

To manage IP filter lists and actions that apply to all IPSec policies on the local computer, rather than on a single IPSec policy, follow these steps.

1. From the **Start** menu, choose **Programs**, **Accessories** and then select **Command Prompt**.

2. Type **MMC** at the command prompt and press the **Enter** key.

3. From the console tree, choose the **IP Security Policy Management** snap-in.

4. Right-click **Security Policies on Local Machine**, and choose **Manage IP filter lists and filter actions**.

5. You can add, remove or edit the items in the **Manage IP Filter Lists** and **Manage Filter Actions** property pages.

6. Choose **Apply** and then select **Close**.

Comprehensive network security can also be configured using Microsoft Proxy Server 2.0 on Windows 2000 Server.

Network Traffic Management

To help you optimize your network infrastructure and to assist you in placing resources in the right places, you will need to monitor the performance of your network. The key is to know what to look for, because you can examine the function of almost any piece of hardware or service. Unless you know what to look for, you will clog your system gathering irrelevant data that you will be unable to interpret. Use network bandwidth wisely to gather only the needed data, and only for the duration that you need it.

Monitoring Network Traffic

Network activity can affect the performance of your system as a whole. However, you cannot detect anomalies in network traffic without having a baseline of regular activity to compare it with. To create a baseline of the level of performance you expect under typical workloads and usage, you would monitor objects over a period of time ranging from days to weeks, depending on the object.

You would then monitor traffic on a regular basis. By comparing the baseline performance with the most recent performance, you can identify performance trends indicating impending problems or need for changes to your network infrastructure. When you have performance data that does not compare with baseline values, you can investigate the problem.

System Monitor

With System Monitor you can track network and system activity with one tool. The System Monitor replaces Windows NT 4.0 Performance Monitor, and can be installed and accessed like any other Microsoft Management Console (MMC) snap-in. It has two components: the System Monitor, which provides a real-time graphical interpretation of system function (Figure 5.13), and the related logging function called Performance Logs and Alerts.

Figure 5.13 System Monitor

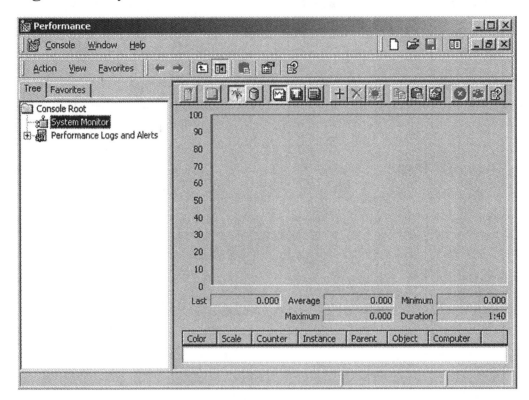

To monitor network activity, you can examine performance data at each layer of the OSI model. System Monitor has objects for network performance data including transmission rates and packet queue lengths, as you can see in Table 5.10.

Tip: Abnormal network counter values on a server often indicate hardware problems such as insufficient memory, processor or disks.

Table 5.10 Network Layers and Their Associated Performance Objects

OSI Layer	Performance Objects
Application, Presentation, Session	Server Work Queues NetBT Connection
Transport	TCP, UDP, NetBEUI, AppleTalk
Network	Network Segment, IP , NWLink IPX/SPX

Network Monitor

The Network Monitor in Windows 2000 focuses on capturing and displaying statistics about the frames that a server receives from the LAN. With this information you can analyze network traffic and troubleshoot networking problems. Network Monitor watches traffic only on the local network segment. If you would like to monitor remote traffic, you need to use the version of Network Monitor that ships with Microsoft System Management Server (SMS) version 1.2 or 2.0. Alternatively, you can purchase a third party sniffer tool that supports more sophisticated monitoring of a wider array of counters along multiple network segments.

Each frame contains the following information:

- The source address of the sending computer

- The destination address of the receiving computer

- Headers from each protocol used to send the frame

- Data

- A trailer verifying frame integrity

You can choose to capture all local network traffic or a particular subset of frames. You can also decide to initiate a predefined action in response to a set of conditions on the network. After capturing the data, you can view it in the Network Monitor console snap-in immediately, or save it in a file for future analysis.

Network Monitor is composed of two parts: the Network Monitor and the Network Monitor driver. To install both, follow these steps:

1.   From the **Start** menu, choose **Settings** and then select **Control Panel**.

2.   Double-click **Add/Remove Programs**, and choose **Add/Remove Windows Components**.

3.   Highlight **Management and Monitoring Tools**, and choose **Details, Network Monitor Tools** and then click **OK**.

4.   Choose **Next**, and from the **Completing the Windows Components Wizard**, select **Finish**.

To capture data, follow these steps:

1.   From the **Start** menu, choose **Programs, Administrative Tools**, and then selelct **Network Monitor**.

2.   From the **Capture** menu, choose **Start**.

Live statistics about the frames are displayed in the Network Monitor Capture window, seen in Figure 5.14. You can see the session statistics for the first 100 network sessions. Then you reset the statistics for another capture by selecting Clear Statistics from the Capture menu. The Capture window has four panes displaying frame statistics:

Graph—This pane displays the following total capture statistics of current network activity:

•   % Network Utilization

•   Frames Per Second

•   Bytes Per Second

•   Broadcasts Per Second

•   Multicasts per Second

Session Statistics—This pane contains the statistics on a current communication session between two participants.

Station Statistics—This pane contains the statistics on communication from or to the local computer.

Total statistics—This pane contains statistics on overall network activity from the time the current capture began.

Figure 5.14 Network Monitor Capture

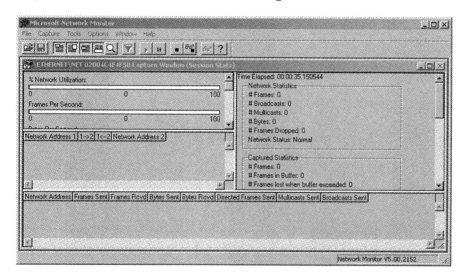

You can specify a capture filter to monitor only a subset of the traffic. This saves data analysis time and buffer resources. You can include or exclude information from the capture specifications to create a decision tree within the Capture Filter window (Figure 5.15).

The following filtering options are available from the Capture Filter window:

1. Filtering by protocol, captures frames using a specific protocol if you specify the protocol on the SAP/ETYPE= line

2. Filtering by address, captures frames from specific computers on your network if you specify up to four address pairs of communicating computers

3. Filtering by data pattern, captures frames matching a specified pattern

Figure 5.15 Network Monitor Capture Filter

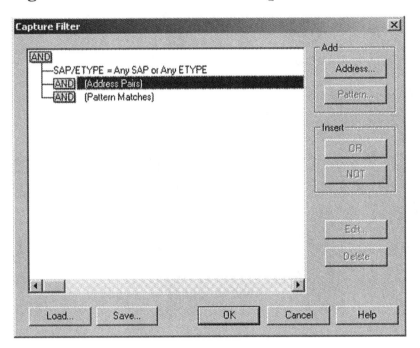

You can load a capture filter by following these steps:

1. From the **Start** menu, choose **Programs**, **Administrative Tools**, and then select **Network Monitor**.

2. From the **Capture** menu, choose **Filter**.

3. From **Capture Filter**, choose to filter by protocol, by address or by data pattern.

4. Alternatively, you can load or edit a pre-existing filter.

5. Click **OK**.

You can also use display filters to determine which frames to display, in the same way you configure capture filters. Since a display filter operates only on data that has already been captured, different subsets of data can be taken from the Network Monitor capture buffer.

Frames can be filtered using the following information:

- The source or destination address of the frame

- The protocols used to send the frame

- The properties and values in the frame

You can load a display filter by following these steps:

1. From the **Start** menu, choose **Programs**, **Administrative Tools**, and then select **Network Monitor**.

2. From the **Capture** menu, choose **Start** and let the capture proceed.

3. From the **Capture** menu, choose **Stop and View**.

4. From **Frame Viewer**, choose **Display Filter** from the **Display** menu.

5. From **Display Filter** (Figure 5.16), choose to filter by the sending protocol, by source or destination address or by the frame properties and values.

6. Alternatively, you can load or edit a pre-existing filter.

7. Click **OK**.

Tip: Make sure you create a capture buffer large enough to hold the traffic you need. To save on buffer space, you can store only the part of a frame that interests you.

Figure 5.16 Network Monitor Display Filter

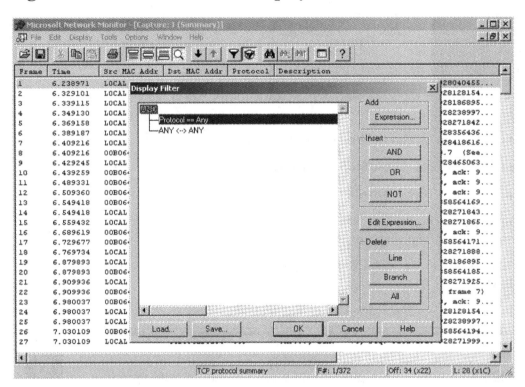

Tip: To reduce the system resources needed for monitoring, run Network Monitor in the background by choosing Dedicated Capture Mode from the Capture menu.

Network Binding Configuration

Network protocol binding is the process, used by Windows 2000, of linking network components from the different levels of the network architecture to support and control communication between those components. You can bind a component to one or more components above or below it. The services provided by a component can then be shared by all components bound to it.

Protocols can be selectively bound to all network interfaces in a multi-homed computer. The default binding order depends on the original sequence in which the protocols were installed. However, you can change the order at any time on a per-interface basis. Network services can also be selectively enabled or disabled on a per-adapter or per-protocol basis. This increases security on public interfaces directly connected to the Internet.

The bindings of installed network components are listed in order of upper-layer services and protocols to lower-layer network adapter drivers. By default, Windows 2000 enables all possible bindings between services, protocols and adapters. To optimize network bandwidth usage and connection times, order your bindings to enhance the computer's function. For example, if your workstation has both TCP/IP and NWLink installed, and most network devices use TCP/IP, the workstation should bind TCP/IP first and NWLink second. This is because protocols are accessed in the order that they are bound every time network communication is initiated, so the most frequently used protocol should be bound first.

To increase performance, you should also remove any unneeded protocols or disable the protocol binding. This would reduce traffic from connection requests, which are sent over all protocols at the same time. Another consideration is to bind the protocols that use the least amount of resources first. For example, if you have a small network whose needs can often be served equally well by NWLink or TCP/IP, bind the simpler NWLink protocol first, because it will be used to transfer files.

Since servers use the protocol sent to them by a client, the binding order should be changed on each workstation rather than on the server. To configure network bindings on Windows 2000 Professional, follow these steps:

1. From the **Start** menu, choose **Settings** and then select **Network And Dialup Connections**.

2. Right-click the connection you want to bind, and then choose **Properties**.

3. Choose **Advanced** and then select **Advanced Settings**.

4. Choose to bind to or unbind the protocol from the selected adapter, and click **OK**.

To change the binding order on Windows 2000 Professional, follow these steps:

1. From the Start menu, choose Settings and then select Network And Dialup Connections.

2. Right-click the connection you want to bind, and then choose **Properties**.

3. Choose **Advanced** and then selelct **Advanced Settings**.

4. Choose the protocol for which you want to change the binding order.

5. Use the **Up Arrow** to move the protocol higher in the binding order, and use the **Down Arrow** to move the protocol lower in the binding order.

6. Click **OK**.

Warning: Changing the network binding settings can have unexpected effects on software. Only configure network bindings if you are familiar with the needs of your software.

TCP/IP Packet Filter Configuration

TCP/IP packet filtering is an important security feature. It allows you to specify what traffic is allowed in and out of each network interface. This is based on filters defined by the source and destination IP addresses, TCP and UDP port numbers, ICMP types and codes, and IP protocol numbers.

Using IPSec Filtering

1. You can filter IP packets using IPSec. To create and configure an IP filter or other rules within a policy, follow these steps:

2. From the **Start** menu, choose **Programs, Accessories** and then selelct **Command Prompt**.

3. Type **MMC** at the command prompt and press the **Enter** key.

4. From the console tree, select the **IP Security Policy Management** snap-in.

5. Right-click the desired security policy on the right pane of the console, and choose **Properties**.

6. Choose the **Rules** property page, **Use Add Wizard**, and then select **Add**.

7. From **Welcome to the Create IP Security Rule Wizard**, choose **Next**.

8. From **Tunnel Endpoint**, specify a tunnel endpoint if desired and choose **Next**.

9. From **Network Type**, specify the network type on which the security rule is applied and choose **Next**.

10. From **Authentication Method,** specify the authentication method and choose **Next**.

11. From **IP Filter List**, choose **Use Add Wizard** and then select **Add**.

12. From **Welcome to the IP Filter Wizard**, choose **Next**.

13. From **IP Traffic Source**, specify the source address of the IP traffic, the options being **Any IP address**, your IP address, a specific DNS name, a specific IP address or a specific subnet.

14. Choose **Next**.

15. From **IP Traffic Destination**, specify the destination of the IP traffic, the options being **Any IP address**, your IP address, a specific DNS name, a specific IP address or a specific subnet.

16. Choose **Next**.

17. From **IP Protocol Type**, choose the IP Protocol types, specify the IP port and then select **Next**.

18. From **Completing the IP Filter Wizard**, choose **Finish**.

19. Choose **Close**, and **IP Filter List** reappears. Choose **Next**.

20. From **Filter Action**, choose **Use Add Wizard** and then selelct **Add**.

21. From **Welcome to the IP Security Filter Action Wizard**, choose **Next**.

22. From **Filter Action Name**, type a name and description for the filter action and choose **Next**.

23. From **Filter Action General Options**, choose to **Permit**, **Block** or **Negotiate security**, and then select **Next.**

24. From **Communicating with computers that do no support IPSec**, decide if you want to resort to ensecured communication with those computers that do not support IPSec, and choose **Next**.

25. From **IP Traffic Security**, specify a **High (Encapsulated Secure Payload)**, **Medium (Authenticated Header)** or **Custom** security method for IP traffic, and choose **Next**.

26. From **Completing the IP Security Filter Action Wizard**, choose **Finish**.

27. **Filter Action** reappears. Choose **Next**.

28. From **Completing the New Rule Wizard**, choose **Finish** and then select **Close**.

Proxy Server 2.0 Filtering

You can also configure extensive packet filtering on your Windows 2000 network using Microsoft Proxy Server 2.0, part of the Microsoft Back Office Suite. Proxy Server helps you build a secure firewall to the Internet by hiding the internal details and IP addresses of your network while increasing your Internet access speed and reducing bandwidth needs. A Windows 2000 Server running Proxy Server supports Internet connectivity while isolating your internal network by having two Network Interface Cards (NICs). One is connected to the Internet, while the other is connected to your internal network. All packets must pass through the Proxy Server software to get through the connection.

The three techniques used are:

Network Address Translation (NAT)—Windows 2000 has a limited ability to perform address translation. Using NAT can hide your actual IP address from computers beyond the device doing the translation, and can assign any IP addresses to your internal workstations and servers that you want, not necessarily official ones. Also, you can configure Proxy Server so that, to the outside world, all of the computers in your internal network appear to have the same IP address, the outside, official address of the Proxy Server.

Packet Filtering—As a gatekeeper, Proxy Server 2.0 examines each packet to see which protocol is being used and if a connection is permitted. You can also restrict access to particular external sites. Functionality can be extended with third-party plug-ins.

Caching—Proxy Server 2.0 can cache information from frequently accessed Internet sites. When users connect to the site, much of the information can be delivered from the Proxy Server. This speeds up access time and decreases WAN bandwidth usage.

The requirements of Proxy Server are:

- Two NICs, one for internal connections and the other for connection to your Internet gateway

- Minimum 12MB hard drive space for Proxy Server, plus caching room for Internet pages

- A valid IP address for your external NIC, which is on a different physical network segment from the private NIC

- Either valid IP addresses or private addresses for internal NIC and computers

To install Proxy Server on a Windows 2000 Server, follow these steps:

1. Close all applications prior to installation.

2. Obtain access to the **Microsoft Proxy Server Setup Wizard** (Mspwizi.exe) on the Microsoft Web site at www.microsoft.com/proxy.

3. Choose **Yes** to the license agreement, and at the main wizard screen, insert the Microsoft Proxy Server CD or BackOffice 4.5 CD #3, and choose **Continue**.

4. Choose **Continue**, type in the product license key, click **OK**, and click **OK**.

5. From **Installation Options**, you can change the installation location by choosing **Change Folder**.

6. Begin the installation by choosing the computer icon.

7. From **Installation Options** (Figure 5.17), choose the options you want to install; the default is to install all of the options.

8. Choose **Continue**.

Figure 5.17 Installation Options

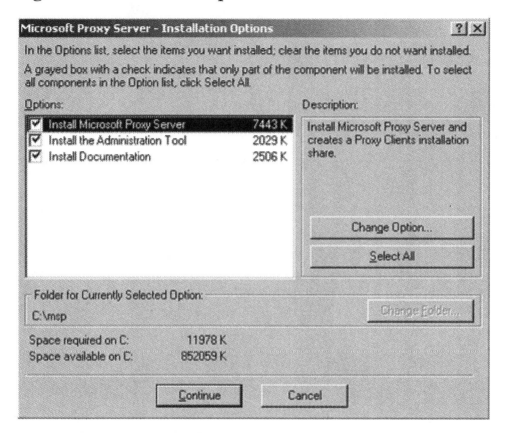

9. From **Microsoft Proxy Server Cache Drives** (Figure 5.18), enable caching, choose the size and location of the cache, and then click **OK**.

Figure 5.18 Microsoft Proxy Server Cache Drives

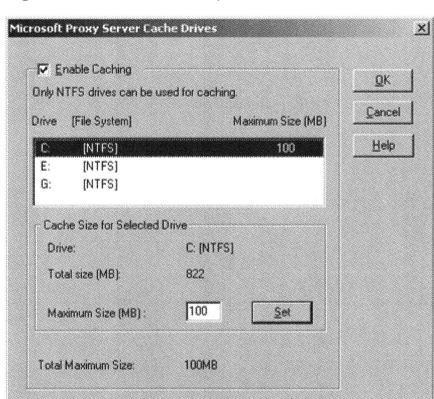

10. The default is one 100MB cache; larger networks can require 2GB or more of cache, which is best distributed across your NT file system (NTFS) volumes.

11. From within **Local Address Table Configuration**, type the IP address ranges of your local network, choose **Add** in between each address range, and then select **Construct Table**.

12. From **Construct Local Address Table**, choose **Add private ranges to the table** to add private private IP addresses.

13. To allow Windows 2000 to use the internal IP routing table, choose the NICs from which it should read, and then double-click **OK**.

14. Click **OK**, edit any errors in the **Local Address Table**, and click **OK**.

15. From **Client Installation and Configuration** (Figure 5.19), set options that define how clients connect to Proxy Server, and click **OK**.

16. The defaults are to use the client's NetBIOS name and to automatically configure the client during intitial client setup.

Figure 5.19 Client Installation and Configuration

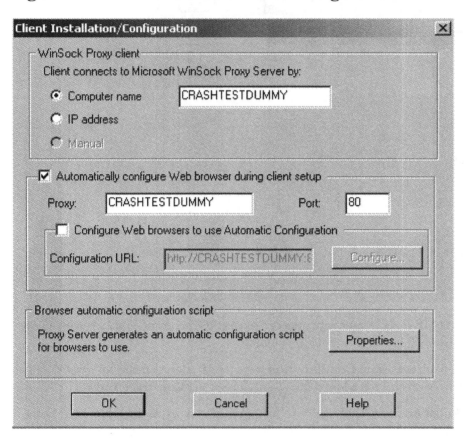

1. From **Access Control**, enable only those clients with assigned permisissions to have access to the Internet through the Proxy server and click **OK**.

2. A message appears saying packet filtering can be enabled later.

3. Click **OK**, choose **Finish** and reboot your computer.

You can use the set of predefined packet filters that come with Proxy Server 2.0 or create your own.

To implement IP packet filtering, follow these steps:

1. From the **Start** menu, choose **Programs**, **Administrative Tools** and then select **Internet Information Services**.

2. Right-click **Web Proxy**, and choose **Properties**.

3. From the **Service** property page, choose **Security** (Figure 5.20).

Figure 5.20 Web Proxy Service Property Page

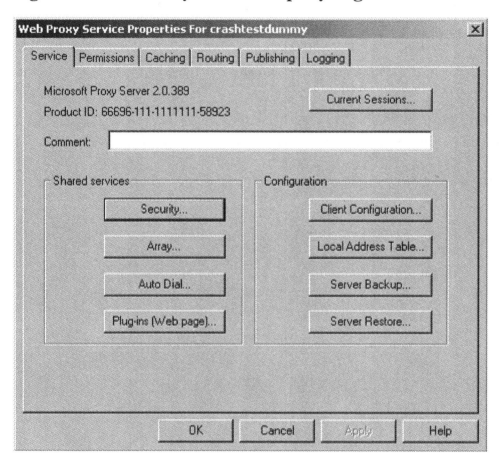

4. From **Packet Filters** (Figure 5.21) choose **Enable packet filtering on external interface**.

Figure 5.21 Packet Filters Property Page

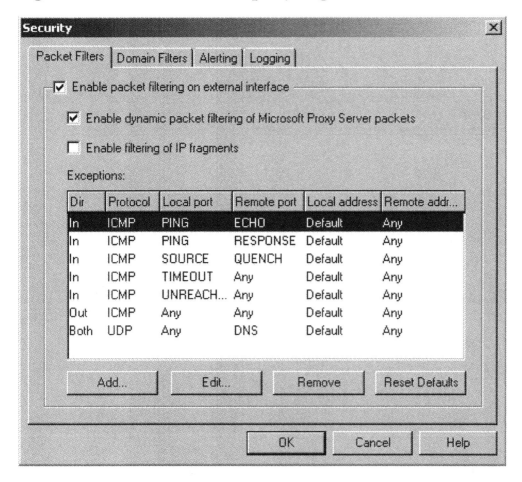

5. You can add custom packet filters to the displayed predefined packet filters by choosing **Add**, selecting the desired packet filtering options (Figure 5.22), and clicking **OK**.

6. Click **OK** to exit.

Figure 5.22 Packet Filter Properties Page

Tip: Packet filter settings are not applied to NICs that are added or enabled while Proxy services are running. You will need to reboot your computer after enabling or disabling an external network adapter to apply the filter settings; restarting Proxy services is not enough.

Options for Custom Packet Filters are described in Table 5.11.

Table 5.11 Options for Custom Packet Filters

Option	Description
Protocol ID	TCP, UDP or ICMP
Direction	Incoming, outgoing or both
Local port	Any port, a fixed port or dynamic ports
Remote port	Any port or a fixed port
Default proxy external IP addresses	Specifies the computer that exchanges packets with the remote host
Specific proxy ID	Permits a specific external interface of the proxy server to exchange packets for this custom filter
Internal computer	Allows a specific computer, normally hidden behind the proxy server, to exchange this type of packet with the remote host
Remote host	Allows the remote host to exchange this type of packet with the local host. You can choose a single host or any host.

Network Protocol Administration

Once you have installed and configured the necessary network protocols, you need to manage and troubleshoot any problems with them. System Monitor and Network Monitor are two tools useful for analyzing and troubleshooting network protocols in general.

As TCP/IP is the most complex set of enterprise networking protocols and NWLink is likely to be used only to connect to NetWare resources, you will need to become familiar with TCP/IP troubleshooting utilities.

Troubleshooting TCP/IP

Windows 2000 has a number of built-in command line utilities, described in Table 5.12, to help you troubleshoot TCP/IP.

Table 5.12 Windows 2000 TCP/IP Troubleshooting Utilities

Option	Description
PING	Verifies configuration and tests connections
ARP	Displays locally resolved IP addresses as Media Access Control (MAC) or hardware addresses
IPCONFIG	Displays the current TCP/IP configuration
NBTSTAT	Displays statistics and connections using NetBIOS over TCP/IP
NETSTAT	Displays TCP/IP protocol statistics and connections
ROUTE	Displays or modifies the local routing table
HOSTNAME	Prints the name of the host on which the command is entered
TRACERT	Checks the route to a remote system

Whenever you reconfigure TCP/IP and restart your computer, you can test the configuration and connections to other TCP/IP hosts and networks to verify functionality. Two of the more frequently used utilities are IPCONFIG and PING.

IPCONFIG—This utility verifies the TCP/IP configuration parameters on a host. You can use IPCONFIG with different switches, the most useful being All (Figure 5.23), which provides the following information:

- Host name, IP address, subnet mask, default gateway, DNS suffix and DNS servers

- If a duplicate IP address exists, the IP address and default gateway can be seen but the subnet mask is 0.0.0.0

- If the computer cannot get an IP address from the DHCP server, an IP address from the reserved private network range is displayed

Figure 5.23 IPCONFIG/ALL

```
Command Prompt                                                    _ □ x
(C) Copyright 1985-1999 Microsoft Corp.

C:\Documents and Settings\Administrator>ipconfig /all

Windows 2000 IP Configuration

        Host Name . . . . . . . . . . . . : ravetest
        Primary DNS Suffix  . . . . . . . : CRASH.CSP
        Node Type . . . . . . . . . . . . : Hybrid
        IP Routing Enabled. . . . . . . . : Yes
        WINS Proxy Enabled. . . . . . . . : No

Ethernet adapter Local Area Connection:

        Connection-specific DNS Suffix  . :
        Description . . . . . . . . . . . : Microsoft Loopback Adapter
        Physical Address. . . . . . . . . : 02-00-4C-4F-4F-50
        DHCP Enabled. . . . . . . . . . . : Yes
        Autoconfiguration Enabled . . . . : Yes
        Autoconfiguration IP Address. . . : 169.254.25.129
        Subnet Mask . . . . . . . . . . . : 255.255.0.0
        Default Gateway . . . . . . . . . :
        DNS Servers . . . . . . . . . . . :

C:\Documents and Settings\Administrator>
```

PING—If you are having network connectivity problems, you can use PING to pinpoint in which transit step the problem originates. You always PING starting from the origin of traffic to the delivery point. By default, if you can reach a remote host, the intermediary transit points are functional.

Figure 5.24 Response from PING to IBID.com

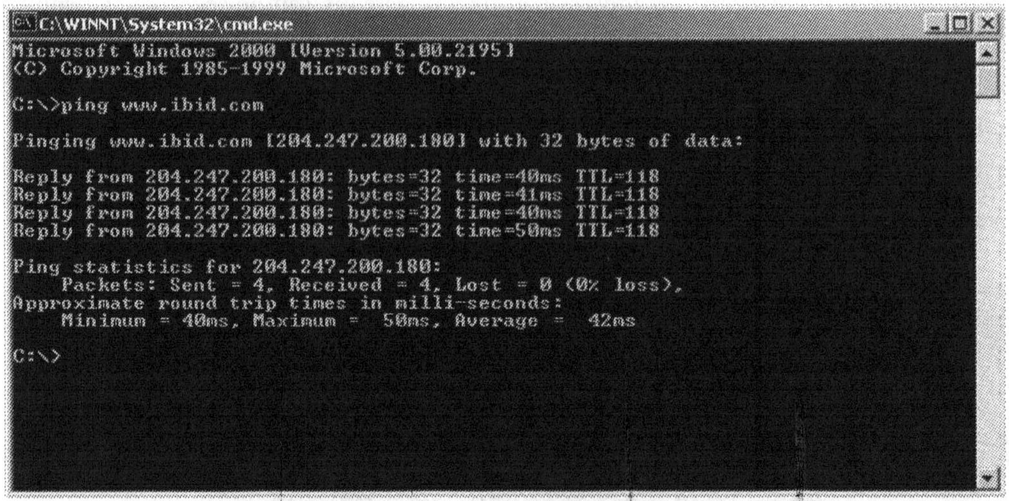

```
C:\WINNT\System32\cmd.exe                                          _ □ ✕

Microsoft Windows 2000 [Version 5.00.2195]
(C) Copyright 1985-1999 Microsoft Corp.

C:\>ping www.ibid.com

Pinging www.ibid.com [204.247.200.180] with 32 bytes of data:

Reply from 204.247.200.180: bytes=32 time=40ms TTL=118
Reply from 204.247.200.180: bytes=32 time=41ms TTL=118
Reply from 204.247.200.180: bytes=32 time=40ms TTL=118
Reply from 204.247.200.180: bytes=32 time=50ms TTL=118

Ping statistics for 204.247.200.180:
    Packets: Sent = 4, Received = 4, Lost = 0 (0% loss),
Approximate round trip times in milli-seconds:
    Minimum = 40ms, Maximum = 50ms, Average =  42ms

C:\>
```

Vocabulary

Review the following terms in preparation for the certification exam.

Term	Description
AppleTalk	The communication protocol used by Macintosh clients is AppleTalk. It must be installed on a computer running Windows 2000 Server for Macintosh clients to connect to it.
ARP	The Address Resolution Protocol is a TCP/IP protocol used to convert an IP address into a physical address.
ATM	Asynchronous Transfer Mode is a networking technology based on transferring packets of a fixed size across a fixed channel.
authentication	In network access, authentication is the process by which the system validates the user's logon information. With IPSec, authentication is the process that verifies the origin and integrity of a message by assuring the identity of each computer.
authorization	This process gives a user access to system objects based on the user's identity.
CA	A Certificate Authority issues and revokes certificates for users, services or devices. A certificate is a file that is used for authentication and secure data exchange.
DHCP	The Dynamic Host Configuration Protocol simplifies TCP/IP network configuration and dynamically configures IP addresses for clients. DHCP ensures that address conflicts do not occur by centralizing address allocation.

Term	Description
DNS	The Domain Name System is a hierarchical naming system used to locate domain names on the Internet and on private TCP/IP networks. The DNS service maps DNS domain names to IP addresses and vice-versa.
Ethernet	This is one of the most widely implemented LAN technology standards. It uses a bus or star topology
FDDI	Fiber Distributed Data Interface is a set of protocols for sending digital data over a fiber optic cable.
FQDN	The Fully Qualified Domain Name is a DNS name that uniquely identifies a computer on the network. It is a concatenation of the host name, the primary DNS suffix, and a period.
frame relay	This packet-switching protocol for connecting devices on a WAN supports data transfer across T1 and T3 lines. Although popular because of low costs, it is being replaced by the faster ATM.
ICMP	The Internet Control Message Protocol supports packets containing error, control and informational messages.
IGMP	The Internet Group Management Protocol supports multicasting, a limited form of broadcasting in which clients having a multicast IP address can message a whole group within an intranet.
IP	The Internet Protocol is the routable protocol in the TCP/IP suite that is responsible for the IP addressing, routing, and fragmentation and re-assembly of IP packets.
IP filter	An IP filter is a subset of potential network traffic based on the IP address, port and transport protocol. The IP filter secures both outbound and inbound traffic.
IP filter list	An IP filter list is a combination of one or more IP filters defining a range of network traffic.

Term	Description
IP filter list	An IP filter list is a combination of one or more IP filters defining a range of network traffic.
IPSec	A set of standard, cryptography-based protection services and protocols, Internet Protocol Security protects all protocols in the TCP/IP suite and Internet communications using Layer 2 Tunneling Protocol (L2TP).
IPX	The Internetwork Packet Exchange is the NetWare protocol that controls addressing and routing of packets within and between LANs.
IPX/SPX	The Internetwork Packet Exchange/Sequenced Packet Exchange is Novell NetWare's networking protocol. Microsoft has its own version of IPX/SPX called NWLink.
Kerberos	The default user and host authentication protocol for Windows 2000. Internet Protocol security uses the Kerberos protocol for authentication.
LAN	A Local Area Network is a communications network connecting computers, printers, and other devices within a limited area.
LMHOSTS	This static file is used for name resolution. It maps NetBIOS (computer) names to IP addresses.
MAC address	The Media Access Control address is used for communication between network adapters on the same subnet. Each network adapter has an associated MAC address.
MMC	The Microsoft Management Console provides a common interface for many Windows 2000 tools, including Proxy Server.

Term	Description
NAT	The Network Address Translation protocol allows a network with private addresses to access information on the Internet through an IP translation process.
NetBEUI	Microsoft's networking protocol for small LANs is NetBIOS Enhanced User Interface.
NetBIOS name	A name recognized by WINS, the service that maps a computer name to its IP address.
NetBT	NetBIOS over TCP/IP is a feature that provides the NetBIOS programming interface over the TCP/IP protocol. It is used for monitoring routed servers that use NetBIOS name resolution.
Network Monitor	This Windows 2000 Server utility captures and displays statistics about frames that it receives from the LAN.
NIC	A Network Interface Card is the expansion board you insert into a computer so it can be connected to a network. NICs are usually designed for a particular network, protocol and media.
NWLink	Novell's transport protocol that supports routing and client-server applications is Microsoft's implementation of IPX/SPX
OSI Reference Model	This standard for communications defines a networking framework for implementing protocols in seven layers.
protocol stack	A protocol suite or stack, is a combination of protocols that work together to achieve network communication.

Term	Description
Proxy Server 2.0	Part of Microsoft's BackOffice suite, Proxy Server separates your internal network from the Internet. It hides the internal IP addresses of your network while increasing your Internet access speed through caching.
public key	Public key technology is a method of cryptography in which two keys are used: a public key for encrypting data and a private key for decrypting data.
rule	A rule is a combination of the various IPSec components that protects a specific subset of network traffic. You can have multiple rules for different traffic subsets.
serial link	A serial WAN link transfers data sequentially.
SMS	Systems Management Server is a Microsoft product that assists in managing computers connected to a LAN.
SNAP	Sub Network Access Protocol specifies a type of data frame similar to Ethernet 802.2., which defaults to 802.2
System Monitor	This utility tracks different processes and objects on a Windows 2000 computer in real time.
TCP	The Transmission Control Protocol enables two hosts to establish a connection and exchange data that is guaranteed.
TCP/IP	The Transmission Control Protocol/Internet Protocol is a set of protocols that provides communication among diverse networks. Since it accommodates different architectures and operating systems, TCP/IP is the most commonly used Internet protocol.

Term	Description
TCP/IP Reference Model	This communications standard for different versions of TCP/IP calls for implementing TCP/IP in four layers.
token ring	This popular LAN technology has computers arranged in a logical circle. The computer that has possession of the token is able to send messages.
UDP	A User Datagram Protocol is a TCP/IP component that transmits data through a connectionless service but does not guarantee the delivery or sequencing delivery of sent packets.
WAN	A Wide Area Network is a computer network that spans a large geographical area. It usually consists of two or more LANs.
WINS	The Windows Internet Naming Service is a Microsoft software service that dynamically maps IP addresses to computer names. This allows users to access resources by name instead of by IP address.
Winsock	Windows Socket is an Application Programming Interface for developing Windows programs that can communicate with other computers through TCP/IP.

In Brief

If you want to...	Then do this...
Install TCP/IP	1. From the **Start** menu, choose **Settings** and then select **Network and Dial-up Connections**.
	2. From **Network and Dial up Connections**, right-click the connection for which you want to install TCP/IP, and choose **Properties**.
	3. Choose **Install**, highlight **Protocols**, and then select **Add**.
	4. From **Select Network Protocol**, highlight **Internet Protocol (TCP/IP)** and click **OK**.
	5. Check that **Internet Protocol (TCP/IP)** is selected and click **OK**.
Configure TCP/IP	1. From the **Start** menu, choose **Settings, Network and Dial-up Connections**, and then select **Local Area Connection**.
	2. From **Local Area Connection Status**, choose **Properties**.
	3. Highlight **Internet Protocol (TCP/IP)** and choose **Properties**.
	4. From the **General** property page, select the method of obtaining an IP address and a DNS server address.
	5. Choose **Advanced** to specify a default gateway, a DNS name resolution method, WINS servers addresses, and security and filtering options, and click **OK**.

If you want to...	Then do this...
Install NWLink	1. From the **Start** menu, choose **Settings**, select **Control Panel**, and double-click **Network and Dial-up Connections**.
	2. Right-click the desired local area network connection, and choose **Properties**.
	3. From the **General** property page, choose **Install.**
	4. Highlight **Protocol**, and choose **Add**.
	5. Choose NWLink IPX/SPX NetBIOS Compatible Transport Protocol from the protocol list, and click OK.
Configure NWLink	1. From the **Start** menu, choose **Settings**, select **Control Panel**, and double-click **Network and Dial-up Connections**.
	2. Right-click the desired local area network connection, and choose **Properties**.
	3. Highlight **NWLink IPX/SPX/NetBIOS Compatible Transport Protocol** and choose **Properties**.
	4. Within the **General** property page, you can type an internal IPX network number.
	5. If you want to manually configure the framing type that Windows 2000 uses for IPX packets, choose **Manual frame type detection**, **Add**, and type the appropriate framing information and IPX nework numbers.
	6. Click **OK**.

If you want to...	Then do this...
Add the IPSec snap-in to the MMC	1. From the **Start** menu, choose **Programs**, **Accessories** and then select **Command Prompt**.
	2. Type **MMC** at the command prompt and press the **Enter** key.
	3. From the console menu, choose **Add/Remove Snap-in**, and then select **Add**.
	4. Choose **IP Security Policy Managment** from the list of snap-ins, and then select **Add**.
	5. From **Select Computer**, choose the range of computers the snap-in will manage, whether the local computer only, the local computer's domain, another domain, or another computer, and then select **Finish**.
Create an IPSec policy	1. From the **Start** menu, choose **Programs**, **Accessories** and then select **Command Prompt**.
	2. Type **MMC** at the command prompt and press the **Enter** key.
	3. From the console tree, choose the **IP Security Policy Management** snap-in.
	4. Right-click **IP Security Policies on Local Machine**, and then choose **Create IP Security Policy**.
	5. From **Welcome to the IP Security Policy Wizard**, and then choose **Next**.
	6. Type a policy name and description, and then choose **Next**.
	7. From **Requests for Secure Communication**, choose **Activate the default response rule** to have the policy allow negotiation with computers requesting IPSec.
	8. Choose **Next**.

If you want to...	Then do this...
Create an IPSec policy	9. If you have enabled **Activate the default response rule**, from **Default Response Rule Authentication Method** choose the authentication method and then select **Next**.
	10. From **Completing the IP Security Policy Wizard**, choose **Finish**.
Install Network Monitor	1. From the **Start** menu, choose **Settings** and then select **Control Panel**.
	2. Double-click **Add/Remove Programs**, and choose **Add/Remove Windows Components**.
	3. Highlight **Management and Monitoring Tools**, choose **Details, Network Monitor Tools** and then click **OK**.
	4. Choose **Next**, and then from the **Completing the Windows Components Wizard**, select **Finish**.
Load a Network Monitor capture filter	1. From the **Start** menu, choose **Programs, Administrative Tools**, and then select **Network Monitor**.
	2. From the **Capture** menu, choose **Filter**.
	3. From **Capture Filter**, choose to filter by protocol, by address or by data pattern.
	4. Alternatively, you can load or edit a pre-existing filter.
	5. Click **OK**.
Load a Network Monitor display filter	1. From the **Start** menu, choose **Programs, Administrative Tools**, and then select **Network Monitor**.
	2. From the **Capture** menu, choose **Start** and let the capture proceed.

If you want to...	Then do this...
Load a Network Monitor display filter	3. From the **Capture** menu, choose **Stop and View**.
	4. From **Frame Viewer**, choose **Display Filter** from the **Display** menu.
	5. From **Display Filter**, choose to filter by the sending protocol, by source or destination address or by the frame properties and values.
	6. Alternatively, you can load or edit a pre-existing filter.
	7. Click **OK**.
Configure network bindings on Windows 2000 Professional	1. From the **Start** menu, choose **Settings** and then select **Network And Dialup Connections**.
	2. Right-click the connection you want to bind, and then choose **Properties**.
	3. Choose **Advanced** and then select **Advanced Settings**.
	4. Choose to bind to or unbind the protocol from the selected adapter, and then click **OK**.

If you want to...	Then do this...
Change the network binding order on Windows 2000 Professional	1. From the **Start** menu, choose **Settings** and then select **Network and Dialup Connections**.
	2. Right-click the connection you want to bind, and choose **Properties**.
	3. Choose **Advanced** and then select **Advanced Settings**.
	4. Choose the protocol for which you want to change the binding order.
	5. Use the **Up Arrow** to move the protocol higher in the binding order, and use the **Down Arrow** to move the protocol lower in the binding order.
	6. Click **OK**.
To create and configure rules within an IPSec policy	1. From the **Start** menu, choose **Programs**, **Accessories** and then select **Command Prompt**.
	2. Type **MMC** at the command prompt and press the **Enter** key.
	3. From the console tree, choose the **IP Security Policy Management** snap-in.
	4. Right-click the desired security policy on the right pane of the console, and then choose **Properties**.
	5. Choose the **Rules** property page, **Use Add Wizard**, and then select **Add**.

If you want to...	Then do this...
	6. From **Welcome to the Create IP Security Rule Wizard**, choose **Next**.
	7. From **Tunnel Endpoint**, specify an endpoint and then choose **Next**.
	8. From **Network Type**, specify the network type on which the security rule is applied and then choose **Next**.
	9. From **Authentication Method,** specify the authentication method and then choose **Next**.
	10. From **IP Filter List**, choose **Use Add Wizard** and then select **Add**.
	11. From **Welcome to the IP Filter Wizard**, choose **Next**.
	12. From **IP Traffic Source**, specify the source address of the IP traffic, the options being **Any IP address**, your IP address, a specific DNS name, a specific IP address or a specific subnet.
	13. Choose **Next**.
	14. From **IP Traffic Destination**, specify the destination of the IP traffic, the options being **Any IP address**, your IP address, a specific DNS name, a specific IP address or a specific subnet.
	15. Choose **Next**.
	16. From **IP Protocol Type**, choose the IP Protocol types, specify the IP port and then select **Next**.
	17. From **Completing the IP Filter Wizard**, choose **Finish**.
	18. Choose **Close**, and when **IP Filter List** reappears, and then select **Next**.
	19. From **Filter Action**, choose **Use Add Wizard** and then select **Add**.

If you want to...	Then do this...
	20. From **Welcome to the IP Security Filter Action Wizard**, choose **Next**.
	21. From within **Filter Action Name**, type a name and description for the filter action and then choose **Next**.
	22. From **Filter Action General Options**, choose to **Permit**, **Block** or **Negotiate security**, and then select **Next**.
	23. From **Communicating with computers that do not support IPSec**, decide if you want to resort to unsecured communication with those computers that do not support IPSec, and then choose **Next**.
	24. From **IP Traffic Security**, specify a **High (Encapsulated Secure Payload)**, **Medium (Authenticated Header)** or **Custom** security method for IP traffic, and then choose **Next**.
	25. From **Completing the IP Security filter action Wizard**, choose **Finish**.
	26. **Filter Action** reappears. Choose **Next**.
	27. From **Completing the New Rule Wizard**, choose **Finish** and then select **Close**.

If you want to...	Then do this...
Install Proxy Server 2.0 on Windows 2000 Server	1. Close all applications prior to installation.
	2. Obtain access to the **Microsoft Proxy Server Setup Wizard** (Mspwizi.exe) on the Microsoft Web site at www.microsoft.com/proxy.
	3. Choose **Yes** to the license agreement, and at the main wizard screen, insert the Microsoft Proxy Server CD or BackOffice 4.5 CD #3, and then select **Continue**.
	4. Choose **Continue**, type in the product license key, click **OK**, and click **OK**.
	5. From **Installation Options**, you can change the installation location by choosing **Change Folder**.
	6. Begin the installation by choosing the computer icon.
	7. From **Installation Options**, choose the options you want to install; the default is to install all of the options.
	8. Choose **Continue**.
	9. From **Microsoft Proxy Server Cache Drives**, enable caching, choose the size and location of the cache, and click **OK**.
	10. The default is one 100MB cache; larger networks can require 2GB or more of cache, which is best distributed across your NTFS volumes.

If you want to...	Then do this...
	11. From within **Local Address Table Configuration**, type the IP address ranges of your local network, choose **Add** in between each address range, and then select **Construct Table**.
	12. From **Construct Local Address Table**, choose **Add private ranges to the table** to add private IP addresses.
	13. To allow Windows 2000 to use the internal IP routing table, choose the NICs from which it should read, and click **OK**.
	14. Click **OK**, edit any errors in the **Local Address Table**, and click **OK**.
	15. From **Client Installation and Configuration**, set options that define how clients connect to Proxy Server, and click **OK**.
	16. The defaults are to use the client's NetBIOS name and to automatically configure the client during intitial client setup.
	17. From **Access Control**, enable only those clients with assigned permisissions to have access to the Internet through the Proxy server and click **OK**.
	18. A message appears saying packet filtering can be enabled later.
	19. Click **OK**, choose **Finish** and reboot your computer.

Implement Proxy Server 2.0 packet filtering	1.	From the **Start** menu, choose **Programs, Administrative Tools** and then select **Internet Information Services**.
	2.	Right-click **Web Proxy**, and choose **Properties**.
	3.	From the **Service** property page, choose **Security**.
	4.	From **Packet Filters** choose **Enable packet filtering on external interface**.
	5.	You can add custom packet filters to the displayed predefined packet filters by choosing **Add**, choosing the desired packet filtering options, and clicking **OK**.
	6.	Click **OK** to exit.
Troubleshoot TCP/IP	Use the following Windows 2000 built-in command line utilities:
	1.	PING verifies configuration and tests connections
	2.	ARP displays locally resolved IP addresses as MAC or hardware addresses
	3.	IPCONFIG displays the current TCP/IP configuration
	4.	NBTSTAT displays statistics and connections using NetBIOS over TCP/IP
	5.	NETSTAT displays TPC/IP protocol statistics and connections
	6.	ROUTE displays or modifies the local routing table
	7.	HOSTNAME prints the name of the host on which the command is entered
	8.	TRACERT checks the route to a remote system

Lesson 5 Activities

Complete the following activities to better prepare you for the certification exam.

1. Compare Windows 2000 System Monitor with Network Monitor.

2. Describe how you would make an IPSec policy functional after creating it with the IP Security Policy Wizard.

3. Explain how you would monitor network traffic on a remote subnet of your network.

4. Compare the OSI Reference Model with the TCP/IP Reference Model.

5. Explain the differences between an IP filter, an IP filter list and a filter action.

6. You are having problems connecting to a remote computer using TCP/IP. Describe some command-line utilities you could use.

7. Describe the function of Proxy Server 2.0.

8. Explain the purpose of a network performance baseline.

9. Describe the information found in the four panes of the Network Monitor Capture window.

10. Define network binding.

Answers to Lesson 5 Activities

1. Windows 2000 System Monitor replaces Windows NT 4.0 Performance Monitor. It allows you to track both network and system activity with one tool, and it can be installed and accessed like any other MMC snap-in. It has two components: the System Monitor, which provides a real-time graphical interpretation of system function, and the related logging function called Performance Logs and Alerts. The System Monitor has objects for network performance data at each layer of the OSI model, including transmission rates and packet queue lengths.

   Windows 2000 Network Monitor, on the other hand, focuses on capturing and displaying statistics about the frames that a server receives from the LAN. With this information you can analyze network traffic and troubleshoot networking problems. Network Monitor watches traffic only on the local network segment. Like System Monitor, Network Monitor can be installed and accessed as an MMC snap-in.

2. You need to create rules that govern when and how security is applied to the IPSec policy after creating the policy with the IP Security Policy Wizard. You can create rules either by using other wizards or by right-clicking a policy on the console and choosing Properties.

3. Network Monitor watches traffic only on the local network segment. If you would like to monitor remote traffic, you need to use the version of Network Monitor that ships with Microsoft System Management Server (SMS) version 1.2 or 2.0. Alternatively, you can purchase a third party sniffer tool that supports more sophisticated monitoring of a wider array of counters along multiple network segments.

4. The Open Systems Interconnection (OSI) Reference Model is a seven-layer standard that presents a layered approach to networking. Each layer of the model is responsible for a different part of the communication process. The model simplifies how network hardware and software work together and helps in troubleshooting by defining how components should function. The OSI Reference Model is a general model followed by most networking protocols.

   On the other hand, the TCP/IP Reference Model is a four-layer model that specifically describes how the TCP/IP protocol stack functions. Microsoft's implementation of TCP/IP maps to the TCP/IP Reference Model instead of to the OSI Reference Model.

5. An IP filter is a subset of potential network traffic based on the IP address, port and transport protocol. The IP filter secures both outbound and inbound traffic. An IP filter list is a combination of one or more IP filters defining a range of network traffic. A filter action component describes how the IPSec driver should secure network traffic.

6. You can use the following Windows 2000 built-in command line utilities to help you troubleshoot TCP/IP connection difficulties:

    *   PING verifies configuration and tests connections

    *   ARP displays locally resolved IP addresses as MAC or hardware addresses

    *   IPCONFIG displays the current TCP/IP configuration

    *   NBTSTAT displays statistics and connections using NetBIOS over TCP/IP

    *   NETSTAT displays TPC/IP protocol statistics and connections

    *   ROUTE displays or modifies the local routing table

    *   HOSTNAME prints the name of the host on which the command is entered

    *   TRACERT checks the route to a remote system

7. Proxy Server 2.0 is part of the Microsoft Back Office Suite. Proxy Server helps you build a secure firewall to the Internet by hiding the internal details and IP addresses of your network while increasing your Internet access speed and reducing bandwidth needs. A Windows 2000 Server running Proxy Server supports Internet connectivity while isolating your internal network by having two NICS, one of which is connected to the Internet, while the other is connected to your internal network. You can configure extensive packet filtering on your Windows 2000 network using Proxy Server. All packets must pass through the Proxy software to get through the connection.

8. Network activity can affect the performance of your system as a whole. However, you cannot detect anomalies in network traffic without having a baseline of regular activity to compare it with. To create a baseline of the level of performance you expect under typical workloads and usage, you would monitor objects over a period of time ranging from days to weeks, depending on the object.

    You would then monitor traffic on a regular basis. By comparing the baseline performance with the most recent performance, you can identify performance trends indicating impending problems or the need for changes to your network infrastructure. When you have performance data that does not compare with baseline values, you can investigate the problem.

9. The Network Monitor Capture window has four panes displaying frame statistics:

    *   Graph shows the total capture statistics of current network activity

- Session Statistics shows the statistics on a current communication session between two participants

- Station Statistics shows the statistics on communication from or to the local computer

- Total Statistics shows statistics on overall network activity from the time the current capture began

10. Network protocol binding is the process of linking network components from the different levels of the network architecture to support and control communication between those components. You can bind a component to one or more components above or below it. The services provided by a component can then be shared by all components bound to it.

Protocols can be selectively bound to all network interfaces in a multi-homed computer. The default binding order depends on the original sequence in which the protocols were installed. However, you can change the order at any time on a per-interface basis. Network services can also be selectively enabled or disabled on a per-adapter or per-protocol basis.

The bindings of installed network components are listed in order of upper-layer services and protocols to lower-layer network adapter drivers. By default, Windows 2000 enables all possible bindings between services, protocols and adapters.

Lesson 5 Quiz

These questions test your knowledge of features, vocabulary, procedures, and syntax.

1. Which of the following protocols converts an IP address into a physical address?
    A. ICMP
    B. ARP
    C. UDP
    D. IP

2. You want to improve the connectivity speed on your multiple protocol network. What can you do?
    A. Change the protocol binding order on the servers
    B. Change the protocol binding order on the domain controllers
    C. Change the protocol binding order on the workstations
    D. Remove unneeded protocols

3. You need to connect to a mixture of NetWare 3.11 and NetWare 4.11 computers on your Ethernet network. How do you configure the frame type on NWLink?
    A. NWLink automatically detects the 802.3 frame type only
    B. NWLink automatically detects the 802.2 frame type only
    C. NWLink automatically detects the 802.2 and 802.3 frame types and will support both
    D. Manually configure the frame type

4. Which of the following can help you troubleshoot TCP/IP problems?
    A. TRACERT
    B. NBTSTAT
    C. IPCONFIG
    D. PING

5. Which of the following protocols supports multicasting?
    A. ICMP
    B. IGMP
    C. TCP
    D. NetBT

6. You want to reduce the administrative burden of TCP/IP on your enterprise network. Which of the following do you implement?
   A. DNS
   B. DHCP
   C. LMHOSTS
   D. WINS

7. Besides data, what does each packet contain?
   A. Source address of the sending computer
   B. Destination address of the receiving computer
   C. Headers from each protocol used to send the frame
   D. A trailer verifying frame integrity

8. Which of the following are predefined IPSec policies?
   A. Secure Server (Require Security)
   B. Server (Request Security)
   C. Client (Request Security)
   D. Client (Respond Only)

9. How can you reduce the resources needed to support a Network Monitor capture?
   A. Use Network Monitor only when you encounter problems
   B. Use Dedicated Capture Mode
   C. Use a capture filter
   D. Use a display filter

10. What is the Windows 2000 IPSec default authentication response rule?
   A. Kerberos v5 protocol
   B. A certificate from a CA
   C. A pre-shared key
   D. No authentication needed

Answers to Lesson 5 Quiz

1. Answer B is correct. The Address Resolution Protocol (ARP) converts an IP address into a physical address. A host wanting to know a physical address broadcasts an ARP request that the host with the requested IP address answers with its physical or MAC address.

    Answer A is incorrect. The Internet control Message Protocol (ICMP) supports packets containing error, control and informational messages.

    Answer C is incorrect. The User Datagram Protocol (UDP) is a connectionless protocol that does not guarantee packet delivery. It is used primarily for sending broadcast messages over the network.

    Answer D is incorrect. The Internet Protocol (IP) specifies the packet format and addressing scheme, but does not guarantee packet arrival or the correct packet sequence.

2. Answers C and D are correct. Because protocols are accessed in the order that they are bound every time network communication is initiated, the most frequently used protocol should be bound first to speed up connectivity. Servers use the protocol sent to them by a client, so the binding order should be changed on each workstation rather than on the server. To increase performance, you should also remove any unneeded protocols or disable the protocol binding. This would reduce traffic from connection requests, which are sent over all protocols at the same time.

    Answer A is incorrect. Servers use the protocol sent to them by a client, so the binding order should be changed on each workstation rather than on the server.

    Answer B is incorrect. Domain controllers use the protocol sent to them by a client, so the binding order should be changed on each workstation rather than on the domain controller.

3. Answer D is correct. On Ethernet networks, the standard frame type for NetWare 3.11 is 802.3, while newer versions of NetWare have the standard frame type of 802.2. NWLink automatically detects the frame type when loaded. If multiple frame types are detected in addition to the 802.2 frame type, NWLink defaults to the 802.2 frame type. So if you want NWLink to support communication from both NetWare 3.11 and NetWare 4.11 computers, you need to manually configure the frame type.

    Answer A is incorrect. NWLink can detect both the 802.2 and 802.3 frame types.

    Answer B is incorrect. NWLink can detect both the 802.2 and 802.3 frame types.

Answer C is incorrect. While NWLink can detect both the 802.2 and 802.3 frame types, it will not automatically support both. Instead, NWLink defaults to the 802.2 frame type. To support multiple frame types simultaneously, you need to manually configure the frame type.

4. Answers A, B, C and D are all correct. All of these built-in Windows 2000 command line utilities can help you troubleshoot TCP/IP problems. TRACERT checks the route to a remote computer, NBTSTAT displays statistics and connections using NetBIOS over TCP/IP, IPCONFIG displays the current TCP/IP configuration, and PING verifies a configuration and tests connections.

5. Answer B is correct. The Internet Group Management Protocol (IGMP) supports multicasting, a limited form of broadcasting in which clients having a multicast IP address can message a whole group within an intranet.

   Answer A is incorrect. The Internet Control Message Protocol (ICMP) supports packets containing error, control and informational messages.

   Answer C is incorrect. The Transmission Control Protocol (TCP) provides connection packet delivery, so that both the delivery of data and the order in which the packets are delivered are guaranteed.

   Answer D is incorrect. NetBIOS over TCP/IP (NetBT) provides a standard interface for NetBIOS services as well as interactions between NetBIOS-based applications and TCP/IP protocols.

6. Answers A, B and D are correct. The Domain Name Service (DNS) is a distributed database of host and domain name to IP address mappings. DNS provides name resolution services for TCP/IP client applications. Each DNS server is responsible for maintaining a database of mappings for its LAN, and is usually configured to contact other DNS servers when it cannot find a mapping requested by a client. The Dynamic Host Configuration Protocol (DHCP) is the Microsoft service that provides automatic configuration of an IP address, a subnet mask, a default gateway, and DNS or WINS server addresses for Windows clients. It supports centralized IP address management. The Windows Internet Naming Service (WINS) dynamically resolves NetBIOS names to IP addresses. You need WINS in a mixed network environment where computers are running legacy versions of Windows and NetBIOS computer names need to be resolved for communication. WINS clients register their name and corresponding IP address with a WINS server. Whenever the client's IP addressing information changes, the client sends updated information to the WINS database. When a WINS client wants to communicate with another network resource, it issues a NetBIOS name query request to the WINS server. The WINS server

looks for the relevant NetBIOS name / IP address mapping for the destination resource in its database, and returns the IP address to the client.

Answer C is incorrect. An LMHOSTS file mapping NetBIOS (computer) names to IP addresses can be imported and used to perform name resolution. However, because LMHOSTS files are static, it can be an administrative burden to keep an LMHOSTS file current. This is not compensated by the small reduction in network traffic offered by an LMHOSTS file. LMHOSTS files are best reserved for small, relatively static networks.

7. Answers A, B, C and D are all correct. Each frame contains the source address of the sending computer, the destination address of the receiving computer, headers from each protocol used to send the frame and a trailer verifying frame integrity. You can use these frame components to create capture or data filters on Network Monitor.

8. Answers A, B and D are correct. Three predefined IPSec policies are available to be used as they are, or they can be changed to suit your particular needs. The Secure Server (Require Security) policy protects all outbound and inbound transmissions. The Server (Request Security) policy protects all outbound transmissions; unsecured inbound transmissions are accepted but not resolved until IPSec requests security from the sender. It is used on both clients and servers to initiate secure communications. The Client (Respond Only) policy ensures that if security is requested by the server, the client will respond by securing the requested protocol and port traffic with that server.

Answer C is incorrect. A Client (Request Security) policy does not exist.

9. Answers B and C are correct. To reduce the system resources needed for monitoring, run Network Monitor in the background by choosing Dedicated Capture Mode from the Capture menu. You can also use a capture filter to save only the part of a frame that interests you, saving buffer space in the process.

Answer A is incorrect. You should use Network Monitor on a regular basis to detect anomalies from the baseline performance as well as to identify performance trends indicating impending problems or need for network infrastructure changes.

Answer D is incorrect. A display filter allows you to see a subset of captured data, which needed network resources to be gathered and is using network resources currently to be saved.

10. Answers A, B and C are all correct. Kerberos v5 is the Windows 2000 default authentication protocol and is supported only on computers that are members of a domain. Use a certificate from this Certificate Authority (CA) is a response rule option that supports a chosen public-key

authentication. Use this string to protect the key exchange (pre-shared key) allows you to type in a pre-shared key known to the requesting computer for key exchange.

Answer D is incorrect. No authentication needed is not a response rule option.

WINS Installation and Administration

The Windows Internet Naming Service (WINS) dynamically resolves Network Basic Input/Output System (NetBIOS) or computer names to Internet Protocol (IP) addresses. You will need WINS in a mixed network environment, where computers are running legacy versions of Windows and NetBIOS computer names will need to be resolved for communication.

WINS clients register their name and corresponding IP address with a WINS server. These clients can then query the WINS servers to locate and communicate with other Windows resources on the network.

After completing this lesson, you should have a better understanding of the following topics:

- WINS Overview

- WINS Server Configuration

- WINS Clients Configuration

- WINS Replication Configuration

- Non-WINS Clients Support

- WINS Monitoring

- WINS Database Maintenance

WINS Overview

Every WINS client is configured with the Internet Protocol (IP) address of a primary WINS server, and for redundancy, a secondary WINS server. IP is the routable protocol in the Transmission Control Protocol/Internet Protocol (TCP/IP) suite responsible for the IP addressing, routing, and fragmentation and reassembly of IP packets. TCP/IP is the collection of communications protocols used to connect hosts on the Internet. Each time a WINS client boots up, it registers its current NetBIOS name and IP address mapping with the database on the designated WINS server. The client also sends updated information to the WINS database whenever its IP addressing information changes. A WINS server only registers NetBIOS names on a temporary basis, so a WINS client must renew its name periodically or the lease will expire.

When the WINS client wants to communicate with another network resource, it first checks its NetBIOS name cache for the NetBIOS name/IP address mapping of the destination computer. If it cannot resolve the name from its cache, the WINS client issues a NetBIOS name query request to the primary WINS server. The primary WINS server looks for the relevant NetBIOS name/IP address mapping for the destination resource in its database, and returns the IP address to the client.

If a WINS client fails after three attempts to find the primary WINS server, it will try to access the secondary WINS server. If the secondary WINS server also proves inaccessible, the client generates three broadcast messages on the local network. If the NetBIOS name is found on the local network, the name is then resolved to an IP address. This WINS name resolution process is shown in Figure 6.1.

Figure 6.1 WINS Name Resolution Process

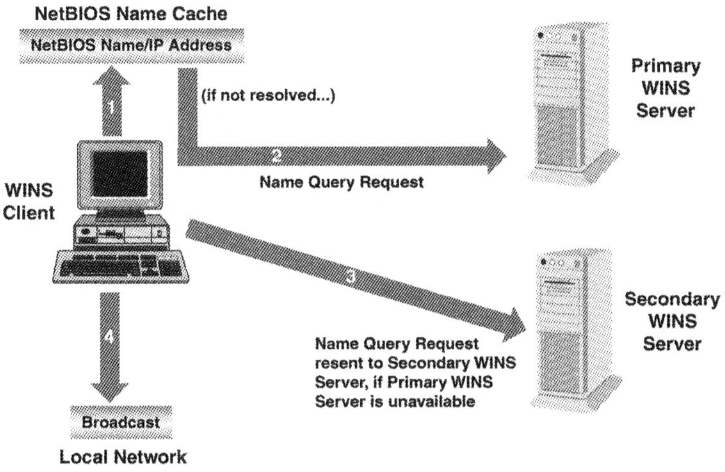

Determining Need for WINS

Before installing WINS on your network, you need to determine if you need the service. While most large networks need WINS to provide NetBIOS name resolution for Windows clients, WINS is unnecessary for the following network infrastructures:

- All the network clients are configured to use another method of name resolution, such as the Domain Name System (DNS), which locates hierarchical domain names on the Internet and on private TCP/IP networks

- There are fewer than 50 clients, all on one subnet, so clients can resolve NetBIOS names by broadcast

---

Note: Broadcast messages cannot cross routers by default, and they generate too much network traffic on networks with more than 50 clients.

Configuring WINS Servers

Before you install WINS, configure the TCP/IP settings for WINS on your server by following these steps:

1. From the **Start** menu, choose **Settings, Network and Dial-up Connections**, and **Local Area Connection**.

2. Choose **Properties**, highlight **Internet Protocol (TCP/IP)**, and select **Properties**.

3. Configure the server to use a static IP address, or make sure there is an address reservation for your server configured on the Dynamic Host Configuration Protocol (DHCP) server, which dynamically configures IP addresses for clients.

4. Configure a subnet mask and default gateway.

5. Choose **Advanced** and the **WINS** property page (Figure 6.2).

Figure 6.2 TCP/IP WINS Property Page

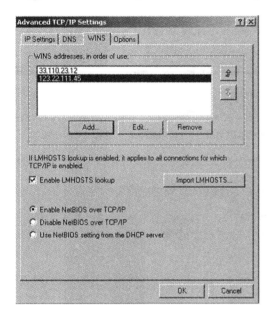

6. Highlight all WINS servers listed on the page and choose Remove to make sure your WINS server registers its address with itself, rather than with another WINS server.

7. Choose **Add** and type the IP address of your own server.

8. Click **OK** three times and choose **Close** to exit.

Installing and Configuring WINS

To install WINS, follow these steps:

1. From the **Start** menu, choose **Settings** and **Control Panel**.

2. Double-click **Add/Remove Programs** and choose **Add/Remove Windows Components** to launch the **Windows Components Wizard**.

3. Highlight **Networking Services**, and choose **Details**.

4. From **Networking Services**, choose **Windows Internet Naming Service (WINS)** and click **OK**.

5. Choose **Next** and, from **Completing the Windows Components Wizard**, select **Finish**.

Warning: Do not install WINS on a multi-homed server. This will cause problems in the replication of a WINS database with databases from other WINS servers.

After installing WINS on a server, you can configure the four property pages:

General—On this page (Figure 6.3), you choose the frequency with which you want to update statistics. You can also type the default database backup path, and choose to back up the database during a server shutdown.

Figure 6.3 WINS General Property Page

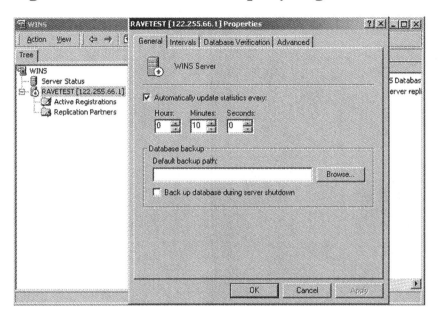

Intervals—On this page (Figure 6.4), you can set the rate at which WINS database records are renewed, deleted and verified.

Figure 6.4 WINS Intervals Property Page

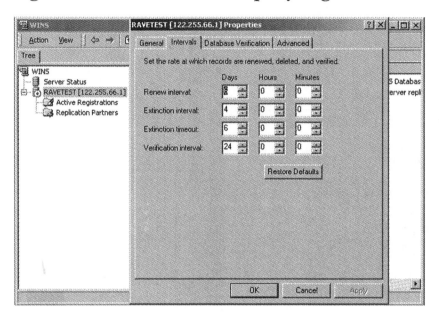

Database verification—On this page (Figure 6.5), you can verify the WINS database consistency at a specific time interval and at a specified time. You can also set the maximum number of records to verify at each interval, and verify the records with the servers who own a particular record or against randomly selected partners.

Figure 6.5 WINS Database Verification Property Page

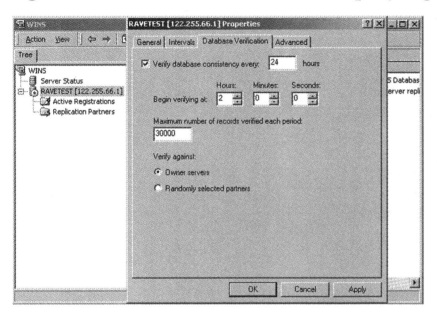

Advanced—On this page (Figure 6.6), you can have detailed events sent to the Windows event log. Another option enables burst handling, where you set the number of requests the server can handle at one time before clients must retry registration or renewal. You can also define the database path.

Figure 6.6 WINS Advanced Property Page

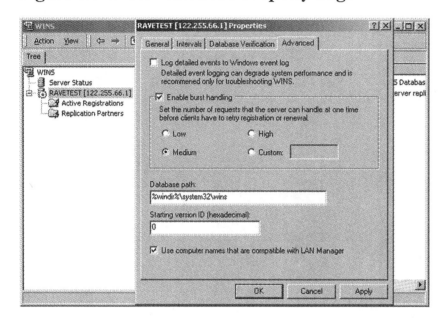

Warning: Detailed event logging has a significant impact on system performance. Use it only for troubleshooting WINS.

All of these properties can be configured on multiple WINS servers in your network from the local WINS server.

To modify the properties for a WINS server, follow these steps:

1. From the **Start** menu, choose **Programs**, **Administrative Tools** and **WINS**.

2. From the **WINS** console, right-click the desired WINS server and choose **Properties**.

WINS Client Configuration

WINS is gradually being phased out of the Windows operating system, and Windows 2000 is the first Microsoft operating system to rely primarily on DNS for name resolution. As a result, you will need WINS to support legacy clients in a typical enterprise network for some time. WINS supports the following Windows clients:

- Windows 2000

- Windows New Technologies (NT) 3.5 or later versions

- Windows 95 or later versions

- Windows for Workgroups 3.11 with TCP/IP 32

- MS-DOS with Microsoft Network Client v3

- MS-DOS with Local Area Network (LAN) Manager v 2.2c

Configuring WINS Clients to Control the NetBIOS Name Resolution

After you have configured the WINS servers, you need to set up the clients to use the WINS servers. This can be done from the client computer or centrally from a DHCP server. By default, Windows 2000 computers rely on DNS for name resolution, so you will need to configure WINS name resolution for Windows legacy clients.

To configure a Windows NT 4.0 workstation to use WINS for name resolution, follow these steps:

1. From the **Start** menu, choose **Settings** and **Control Panel**.

2. Double-click **Network**, choose**TCP/IP** from the list of protocols, and select **Properties**.

3. Choose the WINS Address property page (Figure 6.7), and type the IP address of the primary and secondary WINS servers.

Figure 6.7 Windows NT 4.0 TCP/IP WINS Address Property Page

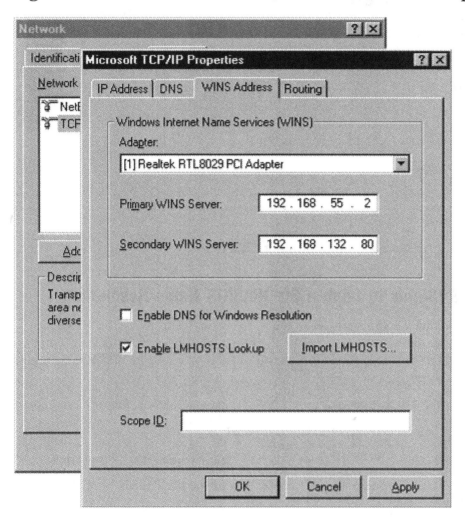

4. Choose **Enable DNS for Windows Resolution,** which allows you to forward unresolved NetBIOS name query requests to a DNS server for name resolution.

5. Choose **Enable LMHOSTS Lookup,** which allows you to import static LMHOSTS file mapping NetBIOS names to IP addresses to help in name resolution.

6. Type the **Scope ID**, which restricts communication to other NetBIOS hosts using the same scope ID.

7. Click **OK**.

For a larger network with a number of Windows legacy clients, it is more efficient to configure WINS NetBIOS name resolution from the DHCP server rather than from each WINS client. To configure a Windows 2000 DHCP server to support WINS name resolution for DHCP clients, follow these steps:

1. From the **Start** menu, choose **Programs, Administrative Tools** and **DHCP**.

2. From **DHCP**, expand the desired server in the left pane, right-click **Server Options** and choose **Configure Options**.

3. From the **Advanced** property page (Figure 6.8), choose the necessary WINS options and click **OK**.

Figure 6.8 DHCP Server Advanced Property Page

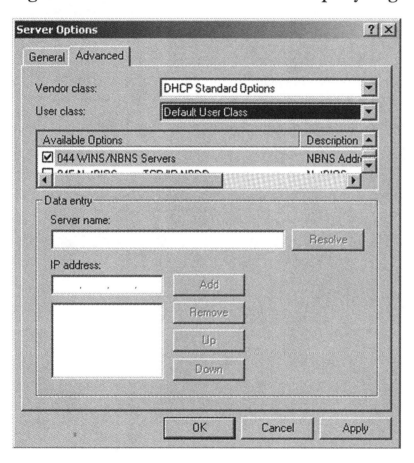

Three options from the Advanced Property page are shown in Table 6.1:

Table 6.1 DHCP Server Advanced Property Page Options

Option	Description
044 WINS/NBNS Servers	This option allows you to enter the IP addresses of WINS/NetBIOS Name Servers (NBNS) in the order the servers are to be contacted.
046 WINS/NBT Node Type	This option allows you to specify the type of NetBIOS over TCP/IP (NBT) name resolution to be used by the client. • B-node, a broadcast mode • P-node, a peer-to-peer communication mode • H-mode, a mixed mode where a direct request for name resolution is made to a WINS server, and if no answer is received, a broadcast request is made • M-node, a hybrid mode where a broadcast request for name resolution is made, and if no answer is received, a direct request to a WINS server is made
047 NetBIOS Scope ID	This option allows you to specify the local NetBIOS scope ID. NetBIOS over TCP/IP will communicate only with other NetBIOS hosts using the same scope ID.

Tip: The H-mode of NetBIOS over TCP/IP name resolution is most frequently used with clients. H-mode reduces network traffic by making a direct name query request to a WINS server, while supporting broadcasts as a backup method of name resolution.

WINS Replication Configuration

To ensure that a name registered with one WINS server is eventually replicated to all other WINS servers, you need to configure the replication of the database entries on all WINS servers within an internetwork. To replicate database entries, each WINS server must be configured as either a pull or push partner, as described in Table 6.2.

Table 6.2 WINS Push/Pull Replication Partners

Option	Description
Push partner	A push partner notifies its pull partner of changes to its WINS database. When the pull partner responds with a request for replication, the push partner sends a copy of its new database entries to its pull partner.
Pull partner	A pull partner requests new database entries, with a higher version number than the last entry it received during the last replication, from its push partner.

It is recommended that replication between WINS servers is set up in a hub pattern (Figure 6.9), with a single master WINS server in the center acting as the hub. You then configure all other WINS servers to replicate only with this central server using the push/pull method. This arrangement reduces WINS replication traffic. In an enterprise network, the WINS server at the head office would be the hub, with branch office WINS servers replicating to it.

Figure 6.9 WINS Hub Replication Arrangement

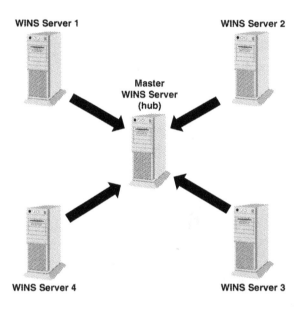

Tip: Deploy as few WINS servers as possible to reduce administrative tasks and bandwidth usage from replication traffic. A standard enterprise network can function well with just a few WINS servers.

Configuring WINS Replication

To establish a WINS replication partner, follow these steps:

1. From the **Start** menu, choose **Programs**, **Administrative Tools** and **WINS**.

2. From the **WINS** console, expand the WINS server that you want to set up for replication.

3. Right-click the **Replication Partners** folder, and choose **New Replication Partner**.

4. Type the name or IP address of the server you want to add as a replication partner, and click **OK**.

5. Double-click the replication partner in the right pane of the **WINS** console, and choose the **Advanced** property page (Figure 6.10).

Figure 6.10 WINS Replication Partner Advanced Property Page

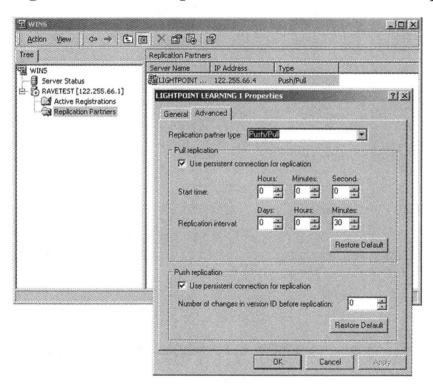

6. Choose the **Replication partner type**.

7. To establish a permanent connection for pull or push replication, choose **Use persistent connection for replication** in either the **Pull replication** or the **Push replication** section, or both sections.

8. From **Start time**, choose the time that you want to begin replication.

9. From **Replication interval**, choose the frequency that you want to replicate with the replication partner.

10. From **Number of changes in version ID before replication**, choose the number of changes to the local copy of the WINS database allowed before your server pushes changes to its replication partner, and click **OK**.

Once you have established a replication partner, you can change the four WINS Replication Partners property pages.

General—On this page (Figure 6.11), you can choose to replicate only with partners and to overwrite unique static mappings at the server.

Figure 6.11 Replication Partners General Property Page

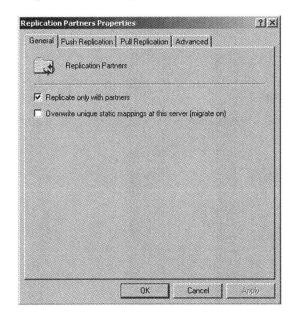

Push Replication—On this page (Figure 6.12), you can choose to start replication at the WINS startup and when addresses change. You can also select the number of changes in the version ID before replication and to use persistent connections for push replication partners.

Figure 6.12 Replication Partners Push Replication Property Page

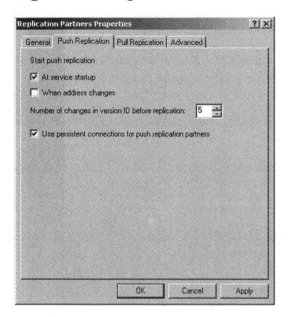

Pull Replication—On this page (Figure 6.13) you can choose the replication start time, the interval time, to start pull replication at the startup of WINS, and to use persistent connections for pull replication partners. You can also choose the number of communication retries between partners before replication attempts are halted.

Figure 6.13 Replication Partners Pull Replication Property Page

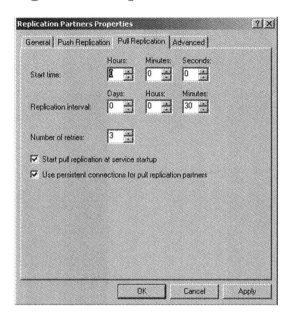

Advanced—On this page (Figure 6.14), you can allow the WINS server to use multicast to automatically configure itself for replication. Multicast is the process of sending a message to a select group of recipients. You can also specify the names or IP addresses of WINS servers from which you want to block database record replication.

Figure 6.14 Replication Partners Advanced Property Page

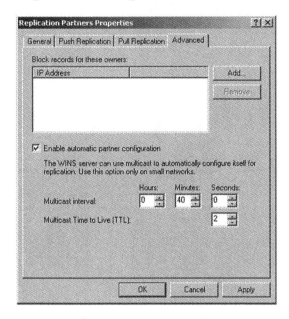

You can manually initiate either a push or a pull replication by following these steps:

1. From the **Start** menu, choose **Programs**, **Administrative Tools**, and **WINS**.

2. From the **WINS** console, right-click the desired WINS server and choose either **Start Push Replication** or **Start Pull Replication**.

3. Type the name or IP address of the replication partner with which you want to start replication and click **OK**.

4. If you have selected push replication, choose to replicate to the specified partner or to all partners, and click **OK**.

Non-WINS Client Support

To support non-WINS clients, you can carry out any of the following alternatives:

*   Import an LMHOSTS file

- Enable DNS to resolve names not in the WINS database

- Configure a WINS proxy agent

Using LMHOSTS Files

For those computers that cannot register dynamically with WINS, an LMHOSTS file holds static NetBIOS name-to-IP address mappings. Static mappings can replicate throughout your WINS environment and write over records on other servers. To add a static entry to the WINS database, follow these steps:

1. From the **Start** menu, choose **Programs, Administrative Tools** and **WINS**.

2. From the **WINS** console, expand the desired WINS server, and right-click **Active Registrations**.

3. From the **General** property page (Figure 6.15), choose **New Static Mapping**, and type the **Computer name**, **NetBIOS scope**, **Type**, and **IP address** of the desired computer.

4. Click **OK**.

Figure 6.15 New Static Mapping General Property Page

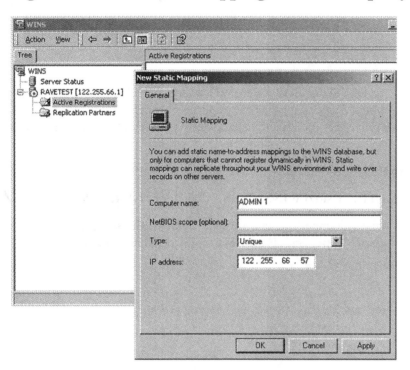

Warning: Microsoft recommends that you not use static entries to resolve names for non-WINS clients. Static entries are hard to eliminate from the WINS database after replication has occurred. A better choice is to configure clients to use DNS to resolve names not in the WINS database.

There are five types of static mapping, as described in Table 6.3.

Table 6.3 Types of NetBIOS Name/IP Address Static Mapping

Option	Description
Unique	A unique name that maps to one IP address
Group	A name that maps to a group with an unlimited number of members
Domain Name	A domain group stores up to 25 addresses for group members
Internet Group	User-defined group that is used to group resources for referencing and browsing
Multi-homed	A computer that has multiple network interface cards and up to 25 IP addresses

To import an LMHOSTS file into a WINS database, follow these steps:

1. From the **Start** menu, choose **Programs**, **Administrative Tools**, and **WINS**.

2. From the **WINS** console, expand the desired WINS server, and right-click **Active Registrations**.

3. Choose **Import LMHOSTS File**, browse for the file name, and select **Open**.

Using WINS Proxy Agents

A WINS proxy agent listens for broadcast name registrations and forwards them to a WINS server. The NetBIOS name is only verified, not registered. The WINS proxy agent also listens for broadcast resolution requests and checks its NetBIOS name cache in an attempt to resolve the name for the non-WINS client. If the name is not in its cache, the WINS proxy agent forwards the request to a WINS server, which then returns the desired IP address to the WINS proxy agent. The proxy agent sends the information to the non-WINS client. This process is seen in Figure 6.16.

Figure 6.16 Name Resolution Using a WINS Proxy Agent

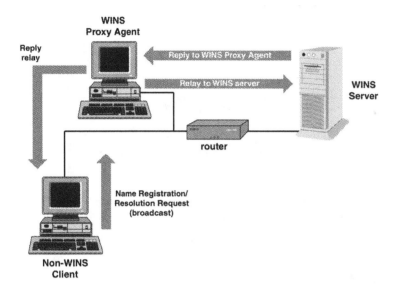

WINS proxy agents are only needed on subnets that do not have a WINS server, because routers do not forward broadcast messages by default.

To configure a WINS proxy agent, follow these steps:

1. From the **Start** menu of a WINS-enabled client, choose **Programs**, **Accessories** and **Command Prompt**.

2. Type **regedt32** and click **Enter**.

3. From within the **Registry Editor**, find the **EnableProxy** entry under **HKEY_LOCAL_MACHINE\SYSTEM\CurrentControlSet\Services\NetBT\Parameters** (Figure 6.17).

Figure 6.17 EnableProxy Entry in Registry Editor

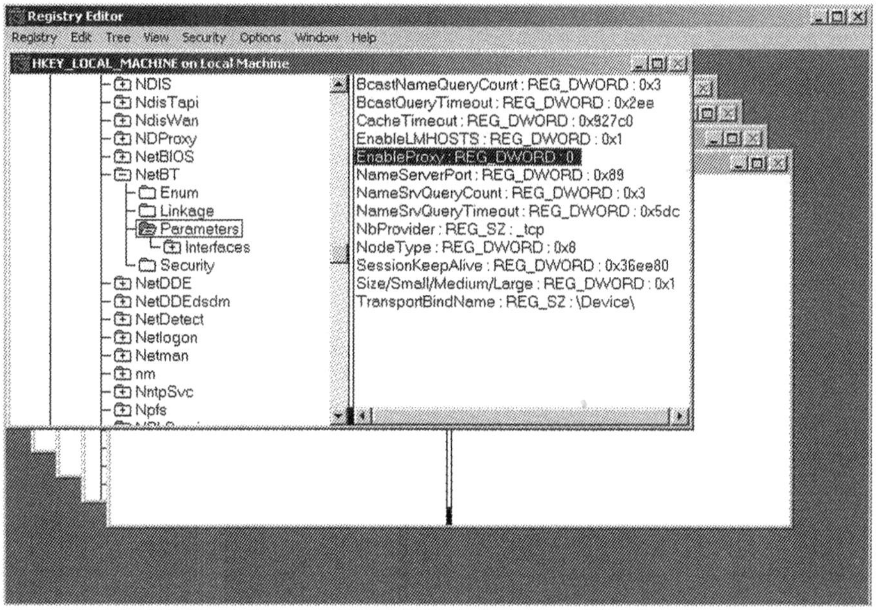

4. Double-click on EnableProxy and set the registry key to 1.

5. Click **OK** to exit.

WINS Monitoring

Using the WINS snap-in, you can manage WINS on multiple servers from the same console. Possible management activities include observing the status of WINS servers, viewing records in a WINS database, and accessing statistics from a WINS server.

Monitoring WINS

To view the status of all your WINS servers, follow these steps:

1. From the **Start** menu, choose **Programs**, **Administrative Tools** and **WINS**.

2. From the **WINS** console, choose **Server Status** in the left pane of the console to see the status of all your WINS servers in the right pane.

3. By default, the status of each server is updated every five minutes; to change this, right-click on **Server Status** and choose **Properties.**

4. Type the desired time in the **Server Status General** property page, and click **OK.**

To view records in the WINS database, follow these steps:

1. From the **Start** menu, choose **Programs, Administrative Tools** and **WINS.**

2. From the **WINS** console, expand the desired WINS server, and right-click **Active Registrations.**

3. Choose either **Find by Name** to search for a specific name or **Find by Owner** to see records for all WINS servers or just yours.

4. If you choose **Find by Owner**, choose the **Record Types** property page (Figure 6.18) and select the desired record types. Select **Add** in between each selection.

5. Choose **Find Now.**

Figure 6.18 WINS Active Registrations Record Types Property Pages

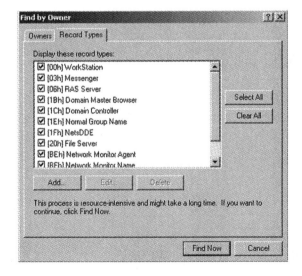

Figure 6.19 shows multiple record types from a WINS database.

Figure 6.19 Records from a WINS Database

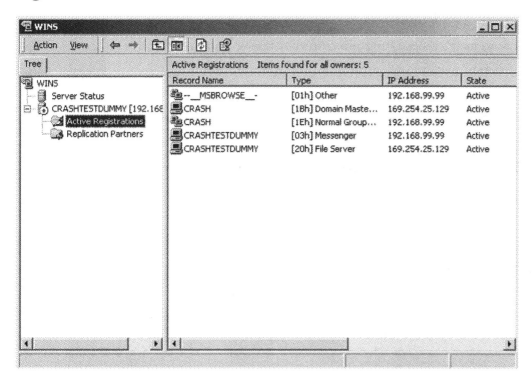

Server statistics are kept for each WINS server. The statistics include information on the following items:

• Replication

• Queries

• Releases

• Unique and group registrations

• Scavenging

- The WINS replication partner

- Database initialization

- The clearing of statistics

To access statistics from a WINS server, follow these steps:

1. From the **Start** menu, choose **Programs**, **Administrative Tools** and **WINS**.

2. From the **WINS** console, right-click the desired WINS server and choose **Display Server Statistics**

3. From **WINS Server Statistics** (Figure 6.20), you can **Reset** or **Refresh** statistics.

Figure 6.20 WINS Server Statistics

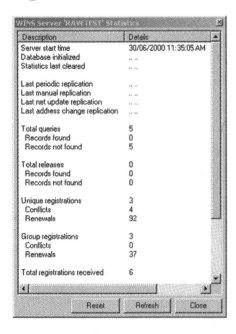

WINS Database Maintenance

Besides database monitoring, you can perform maintenance activities on the WINS databases of multiple servers using the WINS snap-in. Possible database maintenance activities include scavenging, backing up, verifying the consistency, and verifying the version ID consistency. WINS consistency checking is a processing and network-intensive operation. It is best to perform it during off-peak hours to minimize the impact on your servers and the network.

Maintaining the WINS Database

You need to periodically clean and purge the WINS database of old, unnecessary records. To initiate scavenging, follow these steps:

1. From the **Start** menu, choose **Programs**, **Administrative Tools**, and **WINS**.

2. From the **WINS** console, right-click the desired WINS server and choose **Scavenge Database**.

Tip: Microsoft has optimized the scavenging parameters for WINS and does not recommend that you change them.

You can perform other maintenance activities on a WINS database by right-clicking the desired WINS server and choosing the following menu options:

Back Up Database—After you select the folder where the WINS server should place the backed up database files, the database is backed up automatically.

Verify Database Consistency—You can queue a request to verify the WINS database consistency by selecting this option.

Verify Version ID Consistency—This operation retrieves owner-version maps from different WINS servers. It then checks the consistency of the databases by making sure a WINS server always has the highest version number among the network of WINS servers for records it owns.

Vocabulary

Review the following terms in preparation for the certification exam.

Term	Description
DHCP	The Dynamic Host Configuration Protocol simplifies TCP/IP network configuration and dynamically configures IP addresses for clients. DHCP ensures that address conflicts do not occur by centralizing address allocation.
DNS	The Domain Name System is a hierarchical naming system used to locate domain names on the Internet and on private TCP/IP networks. The DNS service maps DNS domain names to IP addresses and vice versa.
IP	The Internet Protocol is the routable protocol in the TCP/IP suite that is responsible for the IP addressing, routing, and fragmentation and reassembly of IP packets.
LAN	A Local Area Network is a communications network connecting computers, printers and other devices within a limited area.
LMHOSTS	This static file is used for name resolution. It maps NetBIOS (computer) names to IP addresses.
multicast	Multicast is the process of sending a message to a select group of recipients.
NBNS	A NetBIOS Name Server resolves NetBIOS names to IP addresses.
NBT	NetBIOS over TCP/IP is a feature that provides the NetBIOS programming interface over the TCP/IP protocol.

Term	Description
NetBIOS name	A Network Basic Input/Output System name is recognized by WINS, the service that maps a computer name to its IP address.
NT	New Technologies is Microsoft's version of Windows previous to Windows 2000.
pull partner	A pull partner requests new database entries, with a higher version number than the last entry it received during the last replication, from its push partner.
push partner	A push partner notifies its pull partner of changes to its WINS database. When the pull partner responds with a request for replication, the push partner sends a copy of its new database entries to its pull partner.
TCP/IP	The Transmission Control Protocol/Internet Protocol is a set of protocols that provides communication among diverse networks. Since it accommodates different architectures and operating systems, TCP/IP is the most commonly used Internet protocol.
WINS	The Windows Internet Naming Service is a Microsoft software service that dynamically maps IP addresses to computer names. This allows users to access resources by name instead of by IP address.
WINS proxy agent	A Windows Internet Naming Service proxy agent extends the name resolution capabilities of a WINS server to non-WINS clients by listening for broadcast name registrations and resolution requests and forwarding them to a WINS server.

In Brief

If you want to...	Then do this...
Install WINS on a server	1. From the **Start** menu, choose **Settings** and **Control Panel**.
	2. Double-click **Add/Remove Programs** and choose **Add/Remove Windows Components** to launch the **Windows Components** wizard.
	3. Highlight **Networking Services**, and choose **Details**.
	4. From **Networking Services**, choose **Windows Internet Naming Service (WINS)** and click **OK**.
	5. Choose Next and, from Completing the Windows Components Wizard, select Finish.
Configure WINS on a server	1. From the **Start** menu, choose **Programs**, **Administrative Tools**, and **WINS**.
	2. From the **WINS** console, right-click the desired WINS server and choose **Properties**.
	The four property pages are:
	General—On this page, you can choose the frequency with which you want to update statistics. You can also type the default database backup path, and back up the database during a server shutdown.
	Intervals—On this page, you can set the rate at which WINS database records are renewed, deleted and verified.
	Database verification—On this page, you can verify the WINS database consistency at a specific time interval and time. You can set the maximum number of records to verify at each time interval, and verify the records against the servers who own a particular record or against randomly selected partners.

If you want to...	Then do this...
Configure WINS on a server	**Advanced**—On this page, you can log detailed events to the Windows event log. Another option is to enable burst handling, in which you set the number of requests the server can handle at one time before clients must retry registration or renewal. You can also set the database path.
Configure a Windows NT 4.0 client to use WINS for name resolution	1. From the **Start** menu, choose **Settings** and **Control Panel**. 2. Double-click **Network**, choose **TCP/IP** from the list of protocols, and select **Properties**. 3. Choose the **WINS Address** property page, and type the IP address of the primary and secondary WINS servers. 4. Choose to **Enable DNS for Windows Resolution**, which allows you to forward unresolved NetBIOS name query requests to a DNS server for name resolution. 5. Choose to **Enable LMHOSTS Lookup**, which allows you to import a static LMHOSTS file mapping NetBIOS names to IP addresses to help in name resolution. 6. Type the **Scope ID**, which restricts communication to other NetBIOS hosts using the same scope ID. 7. Click **OK**.

If you want to...	Then do this...
Configure a Windows 2000 DHCP server to support WINS name resolution for DHCP clients	1. From the **Start** menu, choose **Programs, Administrative Tools** and **DHCP**. 2. From **DHCP**, expand the desired server in the left pane, right-click **Server Options** and choose **Configure Options**. 3. From the **Advanced** property page, choose the desired WINS options and click **OK**.
Configure WINS replication	1. From the **Start** menu, choose **Programs, Administrative Tools** and **WINS**. 2. From the **WINS** console, expand the WINS server that you want to set up for replication. 3. Right-click the **Replication Partners** folder, and choose **New Replication Partner**. 4. Type the name or IP address of the server you want to add as a replication partner, and click **OK**. 5. Double-click the replication partner in the right pane of the **WINS** console, and choose the **Advanced** property page. 6. Select the **Replication partner type**. 7. To establish a permanent connection for pull or push replication, choose **Use persistent connection for replication** in either the **Pull replication** or the **Push replication** section, or both sections. 8. From **Start time**, choose the time that you want to begin replication. 9. From **Replication interval**, choose the frequency that you want to replicate with the replication partner. 10. From **Number of changes in version ID before replication**, choose the number of changes to the local copy of the WINS database allowed before your server pushes changes to its replication partner, and click **OK**.

If you want to...	Then do this...
Support non-WINS clients	a. Import an LMHOSTS file b. Enable DNS to resolve names not in the WINS database c. Configure a WINS proxy agent
Monitor WINS	From the WINS management console, you can: • Observe the status of WINS servers • View records within a WINS database • Access statistics from a WINS server
Perform maintenance activities on a WINS database	From the WINS console, right-click the desired WINS server and choose the following menu options: **Scavenge Database**—This option allows you to clean and purge the WINS database of old, unnecessary records. **Back Up Database**—After you select the folder where the WINS server should place the backed up database files, the database is backed up automatically. **Verify Database Consistency**—You can queue a request to verify the WINS database consistency by selecting this option. **Verify Version ID Consistency**—This operation retrieves owner-version maps from different WINS servers. It then checks the consistency of the databases by making sure a WINS server always has the highest version number among the network of WINS servers for records it owns.

Lesson 6 Activities

Complete the following activities to prepare for the certification exam.

1. Explain the difference between a push and a pull replication partner.

2. Describe the optimum arrangement for the replication of WINS servers and explain the reason for it.

3. Explain the WINS name resolution process.

4. List some WINS server statistics that you can access.

5. Explain how a WINS proxy agent works.

6. List the steps involved in viewing selected records from the WINS database.

7. Explain how you could change the scavenging parameters on a WINS database.

8. Explain why you should not install WINS on a multi-homed server.

9. List the steps involved in adding static entries to the WINS database.

10. Describe the three options you need to configure in the DHCP Server Advanced property page if you want to configure the DHCP server to support WINS name resolution for DHCP clients.

Answers to Lesson 6 Activities

1. A push partner notifies its pull partner of changes to its WINS database. The pull partner responds with a request for new database entries, with a higher version number than the last entry it received during the last replication, from its push partner. The push partner then sends a copy of its new database entries to its pull partner.

2. It is best to set up replication between WINS servers in a hub pattern, with a single master WINS server in the center acting as the hub. You configure all other WINS servers to replicate only with this central server using the push/pull method. This arrangement reduces WINS replication traffic. In an enterprise network, the WINS server at the head office would be the hub, with branch office WINS servers replicating to it.

3. Every WINS client is configured with the IP address of a primary WINS server and, for redundancy, a secondary WINS server. Each time a WINS client boots up, it registers its current NetBIOS name and IP address mapping with the database on the designated WINS server. Whenever the client's IP addressing information changes, the client also sends updated information to the WINS database.

    When the WINS client wants to communicate with another network resource, it first checks its NetBIOS name cache for the NetBIOS name/IP address mapping of the destination computer. If it cannot resolve the name from cache, the WINS client issues a NetBIOS name query request to the primary WINS server. The primary WINS server looks for the relevant

    NetBIOS name/IP address mapping for the destination resource in its database, and returns the IP address to the client.

    If a WINS client fails to find the primary WINS server after three attempts, it will try to access the secondary WINS server. If the secondary WINS server also proves inaccessible, the client generates three broadcast messages on the local network. If the NetBIOS name is found on the local network, the name is then resolved to an IP address.

4. You can access the following WINS server statistics:

    *   Replication

    *   Queries

    *   Releases

    *   Unique and group registrations

- Scavenging

- The WINS replication partner

- Database initialization

- The clearing of statistics

5. A WINS proxy agent listens for broadcast name registrations and forwards them to a WINS server. The NetBIOS name is only verified, not registered. The WINS proxy agent also listens for broadcast resolution requests and checks its NetBIOS name cache to try to resolve the name for the non-WINS client. If the name is not in its cache, the WINS proxy agent forwards the request to a WINS server, which then returns the desired IP address to the WINS proxy agent. The proxy agent sends the information to the non-WINS client. WINS proxy agents are only needed on subnets that do not have a WINS server because broadcast messages are not forwarded by routers by default.

6. To view selected records in the WINS database, follow these steps:

    1. From the **Start** menu, choose **Programs**, **Administrative Tools** and **WINS**.

    2. From the **WINS** console, expand the desired WINS server, and right-click **Active Registrations**.

    3. Choose either **Find by Name** to search for a specific name or **Find by Owner** to see records for all WINS servers or just yours.

    4. If you choose **Find by Owner**, choose the **Record Types** property page and select the desired record types. Select **Add** in between each selection.

    5. Choose **Find Now**.

7. Scavenging is the process of cleaning and purging a database of old, unnecessary records. It is unlikely you would want to change the scavenging parameters for the WINS database as Microsoft has optimized the parameters and does not recommend you change them.

8. If you install WINS on a multi-homed server, you will likely cause problems in the replication of the WINS database with databases from other WINS servers.

9. To add a static entry to the WINS database, follow these steps:

    1. From the **Start** menu, choose **Programs**, **Administrative Tools** and **WINS**.

2. From the **WINS** console, expand the desired WINS server, and right-click **Active Registrations**.

3. From the **General** property page, choose **New Static Mapping**, and type the **Computer name, NetBIOS scope, Type**, and **IP address** of the desired computer. Click **OK**.

10. The three options you need to configure on the DHCP Server Advanced property page on your DHCP server in order to support WINS name resolution for DHCP clients are as follows:

044 WINS/NBNS Servers— This option allows you to enter the IP addresses of WINS/NetBIOS Name Servers (NBNS) in the order the servers are to be contacted.

046 WINS/NBT Node Type— This option allows you to specify the type of NetBIOS over TCP/IP (NBT) name resolution to be used by the client.

- B-node, a broadcast mode

- P-node, a peer to peer communication mode

- H-mode, a mixed mode in which a direct request for name resolution is made to a WINS server; if no answer is forthcoming a broadcast request is made

- M-node, a hybrid mode in which a broadcast request for name resolution is made; if no answer is forthcoming a direct request to a WINS server is made

047 NetBIOS Scope ID— This option allows you to specify the local NetBIOS scope ID. NetBIOS over TCP/IP will communicate only with other NetBIOS hosts using the same scope ID.

Lesson 6 Quiz

These questions test your knowledge of features, vocabulary, procedures, and syntax.

1. Which of the following clients does WINS support?
    A. MS-DOS with LAN Manager v2.2c
    B. Windows for Workgroups with TCP/IP 32
    C. Windows 2000
    D. NetWare 4.11

2. Which of the following is the registry key to configure a WINS proxy agent?
    A. HKEY_LOCAL_MACHINE\SYSTEM\CurrentControlSet\Services\NetBT\Parameters\ EnableProxy
    B. HKEY_LOCAL_MACHINE\SYSTEM\CurrentControlSet\NetBT\Parameters\EnableProxy
    C. HKEY_LOCAL_MACHINE\SYSTEM\CurrentControlSet\Services\ Parameters\EnableProxy
    D. HKEY_LOCAL_MACHINE\SYSTEM\CurrentControlSet\Services\NetBT\ EnableProxy

3. For which of the following network infrastructures is WINS unnecessary?
    A. A mixture of Novell NetWare 5.0 and Windows NT 4.0 clients.
    B. All network clients are configured to use another method of name resolution.
    C. Only Windows 2000 clients exist.
    D. There are fewer than 50 clients on one subnet.

4. What do you need to do before installing WINS on a server?
    A. Remove any WINS servers listed on the TCP/IP WINS property page.
    B. Ensure there is an address reservation for your server configured on the DHCP server.
    C. Configure a subnet mask.
    D. Add the IP address of your server to the TCP/IP WINS property page.

5. When should you perform WINS consistency checking?
    A. After every change in the WINS database.
    B. During peak network usage hours.
    C. During off-peak network usage hours.
    D. Immediately after the WINS installation.

6. What are some methods of supporting name resolution in non-Windows clients?
   A. Change the client registry key
      HKEY_LOCAL_MACHINE\SYSTEM\CurrentControlSet\Services\NetBT\
      Parameters\EnableWINS to 1.
   B. Import an LMHOSTS file.
   C. Enable DNS to resolve names not in the WINS database.
   D. Configure a WINS proxy agent.

7. Which of the 046 WINS/NBT Node Type options in the DHCP Server Advanced property page
   is used most frequently with clients?
   A. B-mode
   B. P-mode
   C. H-mode
   D. N-mode

8. Which of the following are types of static mappings found in an LMHOSTS file?
   A. Unique
   B. Group
   C. Domain name
   D. Multi-homed

9. Which of the following deployment strategies for WINS servers is most appropriate?
   A. Deploy as many WINS servers as possible.
   B. Deploy as few WINS servers as possible.
   C. Deploy one WINS server on each subnet.
   D. Deploy only one WINS server.

10. What method does Microsoft recommend for resolving names for non-WINS clients?
    A. Use static entries
    B. Use DNS
    C. Use a WINS proxy agent
    D. Use an LMHOSTS file

Answers to Lesson 6 Quiz

1. Answers A, B and C are all correct. MS-DOS with LAN Manager v2.2c and Windows for Workgroups with TCP/IP 32 are two Windows legacy clients supported by WINS. Windows 2000 is also supported by WINS, although you would not need to use WINS because DNS is the default name resolution service in Windows 2000.

    Answer D is incorrect. WINS is a service designed to support Microsoft Windows operating systems, not Novell NetWare products.

2. Answer A is correct.
    HKEY_LOCAL_MACHINE\SYSTEM\CurrentControlSet\Services\NetBT\
    Parameters\EnableProxy is the registry key needed to configure a WINS proxy agent. Set this registry key to 1 on a WINS-enabled client.

    Answers B, C and D are all incorrect.
    HKEY_LOCAL_MACHINE\SYSTEM\CurrentControlSet\Services\NetBT\
    Parameters\EnableProxy is the correct registry key.

3. Answers B, C and D are all correct. If all the network clients are configured to use another method of name resolution, then WINS is not necessary. If only Windows 2000 clients exist, you can use DNS as the default name resolution service. In addition, if there were fewer than 50 clients on one subnet, the broadcasts for name registrations and requests would reach the WINS server and would not generate too much network traffic.

    Answer A is incorrect. While Novell NetWare clients cannot use WINS for name resolution, Windows NT 4.0 clients do need the service.

4. Answers A, B, C and D are all correct. Before installing WINS on a server, you need to configure its TCP/IP settings. You should configure the server to either use a static IP address or make sure there is an address reservation for the server on the DHCP server. You also need to configure a subnet mask and gateway. Then remove any WINS servers already listed on the TCP/IP WINS property page to prevent your WINS server from registering with another server instead of with itself. Add your own IP address to the listing on the TCP/IP WINS property page.

5. Answer C is correct. You can perform two types of WINS consistency checking: Database verification and Version ID verification. Both are processing and network-intensive operations. It is best to perform them during off-peak hours to minimize the impact on your servers and the network.

Answer A is incorrect. The WINS database is meant to be dynamic, so depending on the network the database may change a lot. If you performed WINS consistency checking after every change in the WINS database your network bandwidth would be compromised.

Answer B is incorrect. It is preferable to perform WINS consistency checking during off-peak hours to minimize the impact on your servers and network.

Answer D is incorrect. It is unlikely that many new records will be in the database immediately after installing WINS.

6. Answers B, C and D are all correct. To support name resolution in non-Windows clients, you can import an LMHOSTS file having static NetBIOS name-to-IP address mappings, enable DNS to resolve names not in the WINS database, or configure a WINS proxy agent.

   Answer A is incorrect. The HKEY_LOCAL_MACHINE\SYSTEM\CurrentControlSet\Services\NetBT\Parameters\EnableWINS to 1 key does not exist in the Windows 2000 registry.

7. Answer C is correct. The H-mode of NetBIOS over TCP/IP name resolution is used most frequently with clients. The H-mode reduces network traffic by first making a direct name query request to a WINS server, while supporting broadcasts as a backup method of name resolution.

   Answer A is incorrect. B-node is a broadcast mode that creates unnecessary traffic on a large network.

   Answer B is incorrect. While P-node, a peer-to-peer communication mode, does not create much traffic, it also does not support a backup name resolution method.

   Answer D is incorrect. An N-mode option does not exist.

8. Answers A, B, C and D are all correct. There are five types of static mappings found in an LMHOSTS file. A Unique name maps to one IP address. A Group name maps to a group with an unlimited number of members. A Domain name maps to a domain group storing up to 25 addresses for group members. Multi-homed maps to a computer having multiple network interface cards and up to 25 IP addresses.

9. Answer B is correct. You should deploy as few WINS servers as possible to reduce administrative tasks and bandwidth usage from replication traffic. A typical enterprise network can function well with just a few WINS servers.

   Answer A is incorrect. If you deploy too many WINS servers, traffic from the replication of the WINS databases will use up much of your network bandwidth.

Answer C is incorrect. You do not need to deploy one WINS server on each subnet if you have a WINS proxy agent for non-WINS clients on each subnet without a WINS server.

Answer D is incorrect. You should deploy one primary and at least one secondary WINS server for redundancy purposes.

10. Answer B is correct. Microsoft recommends that you configure non-WINS clients to use DNS to resolve names not in the WINS database.

Answer A is incorrect. Microsoft does not recommend that you use static entries to resolve names for non-WINS clients. Static entries are hard to eliminate from the WINS database after replication has occurred. The static mappings write over records of other servers.

Answer C is incorrect. Microsoft neither recommends nor discourages the use of a WINS proxy agent to resolve names for non-WINS clients.

Answer D is incorrect. An LMHOSTS file is composed of the static entries described in Answer A.

Lesson 7

IP Routing Protocols Installation and Administration

Routing is the process of forwarding a packet based on the destination Internet Protocol (IP) address. This can be done using dedicated hardware routers or computers running software that enable them to act as routers. Packets are a transmission unit consisting of both data and a header containing an identification number, source and destination addresses, and error-control information.

Windows 2000 Server offers Local Area Network (LAN)-to-LAN routing through the Routing and Remote Access Service (RRAS). RRAS can dynamically route Transmission Control Protocol/Internet Protocol (TCP/IP), Internetwork Packet Exchange (IPX) and AppleTalk traffic using built-in routing protocols. TCP/IP is the most commonly used Internet protocol because it accommodates different architectures and operating systems.

When a router receives a packet, the network adapter forwards the datagram, an unacknowledged packet of data sent to another network destination, to the IP Layer of the Open System Interconnection (OSI) Reference Model. IP examines the destination address on the datagram and compares it to an IP routing table, and then forwards the packet.

After completing this lesson, you should have a better understanding of the following topics:

* Routing Overview

* IP Routing Configuration

* TCP/IP Filtering Configuration

* Demand-Dial Routing Implementation

* IP Routing Monitoring

* Windows 2000 Router Integration

Routing Overview

Routers connect LANs with different network topologies into Wide Area Networks (WANs) to achieve network interoperability. As each packet sent over a LAN has a header with a source and destination address, the routers match a packet header to a LAN segment. They then choose the most efficient path for the packet. The best path is usually the one with the fewest packet transfers, from one router to an adjoining router (Figure 7.1), called hops.

Figure 7.1 Packet Routing

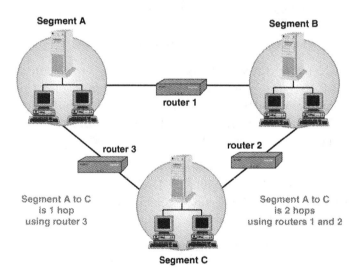

As the packets are transferred from one router to the next and then to the destination host, the routers remember the most efficient path and use this information to route future packets. If a route is not found, an error message is sent to the source computer.

Larger networks generally need the bandwidth, speed, management tools and robustness that dedicated hardware routers, such as the ones from Cisco, offer. If cost is a factor in purchasing dedicated hardware routers or there is not enough traffic to warrant a dedicated hardware router, such as with a smaller branch office, you can configure software routing on a multi-homed Windows 2000 computer. A multi-homed computer has two or more network interfaces installed.

Understanding Routing Concepts

When making routing decisions, the IP Layer consults the routing table stored in a router. The table contains a series of entries detailing the IP addresses of router interfaces to other networks with which the router communicates. A computer running Windows 2000 will automatically build its routing table from its TCP/IP configuration.

Routing tables can be created manually through static routing or automatically by using routing protocols, a process called dynamic routing. In static routing, you need to ensure each router has the necessary routes in its routing table to communicate with any two endpoints on the IP internetwork. Because of their administrative overhead, static routes are best reserved for small, static networks.

Each entry in the routing table is considered one route. There are three types of routes, as described in Table 7.1

Table 7.1 Types of Routing Table Entries

Entry Type	Description
Network route	The network route entry provides a route to a specific network ID in the internetwork.
Host route	The host route entry provides a route to a specific internetwork address consisting of a network ID and node ID. You would use this selection to optimize network traffic by creating custom routes to specific computers.
Default route	The default route is used when a specific route for a particular destination cannot be found in the routing table.

To view the routing information of your computer, type either NETSTAT-RN or ROUTE PRINT at the command prompt, as shown in Figure 7.2.

Figure 7.2 Routing Table

Each entry in a routing table has fields, which differ according to the routable protocol used. Typical information fields for IP are described in Table 7.2.

Table 7.2 Routing Table Fields

Field	Description
Destination	The Destination field describes the network ID for a host route. On IP routers, an additional subnet mask field distinguishes the network ID from the destination IP address.
Gateway	The Gateway field describes the address to which the packet is forwarded. It can be either a hardware address or an internetwork address.
Interface	The Interface field describes the network interface used when packets are forwarded to the network ID. It is a logical identifier, such as a port number.
Metric	The Metric field identifies route preferences, with the lowest metric as the most preferred route. When multiple routes to a particular network destination exist, the route with the lowest metric is used.

Enabling IP Routing

Before you can configure routing between two subnets, you need to establish a Windows 2000 multi-homed computer by following these steps:

1. Install two Network Interface Cards (NICs) on the Windows 2000 Server or Advanced Server that sits between two subnets.

2. Configure each NIC with an IP address of the subnet with which it interfaces (Figure 7.3).

Figure 7.3 A Multi-homed Computer

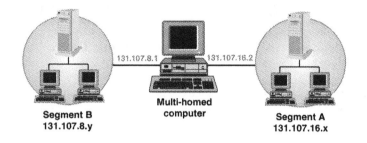

Segment B
131.107.8.y

Multi-homed
computer

Segment A
131.107.16.x

IP Routing Configuration

Installing and configuring IP routing is similar to installing and configuring a remote access server. You can use the same wizard; however, there are fewer configuration steps required.

Configuring IP Routing

If you have previously installed a remote access server, you can turn the computer into a router by following these steps:

1. From the **Start** menu, choose **Programs**, **Administrative Tools**, and then select **Routing and Remote Access**.

2. Right-click the desired server and choose **Properties**.

3. Choose to enable the computer as a router, and click **OK**.

4. When asked if you want the router to be restarted, choose **Yes**.

If you have not previously installed a remote access server, you can install it by following these steps:

1. From the **Start** menu, choose **Programs**, **Administrative Tools**, and then select **Routing and Remote Access**.

2. Right-click the desired server and choose **Properties**.

3. Right-click the desired computer, and choose **Configure and Enable Routing and Remote Access**.

4. From the **Routing and Remote Access Server Setup Wizard**, choose **Next**.

5. From **Common Configurations**, choose **Network Router** and then select **Next**.

6. From **Routed Protocols**, verify that under **Protocols, TCP/IP** is listed, choose **Yes, all of the available protocols are on this list**, and then select **Next**.

7. From **Demand-Dial Connections**, choose **Yes** to allow immediate configuration of demand-dial connections to access remote networks, or **No** to allow for later configuration.

8. Choose **No, Next**, and then from **Completing the Routing and Remote Access Server Setup Wizard**, select **Finish**.

If you right-click on the server and select Properties, five configurable property pages can be seen:

General—This page allows you to enable the computer as either a router for the LAN or for both the LAN and demand-dial routing.

Security—This page allows you to select the authentication provider to validate credentials for demand-dial routers. You can choose to have either Windows Authentication or Remote Authentication Dial-In User Service (RADIUS) Authentication. RADIUS, running on a Windows Internet Authentication Service server, can be used to manage policies governing access to the router. You can also choose to have either Windows Accounting or RADIUS Accounting. The accounting provider maintains a log of connection requests and sessions.

IP—This page allows you to enable IP routing and to allow IP-based demand-dial connections. You can also use this page to define how the server assigns IP addresses, either by using Dynamic Host Configuration Protocol (DHCP) or a static address pool. DHCP simplifies TCP/IP network configuration by dynamically configuring IP addresses for clients.

PPP—This page allows you to set Point-to-Point Protocol (PPP) options. PPP is a method of connecting a computer to the Internet. It is a very stable protocol that supports error checking.

Event Logging—This page allows you to define various event logging settings, including logging errors only, logging errors and warnings, and logging the maximum amount of information.

You can also configure the three IP property pages:

General—This page allows you to define various event logging settings, including log errors only, log errors and warnings, log the maximum amount of information, and disable event logging.

Preference Levels—This page allows you to define the rank of a selected route source by selecting **Move up** or **Move down**. Routes with higher rankings are preferred over lower-ranking routes.

Multicast Scopes—This page allows you to define the scope name, IP address and mask. A multicast is a group of predefined recipients to whom a packet is sent. Windows 2000 supports a limited form of multicast routing. While Windows 2000 can act like a multicast router, the operating system will forward multicast traffic to an interface with direct access to a true multicast router on behalf of local clients.

To configure IP routing, follow these steps:

1. From the **Start** menu, choose **Programs, Administrative Tools**, and then select **Routing and Remote Access**.

2. From **Routing and Remote Access**, expand the desired server.

3. From **IP Routing**, right-click **General** and choose **Properties**.

4. Configure the three properties pages, and click **OK**.

To see the IP routing table, follow these steps:

1. From the **Start** menu, choose **Programs, Administrative Tools**, and then select **Routing and Remote Access**.

2. From **Routing and Remote Access**, expand the desired server.

3. From **IP Routing**, right-click **Static Routes** and choose **Show IP Routing Table**.

To add new entries to the IP routing table, follow these steps:

1. From the **Start** menu, choose **Programs, Administrative Tools**, and then select **Routing and Remote Access**.

2. From **Routing and Remote Access**, expand the desired server.

3. From **IP Routing**, right-click **Static Routes** and choose **New Static Route**.

4. From within **Static Route** (Figure 7.4), type the **Interface, Destination, Network mask, Gateway,** and **Metric**.

5. Choose if you want to **Use this route to initiate demand-dial connections**, and then click OK.

Figure 7.4 Static Route Page

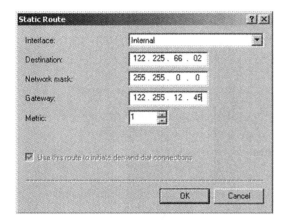

You can also add or modify entries in a routing table by using the ROUTE command with the switches described in Table 7.3.

Table 7.3 ROUTE Command Options

Option	Description
ROUTE add [network] mask [netmask] [gateway]	Adds a route.
ROUTE -p add [network] mask [netmask] [gateway]	Adds a persistent route.
ROUTE delete [network] [gateway]	Deletes a route.
ROUTE change [network] [gateway]	Modifies a route.
ROUTE print	Displays the routing table.
ROUTE -f	Clears all routes.

Configuring Routing Information Protocol (RIP) for IP Routing

Building up routing tables by hand is both tedious and error-prone. Also, static routers do not keep each other informed of changes in their tables and they cannot exchange information with dynamic routers. There is much less administrative overhead when using a routing protocol. A routing protocol enables a Windows 2000 computer, acting as a router, to obtain routing information automatically from nearby routers.

TCP/IP has different types of routing algorithms. Windows 2000 supports the Routing Information Protocol (RIP) v2, Open Shortest Path First (OSPF), and Internet Group Management Protocol (IGMP) v2. You choose the best routing protocol to implement based on your network size and topology.

RIP is a reliable and simple routing protocol that dynamically communicates routing information and changes between neighboring routers. It is a distance-vector routing protocol, so it only learns a limited amount of information about the surrounding network. Routers running RIP broadcast their routing tables every 30 seconds. A computer with RIP listens to the broadcasts and incorporates the information into its own routing table.

Because RIP has a hop limitation of 16, it is best implemented in small to medium sized networks. Also, RIP routers can use up considerable network bandwidth by announcing their entire routing table, causing bottlenecks as a network grows.

RIP uses the hop count as the deciding factor for the best route to deliver a packet. If you want to force a router to preferentially select one link over another, you must configure the more desirable link to have a lower cost.

To install RIP, follow these steps:

1. From the **Start** menu, choose **Programs**, **Administrative Tools**, and then select **Routing and Remote Access**.

2. From **Routing and Remote Access**, expand the desired server.

3. From **IP Routing**, right-click **General** (Figure 7.5) and choose **New Routing Protocol**.

4. From **New Routing Protocol**, choose **RIP Version 2 for Internet Protocol**, and click **OK**.

Figure 7.5 RIP General Property Page

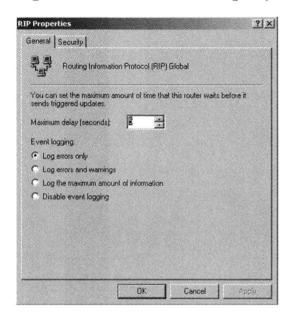

On the Security property page (Figure 7.6) you can specify how to process announcements from routers. You can accept announcements from all routers, accept announcements from listed routers only, or ignore announcements from all listed routers.

Figure 7.6 RIP Security Property Page

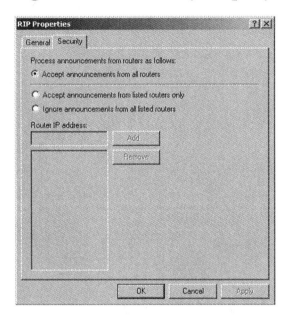

Tip: Windows 2000 supports RIP mostly for backwards-compatibility with existing RIP networks. RIP is considered an outdated routing protocol.

Configuring Open Shortest Path First (OSPF) for IP Routing

OSPF was developed as a robust alternative to RIP. OSPF is a link-state routing protocol that calculates routing table entries by constructing a shortest-path tree of current link states. Because OSPF-based routers communicate with all other routers in their network, they can build a map of the network, allowing for intelligence when redirecting traffic around a failed router. OSPF uses less network bandwidth than RIP, as only changes to the routing tables are propagated. The routing tables are recalculated as soon as changes are received.

OSPF is more complex to set up than RIP. As the size of the OSPF database increases, memory requirements and route computation times increase. As a result, OSPF divides the network infrastructure into groups of contiguous networks called areas, as seen in Figure 7.7. These areas are connected to each other through a backbone area by Area Border Routers (ABRs). Routers that have all interfaces connected to the backbone are internal routers.

Figure 7.7 An OSPF Area Design

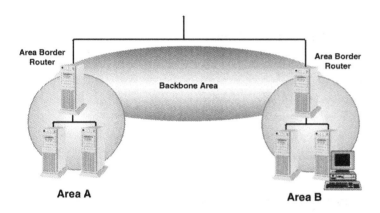

When configuring an OSPF network, follow these guidelines:

- Design areas according to site or administrative boundaries

- Ensure the ABRs for an area are configured with destination and network mask pairs that summarize the area's routes

- The source and route filtering configured on the ABRs are not overly restrictive, thus allowing needed routes to be propagated to other routers

- All ABRs are physically connected to the backbone or logically connected to the backbone through a virtual link

- Routers connect two areas by going through the backbone

- Use the minimum number of routers necessary in an area

Tip: When an ABR cannot physically connect to a backbone network segment, you can connect the new OSPF area to the backbone through a virtual link. Microsoft recommends that you use virtual links as a last resort because they are complicated to set up and error-prone.

Unlike RIP, where packets are dropped after 16 hops, packet transfer with OSPF is not restricted to 16 hop counts. Instead, you can set the accumulated path costs, up to 65,535. This allows you to construct large networks with different link costs. OSPF also supports point-to-point dedicated connections, broadcast networks, and non-broadcast networks.

Tip: Microsoft recommends that OSPF be used in medium to large dynamic internetworks with more than 50 subnets.

To install OSPF, follow these steps:

1. From the **Start** menu, choose **Programs, Administrative Tools**, and then select **Routing and Remote Access**.

2. From **Routing and Remote Access**, expand the desired server.

3. From **IP Routing**, right-click **General** and choose **New Routing Protocol**.

4. From **New Routing Protocol**, choose **Open Shortest Path First (OSPF)**, and click **OK**.

From the General property page (Figure 7.8), you can type the router identification, and choose an autonomous system boundary router. You can also specify the following event logging: Log errors only, Log errors and warnings, Log the maximum amount of information or Disable event logging.

Figure 7.8 OSPF General Property Page

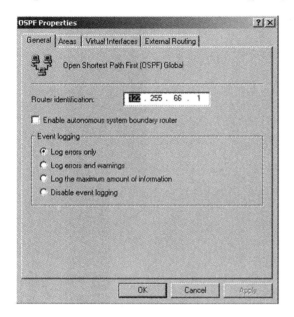

From the Areas property page you can add, edit and remove OSPF areas. By selecting Add, you will see the General and Ranges property pages.

From the General property page (Figure 7.9), you can specify the Area ID, enable a plaintext password, and add a metric for the area. The Ranges property page allows you to specify the destination IP address and Network mask.

Figure 7.9 OSPF Areas General Property Page

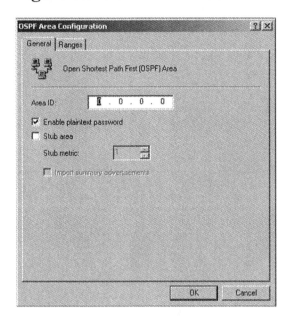

The Virtual Interface property page allows you to add, edit or remove virtual interfaces by specifying the transit area and virtual neighbors.

The External Routing property page (Figure 7.10), allows you to choose to accept or to ignore routes from all route sources except those selected. Route sources include the following:

- Auto Static routes

- Local routes

- RIP Version 2 for Internet Protocol

- Simple Network Management Protocol (SNMP) routes

- Static (non demand-dial routes)

- Static routes

Figure 7.10 OSPF External Routing Property Page

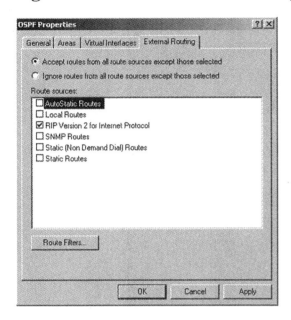

Integrating Software Routing into Existing Networks

Although Microsoft has incorporated routing technology into its server operating systems since Windows NT 3.51, the built-in multi-protocol router was limited in its functionality. In Windows 2000, Microsoft has improved its flexible, extensible routing technology. A Windows 2000 Server can act as a mid-range dynamic software demand-dial or multi-protocol router with the help of RRAS.

As with any other network equipment, the choice of hardware or software routing is largely determined by the expected traffic along connections. A small or medium-sized company can avoid purchasing expensive routing hardware to segment a network by building an entire network infrastructure based only on Microsoft software products.

For larger companies that require high-capacity routing in a complex enterprise environment, you will likely use dedicated hardware routers from specialized router vendors. Using hardware routers prevents bottlenecks in your high-capacity backbone. However, branch offices or individual subnets can still make use of software routing to connect to the backbone.

Windows 2000 supports the following connectivity options when acting as a multi-homed router:

- Dial-up, for low traffic links

- Integrated Services Digital Network (ISDN), for low traffic links

- Frame Relay, packet switching technology that is replacing X.25

- X.25

- Direct physical connection

- Point-to-point Virtual Private Network (VPN) connection through the Internet

Configuring Quality of Service (QoS) Settings

Windows 2000 Quality of Service (QoS) is a set of software components and technologies allowing you to control network traffic more efficiently. This reduces the need to upgrade the network. QoS supports consistent bandwidth results for high-demand traffic, such as video and audio applications.

QoS mechanisms already exist in hardware routers and switches, and the QoS components in Windows 2000 can work with them. This can give you an idea of which applications are in use and their resource requirements. To work correctly, all network hardware needs to support the QoS standards. Before implementing QoS, you need to determine where QoS is needed and what network components support it.

Windows 2000 supports the following QoS standards and components:

Resource Reservation Protocol (RSVP)

With RSVP you can reserve a predetermined amount of bandwidth along a specific path in the network, called the flow. This will reduce the differences in latency that normally occur between packets traveling along different network paths. To reserve a flow, all network hardware that will transfer the packets between two predetermined computers must allocate resources.

The client sends a PATH message to the receiver. As each router having RSVP receives the PATH message, it adds itself to the list and forwards the message. Future packets in the same session will follow the same route. The receiving station responds with a Reservation (RESV) message that travels the same route as the PATH message. As each router forwards the RESV message, it reserves the requested bandwidth (Figure 7.11).

Figure 7.11 How RSVP Functions

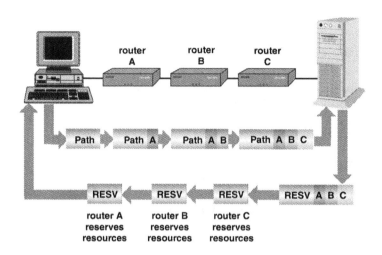

Traffic Control

Traffic Control is an Application Program Interface (API), or a set of routines, protocols and tools for building software applications. It prioritizes different processes within the Windows 2000 operating system, and is used in parts of the network that do not support RSVP.

Packet Scheduling

The QoS Packet Scheduler retrieves packets from outgoing queues and transmits them according to QoS parameters specified by users and applications. If the network is congested, higher priority packets will be moved to the front of the queue.

To install the QoS Packet Scheduler, follow these steps:

1. From the **Start** menu, choose **Settings** and then select **Network and Dial-up Connections**.

2. Choose the desired local area connection, and then from the **File** menu, select **Properties**.

3. Choose **Install**, **Service** and then select **Add**.

4. Highlight **QoS Packet Scheduler** and click **OK**.

External Prioritization

There are three methods of prioritizing packets that are external to Windows QoS. In Internet Engineering Task Force (IETF) Diff-Serv, a 6-bit field in the IP header allows applications to set priority by specifying a level of QoS in the field. In Institute of Electrical and Electronics Engineers (IEEE) 802.1p, the priority is carried as a 2-byte tag in the data portion of the frame in Ethernet networks. In busy network segments, switches can drop low-priority frames in favor of high-priority frames. IP Precedence in layer 3 of the OSI Reference Model allows routers to prioritize traffic and to select packets that must be dropped.

Quality of Service Admission Control Service

The Quality of Service Admission Control Service is the QoS administrative interface you use to manage QoS policies from a centralized location. You create QoS policies based on your network topology, resources, users, groups and applications. Because the policies are stored in Active Directory, they are available throughout the enterprise. You can give specific users priority on the network, prioritize different types of traffic, guarantee a specific amount of bandwidth for particular applications, and prevent protocols that do not support QoS from hoarding network resources. Windows 2000 has prepared QoS templates for your use, so when you have program types that require similar QoS parameters, you do not have to direct the QoS Service provider to prepare and invoke QoS capabilities for each one. The QoS Admission Control Service also controls RSVP Subnet Bandwidth Management, IP Precedence and 802.1p usage.

To install QoS Admission Control on a domain controller in Active Directory, follow these steps:

1. From the **Start** menu, choose **Settings** and then select **Control Panel**.

2. Double-click **Add /Remove Programs**, and choose **Add/Remove Windows Components**.

3. From **Windows Components**, highlight **Networking Services**, and choose **Details**.

4. Choose **QoS Admission Control Service**, **OK**, **Next** and then select **Finish**.

All QoS Admission Control messages can be tracked to obtain network statistics. You can also set up logging to help with troubleshooting, by verifying that RSVP messages are sent and received.

TCP/IP Filtering Configuration

Restricting traffic through filters is a key element of securing your network. Windows 2000 provides IP and IPX packet filters as part of its routing services. With these filters you limit the type of access allowed into and out of the network. Windows 2000 can filter packets based on TCP port, User Datagram Protocol (UDP) port, IP protocol ID, Internet Control Message Protocol (ICMP) type, ICMP code, source address and destination address. This allows you to define which triggers will be secured, blocked or allowed to pass through unfiltered. UDP is a component of TCP/IP that transmits data through a connectionless service, but it does not guarantee the delivery or sequencing of sent packets. ICMP supports packets containing error, control and informational messages.

Take care not to configure packet filters that are too restrictive, impairing the functionality of needed protocols. Filters can be individually configured and grouped together as filter lists to be managed as policies.

Configuring TCP/IP Filtering

You can configure TCP/IP to filter IP packets based on the following criteria:

- TCP port number
- UDP port number
- IP protocol number

To configure TCP/IP filtering, follow these steps:

1. From the **Start** menu, choose **Settings** and then select **Network and Dial-up Connections**.
2. Right-click **Local Area Connection** and choose **Properties**.
3. Highlight **Internet Protocol (TCP/IP)** and choose **Properties**.
4. From the **General** property page, choose **Advanced**.
5. Choose the **Options** property page, **TCP/IP filtering** and then select **Properties**.
6. From **TCP/IP Filtering** (Figure 7.12), configure the desired filters and click **OK**.

Figure 7.12 TCP/IP Filtering Property Page

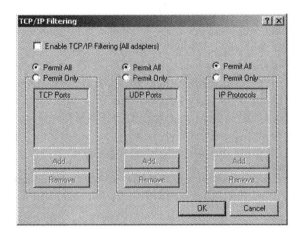

You can configure external source and route filtering for OSPF from the External Routing property page.

IP filtering is also available through Internet Protocol Security (IPSec), which allows you to define filters that specify the network traffic to act on. You can specify and configure filters to include in a customized filter list, which is composed of multiple subnets, IP addresses and protocols. Then you specify what action will happen if traffic matches or does not match a filter. IPSec is generally used for remote access clients and in VPNs.

Demand-Dial Routing Implementation

A demand-dial interface is a router interface brought up on demand, in response to network traffic requirements. The link is only initiated when the routing table shows that the interface is needed to reach the IP destination address. To save on wide area connection costs, you can implement demand-dial routing for those links that do not require full-time connection. Possible WAN connections for demand-dial routing include dial-up and ISDN, as seen in Figure 7.13.

Figure 7.13 LAN/WAN Demand-Dial Routing

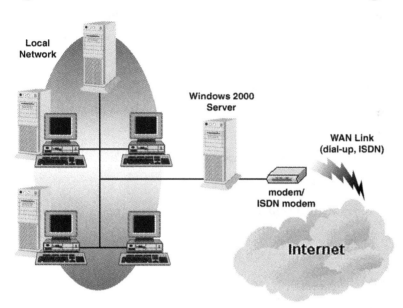

LAN workstations can be connected to a Windows 2000 computer that acts as the gateway server to the Internet. Essentially, the Windows 2000 software router is acting as a Dial-up Networking client computer, and dialing out to the Internet.

Implementing Demand-Dial Routing

To create a demand-dial router if you have not previously installed a remote access server, follow these steps:

Attach the WAN connection device.

1. From the **Start** menu, choose **Programs**, **Administrative Tools**, and then select **Routing and Remote Access**.

2. Right-click the desired server and choose **Properties**.

3. Right-click the desired computer, and choose **Configure and Enable Routing and Remote Access**.

4. From **Routing and Remote Access Server Setup Wizard**, choose **Next**.

5. From **Common Configurations**, choose **Network Router** and then select **Next**.

6. From **Routed Protocols**, verify that **TCP/IP** is listed under **Protocols**, and choose **Yes, all of the available protocols are on this list** and then select **Next**.

7. From **Demand-Dial Connections**, choose **Yes** and then select **Next**.

8. From **IP Address Assignment**, choose to have IP addresses assigned to incoming demand-dial connections either automatically or from a specified range of addresses.

9. From **Completing the Routing and Remote Access Server Setup Wizard**, choose **Finish**.

To create a new demand-dial interface, follow these steps:

1. From the **Start** menu, choose **Programs, Administrative Tools,** and then select **Routing and Remote Access**.

2. Right-click **Routing Interfaces** and choose **New Demand-dial Interface**.

3. From **Welcome to the Demand Dial Wizard**, choose **Next**.

4. In **Interface Name**, type the name of the demand dial interface and choose **Next**.

5. From **Connection Type**, choose the type of demand dial interface: **Connect using a modem, ISDN adapter, or other physical device** or **Connect using virtual private networking (VPN)**.

6. Choose **Connect using a modem, ISDN adapter, or other physical device** and then select **Next**.

7. From **Select a device**, choose the modem or adapter this interface will use, and then select **Next**.

8. From **Phone Number**, type the phone number the modem should dial and choose **Next**.

9. From **Protocols and Security** (Figure 7.14), choose **Route IP packets on this interface** and then select **Next**.

Figure 7.14 Protocols and Security Page of Demand Dial Interface Wizard

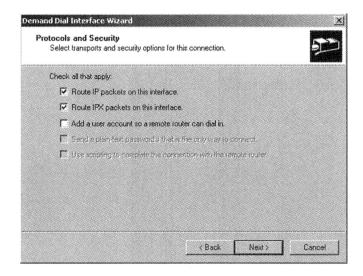

10. From **Dial Out Credentials**, type the **User name, Password** and **Domain,** and choose **Next**.

11. From **Completing the Demand Dial Interface Wizard**, choose **Finish**.

You can configure routing interface options through the following four property pages:

*   General

*   Options

*   Security

*   Networking

General Property Page

The General property page allows you to select and configure the communications device.

Options

The Options property page (Figure 7.15) allows you to specify, for a demand dial connection, the idle time before hanging up. You can also enter the number of redial attempts and the length of the redial intervals.

Figure 7.15 Remote Router Options Property Page

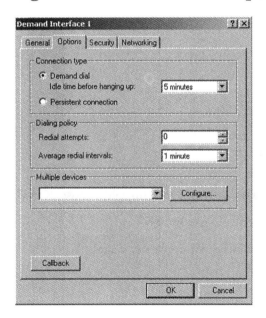

From the Automatic Dialing and Hanging Up property page (Figure 7.16), you can configure Windows to automatically dial and hang up devices depending on how much information is being sent and received. You can configure callback options from the Router Callback property page.

Figure 7.16 Automatic Dialing and Hanging Up Property Page

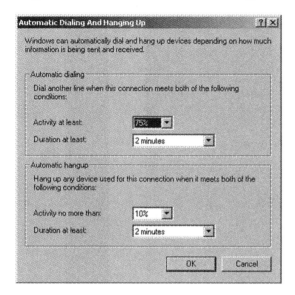

Security

The Security property page allows you to configure security options (Figure 7.17).

Figure 7.17 Remote Router Security Property Page

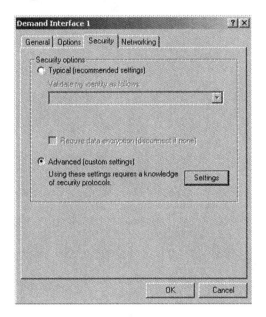

The Advanced Security property page (Figure 7.18) allows you to select data encryption and logon security protocols.

Figure 7.18 Advanced Security Settings Property Page

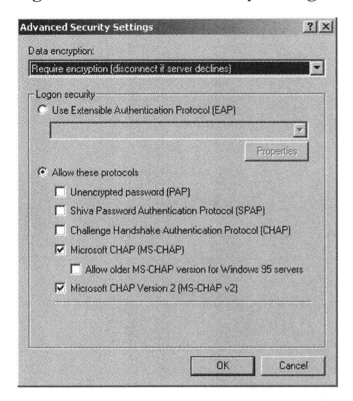

Networking

The Networking property page allows you to select the components used by the connection and specify the type of dial-up server you are calling.

Another configurable option is a demand-dial filter for traffic. If required, you implement demand-dial filters controlling the type of traffic that can initiate a particular demand-dial link. These filters include permitting or denying traffic based on a predetermined source or destination IP address, port, protocols, and time of day. Through RRAS, you use information found in the IP, TCP and UDP headers and in ICMP packets to create demand-dial filters.

An IP header of 20 bytes contains the following information:

- IP protocol identifier, such as a protocol ID of 6 for TCP

- Source IP address

- Destination IP address

A TCP header contains the following information:

- TCP source port, which describes the source process sending the TCP segment

- TCP destination port, which describes the destination process for the TCP segment

A UDP header contains the following information:

- UDP source port, which identifies the source process sending the UDP message

- UDP destination port, which describes the destination process for the UDP message

ICMP packets are encapsulated within IP datagrams before they are routed through an internetwork. ICMP packets contain the following information:

- ICMP type, identifies the type of ICMP packet, such as a request or reply

- ICMP code, identifies the specific function within an ICMP type

To configure demand-dial filters, follow these steps:

1. From the **Start** menu, choose **Programs, Administrative Tools**, and then select **Routing and Remote Access**.

2. For the desired server, highlight **Routing Interfaces**, right-click the demand-dial interface, and choose **Set IP Demand-dial Filters**.

3. From **Set Demand-dial Filters** (Figure 7.19), choose **Add**.

Figure 7.19 Set Demand-Dial Filters

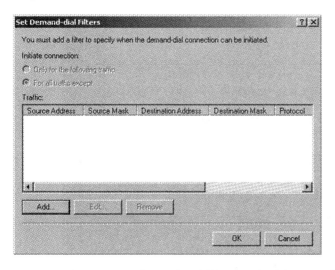

4. Type the options shown in Table 7.4: IP address and subnet mask of the source network and destination network, and the protocol.

5. Click **OK** twice to exit.

Table 7.4 Options in Set Demand-Dial Filters

Option	Description
Source address	IP address of packet source.
Source mask	Subnet mask of packet source. By altering the subnet mask, you can specify a range of addresses. Ex: 10.0.0.0 mask 255.0.0.0 applies to all Class A addresses
Destination address	IP address of packet destination
Destination mask	Subnet mask of packet destination
Protocol	Different protocols can be used for a filter. • TCP and UDP are configured with source and destination ports • ICMP is configured with ICMP type and ICMP code • ANY refers to any protocol • OTHER specifies an IP protocol ID, which in turn is resolved to a protocol number using the protocol file in the %winroot%\system32\drivers\etc directory
Action	You can either initiate connection only for the traffic defined by the filters or deny connection only for the traffic defined by the filters

You can also specify the hours when the demand-dial connection can be made. To configure restrictions for demand-dial connections, follow these steps:

1. From the **Start** menu, choose **Programs, Administrative Tools,** and then select **Routing and Remote Access**.

2. Highlight **Routing Interfaces** on the desired server, right-click on the demand-dial interface, and choose **Dial-out Hours**.

3. From **Dial-out Hours** (Figure 7.20), choose the desired hours to allow or deny demand-dial connections, and click **OK**.

Figure 7.20 Dial-Out Hours Property Page

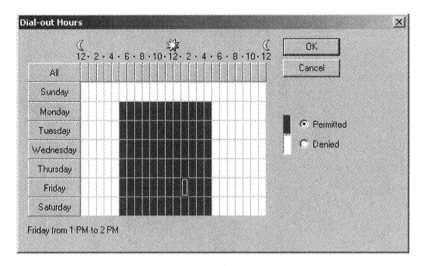

IP Routing Monitoring

A number of software tools are available to help you administer IP traffic on your Windows 2000 software routers. Some offer friendly Graphical User Interfaces (GUIs), unlike most hardware routers' text-based interfaces.

Monitoring IP Routing

Windows 2000 has the following built-in tools to help you monitor IP routing:

Logging—You can configure logging for RIP, OSPF, IP and the server itself through their respective property pages. By default, the log files are located in the %systemroot%\system32\LogFiles folder, but you can specify another location.

NETSH—This command-line and scripting tool supports many Windows 2000 components by adding NETSH helper Dynamic Link Libraries (DLLs). Each DLL provides a group of commands, called a context, for a specific networking component. The Routing context allows you to use commands to configure IP and IPX routing.

Network Monitor—Using the Network Monitor, you can identify network traffic patterns and problems. Network Monitor captures traffic on the local network segment, and displays and filters the captured packets.

The Resource Kit Utilities described in Table 7.5 can also help you manage and monitor routing.

Table 7.5 Resource Kit Utilities that Help in Monitoring

Utility	Description
RASLIST.EXE	The RASLIST command-line tool displays RRAS server announcements on all active network cards in the computer from which it is run.
RASSRVMON.EXE	With the RASSRVMON utility, you can obtain the following monitoring information: • Server information • Per port information • Summary information • Individual connection
TRACEENABLE.EXE	The TRACEENABLE tool is a Graphical User Interface (GUI, pronounced goo-ee) supporting tracing and its options.

Windows 2000 Router Integration

Windows 2000 software routing needs to be integrated into your overall network design infrastructure. You must design your TCP/IP addressing and subnetting carefully to minimize traffic. Software routers can be used to reduce broadcast traffic on LANs, with WAN routers determined by the expected traffic from T1, T3, Frame Relay or Asynchronous Transfer Mode (ATM) links. T1 and T3 are leased line options. Frame Relay is a packet-switching protocol for connecting devices across a WAN, and ATM is a networking technology based on transferring packets of a fixed size across a fixed channel.

Integrating Network Services

Windows 2000 network services all work together to minimize administrative overhead while maximizing functionality. These network services include:

- Domain Name System (DNS), the industry standard name resolution service that allows clients to locate Active Directory services and translates an IP address into a domain name

- DHCP

- Windows Internet Naming Service (WINS), which dynamically maps IP addresses to Network Basic Input/Output System (NetBIOS) names

- RRAS

- Microsoft Certificate Services, which creates and manages the Certification Authorities that issue digital certificates certifying the identities of users, organizations and computers

- Network Address Translation (NAT), which hides internally managed IP addresses from external networks by translating a private internal address to a public external address

Configuring DHCP and DNS Integration

DHCP implementation is so closely linked to WINS, and to DNS in particular, that you can think of the three services as a unit when planning deployment.

DHCP simplifies the administration and management of IP addresses on a TCP/IP network by automating address configuration for network clients. It provides:

- Integration with Active Directory and DNS

- Enhanced monitoring and statistical reporting

- Vendor-specific options and user-class support

- Multicast address allocation

- Rogue DHCP server detection

If you use DHCP servers for Microsoft clients, you will need a name resolution service to match IP addresses with user-friendly names. By default, this is the DNS service in Windows 2000 computers.

Networks supporting legacy versions of Windows must use WINS servers, while networks having a mixture of Windows 2000 and earlier clients require both WINS and DNS.

A DHCP server can be configured to provide DHCP clients with the addresses of the WINS and DNS servers and access methods on DNS server, scope and client levels. You can configure DNS and DHCP services to centralize control or to increase self-sufficiency for branch office address management. From the General property page of a DHCP server, you can specify more than 75 TCP/IP options. From the DNS property page of a DHCP server, you can support advanced options such as allowing automatic updates of DHCP client information in DNS.

In Windows 2000, DHCP servers can register with the Windows 2000 DNS dynamic update protocol. This integration allows the registration of both name-to-address and address-to-name records, but only for newer DNS servers supporting the dynamic protocol and not for older, static DNS servers.

From the WINS property page of a DNS server, you can configure forward lookups (NetBIOS names to IP addresses), reverse lookups (IP addresses to NetBIOS names), caching and time-out values for WINS resolution. You do this by adding a WINS or WINS-R record to the zone where you want WINS lookup to be supported.

Configuring Routing and Remote Access for DHCP Integration

You can configure a DHCP server to provide the IP addresses of routers (default gateways) from the General property page of a DHCP server. When implementing DHCP on your network, assign client IP addresses in a contiguous manner. By doing this, you condense the range of IP addresses and reduce the number of routing table entries. Ideally, the route to an area office and corresponding subnet could be reduced to one network IP address.

When you configure an RRAS address pool to use DHCP, the DHCP packets do not travel to RRAS clients. Instead, RRAS uses DHCP to lease addresses, in blocks of 10, to RRAS clients and stores them in the registry. When the initial pool of addresses is used up, another block is leased. If the server is multi-homed, you can configure the lease of these addresses in the registry. Unlike earlier versions of Windows, with Windows 2000 the DHCP leases are released when RRAS is shut down.

The RRAS client may also use DHCPINFORM packets to obtain DHCP options such as WINS and DNS addresses and the domain name. DHCPINFORM messages are broadcasts used to obtain related TCP/IP information without also obtaining an IP address. Any DNS or WINS addresses received using DHCPINFORM will override those obtained from the RRAS server.

On a subnet that does not have a DHCP server, you also need to configure a DHCP relay agent to listen for broadcast DHCP client requests. The DHCP relay agent forwards the requests to a DHCP server across a hardware or software router. You configure the DHCP relay agent in Windows 2000 as a routing protocol through the RRAS console.

Benefiting from Network Services Integration

By integrating network services, you can create a finely optimized infrastructure that securely and efficiently meets your organization's particular needs, while reducing your administrative work and the network down time.

Vocabulary

Review the following terms in preparation for the certification exam.

Term	Description
ABR	An Area Border Router is a software router running OSPF that connects a group of contiguous networks, called an area, with the backbone.
Active Directory	The directory service included with Windows 2000 Server stores information about objects on a network in a hierarchical view. It provides a single point of administration for all network objects.
API	An Application Program Interface is a set of routines, protocols and tools for building software applications.
AppleTalk	The communication protocol used by Macintosh clients is AppleTalk. It must be installed on a computer running Windows 2000 Server for Macintosh clients to connect to it.
ATM	Asynchronous Transfer Mode is a networking technology based on transferring packets of a fixed size across a fixed channel.
callback	The callback security feature allows a remote access server to call the remote access client to establish a connection after the user credentials have been verified.
Certificate Services	This Windows 2000 service issues and manages the certificates for a particular certification authority.
certification authority	A certification authority establishes and vouches for the authenticity of public keys belonging to users or other certification authorities.

Term	Description
datagram	A datagram is an unacknowledged packet of data sent to another network destination.
demand-dial router	A demand-dial router supports the routing of packets over point-to-point on-demand WAN links.
DHCP	The Dynamic Host Configuration Protocol simplifies TCP/IP network configuration and dynamically configures IP addresses for clients. DHCP ensures that address conflicts do not occur by centralizing address allocation.
DHCPINFORM	DHCPINFORM messages are broadcasts used to obtain information without also obtaining an IP address.
DLL	Dynamic Link Library allows executable routines serving specific functions to be stored separately as files with .dll extensions. These are loaded only when requested by a program.
DNS	The Domain Name System is a hierarchical naming system used to locate domain names on the Internet and on private TCP/IP networks. The DNS service maps DNS domain names to IP addresses and vice versa.
dynamic routing	With dynamic routing, routing protocols such as RIP and OSPF are used to automatically create and modify routing tables.
forward lookup	This is a query in which the DNS name for the computer is used to determine the IP address.
FQDN	The Fully Qualified Domain Name is a DNS name that uniquely identifies a computer on the network. It is a concatenation of the host name, the primary DNS suffix, and a period.

Term	Description
Frame Relay	The packet-switching protocol for connecting devices on a WAN. It supports data transfer across T1 and T3 lines. Although popular because of low costs, it is being replaced by the faster ATM.
GUI	A Graphical User Interface is a user-friendly program interface that makes use of graphics rather than a command-driven interface.
hop	A hop is an intermediate connection in a string of connections linking two network devices. On the Internet, this refers to the forwarding of a packet to the next router.
ICMP	The Internet Control Message Protocol supports packets containing error, control and informational messages.
IEEE 802.1p	Institute of Electrical and Electronics Engineers 802.1p describes a 2-byte tag in the data portion of the frame in Ethernet networks, which allows switches to drop low-priority frames in favor of high-priority frames in busy network segments.
IETF Diff-Serv	Internet Engineering Task Force Diff-Serv describes a 6-bit field in the IP header that allows applications to set priority by specifying a level of QoS in the field.
IGMP	The Internet Group Management Protocol is used to support multicast messaging.
IP	The Internet Protocol is the routable protocol in the TCP/IP suite that is responsible for the IP addressing, routing, and fragmentation and re-assembly of IP packets.

Term	Description
IP filter	An IP filter is a subset of potential network traffic based on the IP address, port and transport protocol. The IP filter secures both outbound and inbound traffic.
IP filter list	An IP filter list is a combination of one or more IP filters defining a range of network traffic.
IP Precedence	IP Precedence in layer 3 of the OSI Reference Model allows routers to prioritize traffic and to select packets that must be dropped.
IPSec	A set of standard, cryptography-based protection services and protocols, Internet Protocol Security protects all protocols in the TCP/IP suite and Internet communications and the Layer 2 Tunneling Protocol (L2TP) uses IPSec.
IPX	The Internetwork Packet Exchange is the NetWare protocol that controls addressing and routing of packets within and between LANs.
ISDN	Integrated Services Digital Network is a communications standard for sending voice, video, and data over digital phone lines.
LAN	A Local Area Network is a communications network connecting computers, printers, and other devices within a limited area.
metric	The metric value tells IP how may routers it will have to pass to reach a destination.
multicast	Network traffic destined for a set of hosts that belong to a group is known as multicast traffic.
multi-homed	A multi-homed computer has two or more network interfaces installed.

Term	Description
multi-protocol router	An RRAS server can act like a router, routing IP, IPX, and AppleTalk packets simultaneously.
NAT	Network Address Translation is an Internet standard that enables a LAN to use one set of IP addresses for internal traffic and a second set of addresses for external traffic.
NetBIOS name	A Network Basic Input/Output System name is recognized by WINS, the service that maps a computer name to its IP address.
NETSH	Net shell is a command-line utility that supports Windows 2000 networking components for both local and remote computers. You can use NETSH to save a configuration script in a text file for configuring other servers.
Network Monitor	This Windows 2000 Server utility captures and displays statistics about frames that it receives from the LAN.
NIC	A Network Interface Card is the expansion board you insert into a computer so it can be connected to a network. NICs are usually designed for a particular network, protocol and media.
NT	New Technologies is Microsoft's version of Windows previous to Windows 2000.
OSI Reference Model	The Open System Interconnection standard for communications defines a networking framework for implementing protocols in seven layers.
OSPF	Open Shortest Path First is a protocol that defines how routers share routing information. Unlike the older RIP, OSPF transfers only routing information that has changed since the previous transfer, saving bandwidth.

Term	Description
packet	A packet is a transmission unit of a fixed maximum size consisting of both data and a header containing an identification number, source and destination addresses, and error-control information.
packet-switching	This refers to protocols in which messages are divided into packets that are transmitted individually along different routes to their destination, where they are reassembled into the original message.
PPP	The Point-to-Point Protocol is a method of connecting a computer to the Internet. It supports error checking.
QoS	The Quality of Service is a set of quality assurance standards and mechanisms for data transmission in Windows 2000.
QoS Admission Control Service	This software service controls bandwidth and network resources on the subnet to which it is assigned. It can be installed on any Windows 2000 computer.
RADIUS	Remote Authentication Dial-In User Service is the most common authentication protocol used by Internet service providers. RADIUS, running on an Internet Authentication Service server with Windows 2000, can be used to manage the access policies of remote access servers.
RAS	A Remote Access Service is a Windows service that permits remote networking for mobile workers and for system administrators who monitor and manage servers at multiple sites.

Term	Description
RESV	With RSVP, the client sends a PATH message to the receiver. The receiving station responds with a Reservation (RESV) message that travels the same route as the PATH message. As each router forwards the RESV message, it reserves the requested bandwidth.
reverse lookup	This is a query in which the IP address is used to determine the DNS name for the computer.
RIP	The Routing Information Protocol is a reliable, simple and older routing protocol that dynamically communicates whole routing tables between neighboring routers.
RRAS	The Routing and Remote Access Service is the Microsoft feature that integrates remote access and multi-protocol routing services. It can turn a Windows 2000 server into a dynamic software router.
RSVP	The Resource Reservation Protocol allows you to reserve a predetermined amount of bandwidth along a specific path in the network, called the flow. This reduces the differences in latency that would normally occur between packets that travel along different network paths.
scope	This is the range of IP addresses a DHCP server can assign.
SNMP	The Simple Network Management Protocol is a set of protocols for managing complex networks.
static routing	With static routing, you manually create and modify routing tables. This is only done with small, relatively static networks.

Term	Description
TCP/IP	The Transport Control Protocol/Internet Protocol is a set of protocols that provides communication among diverse networks. Since it accommodates different architectures and operating systems, TCP/IP is the most commonly used Internet protocol.
UDP	A User Datagram Protocol is a TCP/IP component that transmits data through a connectionless service but does not guarantee the delivery or sequencing delivery of sent packets.
VPN	A Virtual Private Network is the extension of a private network that encompasses links across shared or public networks, such as the Internet.
WAN	A Wide Area Network is a computer network that spans a large geographical area. It usually consists of two or more LANs.
WINS	The Windows Internet Naming Service is a Microsoft software service that dynamically maps IP addresses to computer names. This allows users to access resources by name instead of by IP address.
X.25	This popular protocol is used in packet-switching networks.

In Brief

If you want to...	Then do this...
Install a Windows 2000 RRAS software router	1. From the **Start** menu, choose **Programs, Administrative Tools,** and then select **Routing and Remote Access.**
	2. Right-click the desired server and choose **Properties.**
	3. Right-click the desired computer, and choose **Configure and Enable Routing and Remote Access.**
	4. From **Routing and Remote Access Server Setup Wizard,** choose Next.
	5. From **Common Configurations,** choose **Network Router** and then select **Next.**
	6. From **Routed Protocols,** verify that TCP/IP is listed under **Protocols,** and choose **Yes, all of the available protocols are on this list** and then select **Next.**
	7. From **Demand-Dial Connections,** choose **Yes** to allow immediate configuration of demand-dial connections to access remote networks, or **No** to allow for later configuration.
	8. Choose **No, Next,** and then from **Completing the Routing and Remote Access Server Setup Wizard,** select **Finish.**

If you want to...	Then do this...
Configure IP routing	1. From the **Start** menu, choose **Programs, Administrative Tools,** and then select **Routing and Remote Access.** 2. From **Routing and Remote Access,** expand the desired server. 3. From **IP Routing,** right-click **General** and choose **Properties.** 4. Configure the three property pages, and click **OK.** Following are the three IP property pages: **General**—Various event logging settings are available, including log errors only, log errors and warnings, log the maximum amount of information, and disable event logging. **Preference Levels**—In this page you define the rank of a selected route source. Routes with higher rankings are preferred over lower-ranking routes. **Multicast scopes**—This page allows you to define the scope name, IP address and mask. Windows 2000 supports a limited form of multicast routing.

If you want to...	Then do this...
Add entries to the IP routing table	1. From the **Start** menu, choose **Programs**, **Administrative Tools**, and then select **Routing and Remote Access**. 2. From **Routing and Remote Access**, expand the desired server. 3. From **IP Routing**, right-click **Static Routes** and choose **New Static Route**. 4. In **Static Route**, type the **Interface**, **Destination**, **Network mask**, **Gateway**, and **Metric**. 5. Choose if you want to **Use this route to initiate demand-dial connections**, and then click **OK**. You can also add or modify entries in a routing table by using the ROUTE command with switches.
Install RIP	1. From the **Start** menu, choose **Programs**, **Administrative Tools**, and then select **Routing and Remote Access**. 2. From **Routing and Remote Access**, expand the desired server. 3. From **IP Routing**, right-click **General** and choose **New Routing Protocol**. 4. From **New Routing Protocol**, choose **RIP Version 2 for Internet Protocol**, and click **OK**.

If you want to...	Then do this...
Configure RIP	You can configure RIP with the following two property pages: **General**—From this page you can type the maximum amount of time that the router waits before it sends triggered updates. You can also specify event logging. **Security**—This page allows you to specify how to process announcements from routers.
Install OSPF	1. From the **Start** menu, choose **Programs**, **Administrative Tools**, and then select **Routing and Remote Access**. 2. From **Routing and Remote Access**, expand the desired server. 3. From **IP Routing**, right-click **General** and choose **New Routing Protocol**. 4. From **New Routing Protocol**, choose **Open Shortest Path First (OSPF)**, and click **OK**.

If you want to...	Then do this...
Configure OSPF	You can configure OSPF with the following four OSPF property pages: **General**—From this page you can type the router identification, and choose an autonomous system boundary router. You can also specify event logging. **Areas**—This page allows you to add, edit and remove OSPF areas. If you choose Add, you will see the General and Ranges property pages. From the General property page, you can specify the Area ID, Enable a plaintext password, and add a metric for the area. The Ranges property page allows you to specify the destination IP address and Network mask. **Virtual Interfaces**—This page allows you to add, edit or remove virtual interfaces by specifying the transit area and virtual neighbors. **External Routing**—From this page you can choose to accept or to ignore routes from all route sources except those selected. The OSPF External Route Filters property page allows you to type the destination IP address and network mask of routes to ignore or accept.

If you want to...	Then do this...
Install QoS Admission Control	1. From the **Start** menu, choose **Settings** and then select **Control Panel**. 2. Double-click **Add /Remove Programs**, and choose **Add/Remove Windows Components**. 3. From **Windows Components**, highlight **Networking Services**, and choose **Details**. 4. Choose **QoS Admission Control Service**, **OK, Next** and then select **Finish**.
Install the QoS Packet Scheduler	1. From the **Start** menu, choose **Settings** and then select **Network and Dial-up Connections**. 2. Choose the desired local area connection, and then from the **File** menu, select **Properties**. 3. Choose **Install, Service** and then select **Add**. 4. Highlight **QoS Packet Scheduler** and click **OK**.

If you want to...	Then do this...
Configure TCP/IP filters	1. From the **Start** menu, choose **Settings** and then select **Network and Dial-up Connections**.
	2. Right-click **Local Area Connection** and choose **Properties**.
	3. Highlight **Internet Protocol (TCP/IP)** and choose **Properties**.
	4. From the **General** property page, choose **Advanced**.
	5. Choose the **Options** property page, **TCP/IP filtering** and then select **Properties**.
	6. From **TCP/IP Filtering**, configure the desired filters and click **OK**.
	You can configure TCP/IP to filter IP packets based on the following criteria:
	• TCP port number
	• UDP port number
	• IP protocol number

If you want to...	Then do this...
Install a demand-dial router	1. Attach the WAN connection device.
	2. From the **Start** menu, choose **Programs, Administrative Tools**, and then select **Routing and Remote Access**.
	3. Right-click the desired server and choose **Properties**.
	4. Right-click the desired computer, and choose **Configure and Enable Routing and Remote Access**.
	5. From the **Routing and Remote Access Server Setup Wizard**, choose **Next**.
	6. From **Common Configurations**, choose **Network Router** and then select **Next**.
	7. From **Routed Protocols**, verify that **TCP/IP** is listed under **Protocols**, choose **Yes, all of the available protocols are on this list** and then select **Next**.
	8. From **Demand-Dial Connections**, choose **Yes** and then select **Next**.
	9. From **IP Address Assignment**, choose to have IP addresses assigned to incoming demand-dial connections either automatically or from a specified range of addresses.
	10. From **Completing the Routing and Remote Access Server Setup Wizard**, choose **Finish**.

If you want to...	Then do this...
Create a demand-dial interface	1. From the **Start** menu, choose **Programs**, **Administrative Tools**, and then select **Routing and Remote Access**.
	2. Right-click **Routing Interfaces** and choose **New Demand-dial Interface**.
	3. From **Welcome to the Demand Dial Wizard**, choose **Next**.
	4. From within **Interface Name**, type the name for the demand dial interface and choose **Next**.
	5. From **Connection Type**, choose the type of demand dial interface: **Connect using a modem, ISDN adapter, or other physical device** or **Connect using virtual private networking (VPN)**.
	6. Choose **Connect using a modem, ISDN adapter, or other physical device** and then select **Next**.
	7. From **Select a device**, choose the modem or adapter this interface will use, and then select **Next**.
	8. From within **Phone Number**, type the phone number the modem should dial and choose **Next**.
	9. From **Protocols and Security**, choose **Route IP packets on this interface** and then select **Next**.
	10. From within **Dial Out Credentials**, type the **User name**, **Password** and **Domain**, and choose **Next**.
	11. From **Completing the Demand Dial Interface**, choose **Finish**.

If you want to...	Then do this...
Configure demand-dial routing	You can configure routing interface options through the following four property pages: **General**—This page allows you to select and configure the communications device. **Options**—From this page you can specify, for a demand dial connection, the idle time before hanging up. You can also enter the number of redial attempts and the length of the redial intervals. From the Automatic Dialing and Hanging Up property page, you can configure Windows to automatically dial and hang up devices depending on how much information is being sent and received. You can configure callback options from the Router Callback property page. **Security**—Security options can be configured from this page. The Advanced Security property page allows you to select data encryption and logon security protocols. **Networking**—This page allows you to select the components used by the connection and specify the type of dial-up server you are calling.

If you want to...	Then do this...
Monitor IP routing	Use Windows 2000 built-in tools: **Logging**—You can configure logging for RIP, OSPF, IP and the server itself through their respective property pages. **NETSH**—This command-line and scripting tool supports many Windows 2000 components by adding NETSH helper Dynamic Link Libraries (DLLs). Each DLL provides a group of commands called a context for a specific networking component. The Routing context allows you to use commands to configure IP and IPX routing. **Network Monitor**—Using this, you can identify network traffic patterns and problems. Network Monitor captures traffic on the local network segment, and displays and filters the captured packets. The Resource Kit Utilities RASLIST.EXE, RASSRVMON.EXE and TRACEENABLE.EXE can also help you manage and monitor routing.
Integrate network services	Consider how the following services function: • DNS • DHCP • WINS • RRAS • Microsoft Certificate Services • NAT

Lesson 7 Activities

Complete the following activities to prepare for the certification exam.

1. Explain when you would use static routing.

2. List the ways you can view routing information.

3. Describe instances where you would implement RIP.

4. Explain the rationale for implementing demand-dial routing.

5. Define metric when used in routing.

6. List some of the connectivity options that Windows 2000 supports when acting as a multi-homed router.

7. Explain how RSVP works.

8. List the triggers with which you can configure Windows 2000 packet filters.

9. Explain how to integrate DHCP and DNS.

10. Explain how to implement OSPF.

Answers to Lesson 7 Activities

1. Routing tables can be created manually through static routing or automatically by using routing protocols, a process called dynamic routing. In static routing, you need to ensure each router has the necessary routes in its routing table to communicate with any two endpoints on the IP internetwork. Because of their administrative overhead, static routes are best reserved for small, relatively static networks. For dynamic or large networks, you should configure a routing protocol such as OSPF.

2. You can view routing information by typing either NETSTAT-RN or ROUTE PRINT from the command prompt. Alternatively, from the Routing and Remote Access console you can right-click on Static Routes under IP Routing and choose Show IP Routing Table.

3. RIP is a reliable and simple routing protocol that dynamically communicates routing information and changes between neighboring routers. Because of its hop limitation of 16 and propagation of whole routing tables, RIP has largely been replaced by OSPF. However, you would still need Windows 2000 RIP support for backwards-compatibility with existing RIP networks. RIP is also much easier to configure than OSPF, so it can be used in small to medium sized networks.

4. A demand-dial interface is a router interface brought up on demand in response to network traffic requirements. The link is only initiated when the routing table shows that the interface is needed to reach the IP destination address. To save on wide area connection costs, you can implement demand-dial routing for those links that do not require full-time connection.

5. The metric value tells IP how many routers it will have to pass to reach a destination. You can configure the value in the metric field of a routing table, with the lowest metric as the most preferred route. When multiple routes to a particular network destination exist, the route with the lowest metric is used.

6. Windows supports the following connectivity options when acting as a multi-homed router:

    *   Dial-up, for low traffic links

    *   ISDN, for low traffic links

    *   Frame Relay

    *   X.25

    *   Direct physical connection

- Point-to-point VPN connection through the Internet

7. With the Resource Reservation Setup Protocol (RSVP), you can reserve a predetermined amount of bandwidth along a specific path in the network, called the flow. This will reduce the differences in latency that normally occur between packets traveling along different network paths. To reserve a flow, all network hardware that will transfer the packets between two predetermined computers must allocate resources.

    The client sends a PATH message to the receiver. As each router having RSVP receives the PATH message, it adds itself to the list and forwards the message. Future packets in the same session will follow the same route. The receiving station responds with a Reservation (RESV) message that travels the same route as the PATH message. As each router forwards the RESV message, it reserves the requested bandwidth.

8. Windows 2000 can filter packets based on TCP port, User Datagram Protocol (UDP) port, IP protocol ID, Internet Control Message Protocol (ICMP) type, ICMP code, source address and destination address. This allows you to define which triggers will be secured, blocked or allowed to pass through unfiltered.

9. DHCP implementation is so closely linked to WINS, and to DNS in particular, that you can think of the three services as a unit when planning deployment. If you use DHCP servers for Microsoft clients, you will need a name resolution service to match IP addresses with user-friendly names. By default, this is the DNS service in Windows 2000 computers. Networks supporting legacy versions of Windows must use WINS servers, while networks having a mixture of Windows 2000 and earlier clients require both WINS and DNS.

    A DHCP server can be configured to provide DHCP clients with the addresses of the WINS and DNS servers and access methods on DNS server, scope and client levels. You can configure DNS and DHCP services to centralize control or to increase self-sufficiency for branch office address management. From the General property page of a DHCP server, you can specify more than 75 TCP/IP options. From the DNS property page of a DHCP server, you can support advanced options.

    In Windows 2000, DHCP servers can register with the Windows 2000 DNS dynamic update protocol. This integration allows the registration of both name-to-address and address-to-name records, but only for newer DNS servers supporting the dynamic protocol and not for older, static DNS servers.

10. OSPF is recommended for medium to large dynamic internetworks with more than 50 subnets. OSPF divides the network infrastructure into groups of contiguous networks called areas. These

areas are connected to each other through a backbone area by Area Border Routers (ABRs). Routers that have all interfaces connected to the backbone are internal routers. When you are configuring an OSPF network, you should follow these guidelines:

- Design areas according to site or administrative boundaries

- Ensure the ABRs for an area are configured with destination and network mask pairs that summarize the area's routes

- The source and route filtering configured on the ABRs is not overly restrictive, thus allowing needed routes to be propagated to other routers

- All ABRs are physically connected to the backbone or logically connected to the backbone through a virtual link

- Routers connect two areas by going through the backbone

- Use the minimum number of routers necessary in an area

Lesson 7 Quiz

These questions test your knowledge of features, vocabulary, procedures, and syntax.

1. Which of the following are guidelines to follow when designing an OSPF network?
   A. Use the minimum number of routers necessary in an area.
   B. Routers connect two areas by going through the backbone.
   C. Design areas according to site or administrative boundaries.
   D. All ABRs are logically connected to the backbone through virtual rather than physical links.

2. What connectivity options does Windows 2000 support when acting as a multi-homed router?
   A. ISDN
   B. Frame Relay
   C. Dial-up
   D. X.25

3. Which of the following can you administer through the QoS Admission Control Service?
   A. QoS policies
   B. QoS templates
   C. IP Precedence
   D. RSVP Subnet Bandwidth Management

4. What are the types of entries seen in a routing table?
   A. Network route
   B. Host route
   C. Special route
   D. Default route

5. How can you add entries to a routing table?
   A. Use the ROUTE command
   B. Right-click on Static Routes and select New Static Route
   C. Use RIP
   D. Use the NETSH command

6. Which of the following does an IP header contain?
   A. Source IP port
   B. IP protocol identifier
   C. Source IP address
   D. Destination IP address

7. What are some reasons to implement software routing?
   A. Lack of money to purchase dedicated hardware routers
   B. High volume traffic demands software routing
   C. Software routing is faster than hardware routing
   D. GUI interface is user-friendly

8. Why is OSPF an improvement over RIP?
   A. OSPF is easier to configure
   B. OSPF is not restricted to 16 hop counts
   C. OSPF propagates whole routing tables
   D. OSPF is a link-state routing protocol

9. Which of the following actions can help to integrate Routing and Remote Access with DHCP?
   A. Assign DHCP client addresses in a contiguous manner
   B. Configure a DHCP relay agent
   C. Configure a DHCP server to provide the IP addresses of routers
   D. Configure a long lease time so that when RRAS is shut down and restarted the lease does not expire

10. How do you specify a range of addresses when configuring demand-dial filters?
    A. Type the address range in the range box in the Set Demand-dial Filters property page
    B. You cannot specify a range of addresses
    C. Use a resource kit utility
    D. Alter the subnet source mask

Answers to Lesson 7 Quiz

1. Answers A, B and C are correct. The fewer routers in an area, the less packets are delayed as they make hops to their final destination. Routers need to connect two areas by going through the backbone. You can localize traffic by designing areas according to site or administrative boundaries.

    Answer D is incorrect. Only use virtual links if an ABR cannot be physically connected to the backbone. Virtual links are complicated to set up and error-prone.

2. Answers A, B, C and D are all correct. Windows 2000 supports ISDN, Frame Relay, Dial-up and x.25 when acting as a multi-homed router.

3. Answers A, B, C and D are all correct. The QoS Admission Control Service is the Windows 2000 QoS administrative interface that allows you to manage QoS policies, use QoS templates, control IP Precedence and control RSVP Subnet Bandwidth Management.

4. Answers A, B and D are correct. A network route entry provides a route to a specific network ID in the internetwork. A host route entry provides a route to a specific internetwork address consisting of a network ID and node ID. A default route is used when a specific route for a particular destination cannot be found in the routing table.

    Answer C is incorrect. A special route entry does not exist.

5. Answers A and B are correct. You can manually add static routes by using the ROUTE command in the following fashion: **ROUTE add [network] mask [netmask] [gateway]**. You can also add static routes by using the Routing and Remote Access console. Under **IP Routing**, right-click on **Static Routes** and choose **New Static Route**.

    Answer C is incorrect. RIP is a simple routing protocol that dynamically communicates whole routing tables between neighboring routers.

    Answer D is incorrect. NETSH is a command-line utility that supports Windows 2000 networking components for both local and remote computers. You can use NETSH to save a configuration script in a text file for configuring other servers.

6. Answers B, C and D are correct. An IP header of 20 bytes contains an IP protocol identifier, such as a protocol ID of 6 for TCP, a source IP address, and a destination IP address.

Answer A is incorrect. A TCP header contains information on the TCP source port, while a UDP header contains information on the UDP source port.

7. Answers A and D are correct. A lack of money to purchase dedicated hardware routers and the desire for a user-friendly GUI interface are both reasons to implement software routing.

Answer B is incorrect. For high volume traffic, you need dedicated hardware routers.

Answer C is incorrect. Hardware routing is generally faster than software routing.

8. Answers B and D are correct. Unlike with RIP, where packets are dropped after 16 hops, packet transfer with OSPF is not restricted to 16 hop counts. Instead, you can set the accumulated path costs, up to 65,535. This allows you to construct large networks with different link costs. OSPF is a link-state routing protocol that calculates routing table entries by constructing a shortest-path tree of current link states. Since OSPF-based routers communicate with all other routers in their network, they can build a map of the network, allowing for intelligence when redirecting traffic around a failed router.

Answer A is incorrect. OSPF, being a more sophisticated protocol, is more complex to set up than RIP.

Answer C is incorrect. OSPF only propagates changes to the routing tables, rather than whole routing tables like RIP. As a result, OSPF uses up less network bandwidth.

9. Answers A, B and C are correct. When implementing DHCP on your network, assign client IP addresses in a contiguous manner. By doing this, you condense the range of IP addresses and reduce the number of routing table entries. You also need to configure a DHCP relay agent to listen for broadcast DHCP client requests on a subnet that does not have a DHCP server. The DHCP relay agent forwards the requests to a DHCP server across a hardware or software router. You configure the DHCP relay agent in Windows 2000 as a routing protocol through the RRAS console. You can configure a DHCP server to hand out the IP addresses of routers (default gateways) from the General property page of a DHCP server.

Answer D is incorrect. Unlike with earlier versions of Windows, in Windows 2000 the DHCP leases are released when RRAS is shut down.

10. Answer D is correct. To specify a range of addresses when configuring demand-dial filters, configure the **Source mask** option on the **Set Demand-dial Filters** property page. This option refers to the subnet mask of the packet source. For example, 10.0.0.0 mask 255.0.0.0 applies to all Class A addresses.

Answer A is incorrect. There is no range box in the **Set Demand-dial filters** property page.

Answer B is incorrect. It is possible to specify a range of addresses.

Answer C is incorrect. You do not need to use a resource kit utility.

Lesson 8

Network Address Translation Installation and Administration

Network Address Translation (NAT) is an Internet standard where a Local Area Network (LAN) can use one set of Internet Protocol (IP) addresses for internal traffic and a second set of IP addresses for external traffic. This change in IP addresses protects your internal network from the Internet by hiding internal IP addresses. It can also save you the expense of acquiring a public address range for your network computers from an Internet Service Provider (ISP). With the help of NAT, you can use private addressing, and NAT will translate those addresses to one or more public IP addresses allocated to you by your ISP.

A NAT translator, located where the LAN meets the Internet, performs the IP address translations. Most routers and other network devices can perform NAT, as can Proxy Server 2.0. Windows 2000 Server offers basic NAT through the NAT routing protocol in the Routing and Remote Access Service (RRAS) or the Internet Connection Sharing (ICS) feature of Network and Dial-up Connections.

After completing this lesson, you should have a better understanding of the following topics:

- Network Address Translation (NAT)
- Internet Connection Sharing (ICS)

Network Address Translation (NAT)

You can use either a routed or a translated connection to link up a small home or office network to the Internet. Routing requires a viable range of IP addresses to use on your internal network. In a software-routed connection, a Windows 2000 computer acts like an IP router to forward packets between the internal network and the public Internet. In a translated connection, a Windows 2000 computer acts as a network address translator, providing network connectivity without the need for extensive configuration of IP routing protocols in the hosts and on the Windows 2000 router.

You configure translated connections to the Internet in Windows 2000 by using RRAS NAT or ICS. By using NAT, you can avoid acquiring and maintaining a block of valid IP addresses as the network hosts can share one or more public IP addresses. Also, you do not need to implement IP routing. NAT can be used without any actions from your ISP.

The computer configured with NAT can act as a network address translator, a simplified Dynamic Host Configuration Protocol (DHCP) server, a Domain Name System (DNS) proxy and a Windows Internet Naming Service (WINS) proxy. DHCP dynamically configures IP addresses for clients. DNS maps DNS domain names to IP addresses and vice-versa. WINS dynamically maps IP addresses to computer names. A proxy relays the client requests to the computer performing the actual name resolution and forwards the resolved names back to the requesting client.

Understanding NAT Components

NAT has the following components:

*   Translation

*   Addressing

*   Name Resolution

Translation

NAT, running on a Windows 2000 RRAS server, translates the IP addresses and Transmission Control Protocol/User Datagram Protocol (TCP/UDP) port numbers of packets traveling between the private network and the Internet. TCP enables two hosts to establish a connection and exchange data that is guaranteed. UDP transmits data through a connectionless service but does not guarantee the delivery or sequencing delivery of sent packets. If more than one private address is mapped to a public address, NAT uses unique TCP and UDP port numbers requested from the Transmission Control Protocol/Internet Protocol (TCP/IP) protocol stack to differentiate one intranet location from another. TCP/IP is a set of protocols providing communication among diverse networks.

Addressing

The NAT computer can also provide IP address configuration to the hosts on the private network, much like a simplified DHCP server. If you configure the hosts to be DHCP clients, the NAT computer can allocate an IP address, a subnet mask, a default gateway and the IP address of a DNS server. Non-DHCP clients can be manually configured with IP addressing information.

Name resolution

The NAT computer acts as a DNS server for the hosts on the private network. It forwards name resolution requests from hosts to the Internet-based DNS server for which it is configured. The Internet-based DNS server responds to the NAT computer, which then provides the information to the hosts.

Benefiting from Using NAT

Translation provides more security than routing because the addresses of hosts on your private network remain hidden from the Internet. The NAT computer translates addresses for traffic running in both directions. NAT can only translate IP addresses that reside in the standard TCP/IP header field. It cannot translate payloads for applications that use IP addressing in other fields, such as Kerberos and Internet Protocol Security (IPSec). IPSec is a set of standard, cryptography-based protection services and protocols.

 Note: You need to make sure that a NAT computer can support expected traffic, as routing is faster and more efficient.

Understanding NAT Components

NAT can perform the translation of IP addresses and TCP/UDP port numbers of packets as they are being forwarded because it has static or dynamic mappings of all private IP addresses on the network to one or more public IP addresses provided by the ISP. Static mappings are created in the same fashion as for a software router—through the Routing and Remote Access interface. Dynamic mappings are created when the NAT service automatically remembers and adds routes from client-initiated Internet traffic. Dynamic mappings are refreshed with each use. Any dynamic mappings not refreshed after a configurable length of time are removed from the NAT mapping table.

By default, NAT translates IP addresses and TCP/UDP ports. It does this by modifying and recalculating the following fields in the IP, TCP and UDP headers:

- Source IP address

- Source port

- TCP, UDP and IP checksum

A NAT editor is needed when other than IP, TCP and UDP headers require translating and adjusting. A NAT editor is a component you can install to modify other payloads and return the results to the NAT component. Windows 2000 has NAT editors for the following protocols:

- File Transfer Protocol (FTP), which is used to send files over the Internet

- Internet Control Message Protocol (ICMP), which supports packets containing error, control and informational messages

- Point-to-Point Tunneling Protocol (PPTP), which encapsulates Point-to-Point frames for transmission over the Internet or a private intranet

- Network Basic Input/Output System (NetBIOS) over TCP/IP, which provides the NetBIOS programming interface over the TCP/IP protocol

The components in NAT and their relationship to TCP/IP and other router components are shown in Figure 8.1.

Figure 8.1 NAT Components

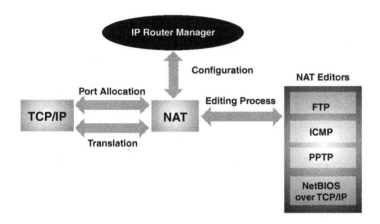

Windows 2000 includes a DHCP allocator in its NAT routing protocol. You cannot configure the DHCP options within the DHCP allocator. The options provided for DHCP clients are described in Table 8.1.

Table 8.1 DHCP Allocator Lease Options

Option #	Option value	Description
1	255.255.0.0	Subnet mask
3	IP address of private interface	Router (default gateway)
6	IP address of private interface	DNS server (if DNS proxy is enabled)
58	5 minutes	Renewal time
59	5 days	Rebinding time
51	7 days	IP address lease time
15	Primary domain name of NAT computer	DNS domain

The DHCP allocator only supports a single scope of IP addresses. If you need to support multiple scopes, superscopes or multicast scopes, you will have to disable the DHCP allocator component of the NAT routing protocol and install a DHCP server.

Understanding Outbound Internet Traffic

When NAT is translating outbound traffic, it first looks for a static or dynamic address and port mapping for a packet. If this is not found, a dynamic mapping is created, depending on whether there is one or more public IP addresses available. If only one public IP address can be used, NAT requests from TCP/IP a new unique TCP or UDP port for the public IP address and will use that as the mapped port. If more than one public IP address is available, NAT maps private IP addresses to public IP addresses without the ports being translated.

NAT then looks for editors. After editing, NAT alters the IP and TCP or UDP headers and forwards the packets using the Internet interface. This process is shown in Figure 8.2.

Figure 8.2 NAT Outbound Internet Traffic

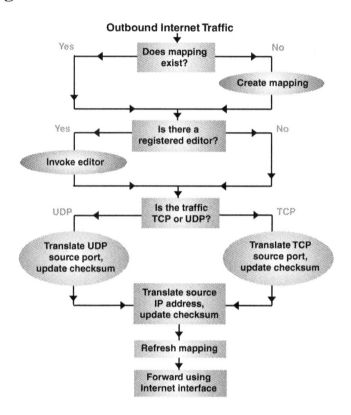

Understanding Inbound Internet Traffic

When NAT is processing inbound traffic, it first looks for a static or dynamic address and port mapping for a packet. If this is not found, NAT discards the packet, protecting the private network. NAT will only forward Internet traffic to the private network user under the following conditions:

- A static map exists for an Internet user to access specific resources on the private network

- Responding to traffic initiated by clients that created a dynamic mapping

Next, NAT looks for editors and invokes one if needed. After editing, NAT modifies the TCP, UDP, and IP headers and forwards the frame. This process is shown in Figure 8.3.

Figure 8.3 NAT Inbound Internet Traffic

Inbound Internet Traffic

Yes / No — **Does mapping exist?**

Discard packet

Yes / No — **Is there a registered editor?**

Invoke editor

UDP / TCP — **Is the traffic TCP or UDP?**

Translate UDP source port, update checksum

Translate TCP source port, update checksum

Translate destination IP address, update checksum

Refresh mapping

Forward using private network interface

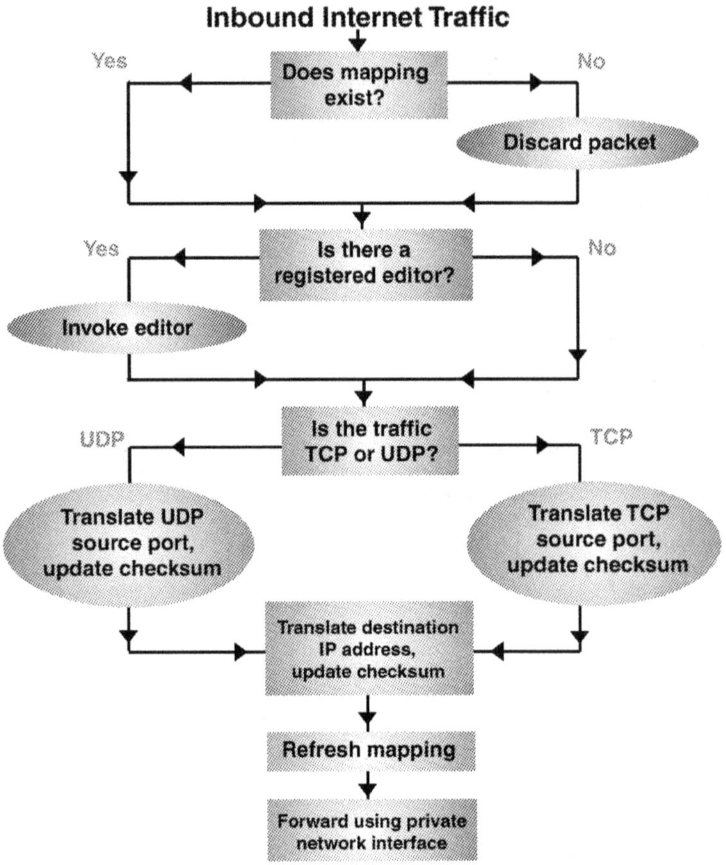

Installing NAT

To reduce costs, you can and will likely run NAT, DHCP, and RRAS all from the same Windows 2000 server. To install NAT on a server that does not yet have routing and remote access abilities, use the Routing and Remote Access Server Setup Wizard, choosing Internet Connection Server and Set up a router with the Network Address Translation (NAT) routing protocol.

To install NAT on a server that is enabled for Routing and Remote Access, follow these steps:

1. Configure the IP address of the home network interface: IP address, subnet mask and no default gateway.

2. Enable routing on your dial-up port.

3. If you do not have a permanent Internet connection, create a demand-dial interface for IP routing using your dial-up equipment and the information you use to dial the ISP.

4. If you have a permanent Internet connection that appears in Windows 2000 as a LAN interface or if you are connecting your Windows 2000 computer to another router before connecting to the Internet, you do not need to create a demand-dial interface.

5. Create a default static route that uses the Internet interface by selecting the demand-dial interface (for dial-up connections) or LAN interface (for permanent connections) that you will use to connect to the Internet.

Tip: Demand-dial filters will not work when you are using NAT on a Windows 2000 computer. One way to work around this is to define static routes for the interface for networks that need to be reached.

6. The destination IP address is 0.0.0.0 and the network mask is 0.0.0.0. The gateway IP address is not configurable for a demand-dial interface.

7. Add the NAT routing protocol.

8. Add the Internet and network interfaces to the NAT routing protocol.

9. Enable NAT addressing and name resolution.

10. Configure the interface IP address ranges

To add the NAT routing protocol, follow these steps:

1. From the **Start** menu, choose **Programs**, **Administrative Tools** and then select **Routing and Remote Access**.

2. From **Routing and Remote Access**, expand the desired server and **IP Routing**.

3. Right-click **General**, and choose **New Routing Protocol**.

4. From **New Routing Protocol**, choose **Network Address Translation (NAT)** and click **OK**.

To enable NAT addressing, follow these steps:

1. From the **Start** menu, choose **Programs, Administrative Tools** and then select **Routing and Remote Access**.

2. From **Routing and Remote Access**, expand the desired server and **IP Routing**.

3. Right-click **Network Address Translation**, and choose **Properties**.

4. From the **Address Assignment** property page, choose **Automatically assign IP addresses by using DHCP**.

5. Configure the range of IP addresses to allocate to DHCP clients in your network by typing the **IP address** and **Mask**.

6. Choose **Exclude**, and then from **Exclude Reserved Addresses**, select **Add** and type addresses to exclude from allocation to DHCP clients.

7. Click **OK** 3 times to exit.

When assigning private IP addresses, use the three blocks of addresses reserved by the Internet Assigned Numbers Authority for private networks. This saves the limited number of IP addresses available for public traffic. Private addresses are not reachable on the Internet. As a result, Internet traffic from a host with a private address must go through an application-layer gateway with a public IP address, such as a proxy server, or be translated into a public IP address by a network address translator before continuing on to the Internet. The following are IP addresses reserved for private use:

*   10.0.0.0 through 10.255.255.255 with a subnet mask of 255.0.0.0 (one Class A network)

*   176.16.0.0 through 172.31.255.255 with a subnet mask of 255.240.0.0 (16 contiguous Class B networks)

*   192.168.0.0 through 192.168.255.255 (256 contiguous Class C networks)

If you are using more than one public IP address for your NAT server, you will need to configure the NAT interface with the range of public IP addresses. Combining an IP address with a subnet mask does this. For example, the public IP addresses 200.100.100.212, 200.100.100.213, 200.100.100.214,

200.100.100.215 can be expressed as 200.100.100.212 with a subnet mask of 255.255.255.252. If you cannot reduce the IP addresses to one address and a subnet mask, enter the starting and ending IP addresses for each range or series of ranges.

To configure interface IP address ranges, follow these steps:

1. From the **Start** menu, choose **Programs, Administrative Tools** and then select **Routing and Remote Access**.

2. From **Routing and Remote Access**, expand the desired server and **IP Routing**.

3. Choose **Network Address Translation**, right-click the desired interface and choose **Properties**.

4. From the **Address Pool** property page, choose **Add**, type the interface IP address range and click **OK** twice to exit.

Administering NAT

Following are four NAT configurable property pages:

The General property page (Figure 8.4) allows you to specify event logging options, including log errors only, log errors and warnings, log the maximum amount of information, and disable event logging.

Figure 8.4 NAT General Property Page

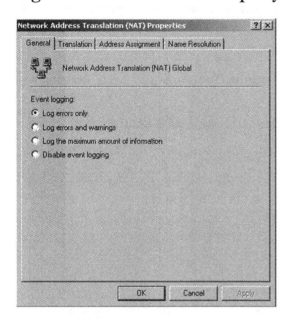

 Note: Several Microsoft services and third-party components can use NAT modules in Windows 2000. These modules can be used by only one service or component at a time. If RRAS NAT or ICS cannot get access to the NAT modules because they are in use by another computer or service, you will get an error message in the event log.

The Translation property page (Figure 8.5) allows you to specify the length of time after which dynamic mappings not refreshed are removed from the NAT mapping table. For TCP connections, the default time-out is 24 hours. For UDP traffic, it is 1 minute. If you select applications, you can make applications on the public network available to private network clients.

Figure 8.5 NAT Translation Property Page

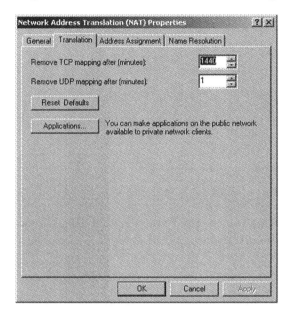

To configure NAT network applications, follow these steps:

1. From the **Start** menu, choose **Programs**, **Administrative Tools** and then select **Routing and Remote Access**.

2. From **Routing and Remote Access**, expand the desired server and **IP Routing**.

3. Right-click **NAT** and choose **Properties**.

4. From the **Translation** property page, choose **Applications**.

5. From **Applications**, choose **Add**.

6. In **Internet Connection Sharing Application** (Figure 8.6), type the name of the application, the remote server port number and the incoming TCO and UDP response ports.

7. Click **OK** three times to exit.

Figure 8.6 Internet Connection Sharing Application Property Page

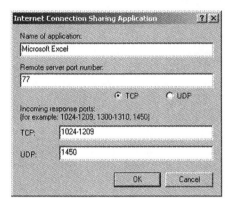

The Address Assignment property page (Figure 8.7) allows you to specify the range of IP addresses that NAT can assign to computers on the private network by using DHCP as well as excluded addresses.

Figure 8.7 NAT Address Assignment Property Page

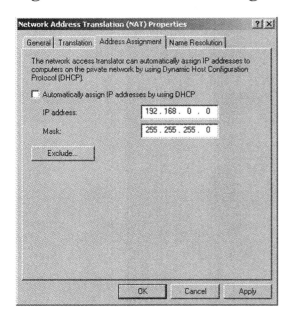

The Name Resolution property page (Figure 8.8) allows you to specify clients to use DNS for IP address resolution. Select the demand-dial interface used to connect to the public network when a name needs to be resolved.

Figure 8.8 NAT Name Resolution Property Page

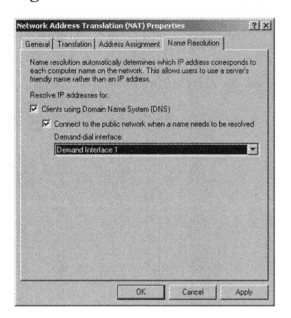

The DHCP Allocator Information page allows you to see DHCP allocator information and details of the various DHCP message types (Figure 8.9).

Figure 8.9 DHCP Allocator Information Page

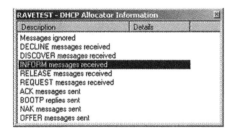

The DNS Proxy Information page allows you to see details on the sent and received DNS queries (Figure 8.10).

Figure 8.10 DNS Proxy Information Page

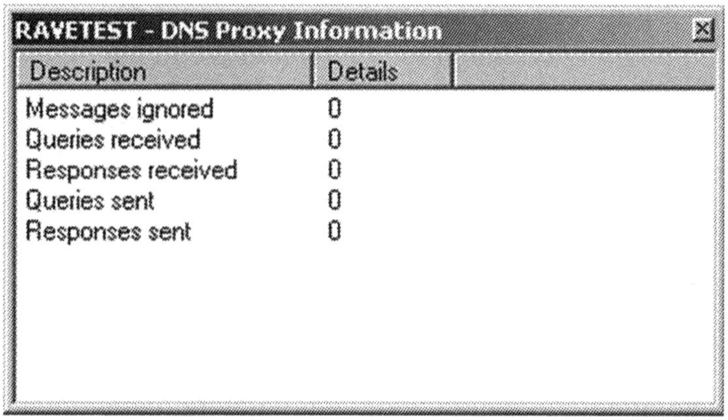

To configure a new interface, right-click Network Address Translation from the Routing and Remote Access console, and choose New Interface.

NAT Interface Properties

Following are three configurable NAT property pages:

General—This page (Figure 8.11) allows you to support other computers in sending and receiving data through this interface.

Figure 8.11 NAT Interface General Property Page

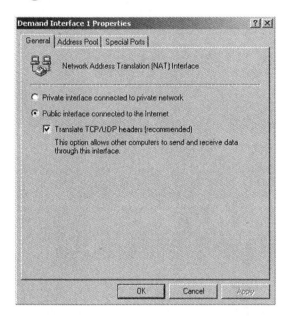

Address Pool—This page (Figure 8.12) allows you to configure interface IP address ranges if you are using more than one public IP address for your NAT server. You do this by combining an IP address with a subnet mask or by entering the starting and ending IP addresses of each range or series of ranges.

Figure 8.12 NAT Interface Address Pool Property Page

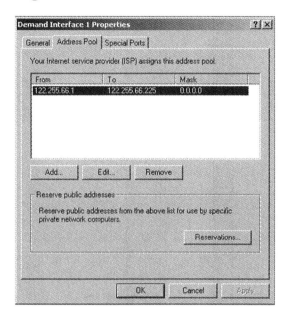

Special Ports—This page allows you to map incoming traffic to specific ports and addresses on the private network. If you choose **Add**, you will see the **Add Special Port** property page (Figure 8.13), where you can designate the port and address to which packets should be sent when they arrive on a special port on this interface's address or on a specific address pool entry.

Figure 8.13 Add Special Port Property Page

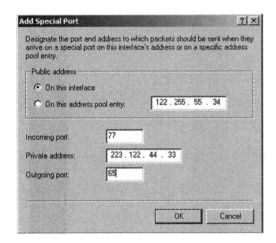

Normally, NAT supports outbound connections from your private network to the public network. Because the connection was initiated from the private network, return traffic from the Internet is passed by NAT. The Special Ports property page lets you give Internet users access to resources on your private network. To allow inbound connections, follow these steps:

1. Configure a static IP address (one IP address from the range allocated by the NAT computer) for the target server on your private network with a subnet mask (range of IP addresses allocated by the NAT computer), default gateway (private IP address of the NAT computer), and DNS server (private IP address of the NAT computer).

2. Exclude the IP address used by the target server from the range of IP addresses allocated by the NAT computer.

3. Configure a static mapping of a public address and port number to a private address and port number.

4. This special port maps an inbound connection from an Internet user to the target server, creating a Web server.

To configure a special port, follow these steps:

1. From the **Start** menu, choose **Programs**, **Administrative Tools** and then select **Routing and Remote Access**.

2. From **Routing and Remote Access**, expand the desired server and **IP Routing**.

3. Right-click the desired interface, and Choose **Properties**.

4. From the **Special Ports** property page, in **Protocol**, choose either **TCP** or **UDP** and **Add**.

5. From within **Incoming Port**, type the **port number** of the incoming traffic.

6. If a range of public IP addresses is configured, choose **On this address pool entry** and type the public IP address of the incoming traffic.

7. From within **Outgoing Port**, type the port number of the private network resource you want to share.

8. From within **Private Address**, type the private address of the private network resource.

9. Click **OK** twice to exit.

The NAT Session Mapping (Figure 8.14) page allows you to see private addresses and ports mapping to public addresses and ports for different protocols.

Figure 8.14 NAT Session Mapping Page

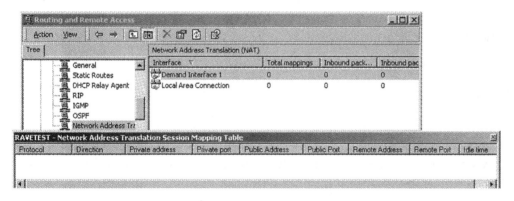

Virtual Private Networks (VPNs) and NAT

Encrypted applications and applications with IP addresses that are embedded in packet locations other than in the IP header cannot be translated by NAT. However, you can use PPTP to tunnel through NAT. A built-in Windows 2000 editor for PPTP traffic translates the IP and Generic Routing Encapsulation (GRE) headers without affecting the original IP datagrams. Only the encapsulation or packet envelope is translated by NAT.

The Virtual Private Network (VPN) arrangement with NAT is useful for branch offices or home users wanting to tunnel to a corporate network. A VPN connection provides secure remote access to networks over the Internet.

Internet Connection Sharing (ICS)

NAT services are also supported by the Internet Connection Sharing (ICS) feature in the Network and Dial-up Connections folder. Easy to use, ICS consists of DHCP, NAT and DNS. With it, you supply your network computers with access to Internet resources, such as e-mail, Web site and FTP sites. ICS carries out a similar function to NAT, but it is far less configurable. Once enabled, you can only configure applications and services. As a result, ICS is best used to connect a home or small business network to the Internet through a dial-up connection. NAT is used when multiple network connections, routing protocols or demand-dial connections need to be supported.

ICS has the following features:

- Simple configuration

- One public IP address

- Fixed address range for hosts

- DNS proxy for name resolution

- Automatic IP addressing

Once ICS is enabled on the computer that uses the dial-up connection, users can use Internet connections as if they were directly connected to the ISP. Although ICS provides many features beyond that of address translation, it has the following limitations:

- Do not use ICS in a network with other Windows 2000 Server domain controllers, DNS servers, gateways, DHCP servers, or systems configured for static IP

- When you enable ICS on a computer, the network adapter is given a new IP address configuration and all existing TCP/IP connections on the computer are lost

- Users on the network must configure TCP/IP on their local area connection to obtain an IP address automatically

- You must select Enable On-Demand Dialing if the ICS computer is using ISDN or a modem to connect to the Internet

To install ICS on a server that does not yet have Routing and Remote Access, choose ICS instead of the NAT routing protocol from within the Internet Connection Server Setup page of the Routing and Remote Access Server Setup Wizard.

If Routing and Remote Access has already been installed on a Windows 2000 server, several steps need to be taken to install ICS. To enable ICS on a connection, follow these steps:

1. From the **Start** menu, choose **Settings**, and then select **Network and Dial-up Connections**.

2. Right-click the desired dial-up, Virtual Private Network (VPN) or incoming connection you want to share and then choose **Properties**.

3. From the **Sharing** property page (Figure 8.15), choose **Enable Internet Connection Sharing for this connection**.

Figure 8.15 Connection Sharing Property Page

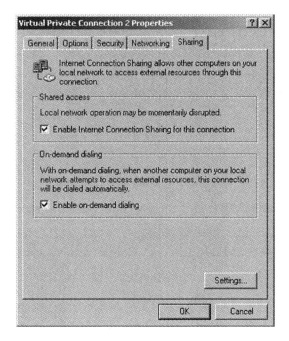

4. If you want this connection to dial automatically in response to traffic requirements, choose **Enable on-demand dialing** and click **OK**.

5. You are warned that your LAN adapter will be set to use another IP address (192.168.0.1) and that your computer may lose connectivity with other computers on your network; choose **Yes** and then click **OK**.

To install Connection Sharing, follow these steps:

1. From the **Start** menu, choose **Programs, Administrative Tools** and then select **Routing and Remote Access**.

2. From **Routing and Remote Access**, expand the desired server and **IP Routing**.

3. Right-click **General**, and choose **New Routing Protocol**.

4. From **Select Routing Protocol**, choose **Connection Sharing** and click **OK**.

5. Next, establish an Internet connection. If you have already have one, you need to configure Internet options for ICS by performing the following steps:

6. From the desktop, double-click on **Internet Explorer**.

7. From the **Tools** menu, choose **Internet Options**.

8. From the **Connections** property page, choose **Never dial a connection** and then select **LAN Settings**.

9. From **Local Area Network (LAN) Settings** (Figure 8.16), deselect **Automatically detect settings**, **Use automatic configuration script** and **Use a proxy server**.

10. Click **OK** twice to exit.

Figure 8.16 Local Area Network (LAN) Settings Property Page

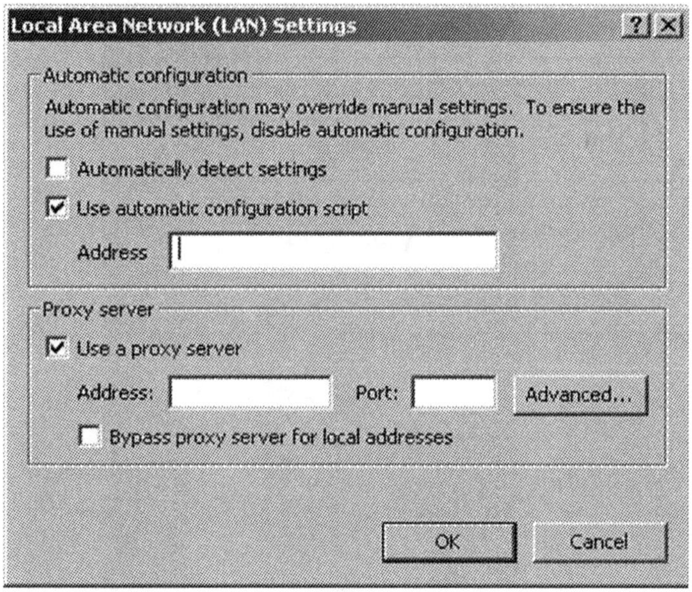

Comparing ICS and NAT

Both ICS and NAT are used to connect small networks to the Internet. They are not designed to act as routers, so they cannot perform the following functions:

- Directly connect separate private networks together

- Connect networks within an intranet

- Directly connect branch office networks to a corporate network

- Connect branch office networks to a corporate network over the Internet

As seen in Table 8.2, ICS and NAT have differences.

Table 8.2 ICS and NAT Feature Comparisons

ICS	NAT
One option configuration	Manual configuration
One public IP address	Multiple public IP addresses
Fixed address range for internal network hosts	Configurable address range for internal network hosts
One internal interface	Multiple internal interfaces

Vocabulary

Review the following terms in preparation for the certification exam.

Term	Description
DHCP	The Dynamic Host Configuration Protocol simplifies TCP/IP network configuration and dynamically configures IP addresses for clients. DHCP ensures that address conflicts do not occur by centralizing address allocation.
DNS	The Domain Name System is an industry-standard name resolution service that allows clients to locate Active Directory services. DNS can translate an IP address into a domain name.
FTP	The File Transfer Protocol defines how to transfer files from one computer to another over the Internet. It is also a client/server application that moves files using this protocol.
ICMP	The Internet Control Message Protocol supports packets containing error, control and informational messages.
ICS	Internet Connection Sharing is a feature of Windows 2000 that allows you to provide your network computers with access to Internet resources. ICS is an easy-to-use package consisting of DHCP, NAT and DNS.
IP	The Internet Protocol is the routable protocol in the TCP/IP suite that is responsible for the IP addressing, routing, and fragmentation and re-assembly of IP packets.
IPSec	A set of standard, cryptography-based protection services and protocols, Internet Protocol Security protects all protocols in the TCP/IP suite and Internet communications.
ISP	An Internet Service Provider is a company that provides access to the Internet.

Term	Description
Kerberos	The Kerberos protocol is the primary authentication procedure in Windows 2000. It is a security system that authenticates users. At logon, it establishes identity, which is used throughout the session.
LAN	A Local Area Network is a communications network connecting computers, printers, and other devices within a limited area.
NAT	Network Address Translation is an Internet standard that allows a LAN to use one set of IP addresses for internal traffic and a second set of IP addresses for external traffic. Windows 2000 offers basic NAT features.
NetBIOS	A Network Basic Input/Output System name is recognized by WINS.
PPTP	The Point-to-Point Tunneling Protocol is a tunneling protocol that encapsulates Point-to-Point frames for transmission over the Internet or a private intranet.
proxy	A proxy relays client requests to the computer that performs the actual name resolution and forwards the resolved names back to the requesting client.
RRAS	The Routing and Remote Access Service is a Microsoft feature that integrates remote access and multi-protocol routing services. It can turn a Windows 2000 server into a dynamic software router.
TCP	The Transmission Control Protocol enables two hosts to establish a connection and exchange data that is guaranteed.

Term	Description
TCP/IP	The Transmission Control Protocol/Internet Protocol is a set of protocols that provides communication among diverse networks. Because it accommodates different architectures and operating systems, TCP/IP is the most commonly used Internet protocol.
UDP	A User Datagram Protocol is a TCP/IP component that transmits data through a connectionless service but does not guarantee the delivery or sequencing delivery of sent packets.
VPN	A Virtual Private Network is the extension of a private network that encompasses links across shared or public networks, such as the Internet.
WINS	The Windows Internet Naming Service is a Microsoft software service that dynamically maps IP addresses to computer names. This allows users to access resources by name instead of by IP address.

In Brief

If you want to...	Then do this...
Install NAT on a Windows 2000 server that does not yet have routing and remote access abilities	Use the Routing and Remote Access Server Setup Wizard, choosing Internet Connection Server and Set up a router with the Network Address Translation (NAT) routing protocol.
Install NAT on a Windows 2000 server that is enabled for Routing and Remote Access	1. Configure the IP address of the home network interface: IP address, subnet mask and no default gateway.
	2. Enable routing on your dial-up port.
	3. If you do not have a permanent Internet connection, create a demand-dial interface for IP routing using your dial-up equipment and the information you use to dial the ISP.
	4. If you have a permanent Internet connection that appears in Windows 2000 as a LAN interface or if you are connecting your Windows 2000 computer to another router before connecting to the Internet, you do not need to create a demand-dial interface.
	5. Create a default static route that uses the Internet interface by selecting the demand-dial interface (for dial-up connections) or LAN interface (for permanent connections) that you will use to connect to the Internet.
	6. The destination IP address is 0.0.0.0 and the network mask is 0.0.0.0. The gateway IP address is not configurable for a demand-dial interface..

If you want to...	Then do this...
Install NAT on a Windows 2000 server that is enabled for Routing and Remote Access	7. Add the NAT routing protocol. 8. Add the Internet and network interfaces to the NAT routing protocol. 9. Enable NAT addressing and name resolution. 10. Configure the interface IP address ranges.
Configure NAT	Right-click on **NAT** and select **Properties** to see four configurable properties pages: The General property page allows you to specify event logging options. The Translation property page allows you to specify the length of time after which dynamic mappings not refreshed are removed from the NAT mapping table. If you select Applications, you can make applications on the public network available to private network clients. The Address Assignment property page allows you to specify the range of IP addresses that NAT can assign to computers on the private network. The Name Resolution property page allows you to specify clients to use DNS for IP address resolution.
See DHCP allocator information	Right-click on **Network Address Translation** in the **Routing and Remote Access** console, and choose **Show DHCP Allocator Information**.

If you want to...	Then do this...
See DNS proxy information	Right-click on **Network Address Translation** in the **Routing and Remote Access** console, and choose **Show DNS Proxy Information**.
Configure a new interface	Right-click on **Network Address Translation** in the **Routing and Remote Access** console, and choose **New Interface**.
Configure a NAT interface	Right-click a NAT interface from the **Routing and Remote Access** console and choose **Properties** to see the following configurable property pages: **General**— This page allows you to support other computers in sending and receiving data through this interface. **Address Pool**— This page allows you to configure interface IP address ranges if you are using more than one public IP address for your NAT server. **Special Ports**— This page allows you to map incoming traffic to specific ports and addresses on the private network.
See port number and IP address mappings	Right-click the NAT interface from within the **Routing and Remote Access** console, and choose **Show Mappings**.

If you want to...	Then do this...
Install ICS on a server that does not yet have Routing and Remote Access	Choose ICS instead of the NAT routing protocol from within the **Internet Connection Server Setup** page of the **Routing and Remote Access Server Setup Wizard**.
Install ICS on a server that is enabled for Routing and Remote Access	1. Enable ICS on a connection. 2. Install Connection Sharing. 3. Establish an Internet connection. 4. Configure Internet options for ICS.

Lesson 8 Activities

Complete the following activities to better prepare you for the certification exam.

1. List the benefits of NAT.

2. Describe what happens to the dynamic mappings in NAT.

3. Demand-dial filters do not work when you are using NAT on a Windows 2000 computer. Explain how you would work around this.

4. Describe the role a NAT editor plays in translating inbound traffic.

5. Describe the biggest drawback of NAT.

6. List some of the features of ICS.

7. List circumstances when you would need to implement routing instead of ICS or NAT.

8. Explain which IP addresses to use when assigning private IP addresses.

9. Explain how you can map more than one private address to a public address.

10. Explain how NAT translates outbound traffic.

Answers to Lesson 8 Activities

1. NAT has many benefits, including increased security for your network, because the internal IP addresses are hidden from the Internet. NAT provides network connectivity without the need for extensive configuration of IP routing protocols in the hosts and on the Windows 2000 router. Also, you can avoid the time and expense of acquiring and maintaining a block of valid IP addresses because the network hosts can share one or more public IP addresses.

2. Dynamic mappings are created when the NAT service automatically remembers and adds routes from client-initiated Internet traffic. Dynamic mappings are refreshed with each use. Any dynamic mappings not refreshed after a configurable length of time are removed from the NAT mapping table. You configure the time in the NAT Translation property page. For TCP connections, the default time-out is 24 hours. For UDP traffic, it is one minute.

3. One method to support only selected Internet traffic without using demand-dial filters is to define static routes for the interface for networks that need to be reached.

4. When NAT is processing inbound traffic, it first looks for a static or dynamic address and port mapping for a packet. Next, NAT looks for editors and invokes one if needed. A NAT editor is needed when more than IP, TCP and UDP headers require translating and adjusting. A NAT editor is a component you install that modifies other payloads and returns the results to the NAT component. Windows 2000 has NAT editors for FTP, ICMP, PPTP and NetBIOS over TCP/IP. After editing, NAT modifies the TCP, UDP and IP headers and forwards the frame.

5. The biggest drawback of RRAS NAT is that translated connections do not allow all IP traffic to pass between computers on your network and Internet hosts. There are only four NAT editors, and none for IPSec or Kerberos. To support all IP traffic and allow for address translation, you need to implement routing and Proxy Server 2.0.

6. Internet Connection Sharing (ICS) has the following features:

    *   Simple configuration

    *   One public IP address

    *   Fixed address range for hosts

    *   DNS proxy for name resolution

    *   Automatic IP addressing

7. Both ICS and NAT are used to connect small networks to the Internet. They are not designed to act as routers, so you need to implement software or hardware routing if you want the following functions performed:

    •   Directly connect separate private networks together

    •   Connect networks within an intranet

    •   Directly connect branch office networks to a corporate network

    •   Connect branch office networks to a corporate network over the Internet

    •   Support all IP traffic

8. When assigning private IP addresses, use the three blocks of addresses reserved by the Internet Assigned Numbers Authority for private networks. This saves the limited number of IP addresses available for public traffic. It also prevents you from inadvertently duplicating a public IP address and distorting traffic. The following are IP addresses reserved for private use:

    •   10.0.0.0 through 10.255.255.255 with a subnet mask of 255.0.0.0 (one Class A network)

    •   176.16.0.0 through 172.31.255.255 with a subnet mask of 255.240.0.0 (16 contiguous Class B networks)

    •   192.168.0.0 through 192.168.255.255 (256 contiguous Class C networks)

9. If more than one private address is mapped to a public address, NAT uses unique TCP and UDP port numbers requested from the TCP/IP protocol stack to differentiate one intranet location from another.

10. When NAT is translating outbound traffic, it first looks for a static or dynamic address and port mapping for a packet. If one is not found, a dynamic mapping is created, depending on whether there are one or more public IP addresses available. If only one public IP address can be used, NAT requests from TCP/IP a new unique TCP or UDP port for the public IP address and uses that as the mapped port. If more than one public IP address is available, NAT maps private IP addresses to public IP addresses without the ports being translated.

    NAT then looks for editors. After editing, NAT alters the IP and TCP or UDP headers and forwards the packets using the Internet interface.

Lesson 8 Quiz

These questions test your knowledge of features, vocabulary, procedures, and syntax.

1. NAT translates IP address and TCP/UDP ports. It does so by modifying and recalculating which of the following fields in the IP, TCP and UDP headers?
   A. Source IP address
   B. Source UDP address
   C. Source port
   D. TCP, UDP and IP checksum

2. Windows 2000 has NAT editors for which of the following protocols?
   A. FTP
   B. PPTP
   C. ICMP
   D. IPSec

3. Which of the following IP address scopes does the DHCP allocator in NAT support?
   A. Multiple scopes
   B. Superscopes
   C. Multicast scopes
   D. A single scope

4. Under what conditions will NAT forward Internet traffic to the private network user?
   A. If an intermediary router exists between the Internet and the NAT server
   B. If a static map exists for an Internet user to access specific resources on the private network
   C. In response to traffic initiated by clients that created a dynamic mapping
   D. NAT will not forward Internet traffic to the private user for security reasons

5. You want to configure the NAT interface with a range of public IP addresses. How would you do this?
   A. NAT cannot support multiple public IP addresses
   B. Assign a block of addresses reserved by the Internet Assigned Numbers Authority
   C. Combine an IP address with a subnet mask
   D. Enter the start and end IP addresses for each range or series of ranges

6. Which of the following DHCP options can be configured within the NAT DHCP allocator?
   A. IP address lease time
   B. Renewal time

C. Rebinding time

D. IP address of the private interface

7. What happens when the NAT modules in Windows 2000 are in use simultaneously by different components?

A. This cannot happen

B. Microsoft services can share the usage of NAT modules

C. NAT and ICS can share the usage of NAT modules

D. A message is recorded in the event log

8. Which of the following differences between ICS and NAT are true?

A. ICS has one option configuration. NAT can be manually configured with a number of options.

B. ICS has a fixed address range for internal network hosts. NAT has a configurable address range for internal network hosts.

C. ICS has multiple public IP addresses. and NAT has one public IP address.

D. ICS has one internal interface. NAT can have multiple internal interfaces.

9. What are some limitations of ICS?

A. You can only configure applications and services. The rest of ICS is not configurable.

B. You cannot use ICS in a network with other Windows 2000 Server domain controllers, DNS servers, gateways, or DHCP servers.

C. Users on the network must configure TCP/IP on their local area connection to obtain an IP address automatically.

D. When you enable ICS on a computer, the network adapter is given a new IP address configuration and all existing TCP/IP connections on the computer are lost.

10. Applications with IP addresses embedded in packet locations other than in the IP header and encrypted applications cannot be translated by NAT. How would you allow traffic from these applications to pass through NAT?

A. This cannot be done

B. Use a NAT editor

C. Use a Resource Kit Utility

D. Use VPN

Answers to Lesson 8 Quiz

1. Answers A, C and D are correct. NAT modifies and recalculates the source IP address, source port, and TCP, UDP and IP checksums in order to translate IP addresses and TCP/UDP ports.

    Answer B is incorrect. UDP transmits data through a connectionless service but does not guarantee the delivery or sequencing delivery of sent packets. It does not use addresses.

2. Answers A, B and C are correct. Windows 2000 has NAT editors for File Transfer Protocol (FTP), Internet Control Message Protocol (ICMP) and Point-to-Point Tunneling Protocol (PPTP).

    Answer D is incorrect. Windows 2000 does not have a NAT editor for Internet Protocol Security (IPSec).

3. Answer D is correct. The DHCP allocator in NAT supports a single scope.

    Answers A, B and C are incorrect. The DHCP allocator does not have the full functionality of a DHCP server. It cannot support multiple scopes, superscopes or multicast scopes. If you need to support those items, disable the DHCP allocator component of the NAT routing protocol and install a regular DHCP server.

4. Answers B and C are correct. Normally, NAT supports outbound connections from your private network to the public network. Because the connection was initiated from the private network, return traffic from the Internet is passed by NAT. The NAT Interface Special Ports property page lets you give Internet users access to resources on your private network through static mapping.

    Answer A is incorrect. An intermediary router between the Internet and the NAT server will not affect how NAT forwards Internet traffic. NAT will still check its mapping.

    Answer D is incorrect. NAT needs to forward Internet traffic to the private user or communication between your network computers and the Internet will be impossible.

5. Answers C and D are correct. If you are using more than one public IP address for your NAT server, you need to configure the NAT interface with the range of public IP addresses. You can do this by combining an IP address with a subnet mask or by entering the starting and ending IP addresses for each range or series of ranges in the Interface Address Pool property page.

    Answer A is incorrect. NAT can support multiple public IP addresses.

Answer B is incorrect. The three blocks of addresses reserved by the Internet Assigned Numbers Authority is to be assigned for use on private networks, not for public IP usage.

6. Answers A, B, C and D are all incorrect. You cannot configure the DHCP options within the DHCP allocator. The default options are given out to the DHCP clients on the network.

7. Answer A and D are correct. Several Microsoft services and third-party components can use NAT modules in Windows 2000. Only one service or component can use these modules at a time. If RRAS NAT or ICS cannot get access to the NAT modules because they are in use by another computer or service, you will get an error message in the event log.

    Answers B and C are incorrect. NAT modules can be used by only one service or component at a time.

8. Answers A, B, and D are correct. ICS is much less configurable than NAT. ICS has only one option configuration, while NAT can be manually configured with a number of options. ICS has a fixed address range for internal network hosts while NAT's address range is configurable. ICS has a single internal interface while NAT can have multiple internal interfaces.

    Answer C is incorrect. The reverse is true—ICS has one public IP address while NAT has multiple public IP addresses.

9. Answers A, B, C and D are all correct. Although ICS has many features beyond that of address translation, much of it is not configurable. You can only configure applications and services. You cannot configure ICS to function in a network with other Windows 2000 Server domain controllers, DNS server, gateways or DHCP servers. No static IP addresses are allowed, so users must configure TCP/IP on their local area connection to obtain an IP address automatically. The network adapter is given a new IP address configuration by default, so all existing TCP/IP connections on the computer are lost.

10. Answers B and D are correct. You can use PPTP to tunnel through NAT. A built-in Windows 2000 editor for PPTP traffic translates the IP and Generic Routing Encapsulation (GRE) headers without affecting the original IP datagrams. Only the encapsulation or packet envelope is translated by the NAT.

    Answer A is incorrect. You can allow traffic from applications with IP addresses embedded in packet locations other than in the IP header and encrypted applications to pass through NAT.

    Answer C is incorrect. A Resource Kit Utility to perform this function does not exist.

Lesson 9

Certificate Services Installation and Administration

Certificates play a large role in Microsoft's Windows 2000 Public Key Infrastructure (PKI). A PKI is a system of digital certificates, Certification Authorities (CAs), and other registration authorities that verify and authenticate the validity of each party involved in an Internet transaction. Certificates allow users and computers to use smart card logon, send encrypted e-mail messages, and digitally sign documents. Windows 2000 Certificate Services supports a number of CAs, whose function is to issue, manage, renew and revoke certificates.

After completing this lesson, you should have a better understanding of the following topics:

*   Certificates

*   Certificate Services Installation

*   Certificate Services Administration

Certificates

With the growth of the Internet, security has become increasingly important. Central to your network security is the concept of cryptography. Cryptography is a set of mathematical techniques for encrypting and decrypting data for secure transmission so that information can only be read by authorized users. Cryptography uses keys in conjunction with algorithms to protect data. An algorithm is a rule or procedure for solving a problem. The algorithm provides the infrastructure; the key is a value applied to the infrastructure to encrypt or decrypt information. Different cryptographic algorithms support different security operations.

The set of services and administrative tools needed to create, deploy and manage keys and the applications based on those keys in Windows 2000 is PKI. PKI describes a comprehensive system of public key generation and management, including distribution and revocation, and is based on public key technology.

Public key encryption uses a pair of mathematically related keys: a public key that is distributed and a private key that remains secret. To encrypt a message to send to someone, you use the recipient's public key. The message recipient then uses their private key to decrypt the message. This process is called asymmetric key encryption. This transaction allows you to share encrypted data with others, where no secure path exists to pass an encryption key. However, public key encryption algorithms are slow. They are used primarily to protect symmetric keys that encrypt large amounts of data.

In symmetric key encryption, a single encryption key is used to both encrypt and decrypt the data. While this method is fast and safe, you need public key technology to guarantee the secure transmission of the single encryption key when sending encrypted data to a recipient.

The Windows 2000 PKI centers on the use of the X.509 standard, the most widely implemented standard for defining digital certificates. A certificate is a digital document that proves the public key in the certificate belongs to the host or user named in the certificate.

Certificates are used for different applications, such as to secure e-mail or to encrypt files, so each certificate has different information in it. A typical X.509 certificate contains the following information:

- Serial number

- Signature algorithm ID

- Issuer name

- Issuer unique ID

- Validity period

- Subject (user) name

- Subject unique ID

- Subject public key information

- Signature on the above fields

The subject can be an individual, an organization, or even a Certificate Authority (CA). A CA is a trusted service or entity that creates, distributes, publishes and validates keys. The CA answers requests for new key assignments by creating new public/private key pairs and delivering them to clients. The CA also publishes public keys in a directory for user access, and keeps a list of expired and revoked keys.

Microsoft Certificate Services is a component of Windows 2000 Server that you use to create CAs. Certificate Services is integrated with the Active Directory along with the other distributed security services, such as domain logon, Group Policies, and smart card logon as shown in Figure 9.1. Domain logon is the process of an identified user being given permission to access selected network resources. Group Policy is a management technology used to specify options for desktop configurations of groups of computers and users. A smart card is a credit card-like hardware token used to access security-enabled protocols and applications.

Figure 9.1 Certificate Services Integration

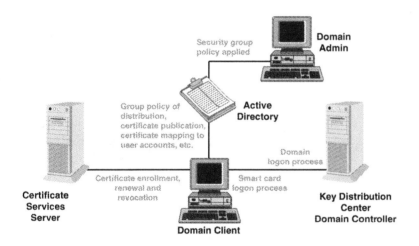

With Certificate Services you can control the policies associated with issuing, managing and revoking certificates, along with the format and contents of these certificates. Because Certificate Services logs all transactions, you can track, audit and manage certificate requests.

Issuing Certificates

The following describes the steps in the process of requesting and issuing a certificate:

Generate a key pair—The applicant generates a public and private key pair or has one assigned by an authority in the organization.

Collect needed information—The applicant collects the personal information required for issuing a certificate, such as the applicant's e-mail address. CAs can have low, medium or high assurance (confidence) depending on the stringency of the identification requirements.

Request the certificate—The applicant sends a certificate request, usually the applicant's public key plus any required information, to the CA. The request can be encrypted with the CA's public key.

Verify the information—The CA applies the policy rules verifying the integrity of the applicant. More stringent verification policies and procedures lead to a certificate with higher assurance.

Create the certificate—The CA creates and signs a certificate containing the applicant's public key and other needed information. By signing with its private key, the CA authenticates the binding of the applicant's name to the applicant's public key.

Send or post the certificate—The CA sends the certificate to the applicant or posts it in a directory.

The certificate can then be verified with the issuer's public key.

Understanding CA Types

A configurable policy module defines what a CA will do when it receives a certificate request. Windows 2000 Certificate Services has policy modules supporting two classes of CAs: enterprise CAs and stand-alone CAs. The two classes of CAs are further subdivided into a root CA and a subordinate CA. The CAs are arranged in a hierarchy, with the most trusted CA, or root CA, at the top. The four types of CAs are described as follows:

Enterprise root CA—An enterprise root CA is the most trusted in an enterprise. All other CAs in the hierarchy are enterprise subordinate CAs. You can have more than one CA hierarchy in a Windows 2000 domain, so you can have more than one enterprise root CA. Each enterprise root CA has a policy module that dictates how certificates are issued, renewed and revoked. The policy information in these modules is stored in Windows 2000 Active Directory.

You can install either an enterprise root CA or an enterprise subordinate CA to issue certificates to users or computers within your organization. Instead of installing a CA in every domain in your organization, have the users in a child domain use a CA in a parent domain.

Tip: In large networks, the enterprise root CA is used solely to issue certificates to subordinate CA types. These enterprise subordinate CAs then issue certificates to users and computers for specific purposes, such as application services and authentication. This provides increased security, because if the enterprise root CA were breached, all issued certificates would not be compromised.

Before you install an enterprise root CA, Active Directory and a Domain Name System (DNS) server must be configured. DNS is an industry-standard name resolution service that allows clients to locate Active Directory services. DNS can translate an Internet Protocol address into a domain name. You must also have administrative privileges on all servers.

Enterprise subordinate CA—An enterprise subordinate CA is subsidiary to an enterprise root CA. It can request certificates from the enterprise root CA that is higher in the hierarchy. Before you install an enterprise subordinate CA, the Windows 2000 DNS Service and Active Directory Service must be configured. You must also have administrative privileges on all servers.

Stand-alone root CA—The stand-alone root CA is the root CA for a trust hierarchy. If you want to issue certificates to entities outside of your organization and the CA needs to be a root CA, you will need to install a stand-alone root CA. A stand-alone root or stand-alone subordinate CA uses a default policy module stored locally, so they do not need the Active Directory. As with the enterprise root CAs, you can only have one stand-alone root CA in a given hierarchy. Before you install a stand-alone root CA, you must have administrative privileges on the local server.

Stand-alone subordinate CA—The stand-alone subordinate CA acts as either a solitary certificate server or a CA in a trust hierarchy, where it requests a certificate from the stand-alone root CA. If you want to issue certificates to users or computers outside of your organization, install a stand-alone subordinate CA. Before you can install one, you must have administrative privileges on the local server.

As long as a certificate can be traced to a known, trusted root CA and it is being used consistently in the application context, the certificate is considered valid. If not, it is considered invalid. Trust relationships are usually established by an enterprise policy. The set of trusted CAs can be configured using the Group Policy editor. They can be configured to apply to specific domain computers, and to all users of a computer. You can also restrict the purposes for which the certificates issued are valid. Restrictions are based on object identifiers, and can be any combination of the following:

- Server authentication

- Client authentication

- Code signing

- E-mail

- IP Security Protocol (IPSec) end system

- IPSec tunnel

- IPSec user

- Time stamping

- Microsoft Encrypted File System (EFS)

IPSec is a set of standard, cryptography-based protection services and protocols that protects all protocols in the Transmission Control Protocol/Internet Protocol (TCP/IP) suite and Internet communications. TCP/IP is a set of protocols that provides communication among diverse networks. Because it accommodates different architectures and operating systems, TCP/IP is the most commonly used Internet protocol. EFS is an extension to Microsoft's file system that provides strong data protection and encryption for files and folders.

The CA trust relationships are automatically propagated to Windows 2000 client computers, who use them to verify certificates. However, users with the appropriate permissions can configure customized trust decisions for themselves within the PKI. They can install or delete trusted root CAs, before using certificate management administrative tools to configure associated usage restrictions. For security reasons, you would normally not grant users permission to do this.

You do not need to verify the public keys for each entity. Instead, to verify a certificate, you verify and trust the public key of the CA by checking it against the Certificate Revocation List (CRL) published by that CA. A CRL is a document maintained and published by a CA that lists certificates that have been revoked. The CA's public key can then be used to verify other certificates.

The Windows 2000 PKI supports roaming for keys and certificates. A user's cryptographic keys and certificates are available regardless of which computer he or she logs onto in the network. If a Microsoft-based Cryptographic Service Provider (CSP) is used, roaming is supported by the roaming profile feature.

A CSP is an independent software module that performs cryptography operations such as secret key exchange, digital signing of data and public key authentication. If a third party CSP is used, roaming is usually supported by hardware devices. These hardware devices, such as smart cards, provide a physical location to store key data. The smart card CSPs that ship with Windows 2000 support roaming by the user carrying the token through any location moves.

Certificate Services Installation

The following points should to be considered when installing Certificate Services:

- If you want to install an enterprise CA, you must set up a domain first

- An enterprise root CA should be installed before any other type of CA

- Information about enterprise CAs is integrated into Active Directory during Certificate Services installation, giving domain clients information about available CAs and the certificates they will issue

- Although a root CA can be installed on any Windows 2000 server, you must factor in security and connectivity requirements, and the expected load

- You cannot rename a computer running Certificate Services because CA names are bound to their certificates to identify the CA object in the Active Directory for an enterprise CA

- Once a computer is running Certificate Services, you cannot remove it from or add it to a domain

- During Certificate Services installation, a unique public/private key pair is generated

- During installation, a root CA will generate and then sign its own CA certificate using its public/private key pair

- Once you have installed a root CA, you can install intermediate or certificate-issuing CAs subordinate to the root CA.

- During installation of a subordinate (child) CA, you can generate a CA certificate through an intermediate CA or root CA higher in the hierarchy by configuring the policy

- During installation of an enterprise or a stand-alone CA, the default enterprise or stand-alone policy module is automatically installed and configured, but you can substitute a custom policy module

Your enterprise CA trust model does not have to correspond to the Windows 2000 domain trust model. A given domain can have multiple enterprise CAs or one CA can fulfill certificate requirements for multiple domains or for entities outside the domain.

To install an enterprise root CA, follow these steps:

1. From the **Start** menu, choose **Settings** and then select **Control Panel**.

2. From **Control Panel**, double-click **Add/Remove Programs** and choose **Add/Remove Windows Components**.

3. From **Windows Components**, choose **Certificate Services**.

4. Choose **Yes** to the warning that the computer cannot be renamed or join another domain once you have installed Certificate Services, and then select **Next**.

5. From **Certification Authority Type** (Figure 9.2), choose **Enterprise root CA, Advanced options** and then select **Next**.

Figure 9.2 Certification Authority Type Page

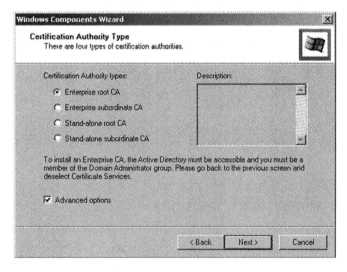

6. From **Public and Private Key Pair** (Figure 9.3), specify the key length, use an existing key installed on the computer or import a key.

Figure 9.3 Public and Private Key Pair Page

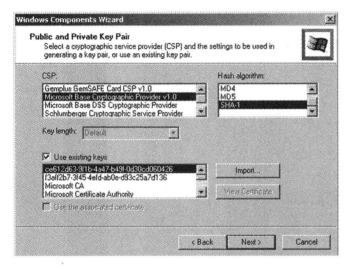

7. Choose the Cryptographic Service Provider (CSP) that uses the desired algorithm to generate key pairs, the desired Hash algorithm and then select Next.

8. From within **CA Identifying Information** (Figure 9.4), type the information to identify the CA and the validity period, and choose **Next**.

Figure 9.4 CA Identifying Information Page

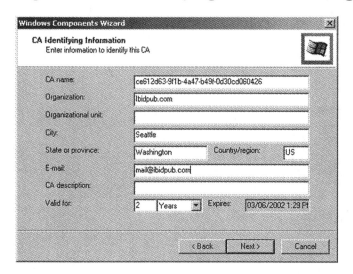

9. From **Data Storage Location** (Figure 9.5), specify the storage location for the configuration data, database and log, and then choose **Next**.

Figure 9.5 Data Storage Location Page

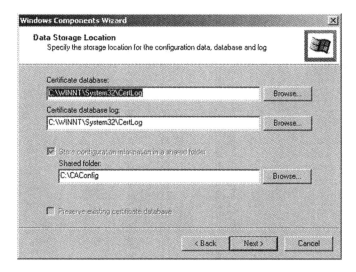

10. By default, the storage location is **drive:\WINNT\System32\CertLog**.

11. During the CA installation process, you may need to click **OK** to stop services, and you will need to give the location of the Windows 2000 installation files.

12. From **Completing the Windows Components Wizard**, choose **Finish**.

13. Close **Add/Remove Programs** and the Control Panel.

After you have installed Certificate Services, both the Certificate Authority and Certificates snap-ins can be added to a console. Once the CA service is started, a green check mark appears next to the CA server on the Certificate Authority console.

 Note: The certificates can physically reside on different stores, but the logical stores give a system wide view of available stores.

The cryptographic keys, as well as their associated certificates and properties, are stored and managed by the subsystem in the Microsoft PKI. The five default certificate stores are described in Table 9.1.

Table 9.1 Default PKI Certificate Stores

Store	Description
MY	This store holds the user's or computer's certificates that have an associated private key.
CA	This store holds the issuing or intermediate CA certificates to use in building certificate verification chains. The issuing CA signs the certificate that is delivered to the applicant, while an intermediate CA directs the applicant's certificate request to another CA higher in the hierarchy.
TRUST	This store holds certificate trust lists and is a way to designate a collection of trusted CAs. Because the trust lists are digitally signed, they can be transmitted over nonsecure links.
ROOT	This store holds self-signed CA certificates for trusted root CAs.
UserDS	This store simplifies access to repositories by giving a logical view of a certificate repository stored in the Active Directory.

Enrolling

Enrollment is the process of obtaining a digital certificate. The subcomponents of Certificate Services include both the service used to create a CA and a Web enrollment form for submitting requests and retrieving certificates from the computer running as a CA. The Windows 2000 PKI supports certificate enrollment for Microsoft enterprise CAs, stand-alone CAs and third-party CAs.

Windows 2000 can provide certificates supporting Rivest Shamir Adelman (RSA), Digital Signature Algorithm (DSA) and Diffie-Hellman. RSA is a general-purpose algorithm supporting digital signatures and distributed public key encryption that is the standard for Internet data encryption. DSA is a public key algorithm used for producing digital signatures. Diffie-Hellman is a public key cryptography algorithm that allows two entities to agree on a shared key without needing encryption during the key generation.

Certificates are issued in the following manner:

- The applicant (except for personal digital certificates) requesting certification generates public/private key pairs

- For personal digital certificates, the CA generates the public/private key pairs and sends them to the users

- The applicant collates the required information as defined by the CA

- The applicant sends the public keys and information, which is usually encrypted using the CA's public key, to the CA

- The CA applies the appropriate policy rules to make sure the applicant should get a certificate

- The CA creates a digital document with information such as public keys and expiration date, and signs it using the CA's private key

- The CA can either send the certificate to the applicant or post it publicly

- The certificate is loaded onto the applicant's computer

There are different ways to enroll. Web-based enrollment and the Certificate Request Wizard are used the most frequently. Auto-enrollment driven by a user's logon policy is also possible.

Web-based Enrollment

To request certificates from a stand-alone CA, you must access web-based enrollment. Microsoft Certificate Services has Hypertext Transfer Protocol (HTTP) enrollment control using forms for custom certificate enrollment and renewal applications. HTTP is the underlying protocol used by the World Wide Web that defines how messages are formatted and transmitted, and what actions Web servers and browsers should take in response to commands. To access enrollment control and to reach the Certificate Services Administrative Tools web page, go to http: //<servername>/CertSrv/default.asp. The Certificate Services web pages are customizable so you can support your users with modified user options or links to online help. Internet Explorer v3.0 or later can be used to access the Certificate Services web pages.

The process of obtaining a client certificate through web enrollment is as follows:

- The user opens the client authentication page from the Certificate Services pages and submits identification information

- Certificate Services responds to the certificate request by creating a client certificate

- Certificate Services returns the client certificate to the browser

- The browser installs the certificate in the client application

To request and install a certificate through web-based enrollment, follow these steps:

1. From the desktop, double-click **Internet Explorer** and connect to **http://<servername>/CertSrv/default.asp**.

2. From the **Microsoft Certificate Services** enrollment page (Figure 9.6), choose **Request a certificate** and then select **Next**.

Figure 9.6 Microsoft Certificate Services Enrollment Page

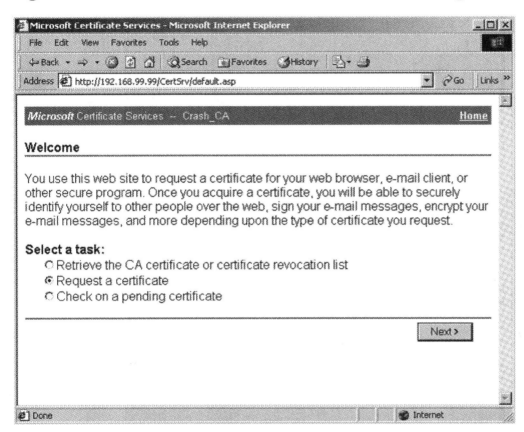

3. From **Choose Request Type** (Figure 9.7), choose **User Certificate Request** and then select **Next**.

Figure 9.7 Choose Request Type Page

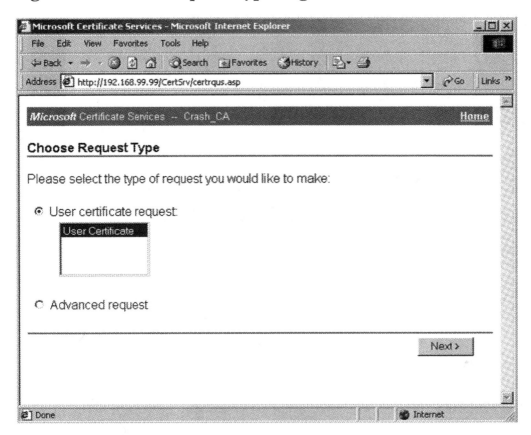

4. From **User Certificate—Identifying Information** (Figure 9.8), choose **More Options**.

Figure 9.8 User Certificate—Identifying Information

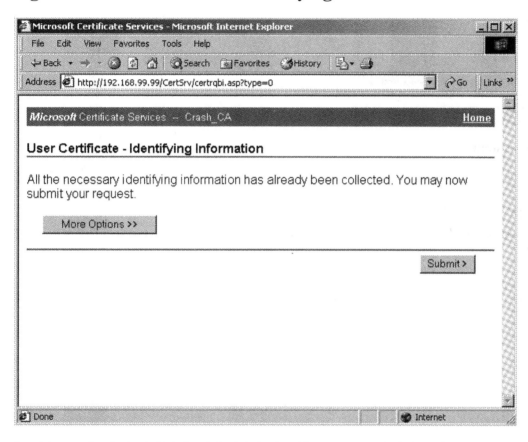

5. Choose the desired CSP; by default it is the CSP type specified during installation of Certificate Services.

6. Choose **Submit,** and then from **Certificate Issued** (Figure 9.9), select **Install This Certificate.**

Figure 9.9 Certificate Issued

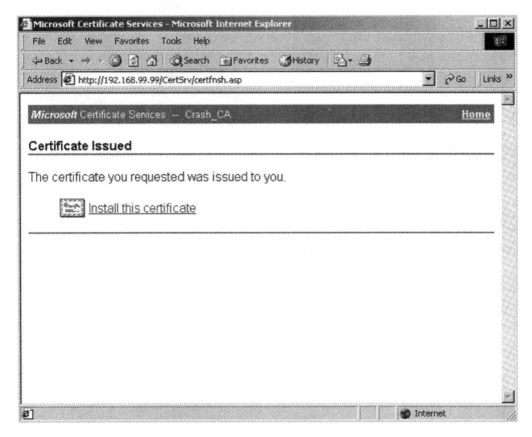

7. The Certificate Installed page appears stating that you have successfully installed a certificate.

8. Close **Internet Explorer.**

Certificate Request Wizard

You can use the Certificate Request Wizard in the Certificates snap-in to request a certificate from an enterprise CA in your domain. The wizard guides you through the process as follows:

1. From the **Start** menu, choose **Run**, type **mmc /a** and press the enter key.

2. From the **Console** menu, choose **Add/Remove** snap-in.

3. From the **Standalone** property page, choose **Add**, highlight **Certificates** and then select **Add**.

4. Choose whether to use the snap-in to manage certificates for your user account, service account or computer account, choose **Finish** and then click **OK**.

5. From the console tree, choose the type of certificate, such as **Certificates—Current User** or **Certificates—Computer Name**.

6. If you are in **Logical Certificate Stores** view mode, choose the **Personal** folder.

7. If you are in **Certificate Purpose** view mode, choose the desired certificate purpose mode.

8. From the **Action** menu, choose **All Tasks** and then select **Request New Certificate**.

9. From **Welcome to the Certificate Request Wizard**, choose **Next**.

10. From **Certificate Template** (Figure 9.10), choose the desired certificate template (predefined configurations providing commons settings for the certificate request) to use for the new certificate.

Figure 9.10 Certificate Template Page

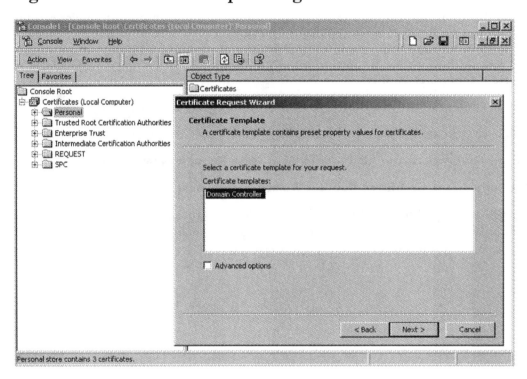

11. Choose **Advanced options**, and then select **Next**.

12. From **Cryptographic Service Provider** (Figure 9.11), choose the desired CSP to generate the key pair associated with the certificate request.

Figure 9.11 Cryptographic Service Provider Page

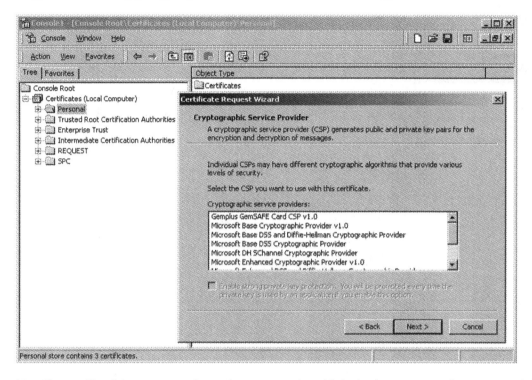

13. Choose **Enable strong private key protection** if desired so you can be prompted for a password every time the private key is used, and then select **Next**.

14. From **Certification Authority** (Figure 9.12), choose the CA to which you want to submit the request and then select **Next**.

Figure 9.12 Certification Authority Page

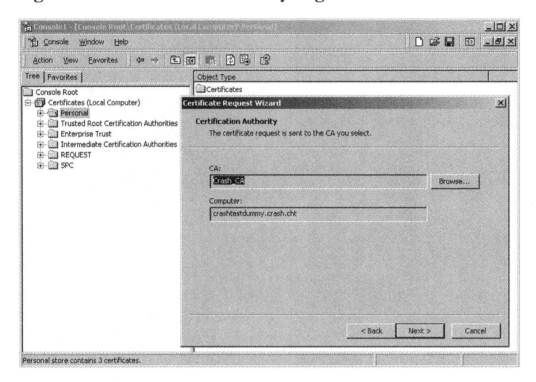

15. From within Certificate Friendly Name and Description, type a friendly name and brief description for the new certificate.

16. From **Completing the Certificate Request Wizard**, choose **Finish**.

17. Choose **Install Certificate** and then click **OK**.

Automated Enrollment

Auto-enrollment can occur as part of a user's logon processing. Certificate types and auto-enrollment objects control the automated enrollment process. These two components are integrated with the Group Policy object and can be defined for sites, domains, Organizational Units (OUs), computers or users. An OU is a logical container within a domain, used to organize objects for easier administration and access.

Certificate types provide a template for a certificate and associate it with a common name for ease in administration. The template defines options including naming requirements, the validity period, allowable CSPs for private key generation, algorithms, and extensions that should be incorporated into the certificate. The certificate types are divided into computer and user types. You can use these certificate types with auto-enrollment objects and with the Certificate Request Wizard.

The auto-enrollment process is integrated with the enterprise CA policy module. The CA service receives a set of certificate types as part of its policy object. These are then used by the enterprise policy module to define the types of certificates the enterprise CA can issue. The CA will reject any certificate request that does not match the specifications of allowable certificates.

Certificate Services Administration

You administer Certificate Services through the Certification Authority snap-in, shown in Figure 9.13. You can use the snap-in to administer a certification authority on the local computer or on another computer. The snap-in allows you to perform the following tasks:

- Start or stop the CA service

- Set security permissions and delegate control of a CA

- View a CA certificate

- Back up a CA

- Restore a CA from a backup

- Renew a root CA

- Renew a subordinate CA

- Manage certificate revocation

- Manage certificate requests

- Manage certificate templates

- Change policy settings

- Map certificate to user accounts

- Modify the Policy Module or Exit Module

Figure 9.13 Certification Authority Snap-in

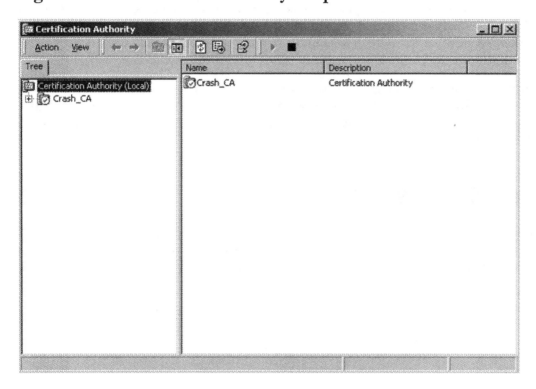

Configuring a CA

By right-clicking the desired CA in the Certification Authority console and choosing Properties, you can see the following five properties pages:

General—This page (Figure 9.14) provides general information, such as the name and a description of the CA, and security settings.

Figure 9.14 CA General Property Page

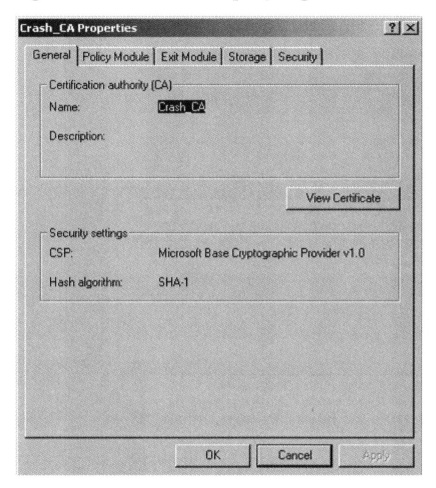

Policy Module—This page provides policy module information. If you select Configure, you will see two other property pages. The Default Action property page allows you to specify the default action for this policy module when it receives a valid certificate request. The X.509 Extensions property page (Figure 9.15) allows you to specify locations from which users can obtain a CRL. From this page, you can also specify locations from which users can obtain the certificate for this CA.

Figure 9.15 CA X.509 Extensions Property Page

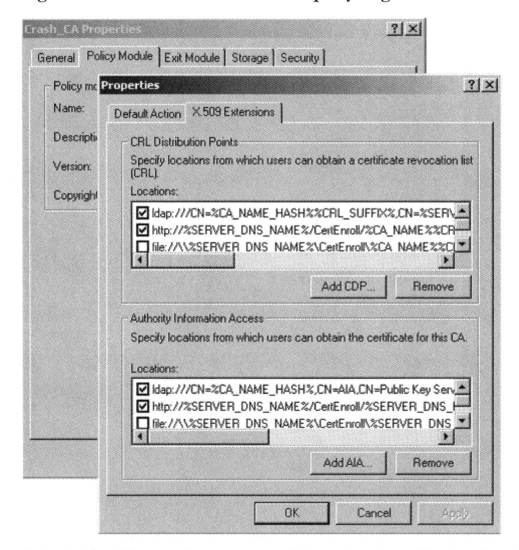

Exit Module—This page allows you to specify the active exit module. An exit module publishes completed certificates and CRLs through a number of transports and protocols. If you select Configure, you will see the Certificate Publication property page where you can select where the certificates will be published.

Storage—This page allows you to see where the certificate database and request log is kept.

Security—This page (Figure 9.16) allows you to provide selected users with the desired administrative permissions. You can also permit inheritable permissions from the parent to propagate to this object.

Figure 9.16 CA Security Property Page

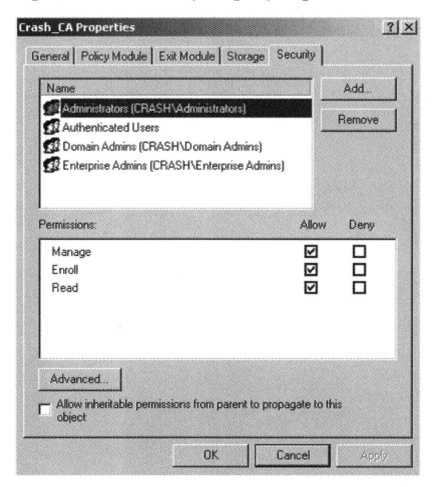

Administering Certificate Services

To stop and start the CA service on a server, from the Certification Authority console right-click the desired server and choose All Tasks and Stop Service or Start Service.

To view the details of the certificates that have been issued, expand the desired CA from the Certificate Authority console, highlight the Issued Certificates folder, right-click the desired certificate and choose Open. You will see the following three Certificate property pages:

General—You can see certificate information including the purpose of the certificate, the issuer, the entity the certificate is issued to and the validity period (Figure 9.17).

Figure 9.17 Certificate General Property Page

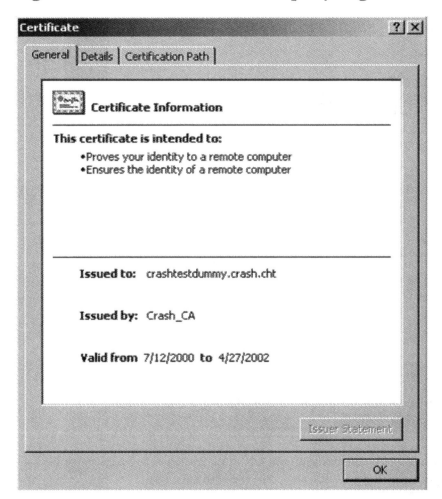

Details—You can see details of the certificate such as the certificate serial number (Figure 9.18). To alter the details, highlight the desired information field and choose Edit Properties.

Figure 9.18 Certificate Details Property Page

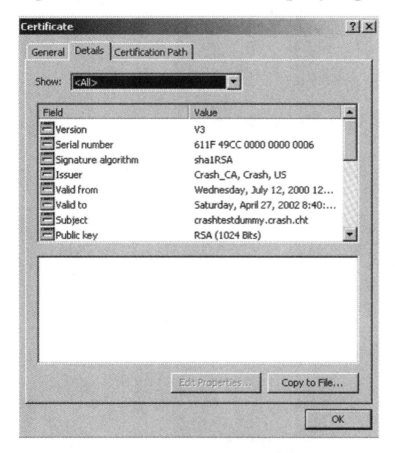

Certification Path—You can see the certification path (chain of related certificates) as well as the certificate status on this page. Select View Certificate to see the certificate itself.

To permit the use of a new certificate template to issue certificates, follow these steps:

1. From the **Start** menu, choose **Programs, Administrative Tools** and then select **Certification Authority**.

2. From **Certification Authority**, expand the **CA**.

3. Right-click **Policy Settings,** choose **New** and then select **Certificate to Issue**.

4. From **Select Certificate Template** (Figure 9.19), choose a certificate template to issue certificates and click **OK**.

Figure 9.19 Select Certificate Template

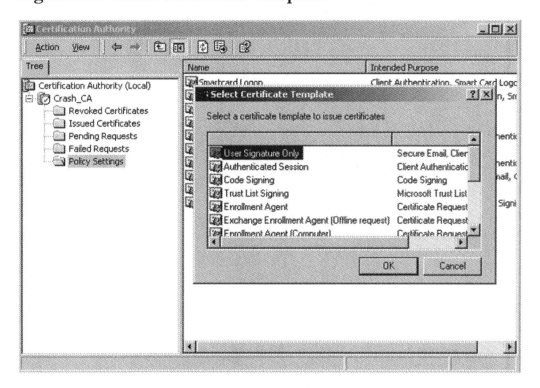

To view the properties of a certificate template, highlight the **Policy Settings** folder, right-click the desired certificate template in the console and choose **Properties**. In the **General** property page (Figure 9.20), you can see information such as the name and purpose of the certificate template.

Figure 9.20 Certificate Template General Property Page

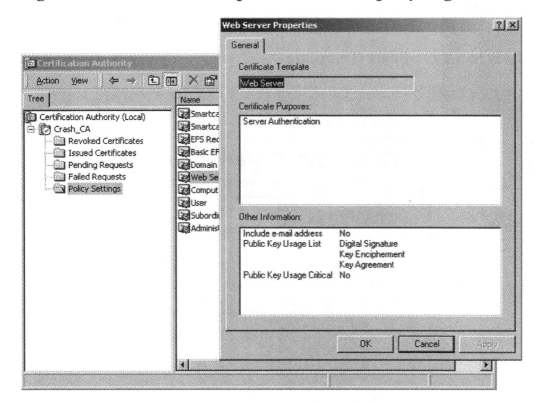

To issue certificates that are waiting in the **Pending Requests** folder, expand the desired CA in the Certificate Authority console, highlight the **Pending Requests** folder, right-click the desired request and choose **Issue**.

To view failed certificate requests, expand the desired CA in the console and highlight the **Failed Requests** folder. When a member of the Cert Publishers or Administrators groups denies a certification request, it will appear as a failed certificate request in the details pane.

Certificate Renewal

Certificate renewal is similar to certificate enrollment. By default, the CA provides to the applicant a new certificate with the same attributes as the existing one and a new validity date. You can use the existing public key or a new public key. Renewal requests are treated as such for automatically enrolled certificates, but for other enrollment mechanisms, a renewal request is treated as a new enrollment.

To renew the CA certificate, follow these steps:

1. From the **Start** menu, choose **Programs**, **Administrative Tools** and then select **Certificate Authority**.

2. From **Certificate Authority**, right-click the desired CA, choose **All Tasks** and then select **Renew CA Certificate**.

3. You will be prompted with need to stop Certificate Services; choose **Yes**.

4. From **Renew CA Certificate**, you are asked if you want to generate a new public and private key pair. Choose **Yes** if the signing key is compromised, you have a program that requires a new signing key with a new CA certificate, or the current CRL is too big and you want to move some of the information to a new CRL.

5. Click **OK** and Certificate Services is restarted.

Certificate Revocation

By default, in Windows 2000 certificates are available for two years after they are issued. However, they can become untrustworthy before the expiration date due to the following reasons:

*   Compromise of an entity's private key

*   Fraud in obtaining a certificate

*   Change in status

You can revoke or withdraw an issued certificate. When you mark a certificate as revoked, it is moved to the Revoked Certificates folder. The next time the CRL is published in Active Directory by an enterprise CA, the revoked certificate will appear in it. Only certificates revoked with the code Certificate Hold can be unrevoked, left on hold until they expire or have their revocation code changed. All other revocation codes are irreversible. Client applications can either download or view online CRLs.

To revoke a certificate, follow these steps:

1. From the **Start** menu, choose **Programs**, **Administrative Tools** and then select **Certification Authority**.

2. From **Certification Authority**, expand the desired CA and choose the **Issued Certificates** folder.

3. Right-click the desired request, choose **All Tasks** and then select **Revoke Certificate**.

4. From **Certificate Revocation** (Figure 9.21), choose the desired **Reason code** and then select **Yes**.

Figure 9.21 Certificate Revocation Page

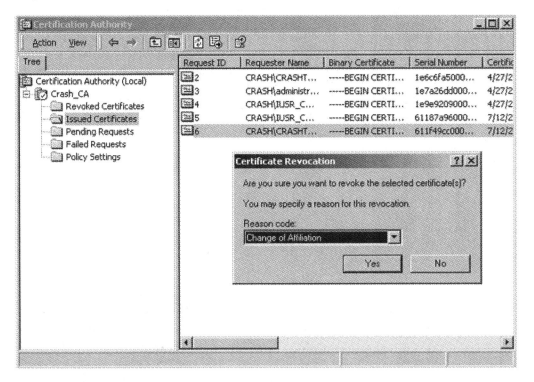

Backup and Restoration of CAs

To protect your CAs, take the following precautions:

• Physically isolate the CA server to reduce the possibility of tampering

- Secure a CA's private key by using cryptographic hardware modules that store the keys and isolate the cryptographic operations from other software running on the server

- Back up your CA so that you can restore it in case of hardware failure, as loss of a CA will cause administrative and operational problems and prevent existing certificates from being revoked

To back up the CA, follow these steps:

1. From the **Start** menu, choose **Programs, Administrative Tools** and then select **Certificate Services**.

2. From **Certificate Services**, right-click the desired CA, and choose **All Tasks** and then select **Backup CA**.

3. From the **Wecome to the Certification Authority Backup Wizard**, choose **Next**.

4. From **Items to Back Up** (Figure 9.22), choose the items you want to back up, the type of backup and the location to back up to, and then select **Next**.

5. From within **Select a Password**, type a password that protects access to the private key and the CA certificate file and choose **Next**.

6. From **Completing the Certification Authority Backup Wizard**, choose **Finish**.

Figure 9.22 Certification Authority Backup Wizard

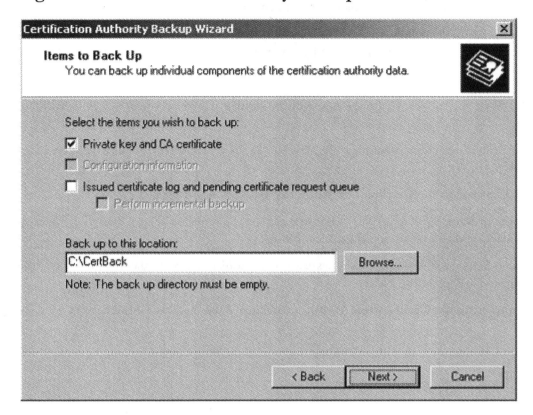

To restore the CA, follow these steps:

1. From the **Start** menu, choose **Programs**, **Administrative Tools** and then select **Certificate Services**.

2. From **Certificate Services**, right-click the desired CA, choose **All Tasks** and then select **Restore CA**.

3. When you are prompted to stop Certificate Services, click **OK**.

4. From the **Welcome to the Certification Authority Restore Wizard**, choose **Next**.

5. From **Items to Restore**, choose the items you want to restore and the location to restore them from, and then select **Next**.

6. From within **Provide Password**, type the password needed to gain access to the private key and the CA certificate file and then choose **Next**.

7. From **Completing the Certification Authority Restore Wizard**, choose **Finish**.

8. When prompted to restart Certificate Services, choose **Yes**.

Command-Line Utilities

Three command-line utilities for administration are included with Certificate Services:

CERTUTIL.EXE—This tool has 40 different modes that allow you to dump and display CA configuration information, configure Certificate Services, backup and restore CA components, and verify certificates, key pairs and certificate chains.

CERTSRV.EXE—This tool is the executable that implements the Certificate Services code. For greater security, you can manually start a root CA server from the command line whenever you want to issue a new certificate instead of using the Certificate Services snap-in. For debugging purposes, you can run CERTSRV with the -z switch to display a log of its activities in the console window.

CERTREQ.EXE—This tool allows you to manually request a certificate from a CA in your domain or retrieve any certificate previously issued by that CA, including revoked or expired certificates. Usually you need to manually request a certificate for subordinate stand-alone CAs. You can also use this tool to request test certificates from a new server to verify that it is working properly.

Managing Certificates

Following are instructions for managing certificates:

1. An entity's certificates are handled through the **Certificates** snap-in, as shown in Figure 9.23.

Figure 9.23 Certificates Snap-in

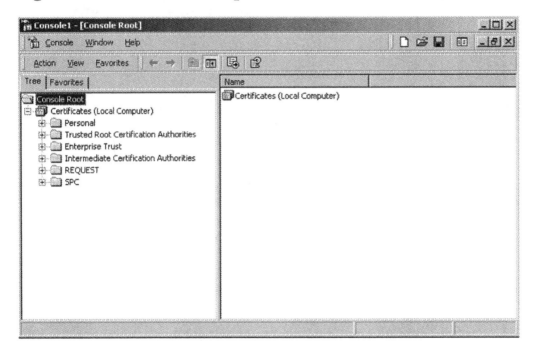

2. To find a particular certificate for an entity, from Certificates right-click the entity and choose Find Certificates. From Find Certificates (Figure 9.24), you can specify the certificate store and data field to search.

Figure 9.24 Find Certificates Page

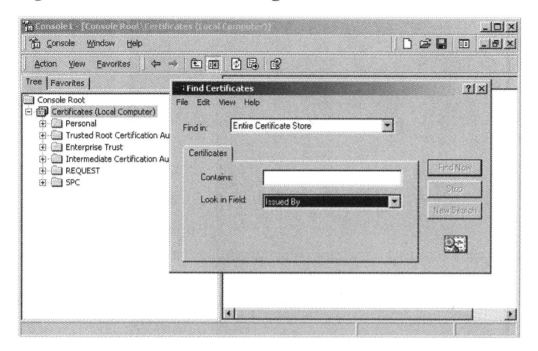

3. To request a certificate using the **Certificate Request Wizard**, from the **Personal** folder of an entity, right-click the **Certificates** folder, choose **All Tasks** and then select **Request New Certificate**.

4. To copy certificates, certificate trust lists, and certificate revocation lists using the **Certificate Import Wizard,** expand the console tree, right-click the desired **Certificates** folder, choose **All Tasks** and then select **Import**.

5. To see the CRL, expand the console tree, highlight **Certificate Revocation List**, right-click the desired CA, and then choose **Open**.

Encrypted File System (EFS) Recovery

You can back up and restore both certificates and associated key pairs through the certificate management administrative tools found in Windows 2000 PKI.

If you ever lose a certificate and its associated private key through tampering or a disk failure, you can recover the data for the EFS. You will need to specify the account of the desired data recovery agent as part of the EFS encrypted data recovery agent policy. By default, the EFS uses the Administrator account as the default recovery agent account. However, in a domain, members of the Domain Admins group can designate another account as the recovery agent account.

The recovery agent account can be used to restore data for all the computers covered by the policy. For example, if a user's private key becomes corrupted, you can back up a file protected by that key. You send the backup by secure e-mail to a recovery agent administrator who can then restore the backup copy.

After opening the file and copying it in plaintext, the administrator then returns the plaintext file to the user by means of secure e-mail. Although the recovery agent administrator can import the recovery agent certificate and private key to the computer with the encrypted file, this is not recommended for security reasons.

Tip: The beta version of the Microsoft certification exam 70-216 Implementing a Windows 2000 Network has long questions involving a large amount of text and one or more exhibits to view. The exhibits are usually network diagrams or Windows 2000 screens mixed with text. You will need to use your exam time wisely.

To add a recovery agent, follow these steps:

1. From a console that has the **Group Policy** snap-in for the local computer, choose **Local Computer Policy**, **Computer Configuration**, **Windows Settings**, **Security Settings**, and then select **Public Key Policies**.

2. Right-click **Encrypted Data Recovery Agents**, and choose **Add** to access the **Add Recovery Agent Wizard**.

Vocabulary

Review the following terms in preparation for the certification exam.

Term	Description
Active Directory	The directory service included with Windows 2000 Server stores information about objects on a network in a hierarchical view. It provides a single point of administration for all network objects.
algorithm	An algorithm is a rule or procedure for solving a problem. Cryptographically-based algorithms are used to encrypt data.
CA	A Certificate Authority is a trusted service or entity that creates, distributes, publishes and validates keys. CA is also a certificate store in the PKI that holds the issuing or intermediate CA certificates to use in building certificate verification chains.
certificate	A certificate is a digital document that proves the public key in the certificate belongs to the host or user named in the certificate.
Certificate Services	The Windows 2000 Certificate Services provides customizable services for issuing and managing certificates for the enterprise.
CRL	A Certificate Revocation List is a document maintained and published by a CA that lists certificates that have been revoked.
cryptography	Cryptography is a set of mathematical techniques for encrypting and decrypting data for secure transmission.

Term	Description
CSP	A Cryptographic Service Provider is an independent software module that performs cryptography operations such as secret key exchange, digital signing of data and public key authentication.
Diffie-Hellman	Diffie-Hellman is a public key cryptography algorithm that allows two entities to agree on a shared key without needing encryption during the key generation.
DNS	The Domain Name System is an industry-standard name resolution service that allows clients to locate Active Directory services. DNS can translate an Internet Protocol address into a domain name.
domain logon	Domain logon is the process of an identified user being given permission to access selected network resources.
DSA	Digital Signature Algorithm is a public key algorithm used for producing digital signatures.
EFS	Encrypted File System is an extension to Microsoft's file system that provides strong data protection and encryption for files and folders.
Enrollment	Enrollment is the process of obtaining a digital certificate.
enterprise root CA	The enterprise root CA is the most trusted CA in an enterprise. It can issue certificates for enterprise subordinate CAs. You install an enterprise CA to issue certificates to entities within your organization.

Term	Description
enterprise subordinate CA	An enterprise subordinate CA is subordinate to the enterprise root CA in the hierarchy. It can request a certificate from the enterprise root CA. You install an enterprise CA to issue certificates to entities within your organization.
Group Policy	Group Policy is a management technology used to specify options for desktop configurations of groups of computers and users.
HTTP	The Hypertext Transfer Protocol is the underlying protocol used by the World Wide Web that defines how messages are formatted and transmitted, and which actions Web servers and browsers should take in response to commands.
IPSec	Internet Protocol Security is a set of standard, cryptography-based protection services and protocols that protects all protocols in the TCP/IP suite and Internet communications.
key	A key is a secret code or number required to read, modify or verify secured data. Keys are used with algorithms to secure data.
MY	This certificate store in the Public Key Infrastructure (PKI) holds the user or computer's certificates that have an associated private key.
OU	An Organizational Unit is a logical container within a domain, used to organize objects for easier administration and access.

Term	Description
PKI	A Public Key Infrastructure is a system of digital certificates, CAs, and other registration authorities that verify and authenticate the validity of each party involved in an electronic transaction.
policy module	A policy module defines what a CA will do when it receives a certificate request and is configurable.
private key	The private key is the secret half of a cryptographic key pair used with a public key algorithm.
public key	The public key is the non-secret, published half of a cryptographic key pair used with a public key algorithm.
public key encryption	Public key encryption, also called asymmetric key encryption, is an encryption method that uses a pair of mathematically related keys: a public key that is distributed and a private key that remains secret. To encrypt a message to someone, you use the recipient's public key. The message recipient then uses the private key to decrypt the message.
ROOT	This certificate store in the PKI holds self-signed certificates for trusted root CAs.
RSA	Rivest Shamir Adelman is a general-purpose algorithm that supports digital signatures and distributed public key encryption. RSA is the standard for Internet data encryption.
smart card	A smart card is a credit card-like hardware token used to access security-enabled protocols and applications.

Term	Description
stand-alone root CA	A stand-alone root CA is the most trusted CA in a hierarchy. It can issue certificates for stand-alone subordinate CAs. You install a stand-alone CA to issue certificates to entities outside of your organization.
stand-alone subordinate CA	A stand-alone subordinate CA acts as either a solitary certificate server or a CA in a trust hierarchy, in which case it can request a certificate from the stand-alone root CA. You install a stand-alone CA to issue certificates to entities outside of your organization.
symmetric key encryption	With symmetric key encryption, a single encryption key is used to both encrypt and decrypt data.
TCP/IP	The Transmission Control Protocol/Internet Protocol is a set of protocols that provides communication among diverse networks. Because it accommodates different architectures and operating systems, TCP/IP is the most commonly used Internet protocol.
TRUST	This certificate store in the PKI holds trust lists, the sequence of trusted CAs.
UserDS	This certificate store in the PKI simplifies access to repositories by giving a logical view of a certificate repository stored in the Active Directory.
X.509	X.509 is the most widely implemented standard for defining digital certificates.

In Brief

If you want to...	Then do this...
Install an enterprise root CA	1. From the **Start** menu, choose **Settings** and then select **Control Panel**.
	2. From **Control Panel**, double-click **Add/Remove Programs** and then choose **Add/Remove Windows Components**.
	3. From **Windows Components**, choose **Certificate Services**.
	4. Choose **Yes** to the warning that the computer cannot be renamed or join another domain once you have installed Certificate Services, and then choose **Next**.
	5. From **Certification Authority Type**, choose **Enterprise root CA**, **Advanced options** and then select **Next**.
	6. From **Public and Private Key Pair**, specify the key length, use an existing key installed on the computer or import a key.
	7. Choose the CSP that uses the desired algorithm to generate key pairs, the desired **Hash algorithm** and then select **Next**.
	8. From within **CA Identifying Information**, type the information to identify the CA and the validity period, and then choose **Next**.
	9. From **Data Storage Location**, specify the storage location for the configuration data, database and log, and then choose **Next**.
	10. By default, the storage location is **drive:\WINNT\System32\CertLog**.
	11. During the CA installation process, you may need to click **OK** to stop services, and you will need to give the location of the Windows 2000 installation files.

If you want to...	Then do this...
Install an enterprise root CA	**12.** From **Completing the Windows Components Wizard**, choose **Finish**.
	13. Close **Add/Remove Programs** and the **Control Panel**.
Request and install a certificate through web-based enrollment	**1.** From the desktop, double click **Internet Explorer** and connect to **http: /< servername> /CertSrv/ default.asp**.
	2. From the **Microsoft Certificate Services** enrollment page, choose **Request a certificate** and then select **Next**.
	3. From **Choose Request Type**, choose **User Certificate Request** and then select **Next**.
	4. From **User Certificate—Identifying Information**, choose **More Options**.
	5. Choose the desired CSP; by default it is the CSP type specified during installation of Certificate Services.
	6. Choose **Submit**, and then from **Certificate Issued**, select **Install This Certificate**.
	7. The **Certificate Installed** page appears stating that you have successfully installed a certificate.
	8. Close **Internet Explorer**.
Add the Certificates snap-in to the console before obtaining a certificate through the Certificate Request Wizard	**1.** If you are in **Logical Certificate Stores** view mode, choose the **Personal** folder.
	2. If you are in **Certificate Purpose** view mode, choose the desired certificate purpose mode.
	3. From the **Action** menu, choose **All Tasks** and then select **Request New Certificate**.
	4. From the **Welcome to the Certificate Request Wizard**, choose **Next**.
	5. From **Certificate Template**, choose the desired certificate template (predefined configurations providing commons settings for the certificate request) to use for the new certificate.

If you want to...	Then do this...
Add the Certificates snap-in to the console before obtaining a certificate through the Certificate Request Wizard	6. If you are in **Logical Certificate Stores** view mode, choose the **Personal** folder.
	7. If you are in **Certificate Purpose** view mode, choose the desired certificate purpose mode.
	8. From the **Action** menu, choose **All Tasks** and then select **Request New Certificate**.
	9. From the **Welcome to the Certificate Request Wizard**, choose **Next**.
	10. From **Certificate Template**, choose the desired certificate template (predefined configurations providing commons settings for the certificate request) to use for the new certificate.
	11. Choose **Advanced options**, and then select **Next**.
	12. From **Cryptographic Service Provider**, choose the desired CSP to generate the key pair associated with the certificate request.
	13. Choose **Enable strong private key protection** if desired so you can be prompted for a password every time the private key is used, and then select **Next**.
	14. From **Certification Authority**, choose the CA to which you want to submit the request and then select **Next**.
	15. From within **Certificate Friendly Name and Description**, type a friendly name and brief description for the new certificate.
	16. From **Completing the Certificate Request Wizard**, choose **Finish**.
	17. Choose **Install Certificate** and then click **OK**.

If you want to...	Then do this...
Administer Certificate Services	Use the Certification Authority snap-in. The snap-in allows you to perform the following tasks: • Start or stop the CA service • Set security permissions and delegate control of a CA • View a CA certificate • Back up a CA • Restore a CA from a backup • Renew a root CA • Renew a subordinate CA • Manage certificate revocation • Manage certificate requests • Manage certificate templates • Change policy settings • Map certificate to user accounts • Modify the Policy Module or Exit Module

Lesson 9 Activities

Complete the following activities to better prepare you for the certification exam.

1. Explain why you would want to use an enterprise root CA solely to issue certificates to subordinate CAs.

2. Explain the main difference between an enterprise and a stand-alone CA, and a root and a subordinate CA.

3. Explain the difference between symmetric and asymmetric key encryption.

4. Define a CA and describe a CA's main activities.

5. Explain why you must install and configure Active Directory before you install an enterprise CA.

6. Explain why you do not have to verify the public keys for each entity.

7. Describe what a recovery agent does.

8. Describe the purpose of certificate types.

9. Describe what happens when you revoke a certificate.

10. List the three command-line utilities used for administration of Certificate Services, and briefly describe what they can do.

Answers to Lesson 9 Activities

1. In large networks, the enterprise root CA is used solely to issue certificates to subordinate CA types. These enterprise subordinate CAs then issue certificates to users and computers for specific purposes, such as application services and authentication. This provides increased security, because if the enterprise root CA were breached, all issued certificates would not be compromised.

2. An enterprise CA is used to issue certificates to users and computers within your organization while a stand-alone CA is used to issue certificates for entities outside the organization. A root CA is the highest or most trusted CA within a given hierarchy while a subordinate CA is subsidiary to the root CA and other subordinate Cas that are higher in a given hierarchy. A subordinate CA can request certificates from an intermediary CA or from the root CA in the hierarchy.

3. In symmetric key encryption, a single encryption key is used to encrypt and decrypt data. Symmetric key encryption is both fast and safe. However, to guarantee the secure transmission of the single encryption key when sending encrypted data to a recipient, you need to use public key technology, also called asymmetric key encryption. In asymmetric key encryption, a pair of mathematically-related keys are used: a public key that is distributed and a private key that remains secret. To encrypt a message to send to someone, you use the recipient's public key. The message recipient then uses their private key to decrypt the message.

4. A Certificate Authority (CA) is a trusted service or entity that creates, distributes, publishes and validates keys. The CA answers requests for new key assignments by creating new public/private key pairs and delivering them to clients. The CA also publishes public keys in a directory for user access, and keeps a list of expired and revoked keys.

5. You must install and configure Active Directory before you install an enterprise CA because the policy information for both an enterprise root and an enterprise subordinate CA is stored in the Active Directory.

6. You do not need to verify the public keys for each entity. Instead, to verify a certificate, you verify and trust the public key of the CA by checking it against the CRL published by that CA. The CA's public key can then be used to verify other certificates.

7. If you ever lose a certificate and its associated private key through tampering or a disk failure, you can recover the data for the EFS. You will need to specify the account of the desired data recovery agent as part of the EFS encrypted data recovery agent policy. The recovery agent account can then be used to restore data for all the computers covered by the policy. For example, if a

user's private key becomes corrupted, you can back up a file protected by that key. You send the backup by secure e-mail to a recovery agent administrator who can then restore the backup copy. After opening the file and copying it in plaintext, the administrator then returns the plaintext file to the user by means of secure e-mail.

8. Certificate types provide a template for a certificate and associate it with a common name for ease in administration. The template defines options including naming requirements, the validity period, allowable CSPs for private key generation, algorithms, and extensions that should be incorporated into the certificate. The certificate types are divided into computer and user types.

9. When you mark a certificate as revoked, it is moved to the Revoked Certificates folder. The next time the CRL is published in Active Directory by an enterprise CA, the revoked certificate will appear in it. Only certificates revoked with the code Certificate Hold can be unrevoked, left on hold until they expire or have their revocation code changed. All other revocation codes are irreversible. Client applications can either download or view online CRLs.

10. Three command-line utilities for administration are included with Certificate Services:

    CERTUTIL.EXE—This tool has 40 different modes that allow you to dump and display CA configuration information, configure Certificate Services, backup and restore CA components, and verify certificates, key pairs and certificate chains.

    CERTSRV.EXE—This tool is the executable that implements the Certificate Services code. For greater security, you can manually start a root CA server from the command line whenever you want to issue a new certificate instead of using the Certificate Services snap-in. For debugging purposes, you can run CERTSRV with the -z switch to display a log of its activities on the console.

    CERTREQ.EXE—This tool allows you to manually request a certificate from a CA in your domain or retrieve any certificate previously issued by that CA, including revoked or expired certificates. You can also use this tool to request test certificates from a new server to verify that it is working properly.

Lesson 9 Quiz

These questions test your knowledge of features, vocabulary, procedures, and syntax.

1. What information is found in the typical X.509 certificate?
   A. Serial number
   B. Issuer name
   C. Validity period
   D. Subject (user) name

2. Which of the following algorithms are supported by Windows 2000 Certificate Services?
   A. RSA
   B. DSA
   C. EFS
   D. Diffie-Hellman

3. Which of the following points about Certificate Services are true?
   A. You can rename a computer running Certificate Services.
   B. You can add or remove a computer running Certificate Services from the domain.
   C. You can install intermediate or certificate issuing CAs subordinate to the root CA.
   D. You can choose to generate a CA certificate through an intermediate CA or root CA by configuring the policy

4. Which of the following items are names of default certificate stores?
   A. USER
   B. CA
   C. TRUST
   D. ROOT

5. Which of the following statements about the certificate issue process are true?
   A. The CA generates public/private key pairs for all applicants.
   B. The applicant collates the information required by the CA.
   C. The CA applies policy rules to make sure the applicant should get a certificate.
   D. The CA can either send the certificate to the applicant or post it publicly.

6. What are some activities that you can perform through the Certification Authority snap-in?
   A. Start or stop the CA service
   B. View a CA certificate
   C. Restore a CA from a backup
   D. Request a certificate

7. How can you protect your CA servers?
   A. Physically isolate the CA server
   B. Use cryptographic hardware modules that store the keys and isolate the cryptographic operations from other software running on the server
   C. Backup your CA
   D. Manually start a root CA server from the command line using the CERTSRV.EXE utility

8. Which of the following are CA types?
   A. Enterprise root CA
   B. Enterprise subordinate CA
   C. External root CA
   D. External subordinate CA

9. You can use object identifiers to restrict the purposes for which certificates can be issued. Which of the following are valid object identifiers?
   A. Server authentication
   B. Time stamping
   C. X.509 signing
   D. EFS

10. Which of the following are methods of obtaining a certificate?
   A. Web-based enrollment
   B. CERTREQ.EXE
   C. Certificate Request Wizard
   D. Autoenrollment

Answers to Lesson 9 Quiz

1. Answer A, B, C and D are all correct. The serial number, issuer name, validity period and subject (user) name are all found in a typical X.509 certificate. Other information include the signature algorithm ID, the issuer unique ID, the subject unique ID, the subject public key information and signature on the above fields.

2. Answers A, B and D are correct. Windows 2000 can provide certificates supporting Rivest Shamir Adelman (RSA), Digital Signature Algorithm (DSA) and Diffie-Hellman. RSA is a general-purpose algorithm supporting digital signatures and distributed public key encryption and is the standard for Internet data encryption. DSA is a public key algorithm used for producing digital signatures. Diffie-Hellman is a public key cryptography algorithm that allows two entities to agree on a shared key without needing encryption during the key generation.

    Answer C is incorrect. Encrypted File System (EFS) is an extension to Microsoft's file system that provides strong data protection and encryption for files and folders.

3. Answers C and D are correct. Once you have installed a root CA, you can install intermediate or certificate issuing CAs subordinate to the root CA. During installation of a subordinate CA, you can choose to generate a CA certificate through an intermediate CA or a root CA higher in the hierarchy by configuring the policy.

    Answer A is incorrect. You cannot rename a computer running Certificate Services because CA common names are bound to their certificates, identifying the CA object in the Active Directory for an enterprise CA.

    Answer B is incorrect. Once a computer is running Certificate Services, you cannot remove it from or add it to a domain.

4. Answers B, C and D are correct. The CA store holds the issuing or intermediate CA certificates to use in building certificate verification chains. The TRUST store holds certificate trust lists and is a way to designate a collection of trusted CAs. The ROOT store holds self-signed CA certificates for trusted root CAs.

    Answer A is incorrect. There is no certificate store named USER.

5. Answers B, C and D are correct. The applicant collates the required information as defined by the CA. The CA applies the appropriate rules to make sure the applicant should get a certificate. The CA can either send the certificate to the applicant or post it publicly.

Answer A is incorrect. Except for personal digital certificates, the applicant requesting certification generates public/private key pairs. For personal digital certificates, the CA generates the key pairs and sends them to the users.

6. Answers A, B and C are correct. You can start or stop the CA service, view a CA certificate or backup and restore a CA from the Certification Authority snap-in.

   Answer D is incorrect. You cannot request a certificate through the Certification Authority snap-in. Typical applicant methods of enrollment are web-based enrollment through a browser, the Certificate Request Wizard through the Certificates snap-in, and autoenrollment driven by a user's logon policy.

7. Answers A, B, C and D are all correct. You can physically isolate the CA server to reduce the possibility of tampering. You can secure a CA's private key by using cryptographic hardware modules that store the keys and isolate the cryptographic operations from other software running on the server. You can backup your CA so that you can restore it in case of hardware failure. You can manually start a root CA server from the command line using the CERTSRV.EXE utility whenever you want to issue a new certificate instead of using the Certificate Services snap-in for greater security.

8. Answers A and B are correct. An enterprise root CA is the most trusted CA in an enterprise, and is used to issue certificates to entities inside an organization. An enterprise subordinate CA is subsidiary to an enterprise root CA. It can issue a certificate or request one from an enterprise CA higher in the hierarchy, such as the enterprise root CA.

   Answers C and D are incorrect. External root CAs and External subordinate CAs do not exist.

9. Answers A, B and D are correct. Server authentication, Time stamping and Encrypted File System (EFS) are all valid object identifiers to use when restricting the purposes for which certificates can be issued.

   Answer C is incorrect. X.509 signing is not an object identifier.

10. Answers A, B, C and D are all correct. Typical applicant methods of enrollment are web-based enrollment through a browser, the Certificate Request Wizard through the Certificates snap-in, and autoenrollment driven by a user's logon policy. You can also use the CERTREQ.EXE command-line utility to manually request a certificate from a CA in the domain.

Network Traffic Security and Cross-Platform Authentication

In order to secure your entire network infrastructure, you will need to think of your system security as a whole, rather than as an assortment of protocols, methods and algorithms pieced together. A well-designed system is complete and easy to maintain. It contains policies that determine how, when and at what level security is applied. A robust system offers multi-level security that is transparent to the user. An administrator, who can track important events, can centrally manage this kind of security.

Windows 2000 offers security features such as public key cryptography, Internet Protocol Security (IPSec) and Transmission Control Protocol/Internet Protocol (TCP/IP) filters through Natural Address Translation (NAT) and Proxy Server 2.0.

In depth auditing is supported. You can apply these security policies on an individual computer or user level, up to domains or whole enterprises. The Internet data protection offered by IPSec, when used with the strong user access control found in Certificate Services and the perimeter defenses available through network protocol filters, constitutes a solid defense of your network data.

After completing this lesson, you should have a better understanding of the following topics:

- Public Key Infrastructure (PKI)

- Certificate Services Installation and Certificate Authority (CA) Creation

- Certificate Services Configuration

- Certificate Creation and Management

- Internet Protocol Security (IPSec) Implementation

- Transmission Control Protocol/Internet Protocol (TCP/IP) for Server Security

Public Key Infrastructure (PKI)

A Public Key Infrastructure (PKI) is a system of public key certificate generation and management, including both distribution and revocation. Key components of a PKI are the Certificate Authorities (CAs) that issue certificates, clients that use certificates and directories that store certificates. Most PKIs use a registration authority that vouches for the user identity and authorization before they grant certificates. A Windows 2000 PKI is shown in Figure 10.1.

Figure 10.1 Windows 2000 Public Key Infrastructure

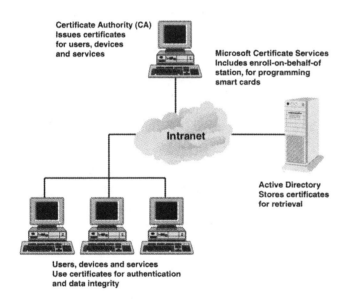

Since public key certificates are used for authentication, servers no longer have to store and maintain a password list for their individual clients. Identification is based on a trust relationship with the CAs. This means the servers only need to trust the CA that issued the applicant's certificate. Authentication can be determined once the trust chain is established and the certificate is verified.

Defining Public Key Infrastructure (PKI) Concepts

Windows 2000 uses the PKI to define the set of services and administrative tools needed to create, deploy and manage keys and the applications based on those keys. Most PKIs revolve around the use of public key certificates.

Encryption Technology

Data is typically encrypted using a process called symmetric key encryption. A single encryption key is used to both encrypt and decrypt the data. Although fast and safe, you cannot use this method to guarantee the secure transmission of the encrypting key when sending encrypted data to a recipient.

Instead, asymmetric or public key encryption is used to protect the symmetric keys that encrypt large amounts of data. Public key encryption uses a pair of mathematically related keys: a public key that is distributed and a private key that remains secret. First, you use a symmetric key to encrypt your message. You then use the message recipient's public key to encrypt the symmetric key, producing an encrypted symmetric key. The message recipient uses their private key to decrypt the symmetric key, and the decrypted symmetric key can be used to decrypt the message.

Public key technology is also used to encrypt digital signatures. A digital signature is a key pair used to authenticate the message sender's identity. The process is the reverse of encrypting data, in that a user's private key generates a digital signature. The signature is later decrypted and verified by the user's public key, as shown in Figure 10.2.

Figure 10.2 Public Key Authentication

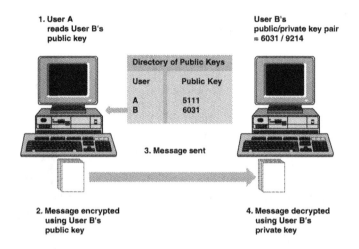

The Windows 2000 PKI uses public key certificates that conform to the X.509 standard, the most widely implemented standard for defining digital certificates. A CA issues a public key certificate. The certificate binds a public key to the user who holds the corresponding private key, proving the identity of the entity named in the certificate. The signature on the certificate is validated through the issuing CA's public key. If the issuing CA is trusted or is on a path of trusted CAs, then the entity named in the certificate has the corresponding private key.

Certificate Authorities (CAs)

Certificates can be issued by a CA to users, subordinate CAs, services, devices and the CA itself. Certificates are also issued for different purposes such as server authentication and file encryption. An entity can have a number of certificates and private keys under different CAs or under the same CA. Each of these keys can be used for different purposes, allow different privileges, and have different algorithms and sizes.

The CA accepts and fulfills certificate requests and revocations. It can also manage the policy-directed registration process that a user follows to get a certificate. In larger organizations, CAs are arranged hierarchically according to functional requirements, as shown in Figure 10.3. Root CAs are at the top of the hierarchy, and use a certificate they issue to themselves. They issue certificates to subordinate authorities, who in turn, can issue certificates to end users or entities, or other subordinate CAs lower in the hierarchy.

Figure 10.3 A CA Hierarchy

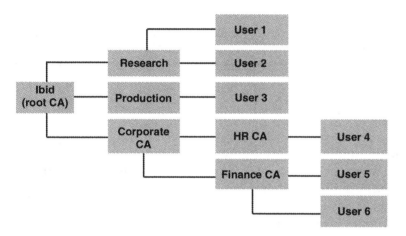

A signer's certificate must be validated before a digital signature can be verified. Tracing a path in a hierarchical chain back to a trusted root CA authenticates the signature. First, if User 4 were trying to verify a signature from User 5, User 4 would try to build a certificate chain for User 5 back to User 4's trusted store: IBID root CA. The chain would be User 5: Finance CA: corporate CA: IBID root CA. Next, User 4 verifies each certificate for validity, starting from the top trusted root. Validity checking ensures the certificate's digital signature has not been tampered with, the certificate has not been revoked and the certificate's validity period has not been exceeded.

Tip: Because the entire trust chain is built upon the root CA certificate, you need to make sure it resides in a protected, trusted certificate store, such as Active Directory.

Requesting a Certificate

A user must obtain a certificate from a CA, a process called enrollment, before being able to use a generated public/private key pair for encryption or digital signatures. This is done through Web-based enrollment, the Certificate Request Wizard in the Certificates snap-in, or auto-enrollment as part of a user's logon processing. For example, a public/private key pair is generated for the user. The public key and any required personal information is collated and sent to the CA. The private key is then saved on the user's computer. The CA receives the certificate request, issues and signs the certificate, and sends the certificate to a directory where others can retrieve it.

For increased security, the user can send the request to a registration authority, which then forwards it to a CA. This enroll-on-behalf feature allows an administrator to use enrollment agent certificates to program smart cards for users. A smart card is a credit card-like hardware token used to access security-enable protocols and applications. Either a Personal Identification Number (PIN) or a password and a card reader is required to access the card, protecting the user's credentials. The smart cards can store public key certificates and private keys and offer support for digital signing. Unlike software private keys, smart cards are portable. Here the private key is written directly to the card, and the certificate is written to a public directory. The smart card can then by used by the user. Figure 10.4 compares the two methods of requesting a certificate.

In a Windows 2000 environment, the certificates for domain clients are stored in Active Directory. Any user or computer with the necessary permissions can get them. You can also map the external user's certificates to Active Directory user accounts.

Figure 10.4 Two Methods of Requesting a Certificate

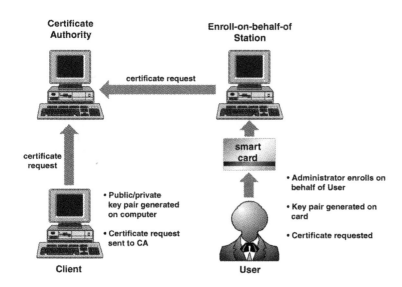

Certificate Revocation List

The CA maintains and publishes its own Certificate Revocation List (CRL), a list of issued certificates that have been recalled. Certificate Services allows CRLs to be published to Active Directory, to a Uniform Resource Locator (URL) for HyperText Transfer Protocol (HTTP) access or to a CRL file. If a user's private key has become compromised, the administrator can place the user's certificate on the CRL. A CRL is digitally signed by the issuing CA and can be verified with the CA's certificate, just like any user certificate. Table 10.1 describes some fields in an X.509 CRL.

Table 10.1 Certificate Revocation List Fields

CRL Field	Description
Signature algorithm	ID of the algorithm (mathematical rule or procedure) that the CA uses to digitally sign the CRL
Issuer	Name of the CA that issues the CRL
Last update	Date and time that the current CRL was issued
Next update	Date and time the next CRL will be issued
List of revoked certificates	Each list entry has the certificate serial number and the date the certificate was revoked
Extensions	Optional information that the CA can include in the CRL
Signature	Digital signature generated by the issuer

Policies govern certificate revocation. The policies determine how frequently CAs refresh their CRLs, what extensions CAs can include in their CRLs, and what circumstances dictate certificate revocation.

Tip: For increased security, set a CRL to be published more frequently, up to once a day if needed.

You can renew certificates using policies that determine if, when and how certificates can be renewed. You can renew certificates with the same key or a different public key.

Tip: Renewing a certificate with a different public key can make it hard to read previously encrypted messages.

Certificate Services Installation and Certificate Authority (CA) Creation

You install Certificate Services using the Windows Components Wizard. You can choose to install the CA, the web enrollment component or both. During installation, you need to decide what type of CA you would like. The four available types are as follows:

- An enterprise root CA is the root CA for a hierarchy and needs Active Directory services

- An enterprise subordinate CA is subsidiary to an enterprise root CA from which it requests a certificate, and it needs Active Directory services

- A stand-alone root CA is the root CA for a hierarchy but does not need Active Directory

- A stand-alone subordinate CA is subsidiary to a stand-alone root CA from which it requests a certificate, and it does not need Active Directory services

During installation, you can choose advanced configuration options including the name of the cryptographic provider, the hash algorithm, using existing public and private keys, and the key length.

You can also specify where the CA's own certificates and log files will be stored.

Tip: To interact with clients that are not using Active Directory, store CA configuration information in a shared folder. To reinstall Certificate Services on a computer that has been acting as a CA, preserve the existing certificate database in order to not overwrite the existing certificates.

If you are installing a subordinate CA, you need to request a certificate for the subordinate CA from the root CA. Bear in mind that the root CA is always the first CA to be installed and configured in a hierarchy.

To install a subordinate CA if your root CA is on line, in the CA Certificate Request screen of the Windows Components Wizard choose Send the request directly to a CA already on the network and specify the computer name of the parent CA server and the desired CA on the parent server (a CA server can host multiple CAs).

To install a subordinate CA if the root CA is not available, in the CA Certificate Request screen of the Windows Components Wizard, choose Save the request to a file, and enter a file name. You can then e-mail or copy the file to the root CA.

If you are using a third party CA, the Windows 2000 CA Service wants to build the full certificate path on startup. If your third-party root CA does not include CA certificates for all CAs in the certificate path, you will need to manually add the CA certificates of parent CAs to the Intermediate Certification Authorities certificate store and the root CA certificate to the Trusted Root Certification Authorities store. Parent CAs are subordinate CAs higher in the hierarchy.

After specifying the certificate path, you need to request and receive a certificate from the newly created subordinate CA. Then you load the certificate into the certificate store from the Certification Authority snap-in. Now the subordinate CA can process any certificate requests.

Certificate Services Configuration

Once you install Certificate Services, both the Certificate Authority and Certificates snap-ins can be added to the console. The Certificate Authority snap-in allows you to administer and configure the CAs, while the Certificates snap-in allows you to manage user, computer and service certificates.

Using the Certificate Authority console (Figure 10.5), you can perform the following tasks:

- Start or stop the CA service
- Set security permissions and delegate control of a CA
- View a CA certificate
- Back up a CA
- Restore a CA from a backup

- Renew a root CA

- Renew a subordinate CA

- Manage certificate revocation

- Manage certificate requests

- Manage certificate templates

- Change policy settings

- Map certificate to user accounts

- Modify the Policy Module or Exit Module

Figure 10.5 Certificate Authority Snap-in

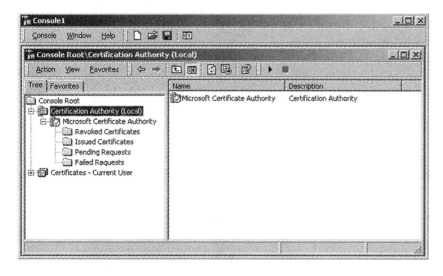

Configuring Certificate Services

Each CA has a set of properties that you can define through its Properties pages. These are accessible by right-clicking a CA object and choosing Properties from the context menu. If you do make changes to a CA, you need to stop and restart it.

General—This page shows the name and description of the CA. It identifies the Cryptographic Service Provider (CSP), the independent software module that performs cryptography operations such as secret key exchange, digital signing of data and public key authentication. It also identifies the hash algorithm, the algorithm used to produce a hash value or number from a string of text, which ensures that a message has not been tampered with.

Policy Module—This page shows which policy module is active on the CA, usually the Enterprise and Stand-Alone Policy module. Choose Select to use another module. Choose Configure to see two other property pages: Default Action and X.509 Extensions. The Default Action page allows you to control what happens to incoming requests. For an enterprise CA, Always issue the certificate is chosen by default. The X.509 Extensions page permits you to customize where CRLs are published and where users can get the CA's certificate.

Exit Module—This page functions like the Policy Module page in that it shows what module is active and allows you to select and configure them. You can designate a series of actions through a sequence of exit modules, although Microsoft only provides one Exit Module with Windows 2000: Certificate Publication. The Certificate Publication Exit Module publishes certificates into Active Directory or to a specified location.

Storage—This page shows where configuration and certificate data are stored.

Security—This page allows you to control what selected users and groups can do with the CA.

 Note: Although you can selectively enable and disable certificate features such as client authentication through a certificate's property pages, you cannot add or remove features not specified in the original template used to issue the certificate.

Certificate Creation and Management

The Certificates snap-in (Figure 10.6) to the Microsoft Management Console (MMC) allows an administrator to manage user, computer and service certificates. Users can manage only their own certificates through their Certificates snap-in. The certificate store consists of five categories: Personal, Trusted Root Certification Authorities, Enterprise Trust, Intermediate Certification Authorities and Active Directory User Object.

Figure 10.6 Certificates Snap-in

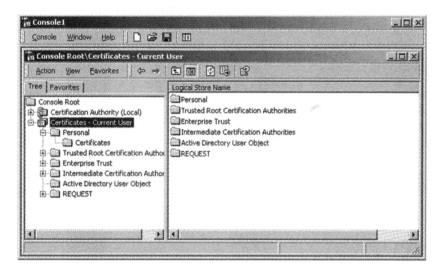

You need to request a certificate before using any application that relies on the public key infrastructure. You can do this through a browser in Web-based enrollment (Figure 10.7), through the Certificate Request Wizard in the Certificates snap-in, or auto-enrollment driven by a user's logon policy.

Figure 10.7 Microsoft Certificate Services Enrollment Page

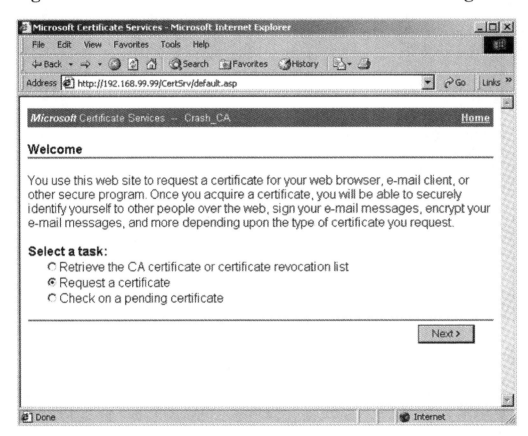

You can export certificates and private keys through the Certificates snap-in. By exporting, you can share a certificate/certificate chain or a certificate/certificate chain and its private key with users and computers that do not have access to a certificate directory.

 Tip: Be careful when exporting private keys. The exported private keys can allow other users to read your encrypted data.

You can import certificates from other sources into any of the certificate store categories using the Certificates snap-in.

Warning: Be careful when importing a root certificate that the certificate originates from a trusted source and that the digital signature matches a trusted publication.

Using Certificates

Public key certificates secure many of the Windows 2000 protocols and processes. Network authentication, IPSec, Encrypted File System (EFS) and Secure Socket Layer (SSL) all use certificates. EFS is an extension to Microsoft's file system that provides strong data protection and encryption for files and folders. Internet browsers use SSL to transmit private documents and information, such as credit card numbers, over the Internet.

Certificates are issued for specific types of uses, as determined in the certificate's extension field. For example, values in the extension field may dictate that a certificate be used for securing e-mail or authenticating a client. You can configure these attributes by right-clicking a certificate and choosing Properties. Choose Enable only the following purposes and select the desired certificate purposes.

On a given certificate, certificate templates determine the purposes available to you for configuration. These templates allow you to quickly create certificates with well-defined purposes. There are 19 predefined templates, none of which you can edit. When a user requests a certificate using web-enrollment, they can choose any of the templates that you have given them permission to access.

Configuring Active Directory for Certificates

Security is integrated with Active Directory through logon authentication and access control to objects in the directory. You use policies to ease administrative overhead. In particular, Certificate Services works closely with Active Directory. First, Active Directory and DNS must be configured on the network prior to installing an enterprise CA, because the policy module and a copy of the certificates are placed into Active Directory. Security support providers such as Kerberos can then query Active Directory services to obtain a certificate containing a public key.

Some configuration of the features provided by Certificate Services can only be done through Group Policies within Active Directory. To configure security permissions on a certificate template, follow these steps:

1. From the **Start** menu, choose **Run**, type **mmc /a** and press the **Enter** key.

2. From the **Console** menu, choose **Add/Remove** snap-in.

3. Choose **Add**, highlight **Active Directory Sites and Services** and then select **Add**.

4. Right-click the **Sites** folder, and from the **View** menu, choose **Show Services Node**.

5. Expand **Services**, **Public Key Services**, and **Certificate Templates** (Figure 10.8).

Figure 10.8 Active Directory Sites and Services Snap-in

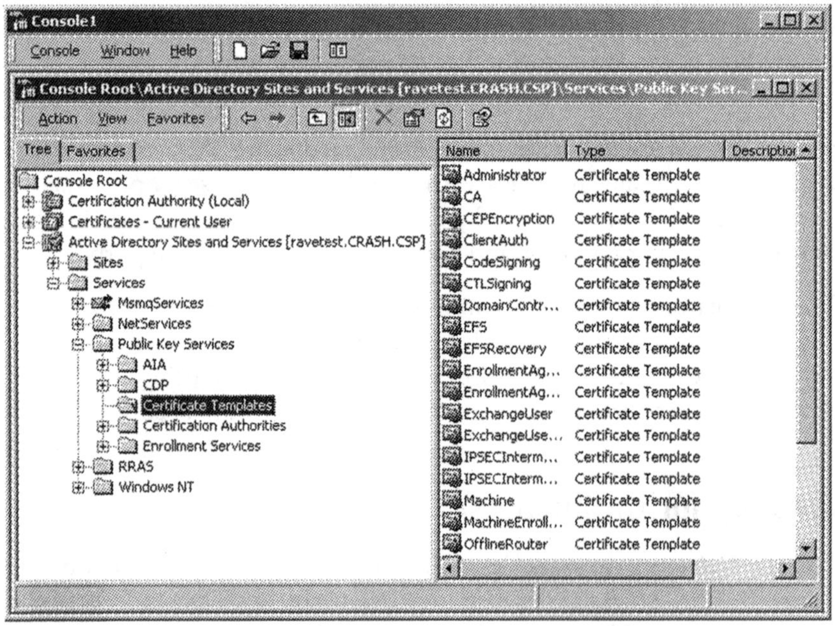

6. Right-click the desired template, and choose **Properties**.

7. From the **Security** property page (Figure 10.9), choose the permissions you want users or groups to have and click **OK**.

Figure 10.9 Template Security Property Page

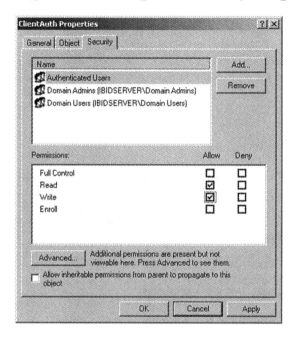

You can also use the Group Policy Object (GPO) to automatically generate, issue and store certificates for computers using the Automatic Certificate Request Setup Wizard. A GPO is a collection of Group Policy settings created by the Group Policy snap-in. To enable automatic enrollment, follow these steps:

1. Use the **Group Policy** snap-in to open the desired GPO.

2. From the console, expand **Computer Configuration**, **Windows Settings**, **Security Settings**, and **Public Key Policies**.

3. Right-click **Automatic Certificate Request Settings**, choose **New** and then select **Automatic Certificate Request**.

4. From **Welcome to the Automatic Certificate Request Setup Wizard**, choose **Next**.

5. From **Certificate Template**, choose the template for the type of certificate you want issued to newly enrolled computers and then select **Next**.

6. Choose the CA in the domain that you want to issue the automatic certificates and then select **Next**.

7. From **Completing the Automatic Certificate Request Setup Wizard**, choose **Finish**.

You can change the root list or set of trusted root certificates that is part of a GPO. This allows you to create a certificate set containing only the trusted CAs available for distribution to a particular group of users.

To add a certificate to the root list, follow these steps:

1. Use the **Group Policy** snap-in to open the desired GPO.

2. From the console, expand **Computer Configuration, Windows Settings, Security Settings**, and **Public Key Policies**.

3. To import a new certificate and begin trusting it, right-click **Trusted Root Certification Authorities**, choose **All Tasks** and then select **Import**.

4. From the **Import Wizard**, type the location of the certificate you want to import.

5. The wizard loads the certificate into the list of trusted roots and displays it.

To remove a root certificate from the list, right-click the desired certificate and choose Delete.

To edit the list of uses for a root certificate, right-click the root certificate and choose Properties. From the General property page, specify what you want the certificate to be able to do.

To use certificates issued by other CAs, you need to put them on the Certificate Trust List (CTL). You can import a CTL created on another Windows 2000 computer or generate a new CTL. To create a new CTL, follow these steps:

1. Use the **Group Policy** snap-in to open the desired GPO.

2. From the console, expand **Computer Configuration, Windows Settings, Security Settings**, and **Public Key Policies**.

3. Right-click **Enterprise Trust**, choose **New** and then select **Certificate Trust List**.

4. From **Welcome to the Certificate Trust List Wizard**, choose **Next**.

5. From **Certificate Trust List Purpose**, specify the prefix identifying the CTL, the validity duration and for what purposes you trust CAs on the CTL, and then choose **Next**.

6. From **Certificates in the CTL,** add the desired CA certificates to the CTL and then choose **Next**.

7. Choose a certificate to use to sign the CTL.

8. Choose an optional timestamp.

9. Type a name and description for the CTL.

10. From **Completing the Certificate Trust List Wizard,** choose **Finish**.

Troubleshooting Certificate Services

Three command line utilities can help you administer and troubleshoot Certificate Services. THE CERTSRV.EXE tool implements the Certificate Services code. If you run CERTSRV with the -z switch, it will display a log of its activities in the console window. With the CERTREQ.EXE tool, you can request and retrieve certificates. Normally, you need to manually request certificates for subordinate stand-alone CAs. This tool also allows you to request test certificates from a new server so that you can verify it is working properly. With the CERTUTIL.EXE tool you can perform a range of activities including creating a backup of the CA's private keys.

Internet Protocol Security (IPSec) Implementation

Another Windows 2000 feature that should be part of a layered enterprise security plan, is Internet Protocol Security (IPSec). IPSec is a security protocol providing end-to-end security for data. Besides data integrity and encryption, IPSec supports network-level authentication to secure intranet, extranet and Internet communications. It uses encryption, digital signatures and hashing algorithms.

The IPSec driver functions at the Internet Protocol (IP) transport layer. It protects each packet before the packet reaches the network and removes the protection once the packet is received. As a result, data from any application can be protected, because the individual application is not involved in the IPSec security model. Only the two communicating computers need to be aware that security has been invoked, because the communication link itself, even for worldwide transmissions, is not protected.

IPSec provides the following security features:

• Digital signature verifies the sender's identity

• Hash algorithms are used to make sure data has not been altered

- Encryption protects data from being read

- Packets cannot be intercepted and resent to the packet origin to gain unauthorized access to your network (anti-replay)

- Public key digital signatures prove the origins of a message

- Keys can be generated during communication so that different keys can protect different parts of a transmission

- Diffie-Hellman, a public key cryptography algorithm that allows two entities to agree on a shared key without needing encryption during the key generation, is supported

- Configurable key lengths accommodate export restrictions or transmissions of data with different sensitivities

Two IPSec-enabled computers negotiate before data is protected and transmitted. During this negotiation, the computers agree on which keys, mechanisms and security policies to use to protect the data, and produce a Security Association (SA).

The initial SA created is called Internet Security Association and Key Management Protocol (ISAKMP). The ISAKMP is then used to negotiate for a pair of IPSec SAs and keys to protect inbound and outbound traffic. The SAs have an agreed algorithm for encryption and an agreed IPSec protocol. The possible IPSec protocols are as follows:

Authentication Header (AH)—Provides data authentication, integrity and anti-replay to IP packets

Encapsulating Security Payload (ESP)—Provides confidentiality, data authentication, integrity and anti-replay to IP packets

Once you create a custom MMC by adding IPSec, you can use the Local Security Settings snap-in to create and configure IPSec policies. IPSec functionality is governed by policies. A policy agent begins running as soon as Windows 2000 is started. It retrieves policy information from Active Directory for domain computers or the registry for standalone computers, and hands it to the IPSec driver.

You can see the default IPSec policies on the Group Policy snap-in to the MMC under Group Policy Object\Computer Configuration\Windows Settings\Security Settings\IP Security Policies on Active Directory.

You can use snap-ins to manage policies centrally through Active Directory, manage policies locally or manage policies for a remote computer. To centrally manage policy for multiple computers, add the IP Security Policy Management snap-in to a console.

Creating and Testing IPSec Policies for Computers

Before implementing IPSec, organize computers in the same domain into groups so that you can apply different IPSec policies to the different groups. Computers in other domains can have complementary IPSec policies supporting secure network communication.

Windows 2000 comes with three predefined IPSec policy entries, however, by default these are not enabled: Client (Respond Only), Secure Server (Require Security) and Server (Request Security). You can modify or remove these. More likely though, you will want to add customized policies.

When planning your IPSec policies, consider the following guidelines:

What the type of information is—Evaluate the type of information being sent over your network to determine the level of security required on a departmental basis. Should you secure the traffic with integrity or with confidentiality or both?

Where the information is stored—To help in performance optimization, you need to determine where the information resides, how it is routed through the network and from what computers it will be accessed. Some questions to ask are: Will the encryption settings you choose work with all relevant computers? Should you secure traffic just between selected computers or on all computers? What about securing selected protocols and ports versus all protocols and ports?

Chances of a network attack—Should the data be secured over remote access connections or also on the Local Area Network (LAN)?

Design and document an enterprise-wide network security plan before implementing IPSec policies, taking into account the security framework of Windows and how security is applied to Group Policy.

Creating an IPSec Policy

All policy settings can be configured through wizards. The wizards are turned on by default, but you can turn then off by deselecting Use Add Wizard. You can also edit policies manually by right-clicking on a policy and selecting Properties.

To create a default IPSec policy using the IP Security Wizard, follow these steps:

1. From the **Start** menu, choose **Programs**, **Administrative Tools** and then select **Local Security Policy**.

2. From the left pane of the console, right-click **IP Security Policies on Local Machine** and then choose **Create IP Security Policy**.

3. From **Welcome to the IP Security Policy Wizard**, choose **Next**.

4. From within **IP Security Policy Name**, type a policy name and brief description, and then choose **Next**.

5. From **Requests for Secure Communication**, accept the default **Activate the default response rule** and then choose **Next**.

6. From **Default Response Rule Authentication Method**, accept **Windows 2000 default (Kerberos V5 protocol)** and then choose **Next**.

7. From **Completing the IP Security Policy Wizard**, choose **Finish** and then select **OK**.

You can also manually configure an IPSec policy through its property pages. Once you have configured an outbound filter specifying your IP address as the source address and another computer's IP address as the destination address, an inbound filter mirroring the outbound one will be configured automatically.

To add a new rule with input and output filters, follow these steps:

1. From the **Start** menu, choose **Programs, Administrative Tools** and then select **Local Security Policy**.

2. Highlight **IP Security Policies on Local Machine**, right-click the desired policy and choose **Properties**.

3. From the **Rules** property page (Figure 10.10), deselect **Use Add Wizard** and then choose **Add**.

Figure 10.10 IPSec Policy Rules Property Page

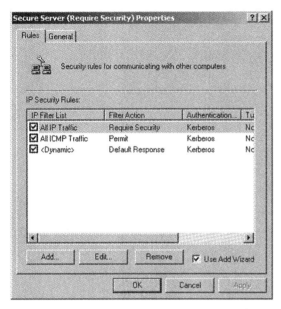

4.   From the **IP Filter List** property page, choose **Add**.

5.   From within **IP Filter List**, type the filter name, deselect **Use Add Wizard**, and then choose **Add**.

6.   From the **Addressing** property page, from within **Source address** type your IP address.

7.   From within **Destination** address, type the IP address of the computer you want to communicate with, click **OK** and then select **Close**.

8.   From the **IP Filter List** property page, choose the filter list you just added in order to activate the filter, choose **Apply** and then select **Close**.

Next, you need to configure the action to take on the filtered packets. To specify a filter action for a rule, follow these steps:

1.   From the **Start** menu, choose **Programs**, **Administrative Tools** and then select **Local Security Policy**.

2. Highlight **IP Security Policies on Local Machine**, right-click the desired policy and choose **Properties**.

3. From the **Rules** property page, deselect **Use Add Wizard** and choose **Add**.

4. From the **Filter Action** property page (Figure 10.11), deselect **Use Add Wizard** and choose **Add**.

Figure 10.11 Filter Action Property Page

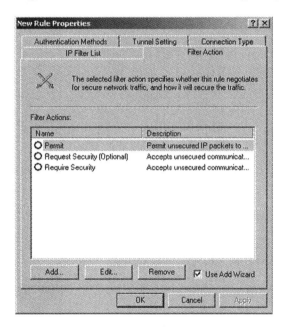

5. From the **Security Methods** property page (Figure 10.12), choose **Negotiate security** and deselect **Allow unsecured communication with non IPSec-aware computer**.

Figure 10.12 Security Methods Property Page

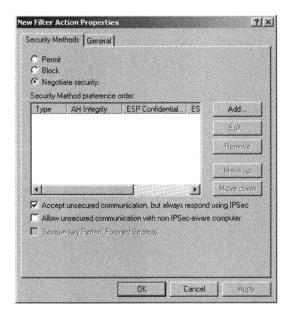

6. Choose **Add**, and from **Security Method**, select the desired level of security, click **OK** and **OK**.

7. To activate the filter you just created, from the **Filter Action** property page choose the desired filter, choose **Apply** and then select **Close**.

You then need to specify the authentication method to be used by the two computers to trust each other when establishing an SA. The Kerberos V5 protocol is used by default. You can also choose to use a certificate from a selected CA or a pre-shared key (a word or phrase that both computers know).

To set the authentication method, follow these steps:

1. From the **Start** menu, choose **Programs, Administrative Tools** and then select **Local Security Policy**.

2. Highlight **IP Security Policies on Local Machine**, right-click the desired policy and choose **Properties**.

3. From the **Rules** property page, deselect **Use Add Wizard** and choose **Add**.

4. From the **Authentication Methods** property page (10.13), choose **Add**.

Figure 10.13 Authentication Methods Property Page

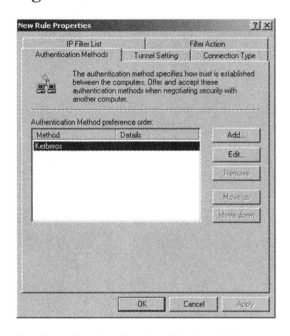

5. From **Authentication Method**, choose to use the Kerberos V5 protocol, a certificate from a CA or a preshared key, and click **OK**.

6. From the **Authentication Methods** property page, highlight the authentication method and choose **Move up** so that the desired authentication method is first in the list, and click **OK**.

You can verify tunnel settings and connection type settings through their respective property pages.

Before you exit, ensure the desired IP Filter list is selected from the Rules property page.

To activate the new policy, follow these steps:

1. From the **Start** menu, choose **Programs**, **Administrative Tools** and then select **Local Security Policy**.

2. Highlight **IP Security Policies on Local Machine**, right-click the policy just created and choose **Assign**.

3. From the **Policy Assigned** column, the value is now **Yes**, as seen in Figure 10.14.

Figure 10.14 Local Security Settings Assigned Policy

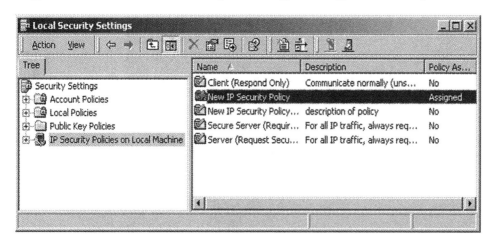

Testing an IPSec Policy

After creating your IPSec policy, you need to test it in a non-production environment to ensure that it functions as you intended. To test communication, follow these steps:

1. Activate the IPSec policy on both the communicating computers.

2. PING the receiving computer.

3. The first PING after enabling the policy generally fails because of timing out during policy negotiation, but future PINGs should work.

You can test the integrity of an IPSec policy by following these steps:

1. From the **Start** menu, choose **Run**, type **mmc** and press the **Enter** key.

2. Open a console with **IP Security Policy Management**, and choose **IP Securities Policies**.

3. From the **Action** menu, choose **All Tasks** and then select **Check Policy Integrity**.

Implementing IPSec

After running the IPSec policies in test labs representing the computing environments for your company, you can conduct pilot programs to further refine your plans. You can get useful feedback by running normal workloads on applications. You view the packet contents with Network Monitor or a third-party sniffer, using the Medium security method level or a custom security method set to AH. You cannot use the High security method level or ESP because that will prevent you from viewing the packets. Once you have decided the policies function well, you can implement them.

Troubleshooting tools are available to help you determine how well the policies are functioning in a production environment. Windows 2000 Server contains a monitoring tool for IPSec called IPSecmon (IP Security Monitor) that will show whether or not the secured communications are successful. Although IPSecmon cannot be used to see failed SAs or other filters, it does show you active SAs on local or remote computers. For example, if you see a pattern of authentication or SA failures, that would indicate incorrect security policy settings.

To access IPSecmon, from the Start menu, choose Run, type **ipsecmon <computer name>** and press Enter. Information on each SA appears as one line in Security Associations. You can see the name of the active IPSec policy, active filter action, IP filter list and tunnel endpoint.

The IP Security Monitor also shows IPSec statistics and ISAKMP/Oakley statistics that help you to optimize performance and troubleshoot. Oakley is a key generation and management protocol. It works with ISAKMP to build the contract between the two communicating computers. The available statistics include:

- The number and type of active SAs

- The number of master and session keys, with functioning SAs usually creating only one master and one session key

- The total number of confidential (Encapsulated Security Payload) or authenticated (Encapsulated Security Payload or authentication header) packets

To troubleshoot errors, you can also examine the System Log using Event Viewer. Polling events that relate to policies stored in Active Directory will be displayed.

You can turn on the policy agent log by changing the registry settings for the log. Then view the systemroot\IPSecPA.log file using a text editor.

Transmission Control Protocol/Internet Protocol (TCP/IP) for Server Security

Besides the PKI and IPSec, there are other means of protecting communication. Firewalls are needed to provide users in your organization with connectivity to the Internet while minimizing the risk of attack on your network computers from inbound traffic. A firewall uses packet filtering, usually Internet Protocol (IP) packet filtering, to allow or forbid the flow of specified types of network traffic. Firewalls can examine each packet coming into your organization's network, and, if it meets certain criteria, it will forward it to the intended recipient. Besides routing, a firewall can also translate IP addresses on the private network, allowing you to use one set of IP addresses for internal traffic and a second set of IP addresses for external traffic.

Windows 2000 Server offers basic NAT capabilities through the Network Address Translation (NAT) routing protocol in the Routing and Remote Access Service (RRAS). The built-in Internet Connection Sharing (ICS) feature of Network and

Dial-up Connections also offers a limited ability to translate connections. However, both RRAS NAT and ICS are meant to connect small home or office networks to the Internet.

To accommodate traffic at an enterprise level, you would need to install a product like Microsoft's Proxy Server 2.0, which provides both address translation and some firewall capability. For heavier traffic, you can use multiple proxy servers, as the traffic between the servers is automatically coordinated.

In particular, RRAS has stringent security. Because you are allowing clients to connect to your network, the potential for security breaches is higher. As a result, Windows 2000 provides multiple security features for RRAS. A client is only permitted access to your network if the following requirements are met:

- Request matches a remote access policy defined for the server

- User's account is enabled for remote access

- Client/server authentication is successful

Various authentication protocols are used to verify the client's identity. Remote access policies used by RRAS and Windows 2000 Internet Authentication Service (IAS) determine whether to accept or reject connection attempts based on predetermined criteria. The policies are stored locally and used on a per-call basis. For centralized policy management, you would use a Remote Authentication Dial-In User Service (RADIUS) server and configure the RRAS servers as RADIUS clients. RADIUS, running on an IAS server with Windows 2000, can be used to manage the access policies of remote access servers.

Configuring TCP/IP for Server Security

To configure TCP/IP to use an IPSec policy on all connections for which it is enabled, follow these steps:

1. From the **Start** menu, choose **Settings** and then select **Network and Dial-up Connections**.

2. Right-click the network connection that you want to configure, and choose **Properties**.

3. From the **General** property page (for a local area connection) or the **Networking** property page (for all other connections), choose **Internet Protocol (TCP/IP)** and then select **Properties**.

4. From the **General** property page, choose **Advanced**.

5. From the **Options** property page, choose **IP security** and then select **Properties**.

6. From **IP Security** (Figure 10.15), choose **Use this IP security policy**, select the desired policy and then click **OK** four times to exit.

Figure 10.15 IP Security Property Page

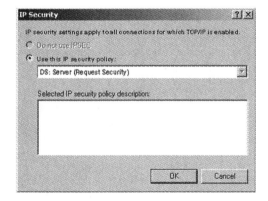

From the Options property page, if you select TCP/IP filtering rather than IP security, you can reach the TCP/IP Filtering property page (Figure 10.16). From this page you can enable TCP/IP filtering for all or specified Transport Control Protocol (TCP) ports, User Datagram Protocol (UDP) ports and IP protocols. TCP enables two hosts to establish a connection and exchange data that is guaranteed. UDP is a TCP/IP component that transmits data through a connectionless service but does not guarantee the delivery or sequencing of sent packets.

Figure 10.16 TCP/IP Filtering Property Page

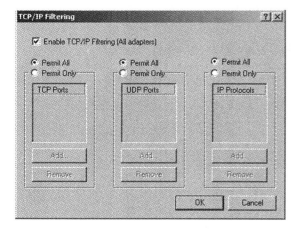

Troubleshooting Network Protocol Security

You need to monitor network security not only to solve problems as they arise but also to optimize the system as your network changes and grows. Several Windows 2000 built-in tools are available to help you.

With the Event Viewer (Figure 10.17), you can monitor program, security and system events on your computer. You decide the specific events you want to record in the logs to be examined later. Of particular interest is the security log that records security events. Examining this log regularly can help you detect areas of potential attack before damage is done to your network. The logs can also provide evidence to help you determine how someone gained forced entry if an attack has already taken place. Events that you can monitor include the following:

- Failure audit for logon/logoff
- Success audit for logon/logoff

- Success audit for security change policies and system events

- Success and failure audit for file access and object access events

Figure 10.17 Event Viewer

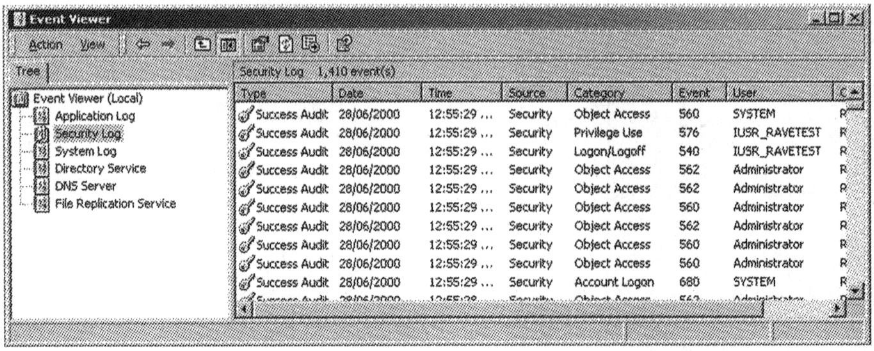

Several System Monitor counters in the Windows 2000 Performance tool also provide information about server security including the following:

- Server\Errors Access Permission

- Server\Errors Granted Access

- Server\Errors Logon

Security is achieved with some performance overhead. Because the Windows 2000 security model and other security services are integrated into different operating system services, you cannot monitor security features separately from other aspects of the services to determine the overhead. Instead, measure performance with and without a security feature using a fixed workload and a fixed server configuration. The objects you should examine using System Monitor and Network Monitor include the following:

- Processor activity and queue

- Physical memory used

- Network traffic

- Latency and delays

Vocabulary

Review the following terms in preparation for the certification exam.

Term	Description
Active Directory	The directory service included with Windows 2000 Server stores information about objects on a network in a hierarchical view. It provides a single point of administration for all network objects.
AH	Authentication Header is an IPSec protocol that provides data authentication, integrity and anti-replay to IP packets.
algorithm	An algorithm is a rule or procedure for solving a problem. Cryptographic algorithms are used to encrypt data.
anti-replay	Anti-replay is a mechanism that prevents transmitted packets from being intercepted and resent to the packet origin to gain unauthorized access to your network.
authentication	Authentication is the process of identifying an entity.
CA	A Certificate Authority is a trusted service or entity that creates, distributes, publishes and validates keys. CA is also a certificate store in the PKI that holds the issuing or intermediate CA certificates to use in building certificate verification chains.
certificate	A certificate is a digital document that proves the public key in the certificate belongs to the host or user named in the certificate.
Certificate Services	The Windows 2000 Certificate Services provides customizable services for issuing and managing certificates for the enterprise.

Term	Description
CRL	A Certificate Revocation List is a document maintained and published by a CA that lists certificates that have been revoked.
cryptography	Cryptography is a set of mathematical techniques for encrypting and decrypting data for secure transmission.
CSP	A Cryptographic Service Provider is an independent software module that performs cryptography operations such as secret key exchange, digital signing of data and public key authentication.
CTL	A Certificate Trust List is a list of the certificates of trusted root CAs.
Diffie-Hellman	Diffie-Hellman is a public key cryptography algorithm that allows two entities to agree on a shared key without needing encryption during the key generation.
digital signature	A digital signature is a key pair that is used to authenticate the message sender's identity.
domain logon	Domain logon is the process of an identified user being given permission to access selected network resources.
EFS	Encrypted File System is an extension to Microsoft's file system that provides strong data protection and encryption for files and folders.
enrollment	Enrollment is the process of obtaining a digital certificate.
enterprise root CA	The enterprise root CA is the most trusted CA in an enterprise. It can issue certificates for enterprise subordinate CAs. You install an enterprise CA to issue certificates to entities within your organization.

Term	Description
enterprise subordinate CA	An enterprise subordinate CA is subordinate to the enterprise root CA in the hierarchy. It can request a certificate from the enterprise root CA. You install an enterprise CA to issue certificates to entities within your organization.
ESP	Encapsulating Security Payload is an IPSec protocol that provides confidentiality, data authentication, integrity and anti-replay to IP packets.
GPO	A Group Policy Object is a collection of Group Policy settings created by the Group Policy snap-in.
Group Policy	Group Policy is a management technology used to specify options for desktop configurations of groups of computers and users.
hash	A hash value or number is generated from a string of text using an algorithm. A hash is used to ensure that a message has not been tampered with.
HTTP	The HyperText Transfer Protocol is the underlying protocol used by the World Wide Web that defines how messages are formatted and transmitted, and what actions Web servers and browsers should take in response to commands.
IAS	The Internet Authentication Service is the central component in Windows 2000 for authenticating, authorizing and auditing users who connect to a network through a virtual private network or dial-up access.
ICS	Internet Connection Sharing is a feature of Windows 2000 that allows you to provide your network computers with access to Internet resources.

Term	Description
IP	The Internet Protocol is the routable protocol in the TCP/IP suite that is responsible for the IP addressing, routing, and fragmentation and re-assembly of IP packets.
IPSec	Internet Protocol Security is a set of standard, cryptography-based protection services and protocols that protect all protocols in the TCP/IP suite and Internet communications.
ISAKMP	The initial SA produced during negotiation between two IPSec-enabled computers is called Internet Security Association and Key Management Protocol. The ISAKMP is then used to negotiate for a pair of IPSec SAs and keys that protect inbound and outbound traffic.
Kerberos	The Kerberos protocol is the primary authentication procedure in Windows 2000. It is a security system that authenticates users. At logon, it establishes identity, which is used throughout the session.
key	A key is a secret code or number required for reading, modifying or verifying secured data. Keys are used with algorithms to secure data.
LAN	A Local Area Network is a communications network connecting computers, printers and other devices within a limited area.
MMC	The Microsoft Management Console provides a common interface for many Windows 2000 tools, including Proxy Server.
NAT	Network Address Translation is an Internet standard that allows a LAN to use one set of IP addresses for internal traffic and a second set of IP addresses for external traffic. Windows 2000 offers basic NAT features.

Term	Description
Network Monitor	This Windows 2000 Server utility captures and displays statistics about frames that it receives from the LAN.
PIN	A Personal Identification Number is a secret number used to identify an entity, known only to the entity and the verifying instrument.
PKI	A Public Key Infrastructure is a system of digital certificates, CAs, and other registration authorities that verify and authenticate the validity of each party involved in an electronic transaction.
policy module	A policy module defines what a CA will do when it receives a certificate request and is configurable.
pre-shared key	A pre-shared key is a word or phrase that both communicating computers know. It is used for authentication.
private key	The private key is the secret half of a cryptographic key pair used with a public key algorithm.
public key	The public key is the non-secret, published half of a cryptographic key pair used with a public key algorithm.
public key encryption	Public key encryption, also called asymmetric key encryption, is an encryption method that uses a pair of mathematically related keys: a public key that is distributed and a private key that remains secret. To encrypt a message to someone, you use the recipient's public key. The message recipient uses the private key to decrypt the message.
RADIUS	Remote Authentication Dial-In User Service is the most common authentication protocol used by Internet service providers. RADIUS, running on an Internet Authentication Service server with Windows 2000, can be used to manage the access policies of remote access servers.

Term	Description
root list	The root list is a set of trusted root certificates that is part of a GPO. This allows you to create a certificate set containing only the trusted CAs available for distribution to a particular group of users.
RRAS	The Routing and Remote Access Service is the Microsoft feature that integrates remote access and multi-protocol routing services. It can turn a Windows 2000 server into a dynamic software router.
SA	A Security Association is created when two IPSec-enabled computers negotiate an agreement on which keys, mechanisms and security policies to use to protect the data.
smart card	A smart card is a credit card-like hardware token used to access security-enabled protocols and applications.
SSL	Secure Socket Layer is used by browsers to transmit private documents and information such as credit card numbers over the Internet.
stand-alone root CA	A stand-alone root CA is the most trusted CA in a hierarchy. It can issue certificates for stand-alone subordinate CAs. You install a stand-alone CA to issue certificates to entities outside of your organization.
stand-alone subordinate CA	A stand-alone subordinate CA acts as either a solitary certificate server or a CA in a trust hierarchy, in which case it can request a certificate from the stand-alone root CA. You install a stand-alone CA to issue certificates to entities outside of your organization.
symmetric key encryption	In symmetric key encryption, a single encryption key is used to both encrypt and decrypt data.

Term	Description
System Monitor	This utility tracks different processes and objects on a Windows 0200 computer in real time.
TCP	The Transmission Control Protocol enables two hosts to establish a connection and exchange data that is guaranteed.
TCP/IP	The Transmission Control Protocol/Internet Protocol is a set of protocols that provides communication among diverse networks. Because it accommodates different architectures and operating systems, TCP/IP is the most commonly used Internet protocol.
UDP	The User Datagram Protocol is a TCP/IP component that transmits data through a connectionless service but does not guarantee the delivery or sequencing of sent packets.
URL	A Uniform Resource Locator is the global address of a document or resource on the World Wide Web.
X.509	X.509 is the most widely implemented standard for defining digital certificates.

In Brief

If you want to...	Then do this...
Install Certificate Services and create a CA	Use the Windows Components Wizard to install the CA, the web enrollment component or both. During installation, decide on the following options: • Type of CA • Name of the cryptographic provider • Hash algorithm • Public key • Private key • Key length • Storage location of the CA's own certificates and log files

If you want to...	Then do this...
Configure Certificate Services from the Certificate Authority console	From the Certificate Authority console, right-click a CA object and choose Properties from the context menu. You will see the following configurable property pages: **General**—This page shows the name and description of the CA. It identifies the CSP and hash algorithm. **Policy Module**—This page shows which policy module is active on the CA. Choose Select to use another module. Choose Configure to see two other property pages: Default Action and X.509 Extensions. The Default Action page allows you to control what happens to incoming requests. The X.509 Extensions page permits you to customize where CRLs are published and where users can get the CA's certificate. **Exit Module**—This page shows what module is active and allows you to select and configure them. You can designate a series of actions through a sequence of exit modules. **Storage**—This page shows where configuration and certificate data are stored. **Security**—This page allows you to control what selected users and groups can do with the CA.

If you want to...	Then do this...
Configure Certificate Services through Active Directory	Use the Group Policy snap-in to open the desired GPO. From the console, expand Computer Configuration, Windows Settings, Security Settings, and Public Key Policies. From here, you can: • Enable automatic enrollment • Change the root list • Edit the list of uses for a root certificate • Use certificates issued by other CAs
Request a certificate	Use one of the following methods: • Microsoft Certificate Services web enrollment, accessible through an Internet browser • Certificate Request Wizard, accessible through the Certificates snap-in • Auto-enrollment, automatically accessible as part of a user's logon processing

If you want to...	Then do this...
Create an IPSec policy using the IP Security Wizard	1. From the **Start** menu, choose **Programs**, **Administrative Tools** and then select **Local Security Policy**.
	2. From the left pane of the console, right-click **IP Security Policies on Local Machine** and choose **Create IP Security Policy**.
	3. From **Welcome to the IP Security Policy Wizard**, choose **Next**.
	4. From within **IP Security Policy Name**, type a policy name and brief description, and then choose **Next**.
	5. From **Requests for Secure Communication**, accept the default **Activate the default response rule** and then choose **Next**.
	6. From **Default Response Rule Authentication Method**, accept **Windows 2000 default (Kerberos V5 protocol)** and then choose **Next**.
	7. From **Completing the IP Security Policy Wizard**, choose **Finish** and then click **OK**.

If you want to...	Then do this...
Manually configure an IPSec policy	1. From the **Start** menu, choose **Programs, Administrative Tools** and then select **Local Security Policy**.
	2. Highlight **IP Security Policies on Local Machine**, right-click the desired policy and then choose **Properties**.
	3. From the **Rules** property page, deselect **Use Add Wizard** and then choose **Add**.
	4. Configure the five property pages in order.
	5. From **IP Filter List**, choose the desired input and output filters.
	6. From **Filter Action**, choose the desired action to take on the filtered packets.
	7. From **Authentication Methods**, choose the desired authentication method to be used by the two computers to trust each other when establishing an SA.
	8. From **Tunnel Setting**, choose the desired settings if you want an IPSec tunnel.
	9. From **Connection Type**, choose the type of connection the rule applies to.
	10. From **Rules,** make sure that the desired **IP Filter List** is selected.
	11. Activate the policy.

If you want to...	Then do this...
Test an IPSec Policy	Use the following tools: • PING, accessible through the command prompt • Policy Integrity, accessible through a console with IP Security Policy Management • IPSecmon, accessible through the Run command • System Log, accessible through Event Viewer • Policy agent log, accessible through systemroot\IPSecPA.log using a text editor
Provide additional TCP/IP security	Use the following: • A firewall, such as Proxy Server 2.0 • Remote access policies • An IPSec policy for all TCP/IP connections • TCP/IP filtering for all or specified TCP ports, UDP ports and IP protocols
Troubleshoot network protocol security	Use the following tools: • Security Log, accessible through Event Viewer • System Monitor • Network Monitor

Lesson 10 Activities

Complete the following activities to prepare for the certification exam.

1. Outline the guidelines you need to consider when planning IPSec policies.

2. Explain why you should be careful when renewing certificates.

3. Explain how you would support certificate access to clients that are not using Active Directory.

4. Explain why you would want to export certificates and private keys.

5. Describe how you would configure an inbound filter in your IPSec policy to match an outbound filter.

6. Explain how you can determine the overhead placed on performance by your security measures.

7. Define a firewall.

8. Explain why an administrator should be careful when exporting private keys.

9. List some of the fields found in an X.509 CRL.

10. Explain how IPSec protects data.

Answers to Lesson 10 Activities

1. When planning your IPSec policies, consider the following guidelines:

    What the type of information is—Evaluate the type of information being sent over your network to determine the level of security required on a departmental basis. Should you secure the traffic with integrity or with confidentiality or both?

    Where the information is stored—To help in performance optimization, you need to determine where the information resides, how it is routed through the network and from what computers it will be accessed. Some questions to ask are: Will the encryption settings you choose work with all relevant computers? Should you secure traffic just between selected computers or on all computers? What about securing selected protocols and ports versus all protocols and ports?

    Chances of a network attack—Should the data be secured over remote access connections or also on the Local Area Network (LAN)?

2. You can renew certificates using policies that determine if, when and how certificates can be renewed. You can renew certificates with the same key or a different public key. However, if you renew a certificate with a different public key, you may not be able to access messages previously encrypted with the old key.

3. During installation of a CA, you can specify where the CA's own certificates and log files will be stored. To interact with clients that are not using Active Directory, you need to store CA configuration information in a shared folder.

4. You can export certificates and private keys through the Certificates snap-in. By exporting, you can share a certificate/certificate chain or a certificate/certificate chain and its private key with users and computers that do not have access to a certificate directory.

5. You can configure an IPSec policy manually through its property pages or automatically using the IP Security Wizard. Once you have configured an outbound filter specifying your IP address as the source address and another computer's IP address as the destination address, an inbound filter mirroring the outbound one will be configured automatically. No additional configuration on your part is needed.

6. Security is achieved with some performance overhead. Because the Windows 2000 security model and other security services are integrated into different operating system services, you cannot monitor security features separately from other aspects of the services to determine the overhead. Instead, measure performance with and without a security feature using a fixed workload and a

588   Implementing a Microsoft Windows 2000 Network Infrastructure

fixed server configuration. The objects you should examine using System Monitor and Network Monitor include the following:

- Processor activity and queue

- Physical memory used

- Network traffic

- Latency and delays

7. Firewalls are needed to provide users in your organization with connectivity to the Internet while minimizing the risk of attack on your network computers from inbound traffic. A firewall uses packet filtering, usually Internet Protocol (IP) packet filtering, to allow or forbid the flow of specified types of network traffic. Firewalls can examine each packet coming into your organization's network, and if it meets certain criteria it will forward it to the intended recipient. Besides routing, a firewall can also translate IP addresses on the private network, allowing you to use one set of IP addresses for internal traffic and a second set of IP addresses for external traffic.

8. You should be careful when exporting private keys because the private keys can allow other users to read your encrypted data.

9. Some of the fields found in an X.509 Certificate Revocation List (CRL) are:

- Signature algorithm, the ID of the algorithm that the CA uses to digitally sign the CRL

- Issuer, the name of the CA that issues the CRL

- Last update, the date and time that the current CRL was issued

- Next update, the date and time the next CRL will be issued

- List of revoked certificates, the certificate serial number and date each certificate was revoked

- Extensions, optional information that the CA can include in the CRL

- Signature, the digital signature generated by the issuer

10. The IPSec driver functions at the IP transport layer. It protects each packet before the packet reaches the network and removes the protection once the packet is received. As a result, data from any application can be protected, because the individual application is not involved in the IPSec security model. Only the two communicating computers need to be aware that security has been invoked, because the communication link itself—even for worldwide transmissions—is not protected.

Lesson 10 Quiz

These questions test your knowledge of features, vocabulary, procedures, and syntax.

1. Which of the following Windows 2000 protocols and processes are secured by public key certificates?
   A. Network authentication
   B. IPSec
   C. EFS
   D. SSL

2. How do you edit certificate templates?
   A. Through the property pages
   B. Using the Certificates snap-in
   C. Using the Certificate Authority snap-in
   D. Certificate templates cannot be edited

3. What are some security features offered by IPSec?
   A. Hash algorithms
   B. Anti-replay
   C. Configurable key lengths
   D. Keys generated during communication

4. What is an SA?
   A. It is created when two IPSec-enabled computers negotiate an agreement.
   B. It is a trusted entity that creates and manages keys.
   C. It is an extension to Microsoft's file system.
   D. It is an independent software module that performs cryptography operations.

5. What are the two IPSec protocols that you can use to protect packets?
   A. Diffie-Hellman
   B. AH
   C. Kerberos
   D. ESP

6. How do you configure TCP/IP to use an IPSec policy on all connections for which it is enabled?
    A. Through Network and Dial-up Connections
    B. Through the Group Policy snap-in
    C. Through the IP Security Policy Management snap-in
    D. Through the Local Security Policy snap-in

7. Which of the following Microsoft products provides translated connections?
    A. Proxy Server 2.0
    B. RRAS NAT
    C. SSL
    D. ICS

8. Which of the following predefined IPSec policy entries does Windows 2000 come with?
    A. Client (Respond Only)
    B. Client (Request Security)
    C. Secure Server (Require Security)
    D. Server (Request Security)

9. To test your IPSec policy, you PING the computer you want to communicate with, and the PING fails. Why would this occur?
    A. Incorrect configuration of IPSec on receiving computer
    B. Incorrect configuration of IPSec policy on your computer
    C. Inactive IPSec policy
    D. Timing out during policy negotiation

10. Which of the following are Windows 2000 tools that can help you troubleshoot security problems?
    A. IPSecmon
    B. CERTSRV
    C. Event Viewer
    D. ISAKMP

Answers to Lesson 10 Quiz

1. Answers A, B, C and D are all correct. Network authentication, Internet Protocol Security, Encrypting File System (EFS) and Secure Socket Layer (SSL) all use certificates.

2. Answer D is correct. There are 19 certificate templates, none of which you can edit. However, you can configure the attributes of the certificates created from the templates. You just cannot add purposes for the certificate that did not exist on the template.

   Answers A, B and C are incorrect. The certificate templates cannot be edited.

3. Answers A, B, C and D are all correct. Hash algorithms are used to make sure data has not been altered. Packets in transit cannot be intercepted and resent to the packet origin to gain unauthorized access to your network. Configurable key lengths accommodate export restrictions or transmission of data with different sensitivities. Keys can be generated during communication so that different keys can protect different parts of a transmission.

4. Answer A is correct. A Security Association (SA) is created when two IPSec-enabled computers negotiate an agreement on which keys, mechanisms and security policies to use to protect the data.

   Answer B is incorrect. A Certificate Authority (CA) is a trusted service or entity that creates, distributes, publishes and validates keys.

   Answer C is incorrect. Encrypted File System (EFS) is an extension to Microsoft's file system that provides strong data protection and encryption for files and folders.

   Answer D is incorrect. A Cryptographic Service Provider (CSP) is an independent software module that performs cryptography operations such as secret key exchange, digital signing of data and public key authentication.

5. Answers B and D are correct. Authentication Header (AH) provides data authentication, integrity and anti-replay to IP packets. Encapsulation Security Payload (ESP) provides confidentiality, data authentication, integrity and anti-replay to IP packets.

   Answer A is incorrect. Diffie-Hellman is a public key cryptography algorithm that allows two entities to agree on a shared key without needing encryption during the key generation.

   Answer C is incorrect. The Kerberos protocol is the primary authentication procedure in Windows 2000. It is a security system that authenticates users. At logon, it establishes identity, which is used throughout the session.

6. Answer A is correct. Right-click the network connection that you want to configure, and choose Properties. From the General property page (for a local area connection) or the Networking property page (for all other connections), choose Internet Protocol (TCP/IP) and then select Properties. From the General property page, choose Advanced. From the Options property page, choose IP security and then select Properties. From IP Security, choose Use this IP security policy and then select the desired policy.

    Answers B, C and D are incorrect. You configure TCP/IP to use an IPSec policy on all connections for which it is enabled through Network and Dial-up Connections.

7. Answers A, B and D are correct. A translated connection protects your internal network from the Internet by hiding internal IP addresses. Microsoft's Proxy Server 2.0, a BackOffice product, can provide both address translation and some firewall capability. Windows 2000 Server offers basic address translation ability through the Network Address Translation (NAT) routing protocol in Routing and Remote Access Service (RRAS). The Internet Connection Sharing (ICS) feature of Windows 2000 Network and Dial-up Connections offers basic, non-configurable Internet access.

    Answer C is incorrect. Internet browsers can transmit private documents and information such as credit card numbers over the Internet using Secure Socket Layer (SSL).

8. Answers A, C and D are correct. Windows 2000 comes with three predefined IPSec policy entries; however, by default these are not enabled: Client (Respond Only), Secure Server (Require Security) and Server (Request Security). You can modify or remove these. More likely though, you will want to add customized policies.

    Answer B is incorrect. A Client (Request Security) IPSec policy does not exist.

9. Answers A, B, C and D are all correct. An incorrectly configured IPSec policy on either of the communicating computers can cause the PING to fail. Even if the policy is correct, you need to activate it before it will take effect. The first PING after enabling the policy usually fails because of timing out during policy negotiation, but future PINGs should work.

10. Answers A, B and C are correct. The IP Security Monitor (IPSecmon) on Windows 2000 Server shows whether secured communications using IPSec are successful. Although IPSecmon cannot be used to see failed SAs or other filters, it does show you active SAs on local or remote computers. The CERTSRV.EXE tool can help you troubleshoot and administer Certificate Services. If you run CERTSRV with the -z switch, it displays a log of its activities in the console window. Event Viewer allows you to monitor program, security and system events on your computer. Of particular interest is the security log that records predetermined security-related events.

Answer D is incorrect. The Internet Security Association and Key Management Protocol (ISAKMP) is the initial SA created during negotiation between two IPSec-enabled computers. The ISAKMP is then used to negotiate for a pair of IPSec SAs and keys to protect inbound and outbound traffic.

Glossary

Term	Description
A	An Address record in the DNS database maps a host name to an IP address.
ABR	An Area Border Router is a software router running OSPF that connects a group of contiguous networks, called an area, with the backbone.
accounting	This process maintains a log of connection requests and sessions.
Active Directory	The directory service included with Windows 2000 Server. Active Directory stores information about objects on a network in a hierarchical view and provides a single point of administration for all network objects.
Active Directory	The directory service included with Windows 2000 Server stores information about objects on a network in a hierarchical view. It provides a single point of administration for all network objects.
ADSL	Asymmetric Digital Subscriber Line is a new technology that supports faster rates of data transfer over existing copper telephone lines.
AH	Authentication Header is an IPSec protocol that provides data authentication, integrity and anti-replay to IP packets.
algorithm	An algorithm is a rule or procedure for solving a problem. Cryptographic algorithms are used to encrypt data.

Term	Description
anti-replay	Anti-replay is a mechanism that prevents transmitted packets from being intercepted and resent to the packet origin to gain unauthorized access to your network.
API	An Application Program Interface is a set of routines, protocols and tools for building software applications.
AppleTalk	The communication protocol used by Macintosh clients. AppleTalk must be installed on a computer running Windows 2000 Server for Macintosh clients to connect to it.
ARP	The Address Resolution Protocol is a TCP/IP protocol used to convert an IP address into a physical address.
ASCII	American Standard Code for Information Interchange is a code for representing English characters as numbers.
ATM	Asynchronous Transfer Mode is a networking technology based on transferring packets of a fixed size across a fixed channel.
auditing	This process of configuring the logging and examination of predetermined events can tell you about potentially dangerous conditions, and besides, it leaves a trail of accountability.
authentication	In network access, authentication is the process by which the system validates the user's logon information. With IPSec, authentication is the process that verifies the origin and integrity of a message by assuring the identity of each computer.
authoritative server	The primary DNS server within a zone that is responsible for keeping an updated master copy of DNS records and the zone's configuration files.

Term	Description
authorization	This process gives a user access to system objects based on the user's identity.
BAP	The Bandwidth Allocation Protocol allows you to dynamically add or drop multiple connection links as needed in response to changing bandwidth needs.
BIND	Berkeley Internet Name Domain is a UNIX service that is equivalent to DNS in Microsoft products.
BOOTP	Bootstrap Protocol is a set of standards enabling computers to connect to one another. It is used mainly on TCP/IP networks to configure diskless workstations. DHCP is based on this protocol.
BOOTP forwarding	The act of forwarding BOOTP broadcasts across subnets.
CA	A Certificate Authority is a trusted service or entity that creates, distributes, publishes and validates keys. CA is also a certificate store in the PKI that holds the issuing or intermediate CA certificates to use in building certificate verification chains.
cache-only server	A server that always passes DNS requests to other servers, but caches DNS information after lookups.
callback	The callback security feature allows a remote access server to call the remote access client to establish a connection after the user credentials have been verified.
caller ID	A security feature is used to verify that an incoming call is coming from a specified telephone number.
certificate	A certificate is a digital document that proves the public key in the certificate belongs to the host or user named in the certificate.

Term	Description
Certificate Services	The Windows 2000 Certificate Services provides customizable services for issuing and managing certificates for the enterprise.
certification authority	A certification authority establishes and vouches for the authenticity of public keys belonging to users or other certification authorities.
CHAP	The Challenge Handshake Authentication Protocol is a challenge-response authentication protocol for PPP connections that uses Message Digest 5 to hash the response to a challenge issued by a remote access server.
CNAME	Canonical Name is a DNS record that establishes an alias for a host name, allowing one host to appear to be multiple computers.
Computer browser service	A service used by Windows computers that maintain an updated list of shared resources on a network or subnet. Computers take on browser roles through elections.
CPU	The Central Processing Unit is the device that processes and transmits data, and where most calculations take place.
CRC	Cyclic Redundancy Check is used to gauge data integrity.
CRL	A Certificate Revocation List is a document maintained and published by a CA that lists certificates that have been revoked.
cryptography	Cryptography is a set of mathematical techniques for encrypting and decrypting data for secure transmission.

Term	Description
CSNW	Client Service for NetWare is a service included with Windows 2000 Professional that allows clients to connect directly to resources on servers running NetWare 2.x and later.
CSP	A Cryptographic Service Provider is an independent software module that performs cryptography operations such as secret key exchange, digital signing of data and public key authentication.
CTL	A Certificate Trust List is a list of the certificates of trusted root CAs.
Daemon	A process that runs in the background and performs a specified operation at predefined times or in response to certain events.
datagram	A datagram is an unacknowledged packet of data sent to another network destination.
demand-dial router	A router that supports the routing of packets over point-to-point on-demand WAN links.
DHCP	Dynamic Host Configuration Protocol is a networking protocol that simplifies TCP/IP network configuration and dynamically configures IP addresses for clients. DHCP ensures that address conflicts do not occur by centralizing address allocation.
DHCP Relay Agent	A DHCP Relay Agent forwards client DHCP requests directly to a DHCP server on another subnet.
DHCPINFORM	DHCPINFORM messages are broadcasts used to obtain information without also obtaining an IP address.

Term	Description
Diffie-Hellman	Diffie-Hellman is a public key cryptography algorithm that allows two entities to agree on a shared key without needing encryption during the key generation.
digital signature	A digital signature is a key pair that is used to authenticate the message sender's identity.
DLL	Dynamic Link Library allows executable routines serving specific functions to be stored separately as files with .DLL extensions. These are loaded only when requested by a program.
DNS	Domain Name System is the hierarchical naming system used to locate domain names on the Internet and on private TCP/IP networks. The DNS service maps DNS domain names to IP addresses and vice-versa.
domain logon	Domain logon is the process of an identified user being given permission to access selected network resources.
DSA	Digital Signature Algorithm is a public key algorithm used for producing digital signatures.
dynamic routing	With dynamic routing, routing protocols such as RIP and OSPF are used to automatically create and modify routing tables.
EAP	The Extensible Authentication Protocol is a method of attaching new security authentication schemes as they are developed.

Term	Description
EAP-TLS	Extensible Authentication Protocol-Transport Level Security is a new protocol devised by Microsoft. It combines the function of EAP, which supports additional authentication methods within PPP, with that of TLS, which supports mutual authentication, negotiation, and key exchange between computers. EAP-TLS also supports the fragmentation and reassembly of packets.
EFS	Encrypted File System is an extension to Microsoft's file system that provides strong data protection and encryption for files and folders.
enrollment	Enrollment is the process of obtaining a digital certificate.
enterprise root CA	The enterprise root CA is the most trusted CA in an enterprise. It can issue certificates for enterprise subordinate CAs. You install an enterprise CA to issue certificates to entities within your organization.
enterprise subordinate CA	An enterprise subordinate CA is subordinate to the enterprise root CA in the hierarchy. It can request a certificate from the enterprise root CA. You install an enterprise CA to issue certificates to entities within your organization.
ESP	The Encapsulation Security Payload is a tunneling mode that supports the encapsulation and encryption of entire IP datagrams for secure transfer across a private or public IP Internetwork.
Ethernet	This is one of the most widely implemented LAN technology standards. It uses a bus or star topology

Term	Description
exclusion range	A small range of IP addresses that are excluded from being leased to DHCP clients.
Group Policy	Group Policy is a management technology used to specify options for desktop configurations of groups of computers and users.
GSNW	Gateway Service for NetWare is a service that creates a gateway in which Microsoft clients can access NetWare resources through a Windows 2000 server.
GUI	A Graphical User Interface is a user-friendly program interface that makes use of graphics rather than a command-driven interface.
FDDI	Fiber Distributed Data Interface is a set of protocols for sending digital data over a fiber optic cable.
forward lookup	A query in which the DNS name for the computer is used to determine the IP address.
FPNW	File and Print Services for NetWare is part of an add-on package called Microsoft Services for NetWare. It runs on a Windows 2000 server and emulates a NetWare server, providing resources for NetWare clients.
FQDN	Fully Qualified Domain Name is a domain name that indicates the precise location of a computer in the hierarchical domain namespace tree.
frame relay	This packet-switching protocol for connecting devices on a WAN supports data transfer across T1 and T3 lines. Although popular because of low costs, it is being replaced by the faster ATM.

Term	Description
FSM	File Server for Macintosh is a Windows 2000 service that manages the publishing of shared files and allows Macintosh users file access.
FTP	File Transfer Protocol is a protocol that defines how to transfer files from one computer to another over the Internet. It is also a client/server application that moves files using this protocol.
Global Catalog	A Windows 2000 service and data store that holds a partial replica of each object found in the Active Directory, along with commonly accessed attributes. When a user begins browsing the network, the associated computer will contact a Global Catalog to look up a specific computer name.
GPO	A Group Policy Object is a collection of Group Policy settings created by the Group Policy snap-in.
hash	A hash value or number is generated from a string of text using an algorithm. A hash is used to ensure that a message has not been tampered with.
HCL	Hardware Compatibility List is maintained by Microsoft and lists approved operating systems.
HINFO	The Host Information DNS record identifies the CPU and operating system used by the host.
hop	A hop is an intermediate connection in a string of connections linking two network devices. On the Internet, this refers to the forwarding of a packet to the next router.

Term	Description
HTTP	The HyperText Transfer Protocol is the underlying protocol used by the World Wide Web that defines how messages are formatted and transmitted, and what actions Web servers and browsers should take in response to commands.
IAS	The Internet Authentication Service is the central component in Windows 2000 for authenticating, authorizing, and auditing users who connect to a network through a VPN or dial-up access.
ICMP	The Internet Control Message Protocol supports packets containing error, control and informational messages.
ICS	Internet Connection Sharing is a feature of Windows 2000 that allows you to provide your network computers with access to Internet resources.
IEEE 802.1p	Institute of Electrical and Electronics Engineers 802.1p describes a 2-byte tag in the data portion of the frame in Ethernet networks, which allows switches to drop low-priority frames in favor of high-priority frames in busy network segments.
IETF Diff-Serv	Internet Engineering Task Force Diff-Serv describes a 6-bit field in the IP header that allows applications to set priority by specifying a level of QoS in the field.
IGMP	The Internet Group Management Protocol supports multicasting, a limited form of broadcasting in which clients having a multicast IP address can message a whole group within an intranet.

Term	Description
IP	The Internet Protocol is the routable protocol in the TCP/IP suite that is responsible for the IP addressing, routing, and fragmentation and reassembly of IP packets.
IP filter	An IP filter is a subset of potential network traffic based on the IP address, port and transport protocol. The IP filter secures both outbound and inbound traffic.
IP filter list	An IP filter list is a combination of one or more IP filters defining a range of network traffic.
IP Precedence	IP Precedence in layer 3 of the OSI Reference Model allows routers to prioritize traffic and to select packets that must be dropped.
IPSec	A set of standard, cryptography-based protection services and protocols, Internet Protocol Security protects all protocols in the TCP/IP suite and Internet communications using Layer 2 Tunneling Protocol (L2TP).
IPX	The Internetwork Packet Exchange is the NetWare protocol that controls addressing and routing of packets within and between LANs.
IPX/SPX	Internetwork Packet Exchange/Sequenced Packet Exchange is Novell NetWare's networking protocol. Microsoft has its own version of IPX/SPX called NWLink.
ISAKMP	The initial SA produced during negotiation between two IPSec-enabled computers is called Internet Security Association and Key Management Protocol. The ISAKMP is then used to negotiate for a pair of IPSec SAs and keys that protect inbound and outbound traffic.

Term	Description
ISDN	Integrated Services Digital Network is a communications standard for sending voice, video, and data over digital phone lines.
ISP	An Internet Service Provider is a private company that offers connectivity to the Internet for individuals or organizations.
Kbps	A measure of data transfer speed, Kilobits per second is 1,000 bits per second.
Kerberos	The default user and host authentication protocol for Windows 2000. Internet Protocol security may use the Kerberos protocol for authentication.
Kernel	The essential part of an operating system that provides basic services. It manages memory, processes, tasks, and disks.
key	A key is a secret code or number required for reading, modifying or verifying secured data. Keys are used with algorithms to secure data.
L2F	Layer 2 Forwarding is a Cisco networking protocol upon which L2TP is based.
L2TP	The Layer Two Tunneling Protocol encapsulates Point-to-Point frames to be sent over IP, X.25, Frame Relay, or ATM networks.
LAN	A Local Area Network is a communications network connecting computers, printers and other devices within a limited area.

Term	Description
LDAP	Lightweight Directory Access Protocol is a directory service protocol that runs over TCP/IP and is the primary access protocol for Active Directory.
lease	The duration a DHCP client is permitted to retain an IP address.
LMHOSTS	This static file is used for name resolution. It maps NetBIOS (computer) names to IP addresses.
LPD	Line Printer Daemon, which originally was a UNIX component, acts like print server. It receives print jobs from LPR clients and sends them to a printer.
LPR	Line Printer Remote is a command-line utility provided by Windows 2000. LPR directs and monitors print jobs aimed for UNIX host printers.
MAC address	Media Access Control address is the address used for communication between network adapters on the same subnet. Each network adapter has an associated MAC address.
MAV	Macintosh Accessible Volume is a Windows shared folder or file that appears as a volume to Macintosh clients who use Apple's file-sharing software to connect to the MAV.
metric	The metric value tells IP how may routers it will have to pass to reach a destination.
Microsoft Certificate Services	An optional component of Windows 2000 that lets you issue digital security certificates, certify them as valid, and revoke undesired certificates.

Term	Description
MMC	Microsoft Management Console is a framework for hosting administrative consoles. A console is defined by the items on its console tree. It has windows that provide views of the tree as well as the administrative properties, services, and events that are acted on by items in the console tree.
MS-CHAP	Microsoft Challenge Handshake Authentication Protocol allows you to encrypt an entire dial-up session, not just the original authentication.
multicast	Multicast is the process of sending a message to a select group of recipients.
Multicast DHCP	DHCP clients having a multicast IP address can message a whole group within an intranet.
multihomed	A computer that has multiple network adapters installed.
Multilink	With Multilink, clients can combine multiple physical connections into one logical connection.
multimaster replication	A replication model in which any domain controller accepts and replicates directory changes to any other domain controller.
multi-protocol router	An RRAS server can act like a router, routing IP, IPX, and AppleTalk packets simultaneously.
MX	A Mail Exchange DNS record identifies a mail exchange server for the domain that processes mail within the domain.
MY	This certificate store in the Public Key Infrastructure (PKI) holds the user or computer's certificates that have an associated private key.

Term	Description
namespace	A set of distinct names for the resources in a network. The names in a namespace can be resolved to the objects they represent. For DNS, namespace is the hierarchical structure of the domain name tree.
NAT	Network Address Translation is a protocol that allows a network with private addresses to access information on the Internet through an IP translation process.
NBNS	A NetBIOS Name Server resolves a computer name to and IP address.
NBT	NetBIOS over TCP/IP is a feature that provides the NetBIOS programming interface over the TCP/IP protocol.
NDS	Novell Directory Services is a distributed database that operates on Novell NetWare 4.x and 5.x networks. NDS maintains information about every resource on the network and provides access to these resources.
NetBEUI	Microsoft's networking protocol for LANs is NetBIOS Enhanced User Interface.
NetBIOS	Network Basic Input/Output System is an Application Programming Interface used by MS-DOS applications on a LAN to enable information transmission and sessions between nodes.
NetBIOS name	A Network Basic Input/Output System name is recognized by WINS, the service that maps a computer name to its IP address.

Term	Description
NetBT	NetBIOS over TCP/IP is a feature that provides the NetBIOS programming interface over the TCP/IP protocol. It is used for monitoring routed servers that use NetBIOS name resolution.
NETSH	Net Shell is a command-line utility that supports Windows 2000 networking components for both local and remote computers. You can use NETSH to save a configuration script in a text file for configuring other servers.
Network Monitor	This Windows 2000 Server utility captures and displays statistics about frames that it receives from the LAN.
NIC	A Network Interface Card is a device that allows the network cable to connect the computer to the network.
NNTP	Network News Transfer Protocol is part of the TCP/IP suite and is used to distribute network news messages on the Internet from a central database on a server.
NS	A Name Server record in the DNS database allows DNS lookup within zones by specifying the primary and secondary name server for the domain.
NT	New Technology is Microsoft's version of Windows previous to Windows 2000.
NTFS	New Technologies File System is a file system designed for Windows NT and Windows 2000. It provides data security, file system reliability, and file system recoverability.
NTLM	New Technologies LAN Manager is a Microsoft client login authentication system that gives a transparent connection to the host while ensuring that clear text passwords do not pass over the network.

Term	Description
NWLink	Microsoft's implementation of IPX/SPX, Novell's transport protocol that supports routing and client-server applications.
ODBC	Open DataBase Connectivity allows you to access any data in any application, no matter which database program handles the data.
OSI Reference Model	The Open System Interconnection standard for communications defines a networking framework for implementing protocols in seven layers.
OSPF	Open Shortest Path First is a protocol that defines how routers share routing information. OSPF transfers only new routing information, to conserve bandwidth.
OU	An Organizational Unit is a logical container within a domain, used to organize objects for easier administration and access.
packet	A packet is a transmission unit of a fixed maximum size consisting of both data and a header containing an identification number, source and destination addresses, and error-control information.
packet-switching	This refers to protocols in which messages are divided into packets that are transmitted individually along different routes to their destination, where they are reassembled into the original message.
PAD	The Packet Assembler/Disassembler is a device that breaks data into packets for transmission over an X.25 network before reassembling them at the destination point.

Term	Description
PAP	The Password Authentication Protocol is the most basic form of authentication in which a user's name and password are transmitted over a network and compared with a table of name / password pairs.
PIN	A Personal Identification Number is a secret number used to identify an entity, known only to the entity and the verifying instrument.
PKI	Public Key Infrastructure includes the laws, standards, policies, and software that regulate certificates and public and private keys. This system of digital certificates and certification authorities authenticate the validity of each party in an electronic transaction.
Pods	Groupings of UNIX hosts that simplify administration.
policy module	A policy module defines what a CA will do when it receives a certificate request and is configurable.
policy module	A policy module defines what a CA will do when it receives a certificate request and is configurable.
PPP	Point-to-Point Protocol is an industry standard suite of protocols for the use of point-to-point links to transport multiprotocol datagrams.
PPTP	Point-to-Point Tunneling Protocol is a tunneling protocol that encapsulates Point-to-Point frames for transmission over the Internet or a private intranet.

Term	Description
pre-shared key	A pre-shared key is a word or phrase that both communicating computers know. It is used for authentication.
primary server	The authoritative DNS server for a domain. Primary servers come in two versions. An Active Directory-integrated primary server is fully integrated with Active Directory and stores all DNS data in the Directory. An ordinary primary server is only partially integrated with Active Directory and stores all DNS data as text files.
private key	The private key is the secret half of a cryptographic key pair used with a public key algorithm.
protocol stack	A protocol suite or stack, is a combination of protocols that work together to achieve network communication.
Proxy	A proxy relays client requests to the computer that performs the actual name resolution and forwards the resolved names back to the requesting client.
Proxy Server 2.0	Part of Microsoft's BackOffice suite, Proxy Server separates your internal network from the Internet. It hides the internal IP addresses of your network while increasing your Internet access speed through caching.
PSM	Print Server for Macintosh is a Windows 2000 service that permits Windows and Macintosh computers to share each other's printers.
PSTN	The Public Switched Telephone Network refers to the telephone system based on copper wires carrying analog voice data.

Term	Description
PTR	A Pointer record in the DNS database maps an IP address to a host name for reverse lookups.
public key	The public key is the non-secret, published half of a cryptographic key pair used with a public key algorithm.
public key encryption	Public key encryption, also called asymmetric key encryption, is an encryption method that uses a pair of mathematically related keys: a public key that is distributed and a private key that remains secret. To encrypt a message to someone, you use the recipient's public key. The message recipient then uses the private key to decrypt the message.
pull partner	A pull partner requests new database entries, with a higher version number than the last entry it received during the last replication, from its push partner.
push partner	A push partner notifies its pull partner of changes to its WINS database. When the pull partner responds with a request for replication, the push partner sends a copy of its new database entries to its pull partner.
QoS	Quality of Service is a set of quality assurance standards and mechanisms for data transmission in Windows 2000.
QoS Admission Control Service	This software service controls bandwidth and network resources on the subnet to which it is assigned. It can be installed on any Windows 2000 computer.

Term	Description
RADIUS	Remote Authentication Dial-In User Service, the most common authentication protocol used by Internet service providers. Running on an Internet Authentication Service server with Windows 2000, RADIUS can be used to manage the access policies of remote access servers.
RAS	Remote Access Service is a Windows service that permits remote networking for mobile workers and for system administrators who monitor and manage servers at multiple sites.
reservation	An IP address that is reserved for a specific client, such as a computer that often needs to be moved to different subnets.
RESV	With RSVP, the client sends a PATH message to the receiver. The receiving station responds with a Reservation (RESV) message that travels the same route as the PATH message. As each router forwards the RESV message, it reserves the requested bandwidth.
reverse lookup	A query in which the IP address is used to determine the DNS name for the computer.
RFC	Request For Comments is a document that defines a TCP/IP standard. RFCs are published by the Internet Engineering Task Force and other working groups.
RIP	Routing Information Protocol. A protocol that specifies how routers exchange routing information. Because RIP exchanges entire routing tables, it is being replaced by the more efficient OSPF protocol.

Term	Description
ROOT	This certificate store in the PKI holds self-signed certificates for trusted root CAs.
root list	The root list is a set of trusted root certificates that is part of a GPO. This allows you to create a certificate set containing only the trusted CAs available for distribution to a particular group of users.
RRAS	The Routing and Remote Access Service is the Microsoft feature that integrates remote access and multi-protocol routing services. It can turn a Windows 2000 server into a dynamic software router.
RSA	Rivest Shamir Adelman is a general-purpose algorithm that supports digital signatures and distributed public key encryption. RSA is the standard for Internet data encryption.
RSVP	The Resource Reservation Setup Protocol allows you to reserve a predetermined amount of bandwidth along a specific path in the network, called the flow. This reduces the differences in latency that would normally occur between packets that travel along different network paths.
rule	A rule is a combination of the various IPSec components that protects a specific subset of network traffic. You can have multiple rules for different traffic subsets.
SA	A Security Association is created when two IPSec-enabled computers negotiate an agreement on which keys, mechanisms and security policies to use to protect the data.
Samba	A popular SMB server freeware that has ports for many versions of UNIX.

Term	Description
scope	The range of IP addresses a DHCP server can assign.
SDLC	Synchronous Data Link Control is a protocol used for communication in IBM's SNA networks.
secondary server	A backup DNS server to the primary server. A secondary server keeps an updated copy of DNS records it receives from a primary DNS server through zone transfers.
serial link	A serial WAN link transfers data sequentially.
SFU	Windows NT Services for UNIX is a Microsoft package that facilitates interoperability between Windows 2000 and UNIX hosts.
SLIP	The Serial Line Internet Protocol is an older and simpler protocol used for connection on the Internet, which is being supplanted by PPP XE "multilink."
smart card	A smart card is a credit card-like hardware token used to access security-enabled protocols and applications.
SMB	Server Message Block is a file-sharing protocol that allows networked computers to transparently access files residing on remote systems over a variety of networks.
SMS	Systems Management Server is a Microsoft product that assists in managing computers connected to a LAN.

Term	Description
SMTP	Simple Mail Transport Protocol is a protocol used to transfer mail on the Internet. SMTP is independent of the transmission subsytem.
SNA	Systems Network Architecture is a communications interface used to establish a link with IBM mainframes and AS/400 hosts.
SNAP	Sub Network Access Protocol specifies a type of data frame similar to Ethernet 802.2., which defaults to 802.2
SNMP	The Simple Network Management Protocol is a set of protocols for managing complex networks.
SOA	The Start Of Authority is a DNS record that is created automatically when you add a zone. It defines the host that has the best DNS information for the zone.
SPAP	The Shiva Password Authentication Protocol is an encrypted password authentication method used by Shiva LAN Rover clients and servers. It is also supported by Windows 2000 Server.
SRV	A Service record in the DNS database lists which servers are hosting a particular service.
SSL	Secure Socket Layer is used by browsers to transmit private documents and information such as credit card numbers over the Internet.
stand-alone root CA	A stand-alone root CA is the most trusted CA in a hierarchy. It can issue certificates for stand-alone subordinate CAs. You install a stand-alone CA to issue certificates to entities outside of your organization.

Term	Description
stand-alone subordinate CA	A stand-alone subordinate CA acts as either a solitary certificate server or a CA in a trust hierarchy, in which case it can request a certificate from the stand-alone root CA. You install a stand-alone CA to issue certificates to entities outside of your organization.
static routing	With static routing, you manually create and modify routing tables. This is only done with small, relatively static networks.
superscope	Multiple scopes grouped together for administrative ease.
symmetric key encryption	With symmetric key encryption, a single encryption key is used to both encrypt and decrypt data.
System Monitor	This utility tracks different processes and objects on a Windows 2000 computer in real time.
TCO	Total Cost of Ownership. The total cost of purchasing an item, including implementation and administrative costs, and lost employee productivity.
TCP	The Transmission Control Protocol enables two hosts to establish a connection and exchange data that is guaranteed.
TCP/IP	Transport Control Protocol/Internet Protocol is a set of protocols that provides communication among diverse networks. Because it accommodates different architectures and operating systems, TCP/IP is the most commonly used Internet protocol.
TCP/IP Reference Model	This communications standard for different versions of TCP/IP calls for implementing TCP/IP in four layers.

Term	Description
Telnet	A terminal emulation program that is used on the Internet to log on to network computers.
token ring	This popular LAN technology has computers arranged in a logical circle. The computer that has possession of the token is able to send messages.
Transitive trust	The trust relationships between Windows 2000 domains in a domain tree or forest, between trees in a forest, or between forests. Transitive trusts are automatically established when a domain joins an existing forest or domain tree.
TRUST	This certificate store in the PKI holds trust lists, the sequence of trusted CAs.
TTL	Time to Live specifies the duration a process can occur or record can be kept before the process is ended or the record discarded.
tunneling	Tunneling technology allows one network to send its data through another network's connections by encapsulating a network protocol within packets carried by the second network.
UDP	User Datagram Protocol is a TCP/IP component that transmits data through a connectionless service but does not guarantee the delivery or sequencing delivery of sent packets.
URL	A Uniform Resource Locator is the global address of a document or resource on the World Wide Web.
UserDS	This certificate store in the PKI simplifies access to repositories by giving a logical view of a certificate repository stored in the Active Directory.

Term	Description
VPN	Virtual Private Network is the extension of a private network that encompasses links across shared or public networks such as the Internet.
WAN	A Wide Area Network spans a large geographical area and typically consists of two or more LANs.
WINS	Windows Internet Name Service is a Microsoft software service that dynamically maps IP addresses to computer names. This allows users to access resources by name instead of by IP address.
WINS proxy agent	A Windows Internet Naming Service proxy agent extends the name resolution capabilities of a WINS server to non-WINS clients by listening for broadcast name registrations and resolution requests and forwarding them to a WINS server.
Winsock	Windows Socket is an Application Programming Interface for developing Windows programs that can communicate with other computers through TCP/IP.
WINS-R	A Windows Internet Name Service Reverse record dynamically maps the reverse of WINS, computer names to IP addresses.
X.25	A popular protocol used in packet-switching networks.
X.25 smart card	This network connectivity hardware attaches directly to an X.25 network and uses the X.25 protocol to establish connections and send and receive data.

Term	Description
X.509	The most widely used standard for defining digital certificates. An X.509 certificate includes the public key and information about the person or entity to whom the certificate is issued, as well as information about the certificate.
zone	In a DNS database, a zone is a domain or an area within a domain that is administered as a distinct entity by a DNS server. The zone contains resource records for all the names within the zone.

Index

AH, 560, 568, 589, 591

algorithm, 485-486, 493, 496-497, 539, 549, 552, 560, 588, 591
  cryptography, 49, 485, 490, 497, 539, 541, 552, 560, 589, 591
  encryption, 28, 170, 181-182, 198, 202-203, 246, 249, 253, 406, 486, 490, 496-497, 534-535, 539, 543-544, 546, 555, 559-561, 587, 591
  hash, 493, 549, 552, 559, 589, 591
  signature, 486, 496, 539, 543-545, 555, 559, 588

American Standard Code for Information Interchange, 139

analog, 162, 166-167, 247

anti-replay, 560, 589, 591

API, 397

Apple Macintosh, 2, 17, 165

AppleTalk, 17-18, 22, 44, 162, 169, 172, 175, 188, 192, 199, 203, 246-247, 251, 256, 379

Application Layer, 259

Application Programming Interface

area, 161-162, 179, 205, 257, 260, 268-269, 336, 343, 161-162, 179, 205, 257, 260, 268-269, 336, 343, 379-380, 391-394, 397, 399-400, 415, 437, 439-440, 442, 445, 467, 469, 482, 484, 561, 570, 587, 592, 379-380, 391-394, 397, 399-400, 415, 437, 439-440, 442, 445, 467, 469, 482, 484, 561, 570, 587, 592, 7, 11, 14, 19, 30-31, 55, 78, 108, 114, 136, 155, 7, 11, 14, 19, 30-31, 55, 78, 108, 114, 136, 155

Area Border Router

ARP, 324-325, 328

array, 283, 323

AS, 1-2, 4-5, 7-13, 15, 17-20, 22-24, 27-29, 32, 44-46, 49-50, 53-56, 59-60, 63, 68-69, 72, 75, 81, 83-84, 98-100, 102, 104-109, 118, 120, 131-132, 134-137, 139, 152, 154, 157-159, 161-165, 169-170, 173, 175-177, 179-180, 183, 186, 188, 191-192, 196, 201-202, 206-207, 209, 211, 213-214, 218-220, 246-247, 249, 253, 256, 272, 277-278, 281-282, 292, 301, 323-324, 329-330, 335, 343, 348-349, 356, 371-373, 375-377, 379-382, 384-385, 388, 390-392, 395-401, 408, 414-416, 436-438, 440, 442-443, 445-448, 450, 453-455, 458, 466, 470, 480, 486-491, 496-497, 502-503, 506-508, 513-517, 519, 522, 524, 535-536, 539-541, 543-544, 546, 549, 552, 555, 559-560, 562, 566-569, 571, 587-588, 591-592
/400,

ASCII, 139

Asymmetric Digital Subscriber Line, 168, 247

Asynchronous Transfer Mode, 162, 168, 247, 256-257, 413

ATM, 50, 162, 168-169, 202, 246-247, 253, 256-257, 413

auditing, 107, 139, 213-214, 246, 250, 252, 541

authentication, 1-2, 6, 8, 19, 22, 49, 170-172, 174-176, 188, 197-199, 201-203, 209, 213-219, 245-252, 254, 271, 273-274, 277-278, 291, 327, 330-331, 385, 489-490, 498, 535, 538, 540-545, 547, 549, 551-552, 555, 557,

WINS-R, 63, 65, 415

wizard, 19, 21-22, 44, 58, 69, 72, 113, 121, 124,
    126, 136-137, 155, 172, 177-178, 186-187,
    203, 207, 215, 245, 248, 251-253, 273-274,
    276, 284, 290-293, 322-323, 337-338, 384-385,
    402-403, 452, 467, 495, 497, 502-503, 506-
    507, 519-521, 523-524, 538, 540, 546, 549-
    550, 553, 557-559, 561-565, 587
    Automatic Certificate Request Setup, 557-558
    Demand Dial Interface,
    Network Connection, 135, 176-178, 186-187,
        204, 269, 570, 592
    Windows Components, 19, 56, 113, 215, 284,
        337-338, 398, 492, 495, 549-550
    Windows Components,

World Wide Web, 49, 497

X.25,

X.509,

zone,
    delegating authority,
    forward lookup,
    replication, 70, 107, 111
    reverse lookup, 61, 62, 71, 95, 106, 109
    root domain configuration, 71

www.ingramcontent.com/pod-product-compliance
Lightning Source LLC
Chambersburg PA
CBHW080129060326
40689CB00018B/3722